POST-COMMUNISM

For Katy and Paul

POST-COMMUNISM

An Introduction

LESLIE HOLMES

Duke University Press, Durham 1997

Copyright © Leslie Holmes 1997

All rights reserved. No reproduction, copy,
or transmission of this publication may be made
without written permission. Any person who
does any unauthorized act in relation to this
publication may be liable to criminal prosecution
and civil claims for damages.

First published 1997

Published in the United States by
Duke University Press
Durham, North Carolina
and in Great Britain by
Polity Press
Cambridge, UK

ISBN 0-8223-1987-X
ISBN 0-8223-1995-0

Library of Congress Cataloging-in-Publication Data
Holmes, Leslie.
    Post-communism : an introduction / Leslie Holmes.
        p.   cm.
    Includes bibliographical references (p.   ) and index.
    ISBN 0-8223-1987-X (alk. paper). — ISBN 0-8223-1995-0 (pbk. :
alk. paper)
    1. Communism. 2. Post-communism. 3. Europe, Eastern—Politics
and government—1989– 4. Soviet Union—Politics and
government—1985–1991. 5. Former Soviet republics—Politics and
government.   I. Title.
HX44.5.H65 1997
320.947—dc21   96-39936
                                                                CIP

Typeset in 10 on 12 pt Times
by Best-set Typesetter Ltd, Hong Kong
Printed in Great Britain by T J International Ltd

This book is printed on acid-free paper

Contents

Contents   **vii**

Figures and Tables

FIGURES

TABLES

Preface

This book is offered as an introduction to the fascinating, but complex and constantly changing, world of post-communism in what used to be known as Eastern Europe and the USSR. Although it would have been worthwhile to have considered some of the other post-communist states (such as Afghanistan, Ethiopia or Mongolia), there is already so much to cover vis-à-vis the European and FSU (Former Soviet Union) post-communist states that it was decided to limit the analysis to 'just' what is by now a group of almost 30 countries. This said, many of the comparative points made in the following chapters could be applied to other post-communist states.

In one sense, it is foolhardy to write a book on a topic that is still very much a moving target. However, three factors suggest that the time is as ripe as it is likely to be for many years to produce an overview of both recent changes and interpretations of these.

First, there has been something of a slowdown of the transition in many countries. Only now are the broad contours of post-communism crystallizing; previously, it was unclear whether or not patterns that *appeared* to be emerging would disappear almost as soon as they had begun to take shape.

Second, while there has been a steady stream of primary and intermediate-level sources since post-communism first appeared (1989), it is only since about 1992 that much secondary material has been appearing on most of the post-communist states. This followed a near drought in 1990 and 1991, as observers both attempted to keep pace with developments and perceived a need to digest them before publishing books and articles interpreting them. A comparative book of this scale and nature will necessarily be highly dependent on such secondary literature, since it would be impossible for any one individual to be a specialist on all the aspects of all the countries touched upon in the present volume.

Third, as someone who has been attempting to teach this subject in recent years, I have been made very aware by my students of the need for at least one source that can be used as a (reasonably detailed) introduction to what is, after all, a very new and very large subject. The earlier point about the drought becoming a deluge is germane here; many of the new books and articles are rather specialized for novices, and there is still a shortage of sources that attempt to provide a broad comparative overview. The present book is a modest contribution to bridging the gap, by providing a single-authored book that does not concern itself exclusively with either the FSU or eastern Europe, but rather with both. It is hoped there will be many more overview books, since there is a pressing need for them.

A book of this kind will not and could never satisfy everyone. Many specialists on a given country or region, for instance, will argue that it is better not even to mention their particular interest if the references are to be as fleeting and superficial as they are bound to be in a book like this. But the comparative approach is a valid one, and should not be seen as being in opposition to or competition with individual country or thematic studies. Ideally, it highlights both similarities *and* differences between groups of people (nations, genders, classes, etc.). Often, it can place important *general* questions on the agenda that might not be as obvious to someone who is focusing on a particular group or problem. Moreover, it is useful to stand back from the canvas sometimes to appreciate the larger picture, even if some of the detail is lost in doing so. As long as it does not attempt to exaggerate the similarities – to imply uniformity where there is none – comparison can also help us better to understand phenomena that are occurring in several countries at about the same time. Conversely, respectable comparative analysis cannot occur *without* the detailed studies of individual phenomena provided by the true specialist. In short, the specialist and the comparativist should interact and learn from each other.

Although this book is long and covers a wide range of topics, it has several limitations. It has been written by a political scientist, and therefore focuses primarily on *political* aspects of post-communism. One very obvious omission is any direct consideration of culture in the various countries analysed, though much can be inferred about *political* culture from the political histories provided.

Precisely because so much has happened so quickly in that part of the world with which this book is concerned, academics (especially comparativists) have had to become even more dependent than usual on more ephemeral sources, such as newspapers. In many parts of this book, there could be at least one reference for almost every sentence, since extensive use has been made of an enormous range of (often short) primary, intermediate and secondary sources in both the printed and electronic media. Sourcing has been kept to what seems to me to be the minimum respectable and useful level, although there will still be more references than some would deem appropriate. For those wishing to pursue any particular topic, a list of further reading is included at the end of each chapter; these provide readers with a guide to many of my own starting points. Like most writers on post-communist topics, I have been heavily dependent on the daily and weekly reports from Radio Free Europe/Radio Liberty until 1994, and from the Open Media Research Institute since the beginning of 1995. Another useful source that is not yet as well known as it might be, and which has been used extensively for up-to-date economic information, is *Business Central Europe*.

A few points need to be made about terminology. The eight communist states that used to comprise Eastern Europe are distinguished here from their successors by referring to the latter collectively as eastern Europe; both Yugoslavia and Albania are included in this group. The term East Central Europe excludes the Balkan states, and is therefore inadequate when generalizing about the former Eastern Europe; it refers here to Czechia, Hungary, Poland, Slovakia and, until 1990, also to the German Democratic Republic. The term FSU is used when referring to a recent phenomenon in all parts of the former USSR, including the Baltic states (Estonia, Latvia and Lithuania); when the Baltic states are excluded from a part of the discussion concerned with the situation since late 1991, the term CIS (Commonwealth of Independent States) is used. The word Czechoslovakia is used to refer to the communist period; Czecho-Slovakia refers to that country from the end of 1989 to the end of 1992; the two successor states are here called Czechia and Slovakia. (The controversial term Czechia is used in preference to the Czech Republic since the latter is the name only of a state, not a country. Conversely, the term Republic of Macedonia – not Macedonia – is used in this book for the successor state to the former Yugoslav republic, so as to distinguish it from those parts of Macedonia located in Greece and Bulgaria.) Readers will find a summary of all these points in the 'Terminology' chart on p. xv, which can be used for quick reference. The lower case is used when referring in a generic way to organizations and offices, the upper case only when referring to the actual title/name of a particular example of these. Since this is intended to be primarily a textbook rather than a specialized monograph, all but the most conventional accents on words and names have been omitted.

The layout of the book will be fairly obvious from the contents page. Basically, the first two chapters are concerned with more theoretical aspects of the topic. These are followed by two chapters that analyse the transition to post-communism in individual countries; one that considers why some countries appear so far to have avoided this transition; and a very short comparative overview of the transition, which includes a brief consideration of the concept of revolution. Chapters 7–11 consider political, economic and social aspects of the post-communist countries, as well as their relationships to the worlds beyond their borders. The final chapter addresses some more abstract issues, and very briefly looks to the future. I would like to thank Steven Kennedy for some helpful suggestions for improving the original layout I had in mind.

Some readers may wonder why there is so much history in a book on what is by most criteria a very new phenomenon. There are three main reasons. First, ethnic conflict is currently a salient feature of politics in many parts of the post-communist world; since those involved in this often link current tensions to the past, the present cannot be understood without some knowledge of history. Second, it is a primary (if obvious) contention of this book that post-communism is a reaction to, yet also emerges from, communism. Hence, readers will be able to make much more sense of the present if they have some knowledge of what immediately preceded it. Third, years of having taught both communism and post-communism have convinced me that most students prefer to have some overview of the historical background to any given contemporary issue.

I wish to thank the University of Melbourne for granting me study leave in the first half of 1993 to research and write this book. I would also like to express my deep appreciation to colleagues at the University of Luneburg (especially Dr Ferdinand Muller-Rommel), St Antony's College, Oxford (especially Professor Archie Brown) and the Russian Research Center at Harvard University (especially Professor Timothy Colton) for allowing me to be attached to their institutions during this study leave.

Among the many specialists who have helped me to refine my knowledge and understanding of their particular areas, I would particularly like to thank the following, listed in alphabetical order, for having commented on various parts of the draft manuscript – Archie Brown, Richard Crampton, Laszlo Csapo, Janina Frentzel-Zagorska and Tony Phillips; thanks also to the two anonymous readers of the manuscript for some very useful suggestions. Naturally, I accept full responsibility for the errors that remain; in a book on a subject that is so new, rapidly changing and wide-ranging, it is inevitable there will be a fair number of these.

Acronyms and Abbreviations

Where a foreign-language acronym is in common usage in the English-language literature, an English rendering of the original full version is provided in parentheses.

ADP	Albanian Democratic Party
AFD	Alliance of Free Democrats
BANU	Bulgarian Agrarian National Union
BCE	*Business Central Europe*
BCP	Bulgarian Communist Party
BSP	Bulgarian Socialist Party
CAPCS	*Communist and Post-Communist Studies*
CEFTA	Central European Free Trade Agreement
CF	Civic Forum
CIS	Commonwealth of Independent States
CMEA	Council for Mutual Economic Assistance
Comecon	(alternative acronym for CMEA)
Cominform	Communist Information Bureau
CPCS	Communist Party of Czechoslovakia
CPE	Centrally Planned Economy
CPRF	Communist Party of the Russian Federation
CPSU	Communist Party of the Soviet Union
CSCE	Conference on Security and Cooperation in Europe
DEMOS	Democratic Opposition of Slovenia
DEPOS	(Serbian Democratic Movement)
EBRD	European Bank for Reconstruction and Development
EC	European Community
ECE	East Central Europe
ECO	Economic Cooperation Organization
EEA	European Economic Area
EECR	*East European Constitutional Review*
EFTA	European Free Trade Association
EIU	Economist Intelligence Unit
EU	European Union
FBIS	Foreign Broadcast Information Service
FRG	Federal Republic of Germany
FSU	Former Soviet Union
GATT	General Agreement on Tariffs and Trade
GDP	Gross Domestic Product
GDR	German Democratic Republic
GNP	Gross National Product
HDF	Hungarian Democratic Forum

HDZ	(Croatian Democratic Alliance)
HSP	Hungarian Socialist Party
HSWP	Hungarian Socialist Workers' Party
IMF	International Monetary Fund
KGB	(Committee for State Security)
KRWE	*Keesings Record of World Events*
KSS-KOR	(Committee for Social Self-Defence – Committee for the Defence of Workers)
LCY	League of Communists of Yugoslavia
LDPR	Liberal Democratic Party of Russia
NACC	North Atlantic Cooperation Council
NAM	Non-Aligned Movement
NATO	North Atlantic Treaty Organization
NMP	Net Material Product
NSF	National Salvation Front
OIEC	Organization for International Economic Cooperation
OMRI	Open Media Research Institute
OSCE	Organization for Security and Cooperation in Europe
PAV	Public Against Violence
PCA	Partnership and Cooperation Agreement
PDP	People's Democratic Party
PLA	Party of Labour of Albania
p.r.	proportional representation
PRC	People's Republic of China
RDC	Russia's Democratic Choice
RFE/RL	Radio Free Europe/Radio Liberty
RSDLP	Russian Social Democratic Labour Party
RSFSR	Russian Soviet Federal Socialist Republic
SEV	Russian abbreviation for CMEA)
SFRY	Socialist Federal Republic of Yugoslavia
UDF	Union of Democratic Forces
UK	United Kingdom
UN	United Nations
UNICEF	United Nations Children's Fund
US(A)	United States (of America)
USSR	Union of Soviet Socialist Republics
WEU	West European Union
WHO	World Health Organization
WTO	Warsaw Treaty Organization (to 1991); World Trade Organization (since 1995)

Terminology and Map

Up to 1989	1989–1992	Post-Communism
USSR All the 15 Soviet republics, including the Baltic republics		**FSU** All the successor states to the Soviet republics **CIS** Successor states to the Soviet republics *excluding* the Baltic states **Baltic states** Estonia Latvia Lithuania
Eastern Europe Albania Bulgaria Czechoslovakia German Democratic Republic (GDR) Hungary Poland Romania Yugoslavia		**eastern Europe** Successor states to all those included in Eastern Europe
Balkan states Albania Bulgaria Romania Yugoslavia		**Balkan states** Albania Bulgaria Romania Former Yugoslavia
East Central Europe Czechoslovakia Hungary Poland GDR	**East Central Europe (Visegrad Three)** Czecho-Slovakia Hungary Poland	**East Central Europe (Visegrad Four)** Czechia Slovakia Hungary Poland
German Democratic Republic East Germany		
Federal Republic of Germany West Germany		**Federal Republic of Germany** Unified east and west Germany

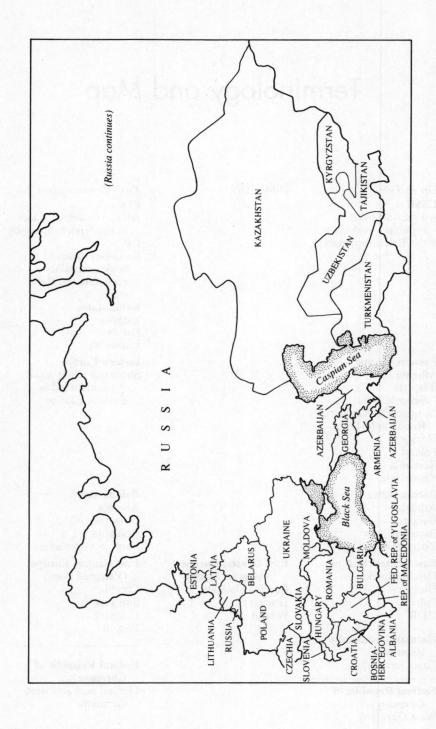

(Russia continues)

Part I

Theories and Approaches

1

On Communism and Post-Communism

This is a book about a very new phenomenon, dating from no earlier than 1989, that is widely labelled 'post-communism'. Quite what is meant by this label is not entirely clear, and it is noticeable how few books dealing with various aspects of post-communism fail to provide even a working definition of the concept. Although this is noteworthy, it is not necessarily surprising, since the phenomena that are collectively being labelled post-communism are not merely diverse but also in many cases hazy. This is largely because the phenomenon is still crystallizing. It is also because it is in many ways assuming a greater variety of forms in the various countries in which it exists than communism did in those same countries. While it was always important to be aware of the considerable variations in the interpretation and implementation of the latter concept in countries with such diverse cultural backgrounds as Czechoslovakia, Vietnam, Cuba and Ethiopia – to name but four states that are or were communist – there is now far less of a basically common blueprint than there was up to 1989.

In seeking to understand what post-communism might mean and what it does not mean, it is necessary to study the goals, policies, structures and behaviours that have emerged in the formerly communist world in the period since 1989. It could even be argued that the *only* way in which to provide an answer to the question 'What is post-communism?' is to study the *practice* of the countries that were previously communist. This is a valid but incomplete methodology. Although there is no distinctive ideology of post-communism, there are a number of premises and assumptions – many of them neither fully articulated by nor even consciously formulated in the minds of those building post-communism – that can help us to form a fuller impression of what it might mean than would be the case if *only* practice were to be studied. Thus it is important to attempt to understand the values, attitudes and orientations of those creating and living in the countries identified as post-communist. The general context and nature of post-communism also need to be examined. Finally, any attempt at understanding post-communism needs to identify what it is reacting to, just as most analyses of postmodernity provide an interpretation of modernity. Hence this book includes brief surveys of both the theory and practice of communism; these have been written in such a way as to enhance our understanding of post-communism.

Before this, however, the parameters and limitations of the present study need to be specified. By the beginning of 1989, some 23 countries could be defined as communist. Five years later, a maximum of five (China, Cuba, Laos, North Korea and Vietnam) could be so described, and there were question marks over even some of these (see chapter 6). This means that at least 18 states (Afghanistan, Albania, Angola, Benin, Bulgaria, Cambodia, Congo, Czechoslovakia, East Germany, Ethiopia, Hungary, Mongolia, Mozambique, Poland, Romania, Soviet Union, South Yemen and Yugoslavia) had moved to something usually called post-communism. Unfortunately, so much has happened in all of these countries in such a relatively short period that it is beyond the scope of a single book to provide even a general overview of these developments. Instead, and based largely on perceived student demand, the focus here is on 'just' what used to be known as Eastern Europe and the USSR. As will become increasingly obvious as the book proceeds, even this narrowing of focus is insufficient to provide in-depth analysis of *any* one country or phenomenon considered here. The book can only raise issues, briefly describe some of the solutions that are being adopted to deal with the problems of post-communism, and suggest further sources for those readers wanting to pursue any particular topic.

The coverage is not the only limitation of this book. A second is its topicality. As mentioned above, post-communism is still crystallizing; although the rate of change has slowed in many post-communist countries, it is still rapid. Thus the book is dealing with a moving target, and some parts of it will necessarily be outdated even by the time it is first published.

This rapid rate of change means it is often difficult to check the validity of reports, data, etc. Thus a third limitation is accuracy. While every effort has been made to check the correctness of information in this book, readers must appreciate that no author can be omniscient and no text entirely reliable.

Having highlighted some of the book's limitations, an analysis of both communism and post-communism as theories and phenomena can be embarked on.

Communism

The ideology of communist states – communist ideology – was called Marxism-Leninism. Three points can be highlighted from this title alone. First, it was named after two *people* – Karl Marx and Vladimir Lenin – rather than two *concepts*. Most ideologies (including liberalism, fascism, conservatism, socialism, and, to the extent that this is a true ideology, feminism) are named after abstract ideas and do not focus on individuals who have made a major contribution to the development of the underlying premises. It is thus ironic that an ideology that purports to play down the role of the individual, and that criticizes ideologies such as liberalism and conservatism for their focus on the individual, is itself focused on two individuals. Another dimension here is that the focus on individuals can be interpreted as symbolic of what was in practice the highly *voluntaristic* nature of the ideology; this point is elaborated below.

Second, the very name of the ideology suggests the possibility of at least complexity, perhaps even contradiction. No two people ever perceive the world from identical perspectives, so that naming an ideology after two revolutionaries suggests possible tensions within it. This point is also explored below.

Third, both individuals were men. Some feminists have argued that communism was a highly patriarchal ideology and system. The more practical ramifications of this are considered in chapter 9; it is worth noting here that many now see Marxism-Leninism's inadequate emphasis on gender issues as one of its major flaws.

The term Marxism-Leninism was not used in either Marx's or Lenin's time. Rather, it appears to have been devised by Stalin, who sought both a name for the USSR's state ideology, and to legitimize this ideology by reference to the 'founding fathers' of communist theory and practice. Very crudely, Marxism provided the broad theoretical underpinnings of Marxism-Leninism, whereas Leninism provided many of the more concrete answers to questions of organization and revolution. These two components can now be considered individually.

Marxism

The writings of Karl Marx (1818–1883) are prolific, rich, often contradictory, and depressingly incomplete on some of the most important questions of socialism. His approach has been described as *historical materialism*, and this concept has served as a bedrock of Marxist analysis since the middle of the nineteenth century. It is essentially a method for interpreting history, especially change in history; although a complex concept for those new to it, it is important to understand its basics.

Most theories of being – ontologies – are either materialist or idealist. In the latter, ideas constitute the basis of reality, whereas in the former, it is the material world (that is, matter) that is real. For materialists, our ideas are conditioned primarily by the material world, not vice versa. Marx's own materialism went beyond this, however. For him there were no permanent or static realities: reality, and our interpretation of this, changes according to time, place and who we are. Hence Marx rejected most notions of universal truths, and instead believed in contextuality.

This *dynamic* approach to reality has been described as *dialectical materialism*, although Marx himself never used this term. It is not appropriate to explain here what is meant by dialectical. Suffice it to say that the approach emphasizes constant change and interaction; when an event occurs, it generates reactions, which in turn generate further reactions. One implication of this is that history is seen never to repeat itself. This said, Marx did believe there were general and identifiable patterns in history; this belief is often described as Marx's *historicism*.

For Marx, the main driving force of history was the relationship between *classes*. He saw the latter as groupings of people who share the same basic relationship to the means of production. Throughout history, most societies have been fundamentally divided between those who own the means of production and those who have to work for these owners. In ancient societies, the two main classes were freepersons and slaves; in feudal societies, they were landowners and peasants; and in capitalist societies, they were the bourgeoisie (owners of capital) and the proletariat (literally, those without property – but in Marxism, usually meaning those who must sell their labour in factories etc. in order to survive). Marx appreciated that societies were more complex than this bipolar picture would suggest, and identified numerous subdivisions and offshoots of the main classes (such as the intelligentsia). Yet he also argued that most citizens more or less related to one or other of the two categories in the various historical epochs. Under capitalism, this bipolarization would become more pronounced than ever.

Although the relationship between classes was for Marx the most important aspect of any given society, it was not typically the relationship between the ruling and subordinate classes that led to revolutionary change. Often, most notably in the transition from feudalism to capitalism, technological innovation was the starting point for a process that would lead to one type of ruling class replacing another. For instance, the coming of the industrial revolution led to the emergence of a new, urban-based class of owners (of factories), the bourgeois capitalists. As this class grew in many European countries, so conflict arose between it and the then dominant ruling class, the large-scale landowners. The bourgeoisies came to realize that their interests could only be properly secured if they were to wrest political power from the big landowners; for Marx, the French Revolution was largely the outcome of this conflict between the old and the new ruling classes. Like all their predecessors, however, the new ruling classes in Europe claimed to represent the whole of society rather than their own vested interests.

According to Marx, the capitalist industrial societies that began to emerge in Europe in the eighteenth century contained within them the seeds of their own destruction. He maintained that the growing tensions between the two main classes would become so great that the proletarian masses would rise up and overthrow their bourgeois oppressors. This would constitute a *socialist* revolution. For this to succeed, however, it would have to be international; a socialist revolution in just one country would result in that country's isolation, and possibly even invasion from bourgeois countries claiming to be threatened by such a radically new type of system. Given this argument, Marx is often described as an *internationalist*.

The socialist revolution would lead to the establishment of a new type of power structure. Although there would still be a state operating in the interests of the ruling class, the new one would differ from all its predecessors in that the ruling class would now constitute the majority of the population, not a small minority. Marx never provided much detail on this post-revolutionary state; however, he did on at least two occasions refer to it as the *dictatorship of the proletariat*. He argued that this state would eventually, in the words of his long-time collaborator Friedrich Engels, 'wither away'. This would occur once the state was no longer required to repress or suppress particular classes. The only way this could occur was by removing the very basis of class division, private ownership. Thus a major task of the state following a socialist revolution was to socialize (take into public ownership) the means of production. Only with the emergence of such a classless society could there be the final disappearance of the state.

This is not to say that there would be no political organization at all under communism. Rather, according to Engels's interpretation of Marx, for the first time in history the government of persons (which implies some form of coercion over people) would be replaced by the administration of things (which was intended to suggest a relatively conflict-free, distributive and arbitral arrangement).

Several points need to be highlighted in the above analysis if Leninism and the reasons for its emergence are to be understood. First, Marx's analysis was based very much on his observations of Western Europe. When approached by Russian revolutionary thinkers in the 1870s and 1880s and asked whether or not his analysis could be applied to their country, Marx agonized for a long time before devising an ambiguous answer. But he did indicate that once a country had taken major steps towards industriali-zation, it would have to proceed through the various stages of capitalism before the conditions would be ripe for a socialist revolution.

Second, Marx provided very little detail on the nature of the socialist revolution itself. In particular, he did not elaborate a theory of the role of a revolutionary party or other important organizational aspects of a revolution.

Third, he painted only the scantiest picture of what a socialist state and society would look like. He never finished a planned major analysis of the state, and most of the available writings focus more on the capitalist state than the socialist.

Finally, Marx often blurred the distinctions between 'socialism' and 'communism'. However, he apparently envisaged the latter gradually emerging out of the former as both classes and the need for a state disap-peared. At this stage – true communism – there would for the first time in history be no structural reasons why individuals should be alienated from the world around them, their work, their fellow humans or themselves.

Leninism

The four points just identified serve as an appropriate introduction to *Leninism*, since Lenin is often seen as someone who plugged gaps or pro-vided relatively clear-cut answers to ambiguities in Marx's own writings. Vladimir Lenin (1870–1924) was not quite a teenager when Marx died. But even as a very young man, Lenin was incensed at many of the injustices of life in Russia, and saw these as responsible for his own brother's execution in May 1887. A mixture of anger and despair attracted him to Marxism, which claimed to show why exploitation and class conflict would one day disappear. By the 1890s, Lenin was involved with a Russian Marxist group in St Petersburg, and was particularly influenced by the so-called father of Russian Marxism, Georgii Plekhanov.

But by the beginning of the twentieth century, Lenin had begun to disagree with many of the other members of the Marxist group he belonged to, the Russian Social Democratic Labour Party (RSDLP). He believed that too many of them were unrealistic in their attitudes towards both the working class and the Tsarist autocracy that ruled the Russian empire. It was in this context that he wrote *What is to be Done?* (published 1902). In this, he advocated an elitist clandestine party that would strive to bring about a revolution in Russia. Although Lenin justified his call for elitism and secrecy in terms of the need to protect the party from Tsarist oppression, many of his comrades believed he was displaying an authoritarian and hierarchal side that many considered inappropriate in what was supposed to be a workers' party.

These differences led to a major split within the RSDLP in 1903, and the emergence of the Mensheviks (led by Yulii Martov) and the Bolsheviks (under Lenin). Despite various attempts in the following years to reunite the two sides, the division represented fundamental differences of interpretation and style, and the two eventually went their own ways.

On one level, the Bolshevik/Menshevik split represented a profound difference in interpreting Marx. Basically, the Mensheviks tended towards a more *deterministic* interpretation. They believed that although historical materialism enabled Marxists to determine in very general terms future social development, history has to unfold largely at its own pace and in ways that cannot be predicted with any precision. While accepting that it was a task of Marxists to alert the masses to their exploitation and to the possibilities of a better future, the Mensheviks also feared that if a revolutionary elite were to attempt to accelerate historical processes too much and artificially, its efforts would backfire. In contrast, the Bolsheviks (particularly Lenin) adopted a much more *voluntaristic* approach. Echoing Marx, Lenin argued that bourgeois propaganda (via the educational system and the mass media, for instance) was so powerful that it was unrealistic to expect ordinary working people – who were often poorly educated, and tired from their arduous and long hours of work – to develop much of an alternative (revolutionary) consciousness. A revolutionary elite would therefore have to work on behalf of the masses, and accelerate historical processes.

In light of Lenin's general approach just outlined, the ways in which he addressed the four aspects of Marxism highlighted earlier can now be considered.

After long deliberation and a change of mind, Lenin eventually (by mid-1917) came to the conclusion that Russia *could* soon have a socialist revolution. This was at odds with Marx's argument that such a revolution would have to start in the most advanced, industrialized countries. Lenin justified his position by referring to Marx's internationalism and arguing that although Russia was not as developed as many of the countries of Western Europe, it constituted the weakest link in an international chain of capitalist and imperialist countries.[1] Lenin further maintained that if this link were to be broken, there would be literally a chain reaction, as the workers of the more industrialized countries were inspired to revolution by the actions and successes of their Russian comrades. Events in both Germany and Hungary in 1918 and 1919 could be seen to have endorsed Lenin's belief that it might be possible to trigger an international revolution by overthrowing the Russian system. In all events, Lenin either modified or distorted (depending on one's perception) classical Marxism so as to justify a 'socialist' revolution in a country not yet ready for one in terms of economic, technological and social development. Once this precedent had been set, revolutionary groups in other countries with very small bourgeoisies and/or proletariats were ready to attempt 'socialist' revolutions in contexts which Marx himself would have seen as highly premature.

Lenin's theory of the role of a revolutionary party also plugged gaps in Marx's own analysis. Some maintain that since Lenin had argued in *What is to be Done?* that his call for an elitist and clandestine party was time and place specific, the views expressed there do not prove he was *generally* elitist. Even if this is accepted, it cannot be denied that in 1921, when the Bolsheviks had consolidated power and were coming under increasing pressure from workers and soldiers to democratize, Lenin tightened control in the party still further. It was then that he not only finally banned all other political parties, but also forbade factionalism *within* the communist party. The organizational principle most associated with Lenin and the Bolsheviks, *democratic centralism* (see chapter 7), at this time came to signify increasing centralization and decreasing democracy, even within the party. This, too, set a precedent for decades to come.

It will be recalled that Marx had provided little guidance on the kind of state to be established following a socialist revolution – let alone a premature one – so that there was yet another theoretical void to be filled. True, Marx had in the *Manifesto of the Communist Party* listed ten policies he believed a post-revolutionary government should implement (these are listed in full in L. Holmes 1986a, p. 6); but Lenin and the Bolsheviks had to decide for themselves how such a government and state should be structured and function.

In fact, Lenin produced no *detailed* theoretical analysis of the post-revolutionary state. *The State and Revolution* (1917) considered the proletarian state in general terms, but there was little detail on its organization and functions; the tract was more concerned with the pre-revolutionary state and the role of the proletariat during a revolution. Thus, although Leninism provides greater detail on the organization of a post-revolutionary state than does Marxism, this is more on the basis of inference from the *actions* and policies of the Bolsheviks in the period 1917 to 1924 than of Lenin's theorizing. In addition to banning other parties, Lenin professed a commitment to a planned economy, and established a secret police force (the Cheka) to deal with so-called enemies of the people. In fact, neither planning nor the use of the secret police were as extensive under Lenin as they subsequently became under Josef Stalin, who ruled the USSR from the late

1920s until his death in March 1953. Nevertheless, Lenin can be seen to have laid the basis for the extremes and horrors of the Stalinist state.

Although *The State and Revolution* provided little analysis of the post-revolutionary state, it did suggest a way of reducing the confusion in Marx's works between socialism and communism. In the *Critique of the Gotha Programme* (1875), Marx had referred briefly to a 'first phase' and a 'higher phase' of communism; Lenin proposed that the former be described as socialism, the latter as communism. Socialism would be an arrangement in which society, rather than individuals, increasingly owned the means of production, but in which there would still be a division of labour and unequal reward based on the individual's input. There would also still be a state. Under communism, not only would there be no classes, but also no fundamental alienation, no clear division of labour and no state. Distribution would be according to need rather than input – the socialist adage of 'from each according to their ability, to each according to their work' would be replaced by the principle of 'from each according to their ability, to each according to their need'.

Stalinism

Clearly, there were many gaps and contradictions in the works of both Marx and Lenin. It is thus obvious that an ideology named after 'the' ideas of both men would contain significant ambiguities. In fact, no analysis of the state ideology of Marxism-Leninism would be complete without reference to *Stalinism*, which for many is a vital component of Marxism-Leninism even though it does not appear in the ideology's title. Waller (1993, p. 1), for example, is not alone in his view that 'Communism took its characteristic shape in the Soviet Union during Stalin's period in power'; Callinicos (1991, esp. p. 2) goes so far as to equate Marxism-Leninism generally with Stalinism. Unfortunately, Stalinism only adds to the complexity and inconsistency of Marxism-Leninism.

As with Leninism, much of what is identified as Stalinism is based as much on Stalin's practice as on his theorizing. Stalin was not a great or prolific theorist. Indeed, there is little theorizing in Stalin's writings of the need either for *high levels of coercion and terror* or for *personality cults*, even though both were salient features of the Stalinist system. Moreover, while it was Stalin who in practice introduced the *centrally planned and directed economy* (also known as the command economy), this was based on ideas and policy proposals dating from Lenin's time.

However, there is one aspect of Stalinism that was at least partly theorized, and which is definitely associated with Stalin rather than Marx or Lenin. This is the concept of *socialism in one country*, which Stalin developed in 1924 and had adopted as party policy in 1925.

For a brief period following Lenin's death in January 1924, Stalin continued publicly to espouse the Marxist and Leninist view that the socialist revolution would have to be internationalized if it were to succeed.[2] But Stalin's position on internationalism soon changed, as he sought to become *the* Soviet leader (that is, Lenin's successor). Since there was no agreed method for replacing a Soviet leader, the battle for the top post had to be fought in terms of personalities, power bases and policies.

It would be inappropriate to rehearse here the details of each of these in the case of the Lenin succession. Suffice it to note that one of Stalin's principal rivals in the leadership struggle was Leon Trotsky. Trotsky had in 1906 devised the concept of *permanent revolution*, which implied constant international upheaval; as 1924 progressed, Stalin began to target this idea as a way of discrediting Trotsky. Stalin exploited the fact that most Soviet citizens were both war weary (following the First World War, 1914–18, and the Russian Civil War, 1918–20) and aware that revolution appeared un-likely elsewhere in Europe. By advocating socialism in one country and contrasting it with permanent revolution, Stalin was promoting a policy both more attractive and apparently more realistic than Trotsky's. In addi-tion, the notion of building a system in the USSR more advanced than any other in the world – of reaching socialism before the West European states – appealed to the national pride of many Soviets. Stalin had found a winner; although it would be quite wrong to suggest that Stalin defeated Trotsky solely because of his more popular policy, it would be equally incorrect to underplay the significance of Stalin's innovation.

Socialism in one country was used to justify the so-called *revolution from above* in the USSR from the late 1920s. The USSR was at that time still far from being the predominantly urbanized and industrialized (let alone capi-talist) type of society Marx had maintained was a necessary precondition for a socialist revolution. In the absence of the international revolution, Stalin now argued that socialism could be built only by dramatically inten-sifying the industrialization process. This was the context in which the first five-year plan was introduced in late 1928. Although this was originally focused primarily on the rapid development of industry, Stalin was soon arguing that industrial development on the scale and at the pace he consid-ered necessary would require a much more efficient and productive agricul-tural base. He used this argument to justify draconian measures against the peasantry from the end of the 1920s. From then until the early 1930s, the communists used high levels of coercion to force often unwilling peasants to work together in collective farms. Some peasants accepted the official jus-tifications for collectivization and were prepared to cooperate for the good of their country. But many others were bitter that the government was coercing them and, allegedly in the name of socialism, grossly exploiting them in order to finance the massive industrialization programme.

The high levels of coercion in the late 1920s and early 1930s generated high levels of resistance, which by the mid-1930s had affected important sections of the communist party itself. Stalin's determination to suppress resistance to and even questioning of his policies and actions, plus his own increasingly paranoiac and megalomaniacal personality, resulted in the emergence of widespread state terror (high levels of coercion, apparently *arbitrarily* applied). For some observers, this became the salient feature of Stalinism in the mid to late 1930s.

The Yugoslav model

After the Second World War, Stalinism spread to most of the countries of
Eastern Europe. But tensions between the USSR and Yugoslavia were by
1948 so high that the two countries essentially broke off relations. The
relevance of this here is that, partly in an endeavour to distance itself from
the Soviet theory and practice of communism, Yugoslavia gradually developed its own version. While it must be acknowledged that the practice of
communism was slightly different in every country, the *Yugoslav model*
differed from the Soviet far more than did any other in Eastern Europe. A
very brief overview of its salient features is therefore necessary if the reader
is to begin to appreciate some of the range of diversity of communism in
practice.

The key concept associated with the Yugoslav model of communism is
self-management. This emerged at the beginning of the 1950s, and was
initially introduced only at the workplace level. Over the years – at least
until 1974, when there was some recentralization – this gradually spread to
the various administrative tiers of the Yugoslav system. In essence, this
principle permitted far more local input to decision-making than did the
highly centralized Soviet model. Although many citizens considered that in
practice they still had insufficient say in the running of their own system,
most commentators agree that the Yugoslav authorities made more serious
efforts to foster a genuine workers' state – a dictatorship *of* the proletariat,
as distinct from the Soviet-style dictatorship *over* the proletariat – than did
any other communist elite (for detailed analyses of the Yugoslav model see
Rusinow 1977; Lydall 1986).

Communism and socialism

In concluding this section, it is worth noting that none of the states here
labelled communist ever themselves claimed to be communist. Rather,
most sooner or later emulated the Soviet example of 1936 by declaring they
had achieved socialism. However, in declaring their end goal (or *telos*) to be
communism, adopting an official ideology called Marxism-Leninism, organizing the political system according to the principle of democratic
centralism, and having a centrally planned and largely socialized economy
(although the level of both varied over time and from country to country),
such states could be readily distinguished from others that also claimed to
be socialist but which did not adopt these features (such as Libya, Burma/
Myanmar). Those who claim it is inappropriate to label these countries
communist because they had not yet created the stateless, classless and
alienation-free society Marx saw as the end goal of communists apparently
do not know their Marxism very well. In *The German Ideology* (1846),
Marx wrote: 'Communism is for us not a *state of affairs* which is to be
established, an *ideal* to which reality [will] have to adjust itself. We call
communism the *real* movement which abolishes the present state of things'

(Marx and Engels 1970, pp. 56–7). Clearly, Marx was labelling as communism the movement towards the ultimate and desired end goal, not just that goal itself.

Unfortunately for their elites, all the European communist states and the USSR were losing their way by the 1980s, for reasons and in a manner to be elaborated in chapters 2–4. At this juncture, the thorny problem of what post-communism might mean can be addressed.

Post-Communism

It is a basic premise of this book that post-communism is better understood as the rejection of the communist power system than as a clear-cut adoption of an alternative system. Consequently, there can be no understanding of what post-communism might mean without an analysis of what communism as a system of power meant *in practice*. Largely for this reason, much of this book has been structured so as to permit direct and ready comparison on any given topic between the situations in late communism (broadly the 1980s) and early post-communism. But what can be said at this point about post-communism as a concept and phenomenon?

There is no readily identifiable and reasonably specific ideology or even theory of post-communism as there was for communism. This is a major reason why it is so difficult to conceptualize post-communism. Nevertheless, tentative steps towards such a conceptualization need to be taken if we are to begin to understand this diverse and complex phenomenon.

Perhaps the first writer to begin to explore what post-communism might mean was Zbigniew Brzezinski, who wrote:

> A new phenomenon – post-Communism – is now appearing . . . a post-Communist system will be one in which the withering away of communism has advanced to the point that neither Marxist theory nor past Communist practice dictate much – if any – of ongoing public policy. Post-Communism, very simply, will be a system in which self-declared 'Communists' just do not treat communist doctrine seriously as the guide to social policy . . . (1989, p. 252)

Two points can be made about this quotation. First, there is a sense of irony in it; Brzezinski is modifying some of Marxism's own terms (for instance, the reference to a 'withering away' of communism) in making his argument. Second – and understandably, given that his book was written *before* the extraordinary changes that became clearly visible only in the latter half of 1989 – Brzezinski's definition appears to imply that the communists themselves would increasingly jettison their past practices and theories, but in one way or another continue to rule.

By now it is clear that most of the anti-communist revolutions of 1989–91 went much further than predicted by Brzezinski (or, to be fair, almost every other commentator). Although former communists continue to exercise some form of power in many post-communist states (see chapters 7 and

12), this is in most cases only *after* they have stopped calling themselves communists, have publicly renounced Marxism-Leninism and many of the salient features of communist structures and policies, *and* have subjected themselves to genuinely competitive elections. In short, it is necessary to move beyond Brzezinski's early definition.

The most obvious, if also unenlightening, definition of post-communism is that it is whatever follows a communist system. This almost tautological statement can be refined by suggesting that post-communism grows out of communism as it was actually practised, and is the product of the anti-communist, *double-rejective* revolutions of 1989–91. By focusing on what was rejected in these revolutions (the issue of whether or not they were revolutions is addressed in chapter 6), some vague contours of post-communism begin to take shape.

The first rejection was of what was perceived to be external domination. In the case of many countries of Eastern Europe, this was by the Soviet Union. In the case of much of the USSR itself, it was by Russia. And in the case of much of Yugoslavia, it was by Serbia.

The second rejection was of communism as a system of power (whether or not the ideal, or end goal, of communism was also rejected cannot be answered with any degree of certainty, and in any case is of little relevance to an understanding of the 1989–91 revolutions). In addition to the rejection of democratic centralism and other formal aspects of the system, it meant a repudiation of the mendacity, hypocrisy, elitism, corruption, incompetence and deteriorating performance of the communists.

There are limits to the validity of the concept of the double-rejective revolution. Communist Albania could not in any meaningful sense have been described as dominated by an external power, and so had in essence merely a single rejection. Conversely, it could be argued that the GDR also rejected its own identity and independence when it merged with West Germany in October 1990; in a sense, this was a triple rejection. Russia did not reject external domination, although it did experience what could, with some conceptual bending, be described as a rejection of its own role as an imperial power. Its double rejection was therefore different from that of most of the other communist states, although there are *some* parallels between the Russian and Serbian experiences.

While the concept of the double-rejective revolution has its limitations, it also has the major advantage that it suggests the abandonment rather than the clear-cut adoption of something. Communism was discredited; but democracy, the market and arguably even sovereignty were not widely and deeply understood (internalized) as they were in the West. Rather, many citizens of the formerly communist world tended at the time of the collapse of communist power and in the immediate aftermath to assume that if something had long been criticized by the communists, then it was probably what was now needed. Indeed, there was a widespread assumption that what was required was whatever was as nearly as possible the opposite of what communism had involved. For instance, if communist power meant in practice an all-powerful state, then a much less interventionist one was needed. If communism involved having an all-embracing ideology that claimed to have answers to everything, then there was bound to be cynicism about any alternative, putatively omniscient ideology. At a more concrete level, if communism meant in practice a one-party state, then a multiparty system was wanted. And if communism involved having a centrally planned and state-owned economy, then what was required was a marketized and largely privately owned economy. Although the *means* for achieving the political and economic objectives have varied, the *ends* themselves have been broadly similar in the numerous post-communist states.

In short, the image of what was to replace domination and communism was for many citizens a deduced, not an induced, concept. True, a few intellectuals did have some experience of the West and a reasonable understanding of it. But most citizens had a limited comprehension of what many of the concepts they and their politicians were advocating meant in practice, and even less direct experience of them. Moreover, much of the demand for democracy and the market, whether from elites or ordinary citizens, was based on two questionable assumptions. The first was that these two concepts are necessarily linked – that there cannot be one without the other. The second was that better standards of living would result from the adoption and achievement of these general goals. While some in the post-communist world appreciate from their knowledge of the Asian 'tigers'[3] that there can be rapidly rising standards of living with relatively little democratization, most people in the early post-communist societies looked to Europe rather than Asia for role models (this is less true of some parts of the FSU than of eastern Europe). It is important to bear all this is mind, since many of the problems of post-communism relate to unrealistic expectations and a poor understanding of the ramifications of concepts such as market economics. This is largely because of the absence during the communist era of the total culture within which market values and competitive politics exist. The full meaning of many important concepts and practices cannot be learnt from books alone.

A FOURTEEN-POINT MODEL

At this juncture, many of the points just made can be systematized, developed and supplemented to create a fourteen-point model of post-communism (see chapter 6 for a model of the transition *to* post-communism) that makes it possible to distinguish post-communist countries from others with which they might initially appear to have much in common. Although some question the uniqueness of post-communism, much of this model is an elaboration of three factors common and unique to post-communist states: a similar starting point and legacy; the comprehensiveness of their attempts at transition; and the global context in which such attempts have been made. Hence, *while several of the following variables apply to numerous countries outside the post-communist world, the particular blend is unique to post-communism.* It is therefore legitimate to identify post-communism as a phenomenon in its own right, even though traditional cultures vary enormously across the individual countries and the paths being taken by them are relatively diverse. In the following analysis, the first factor listed above has been examined in terms of political cultural implications of a common heritage, while the second and third are dealt with in a single section on structural commonalities of early post-communism.

Political cultural implications of a common heritage

Within the limits already identified, the post-communist states that came into existence in the period 1989–91 have a common starting point – the rejection of external domination and of communism as a system of power. However, while it is argued here that communism has been rejected as a system of power, it is also maintained that many aspects of the communist era were deeply and often subconsciously internalized by both citizens and officials. Further, it is clear that current attitudes towards institutions and concepts such as 'political party', 'parliament' and 'democracy' are being heavily influenced by memories of and associations with the communist past. All this is profoundly affecting post-communist political culture and the capacity to create a new order. Thus no post-communist politicians have started with a clean slate; they are having to create a new system with citizens who are carrying a considerable amount of baggage from the past.

This common heritage has a number of closely related ramifications. They are elaborated here as separate variables *solely* in order to render them more readily identifiable; in practice, most of them interact and are mutually dependent.

1 Assertion of independence and the rise of nationalism   The rejection of external domination is just one reason why a salient feature of many post-communist states has been a strong assertion of sovereignty and independence, and a marked rise in various kinds of nationalism. Although both of these features are already being tempered in *some* post-communist states, it is understandable that the recent sense of liberation has resulted in what many outside the post-communist world consider unrealistic and outdated notions of the autonomy of the state, and in several cases undesirable levels and manifestations of nationalism.

2 Near absence of a culture of compromise   There is still a poorly developed democratic culture in most post-communist states. This can largely be explained not only in terms of the decades of communist rule, but also of the fact that none of these countries – with the partial exceptions of what used to be Czecho-Slovakia and the GDR – had had much experience with liberal democracy in the pre-communist era. Hence there is little internalized comprehension of the notions of consensuality and compromise. In addition, and despite the short-lived euphoria over their own achievements in *some* of the countries in the revolutionary period 1989–91, there is still relatively little sense among the mass citizenry of the possibilities of self-empowerment in the political sphere.

To argue that there is an underdeveloped sense of consensuality and compromise does not necessarily imply that there is no desire for homogeneity. On the contrary, there is in some ways too much expectation of homogeneity, partly as a result of past experiences. What is in too short supply is an appreciation that there can and should be conflicting views, but that these can and should be reconciled through negotiation and bargaining within an accepted framework of rules.

3 High expectations of leaders   Following on from this is what many in the more established democracies would consider to be an excessive faith in the ability of individual leaders. It is noteworthy how many post-communist states have opted for strong, charismatic presidents, of whom many citizens probably have unrealistic aspirations in the early stages. Subsequently, if it becomes clear that the president's capacity to bring rapid, significant change is limited, many formerly supportive citizens become either very disillusioned with or even hostile towards the president. Changed attitudes towards presidents Walesa in Poland, Landsbergis in Lithuania, and even Yeltsin in Russia exemplify this point (for 1992 survey evidence of a desire for strong leaders in three FSU states see Reisinger et al. 1994, esp. pp. 191–2).

4 Cynicism towards and/or mistrust of political institutions   Connected to this leader orientation is a comparative lack of regard for institutions – especially parliaments, political parties and 'public authorities' (for survey evidence see Rose and Haerpfer 1994a, esp. pp. 17–18). During the communist era, many citizens had a marked sense of 'them' and 'us', and often turned to private relations as a way of coping with the fact that they had little impact on their often incompetent and corrupt institutions. Thus, in addition to actually establishing new institutions, post-communist politicians have to nurture a communal faith in the very notion of state institutions, the rule of law, constitutionalism, etc.

Another dimension of the deeply ingrained heritage of 'them' and 'us' thinking and the conception of institutions is what Schopflin (1993a, pp. 26–7) identifies as a greater tendency than in many other societies to believe that politics are both highly personalized and conspiratorial.

As Dempsey (1993, p. 281) points out, there is also a communist legacy of corruption (see Los 1990, Clark 1993, L. Holmes 1993a). This corruption is clearly a feature of post-communism too (see Yasmann 1993a and 1993c, Kettle 1995). Among the numerous reasons is the fact that post-communist politicians themselves have been influenced by decades of communist and pre-communist rule and values. In addition, the sorry state of the economy in all early post-communist states has meant that many goods are too expensive even for many officials to afford, so that they turn to corruption to acquire them.

In light of the above, it becomes even clearer why the development of citizen faith in institutions, and the notion of clean politics, will take many years yet to develop.

Schopflin, in a polemical and stimulating article, has referred to much of what has been elaborated in points 2–4 as the legacy of the 'infantilized society' (1993a, p. 24). This is in one sense a most unfortunate term, since it can be interpreted as indicative of the patronizing arrogance of the Western observer. But on another level, the metaphor is a useful one in helping us to make sense of post-communism. The term is infantilized rather than infantile; although it does suggest that the citizens of these countries are politically novices or even immature, another equally important implication is that the paternalistic communist system is to blame for this. The communist systems took almost all important decisions on behalf of the citizens, permitting very little public input (at least until the final stages of communist rule, and even then significant improvement occurred in only a few communist states). Schopflin's term should therefore be read as a criticism of the political legacy of the communists rather than of the citizens of the post-communist world.

5 Rejection of teleologism and grand theories   Although there are signs that many citizens and politicians are searching for some new goal – faith even – in the post-communist era, this is not to be confused with a quest for some putatively omniscient teleological ideology such as Marxism. There is widespread scepticism about 'grand theories' that not only produce images of a (possibly attractive) distant *telos* (the root of the word teleological), but also seek to justify an elitist and hierarchical system on the grounds that this is the optimal arrangement for achieving the end goal as rapidly and efficiently as possible. This is all part of the rejection of the communist power system, which described the party elite as the 'vanguard'.

6 An ideological vacuum   Leading on from the last point, there is still no underlying, widely accepted ideology and set of ground rules in most post-communist societies.[4] This helps to explain the current appeal of nationalism in many post-communist states. Nationalism is not a true ideology (see chapter 10). Nevertheless, it provides a framework for many who have lost their usual referents (an effect of the discrediting of the totalizing ideology of Marxism-Leninism) and who fear losing their own identity as a consequence (for a subtle analysis of the complex relationship between nationalism and the ideological vacuum see J. Hall 1995, esp. pp. 86–8).

In addition to the other problems of nationalism (such as the possibilities of it becoming aggressive and exclusionary), one of its most dangerous aspects precisely in the vacuum of early post-communism is the negative influence it can exert on the development of a democratic political culture. In line with the argument in point 2 above, and again citing Schopflin (1993a, p. 23), 'both nationalism and religion contain clear homogenising imperatives, which are hostile to the bargaining and compromise demanded by democracy.' This reference to religion leads nicely to the next point.

7 *Moral confusion*   The breakdown of Marxism-Leninism has also left something of a moral vacuum. Although the church (as with Catholicism in Poland and Lithuania, Islam in the Central Asian states of the CIS and Azerbaijan) has filled that void for some citizens, many others have been unable to relate closely to religion. Some post-communist leaders have also sought to provide moral guidance and leadership; the best example is Czechia's Vaclav Havel. But such leadership is rare, and has in any case been quite inadequate to overcome the moral deficit in so many early post-communist societies.

This vacuum has contributed to a marked increase in crime rates, which is another feature of many post-communist countries. Such criminality cannot be explained solely in terms of the moral vacuum: one should also factor in variables such as the rise in unemployment coupled with an inadequate welfare state; the marked decline in living standards, which has encouraged many citizens to seek to compensate by means of economic crime; and the fluidity and uncertainty of the new state institutions, which in general exert a negative influence on law enforcement. Nevertheless, evidence of the moral vacuum is highly visible in several post-communist states, and is affecting the general ambience in them (for evidence see Halligan and Mozdoukhov 1995, p. 30).

The commonalities of early post-communism

8 *Comprehensive revolution*   During recent decades, several countries have made the transition to democracy from one kind of authoritarian system or another. They include some of the countries of southern Europe (Spain, Portugal, Greece) and several Latin American countries. Many other states have made or are making the transition from predominantly rural and agricultural economies to urban and industrialized ones; the Asian tigers exemplify this. Yet none of these countries has attempted a *simultaneous* and very rapid transition *from* a centralized and state-run and largely nationalized economy, a highly centralized and relatively closed polity, a society largely devoid of a bourgeoisie, and from long-standing military and trading blocs, *towards* a marketised and privatized economy *and* pluralist democracy *and* a society with a powerful capitalist class *and* to new military allegiances and trading blocs. The intended comprehensiveness and pace of change distinguishes the post-communist states from other transitional ones, and means that caution must be exercised in relating much of the 1980s comparative literature on transitions (see, for instance, Pridham 1984, O'Donnell et al. 1986, Malloy and Seligson 1987) to post-communism.

9 *Temporality*   Clearly, post-communism is a transitional phenomenon. As already indicated, most of the elites and many of the citizens of these

countries want them to become more like 'the West', politically, economically and socially. Once they are perceived to have arrived and settled at this destination – or even at some other, such as a populist dictatorship – they will no longer be post-communist. In this sense, post-communism is a temporary phenomenon, even if it lasts one or two decades.

10 Dynamism   It might initially appear to be tautologous to describe a society as both transitional and dynamic. But a transitional society might appear to stagnate at a given point, moving neither forwards nor backwards. Expressing this metaphorically, a train may break down between stations. In some senses, Russia could be argued to have been in such a situation since 1992. But most post-communist states do appear to be moving (see chapter 12 for a brief overview of the possible destinations), and in this sense are dynamic.

Another point about the dynamics of post-communism is that there are already reasonably distinct *stages*; since an appreciation of these will be easier after a reading of part 3 of this book, they are considered at the beginning of chapter 12.

11 Instability   In addition to the moral and ideological vacuum in so many post-communist states, the fact that there is as yet still no broad consensus in them on such issues as the optimal political arrangements or the pace and sequencing of economic change means that most were as of 1995 still *relatively* unstable. This instability is very obvious in those regions of the formerly communist world where there is overt warfare, notably in parts of the former Yugoslavia and the FSU. But even where there is no actual fighting, there are numerous other symbols of instability. These include the frequency of elections and changes of government; frequent votes of no confidence in the government; either frequent changes of policy or the non-adoption of policies on important issues (such as property rights and privatization); constant re-forming of political parties and coalitions; frequent constitutional changes; and so on.

Finally, and importantly, there is an uncertainty in many parts of the post-communist world about frontiers. For Claus Offe (1991), the actual or possible redrawing of boundaries is one of the three major transitions (along with the economic and political) of post-communism.

12 A widespread sense of insecurity   Whatever other criticisms are levelled against late communism – and there are many legitimate ones – few citizens feared for their jobs or accommodation. In both of these areas, security was high by international standards. Conversely, high unemployment levels in so many post-communist states (Czechia and Russia were apparently two exceptions to this as of 1995, though see chapter 9) and uncertainties about property ownership have resulted in a marked increase in feelings of insecurity. This has been exacerbated by the overall reduction of the the role, scope and capacities of the welfare state in most of these countries (for survey data suggesting feelings of insecurity, because of unemployment and high levels of inflation see Rose and Mishler 1994, esp. pp. 176–7, and Rose and Haerpfer 1994a, esp. pp. 13–14).

13 Unfortunate timing   For many anti-communists, the 1989–91 revolutions occurred some four decades too late in the case of Eastern Europe, and approximately seven decades late in the case of the USSR. But this is not the sense in which the term 'unfortunate timing' is used here. Rather, it refers to the fact that the anti-communist revolutions more or less coincided with a serious downturn in the economies of most First World countries. This meant that it was much more difficult for post-communist countries to obtain economic aid and investment than it would have been in a more healthy international economic climate. The problem was further compounded precisely by the fact that so many countries moved to post-communism at more or less the same time. A major consequence of this was that there was far more demand for the limited supply of funds than would have been the case had only one or two countries made the shift at a time.

14 Legitimation problems   Many of the above problems, plus the inexperience, bickering and what is increasingly perceived by citizenries as incompetence of many of the 'new' – many post-communist politicians were functionaries of one kind or another during the late communist period – political elites have led to serious legitimation problems for virtually all post-communist states. Whether or not these constitute legitimation crises is a question addressed in chapter 12.

Like all models, this one has its problems and limitations. Since it focuses on similarities, it does not *per se* even begin to bring out the richness and diversity of post-communism; what has in recent times been happening in Tajikistan or Turkmenistan is in important ways very different from what is happening in Hungary or Poland, for example. Not all variables apply to all countries. The particular salience of individual variables, and the balance between them, is of course unique to each country. And many of the variables are difficult to prove empirically. Nevertheless, the model serves as a useful heuristic device in attempting to conceptualize post-communism; for some appreciation of the diversity of paths being taken by actual countries, the reader will have to take on chapters 7–11.

Notes

1 In 1917, Lenin published *Imperialism, the Highest Stage of Capitalism*. In this, he argued that the First World War was above all a war between imperialist, capitalist states and was a direct result of the logic of capitalism to compete and ever to increase its profits and markets.
2 Although Lenin himself became increasingly despondent during the early 1920s about the imminent likelihood of a successful revolution in an advanced industrial country, he was too ill (or perhaps confused) to provide any theoretical justification for a continuation of the building of socialism in what had since 1922 been called the USSR.

3 This term originally referred just to the 'four little tigers' or 'four little dragons' of Hong Kong, Singapore, South Korea and Taiwan. Nowadays it is often applied in addition to several other Asian countries, including Indonesia, Malaysia and Thailand.
4 It could be objected that the West does not really have an ideology either. Even if this point is accepted, it would be difficult to refute the notion that the West does have a *relatively* stable and developed set of core values. Moreover, citizens in the post-communist states are *used* to an overt and putatively omniscient official ideology in a way most Westerners are not.

FURTHER READING

Useful and accessible sources on various aspects of Marxism and Marxism-Leninism include, in alphabetical order, Avineri 1968; Carew Hunt 1963; Harding 1983; Kolakowski 1981; McLellan 1980a, 1980b, 1988; Meyer 1984.

Given the widespread interest in it, it is surprising how little there is on what exactly post-communism might mean in a general sense, but useful starting points are Schopflin 1993a and Schopflin 1993b, pp. 256–300, while Wnuk-Lipinski 1995b outlines some of the problems involved in theorizing the phenomenon. For an interesting argument as to why post-communism should be seen more as a *transformational* phenomenon (which focuses on processes emerging from the past) than as a *transitional* one (which, they maintain, focuses on destinations) see Bryant and Mokrzycki 1994b.

2

Theories of the Collapse of Communist Power

At a seminar held in Oxford in May 1993, the eminent Hungarian intellectual Elemer Hankiss argued that were the German sociologist and social theorist Max Weber still alive, he would wait at least a decade before pronouncing on the reasons for the collapse of communist power – and that when he did, he would do so in a book of at least a thousand pages. There can be little doubt that great minds will address the issue of the fall of communism for decades to come, and that, in a few years' time, an overview of the type provided here will be far more complex and sophisticated.

This said, many of the world's leading scholars have already provided early analyses of the reasons for the 1989–91 revolutions, and it is one task of this chapter to provide a brief and critical overview of many of these. A second objective is to suggest interpretations that can be deduced from major recent works that, while not themselves directly addressing the fall of communist power, can nevertheless provide insights for those wishing to consider the revolutions from as many potentially enlightening perspectives as possible. For instance, a brief reference to Paul Kennedy's book *The Rise and Fall of the Great Powers* is included here, even through this does not directly consider the 1989–91 revolutions.

The chapter is divided into ten parts: nine are approaches to and/or theories of the reasons for the revolutions, while the tenth provides conclusions. Not all of the approaches operate at the same level. For example, some are primarily concerned with Eastern Europe, and others with the USSR. The first four focus mainly on short-term precipitating factors, the following five on more long-term, underlying ones. Similarly, the first four are readily accessible, while the following five are more abstract and require longer to assimilate.

Readers should *not* assume that the amount of space devoted to explanations implies anything about their relative significance. Sometimes, a very important point can be made succinctly, while a less significant one is more complex and requires a longer exposition. In other cases – the 'economic failure' argument is the best example – a truncated form of the explanation is provided in this chapter because the point is elaborated elsewhere in the book.

Nor should it be assumed that the theories are mutually exclusive. In fact, many of them coexist very well, sometimes precisely because they are looking at different countries and/or at more short-term or long-term factors.

A final point is that most writers, understandably and to their credit, provide multifactoral analyses. J. F. Brown (1991, pp. 2–4), for instance, identifies six factors leading to the collapse of communist power in Eastern Europe: 40 years of failure; the illegitimacy of communism; societal opposition; the communist ruling elite's loss of confidence in its ability to rule and unwillingness to use the means to maintain its rule; the improvement in East–West relations; and the impact of Soviet developments under Gorbachev. Ralf Dahrendorf (1990, pp. 13–22) focuses on three principal factors: Gorbachev; the fact that 'communism never worked'; and 'the strange history of the 1980s', in which the West did well and Europe regained its self-confidence. And Paul Kennedy (1993, pp. 230–1) identifies three factors leading to the collapse of the Soviet system: a crisis of legitimacy; a crisis of economic production and social provision; and a crisis of ethnic and cultural relationships. Even a consideration of just three analysts' views reveals areas of overlap. Because of this, and since so many commentators have listed several factors, it makes little sense to summarize the views of one writer after another; *inter alia*, this would result in much repetition. Rather, I have chosen to isolate what seem to me to be the core arguments of a number of analyses, and to cite examples of scholars who have subscribed more or less to each of them. Even this method is problematical, in that some factors (such as the role of the media) are included here under one approach, while others would have either located them in a different section or else identified them as categories in their own right. The reader should not be overconcerned with the particular pigeon-holing used in this chapter. The principal aim is to convey as many of the *ideas* as possible, which can then be reclassified as the reader prefers.

The Gorbachev Factor

In addition to J. F. Brown and Ralf Dahrendorf, many analysts have placed 'the blame' for the collapse of communist power, both in Eastern Europe and in the USSR, on one man, Mikhail Sergeevich Gorbachev. At a November 1991 conference held in Miami, the ever-controversial American analyst Jerry Hough summarized his views on Gorbachev's role particularly punchily – 'Gorbachev blew it.'

Gorbachev became General Secretary of the Central Committee of the CPSU in March 1985, and soon introduced reform in the economy (mainly *perestroika* and *uskorenie*), the polity (*demokratisatsiya* and *glasnost*) and foreign policy (new political thinking – for translations of and details on all these, see chapters 4 and 11). The following argument is *based on* the arguments of those who have seen Gorbachev's role as crucial; since there are differences – sometimes subtle, sometimes more obvious – between these various analysts, the overview provided here cannot be taken as a direct reflection of any one of them. Rather, it is an amalgam, designed to highlight the most common strands of the arguments.

The argument about Gorbachev's role focuses essentially on three elements. The first is Gorbachev's own personality and political orientations. Most analysts agree that Gorbachev was a genuine reformer but not a revolutionary – a leader who knew that the USSR needed significant change, but who continued to believe that the necessary extent and type of change required was possible within a socialist framework. The complexity of Gorbachev's personality is also usually highlighted. On the one hand, he knew he would have to be a strong and relatively radical leader to bring about the changes in the Soviet system he considered vital. On the other hand, he was, as Goldman expressed it, 'willing to listen and learn' (1991, p. 226). He was not dictatorial by nature but was prepared to compromise and change if this seemed appropriate.

One aspect of Gorbachev's personal role identified by former Politburo member Yegor Ligachev in his memoirs (1993, pp. 348–9) is that Gorbachev was subject to what political scientists often call overload. According to Ligachev, Gorbachev was so closely involved in so many areas that 'it was difficult to think fundamental issues through deeply.' Thus, to the extent that Gorbachev's failures and vacillations were important in bringing about the collapse of Soviet communist power, his excessive workload becomes a significant factor.

The second element is closely linked to the first. Gorbachev's policies reflected his radical reformism on the one hand (described by Sakwa 1990, esp. p. 61, as 'revolutionary reformism'), and on the other the tensions between his strong commitments, his willingness to change if this seemed appropriate, and his desire to act as a conciliatory force up to a certain point. In a manner not dissimilar from Lenin's in the early 1920s, he introduced a very generalized notion of economic reform in the mid-1980s, having only a hazy image of the policy's details and how it would develop over time. In this sense, his economic *perestroika* can be compared with Lenin's New Economic Policy introduced in 1921. Indeed, whether *glasnost* or *demokratisatsiya* or 'new political thinking' (see A. Brown 1992a) is examined, it is clear that all of Gorbachev's policies were general ideas for improvement, which were to crystallize and be modified as they were put into practice. This is not necessarily a criticism; as writers from Popper (1957) to Braybrooke and Lindblom (1970) have pointed out, much of the policy-making in the West is and *should* be done in a piecemeal or 'disjointed incrementalist' manner. Conditions in the USSR in 1980s were not as basically sound as they were in most Western systems, however, and Gorbachev has been criticized by some for not having provided sufficiently firm leadership in a situation Gorbachev himself (1987, p. 51) described as a 'pre-crisis' one.

Third, many analysts focus on the unique position of Gorbachev as Soviet leader. While all communist states – obviously – had their leaders, there was only one 'home of the first socialist revolution' and centre of the

Soviet bloc. This argument is more fully explored in subsequent sections. For now, the most important point is that Gorbachev is seen as having given the go-ahead to Eastern Europeans to pursue their own goals, even if this involved overthrowing communism. This approach (encouraging countries to take their own paths independently of the Soviet Union, and on the assumption that the USSR would not interfere under any circumstances) has been described as Gorbachev's 'Sinatra Doctrine', after the American crooner's hit 'I Did it My Way'. This argument can be used to explain not only the East European revolutions, but also the Soviet one, in that many of the republics of the USSR were inspired by what they saw happening and being tolerated in Eastern Europe.

But the impact of his 'Sinatra Doctrine' was not the only aspect of Gorbachev that is linked with his unique position as the Soviet leader. Another is that it was precisely his criticisms of past practices, his calls for radical change and his ambiguity that helped to undermine the legitimacy of communists everywhere. This point, too, is more fully elaborated later in the chapter.

Economic Failure

The communist economies achieved much in their early stages, with impressively high growth rates, but slowed down over time (the role of this point in the collapse of communist power is strongly emphasised by Batt 1991). This slowdown had many ramifications. One was that the communist world generally (the People's Republic of China during the 1980s being a notable exception) was not merely not catching up with the West, but was actually falling behind. If the communist economies generally had been better able to satisfy the consumer, the fact that overall growth rates were declining might have been less significant. But many of the economies had been structured more or less along the lines laid down by Stalin for the Soviet economy in the 1930s, which meant that producer goods' industries were generally privileged over consumer goods' industries. Consumers were badly treated in comparison with West Europeans, and many East Europeans, plus a growing number of Soviets, were aware of this.

Since the problems of the economies are dealt with in chapter 8, it is inappropriate to provide details here. But before moving to the next section, it is worth considering one rather technical aspect of Soviet economic policy that the former number two in the party to Gorbachev, Yegor Ligachev, identifies as the single most important factor leading to the crisis of the Soviet economy in the late 1980s. Ligachev cites a decision taken by the Politburo at the end of 1987 to shift more rapidly from central planning towards contractual arrangements between suppliers and producers as the point at which the Soviet economy began to go into free fall. Following this, wages and hence demand rose much faster than supply; this led to the economic chaos that typified the USSR by the end of the 1980s (Ligachev 1993, pp. 339–51).

The Role of Opposition Forces

It will be recalled that J. F. Brown has identified 'societal opposition' to communism as one of the factors leading to its collapse. There is no question that ordinary citizens vented their dissatisfaction with their communist governments on numerous occasions in recent decades (most notably in the GDR in 1953, Poland and Hungary in 1956, Czechoslovakia in 1968, and Poland again in 1970–1, 1976, 1980–1; there were also lesser outbursts in Bulgaria and Czechoslovakia in 1953, Romania in 1977 and 1987, Yugoslavia in 1971 and 1981, the USSR in 1962, etc. – for details see L. Holmes 1986a, pp. 284–319). By the end of the 1980s, *open displays of mass discontent* had become a salient feature of the politics of many communist states, and for some commentators (such as Reddaway 1993), they contributed in a significant way to the collapse of communist power.

Another source of opposition were the *dissidents* in so many countries, although their profile was much lower in the Balkan states than in East Central Europe. Some analysts maintain that the writings and protests of these critical intellectuals (often Marxists) served to undermine the communist system in several countries. Thus, in his introductory chapter to a full-length edited study of this phenomenon, Ray Taras (1992b, p. 4) writes:

> The central thesis that informs this study is . . . the existence of linkage, however tenuous and indirect, between recent political change and past Marxist dissent in the Soviet alliance system . . . we might want to argue that what undermined Marxism in the Soviet bloc was precisely the co-existence of the 'two Marxisms' about which Alvin Gouldner wrote – the 'scientific' Marxism adopted by socialist states and the 'critical' Marxism appropriated by those opposed to monolithic Muscovite ideology.

It should be noted, however, that some commentators have warned strongly against overemphasizing the role of the dissidents (see, for instance, Brzezinski 1993a, p. 60).

A third variant of this 'opposition forces' argument is the notion that *civil society* began to emerge and develop in many communist countries in the 1980s, and then challenged the communist authorities (see, for instance, Kukathas et al. 1991, R. Miller 1992a); this argument is elaborated in chapter 10.

Competition with the West

From early in its existence, but particularly from Stalin's time, the USSR saw itself as being in competition with the West. When Stalin called in the 1920s for 'socialism in one country', he was not advocating a society totally in isolation from the rest of the world. Rather, the policy was said to mean that the USSR would establish a model of socialism other countries would study and seek to emulate. This was alleged to be a less threatening approach to the internationalization of socialism than direct export of revolution, and Stalin apparently hoped the capitalist world would leave the USSR in peace.

But this was a vain hope. Despite having signed a non-aggression treaty with the Soviets in 1939, the Germans invaded the USSR in 1941. Almost exactly a decade before, Stalin had used the threat from the capitalist world to justify allocating a substantial proportion of state funds to a build-up of the Soviet military and military-related industry. Many Soviet historians maintained that the Second World War would have had an even worse outcome for the USSR had Stalin not invested so much in the Soviet war machine. Whether this is a convincing argument or not, the fact is that the Soviet leadership identified a threat in the early 1930s and adopted policy decisions on the basis of this. Given that the new Soviet system had been invaded by several foreign powers (including the USA, the UK, France, Germany, Japan and Turkey) in 1918, and that the numbers of violently anti-communist fascists in Europe were on the rise in the late 1920s and early 1930s, Stalin's warnings were probably realistic enough. In all events, they set a pattern for the future.

The Soviets cooperated closely with the Western Allies from 1941 to 1945. But with the defeat of fascism, old tensions between the capitalist West and the communist USSR soon resurfaced. Indeed, with the spread of communism in the 1940s, the tensions worsened. By the late 1940s, relations had deteriorated so much that observers began to refer to a Cold War between East (especially the USSR) and West. Stalin now attempted to isolate his country from the West as far as possible, at the same time as he was determined to catch up with and overtake it.

Following Stalin's death in 1953, the situation began to change. While Stalin's successor Khrushchev did not subscribe to the view that 'if you can't beat 'em, join 'em', he accepted that if the Soviets were to surpass the West, they would have to learn from it. He did not end the Cold War, but he did favour less hostility between East and West; there was nothing during his reign to compare with the Korean War of 1950–3, when East and West essentially fought a war by proxy. Instead, the new Soviet leader pursued a policy of 'peaceful coexistence'. One practical ramification of this was that Soviet natural scientists could now have easier access to Western scientific journals.

Despite the modest improvement in East–West relations, Khrushchev remained committed to the idea of eventually surpassing the West. During the 1950s he boasted that the USSR would soon overtake the USA in areas such as meat and milk consumption. Khrushchev also oversaw the publication of the CPSU's party programme of 1961, which claimed that the USSR would reach basic communism by 1980. This could hardly be interpreted as suggesting that the USSR would become an alternative *capitalist* model.

In 1962, the world went on to nuclear alert as a result of the Cuban missile crisis (see chapter 5). The Soviet backdown humiliated not only their leader, but the Soviet people collectively; when Khrushchev was removed from power by his colleagues in October 1964, his successors determined that the USSR would never again be made to look so weak to the rest of the world.

An increase in Soviet defence expenditure that had already started in the last year or two of Khrushchev's reign therefore intensified in the Brezhnev era (1964–82). The expenditures and military developments were such that the West was by the late 1960s acknowledging that the USSR had caught it up in many areas of military technology and expertise, and in some areas might even have surpassed it. There was intense competition between the USA and the Soviet Union in the area of space research, for instance. While the USA was the first nation to put a person on the moon (Neil Armstrong in 1969), the Soviets had been first at putting one into space (Yurii Gagarin in 1961).

It was in this climate of escalating military competition and expenditure on both sides that Western leaders such as the German chancellor from 1969, Willy Brandt, called for an improvement in relations between East and West (his so-called *Ostpolitik* – literally policy towards the East). Fortunately, the Soviets and most of the Soviet bloc responded favourably. After all, the West was offering increased economic and technological assistance and interaction in return for a reduction of international tensions.

Thus a marked improvement in relations, *détente*, typified the early to mid 1970s. The zenith of détente was the 1975 Helsinki agreement of the Conference on Security and Cooperation in Europe (CSCE). But the improvement in relations was short-lived. As part of the Helsinki agreement, the West had insisted the Soviet bloc start respecting human rights better, notably by ceasing to harass dissidents. While some countries, notably Hungary, did more or less respect this part of the agreement, the Soviet Union, Czechoslovakia and other states continued to hound critical intellectuals. This was unacceptable to Western leaders such as US President Jimmy Carter, who were not prepared to permit a continuing improvement in East–West relations while so many communist states continued to demonstrate a blatant disregard for freedom of speech, association, assembly and travel.

By the late 1970s, the Cold War was again intensifying. The situation deteriorated markedly at the end of 1979, following the Soviet intervention in Afghanistan. By this stage, not only was the West – particularly the USA – increasingly irritated by the East's contempt for human rights, but it was also recovering from its own loss of self-confidence during the final stages of the Vietnam War (from which the USA withdrew in 1973). With more hawkish leaders coming to power in the West (Margaret Thatcher in 1979; Ronald Reagan in 1981; Helmut Kohl in 1982), the leadership of the Soviet bloc realized they would either have to intensify their competition with the West or else *de facto* acknowledge defeat in the greatest ideological war of the twentieth century.

In December 1979, NATO offered to delay installation of new cruise and Pershing nuclear missiles in Western Europe if the Soviets would remove their own newly installed nuclear missiles in Eastern Europe. But this offer was made shortly before the Soviet intervention in Afghanistan and before its new leaders had begun to formulate a much tougher anti-communist foreign policy. Soviet involvement in Afghanistan and determination to forge ahead with a weapons modernization program in Europe meant that the West felt compelled to proceed with its new missile programme in Europe from 1983.

Two changes of leadership in the USSR in the period 1982–4 made it unlikely that there would be any major reorientation in foreign policy; Andropov and Chernenko were too busy consolidating power and attempting to deal with the multitude of domestic problems that constituted the Brezhnev legacy. In addition, the defence lobby in Moscow was one of the most powerful. It is hardly surprising then that Soviet defence expenditure did not dramatically decline in this period.

The situation began to change only with Gorbachev's accession. By this stage the USA had made clear to the USSR its commitment to compete in – and win – the arms race. Reagan was referring to the USSR as the 'evil empire', and his administration was far more convinced of the correctness of its anti-communist policy than was Nixon's or Ford's in the early 1970s. Gorbachev had doubts about the correctness of *his* predecessors' policies, and made rapid progress in agreeing with the USA to reduce the respective nuclear arsenals.

Despite these improvements, Reagan was determined to push ahead with a new form of defence shield in outer space, the *Strategic Defence Initiative* (SDI or, more popularly, Star Wars). After all, the Soviets had not proved very reliable in the past, and the US administration saw little reason to be overly trusting of them now. The costs of developing the SDI were exorbitant, even for the prosperous USA. Given the sorry state of the Soviet economy, Gorbachev knew that attempting to match the USA on this new technology could bankrupt his country. He therefore did everything possible to persuade the USA to renounce its commitment to the project. But it was to no avail (the USA finally abandoned SDI only in 1993, under the new Clinton administration).

In one sense, SDI could be seen as the straw that broke the camel's back (for a leading Western economist emphasizing the significance of SDI to the collapse of the Soviet system see Ellman 1993, p. 56). It is thus particularly ironic that the development of the SDI was much less advanced than the Soviets (and others) had believed; in August 1993, US authorities revealed that many of the early test results had been fabricated! But the USSR had already failed to meet its own target of reaching communism by the year 1980, or even the more modest target of surpassing US per capita meat and milk consumption. Now, according to this interpretation, as Gorbachev and the Soviet leadership appreciated that they could not move to the next stage of competition with the West represented by Star Wars, they realized that the competition *generally* with the West had been lost. This in turn led to *self-doubt* among many of the top leaders, a factor considered in greater detail later in the chapter.

But there is more to the explanation that emphasizes East–West competition. Another dimension focuses on the very fact that East–West relations improved from the late 1960s, despite the hiccup of the early 1980s. According to this line of argument, the more communist leaderships were prepared to recognize positive aspects of the West and cooperate with it – albeit still in a limited way – the more ordinary citizens and lower ranking officials in the communist countries questioned the validity of ideological attacks on the West. The increased cooperation also led to an increase in tourism from the West, which, though still very controlled by Western standards, meant that more and more citizens in more and more communist countries began to learn 'from the horse's mouth' about life in the West.

Then there was the fact that the West – not only the USA, but also Europe – recovered strongly in the 1980s after the serious economic downturn of the 1970s. This is the major point of Dahrendorf's reference above to 'the strange history of the 1980s'. All this undermined the respect of ordinary citizens for communist ideologists who had predicted the imminent demise and collapse of the Western capitalist system.

Finally, the *basically* improved relations with the West meant that radio jamming was less pronounced in the 1970s, and again from the mid-1980s, in many communist states than had once been the case. Thus Western radio broadcasts to Eastern Europe and the USSR (notably from the US-funded Radio Free Europe and Radio Liberty, and from the UK-funded BBC World Service) are seen as having played a role in alerting citizens to what was happening inside their own countries, thus raising dissatisfaction with the communist political and economic system. One major event reported by the West, and which helped to weaken faith in the communists' putative omniscience and omnipotence, was the Chernobyl nuclear disaster of 1986. Western reporting of this acted as a major stimulus to *glasnost*, which until then had still constituted a rather modest reform. To the extent that Soviet *glasnost* spun out of control and contributed in a substantial way to the collapse of communism, the role of the Western media comes into focus. Their role in raising consciousness and spreading the message specifically in 1989 was also significant.

The Marxist Corrective

While many, including ex-Marxists, have argued since 1989 that the anticommunist revolutions demonstrated once and for all the impossibility of the Marxist project, a few Marxists – in particular the 'state capitalist' theorists – have adopted a radically different position. For them, the recent revolutions were in fact anti-Stalinist and may have given Marxism new life.

A leading exponent of this argument is Alex Callinicos. In his 1991 book *The Revenge of History*, he maintained that a sharp distinction should be drawn between Marxism and Leninism on the one hand, and Stalinism on the other (see esp. pp. 15–20). For Callinicos, Marxism is not redundant; on the contrary, it provides an excellent tool for making sense both of the recent revolutions and future developments.

Consistent with earlier state capitalist interpretations of the Soviet and East European systems (see, for instance, Cliff 1974, Harman 1983), Callinicos argues that there was a peculiar form of capitalism in the communist states, 'bureaucratic state capitalism'. According to this argument, the communist elites may not have formally *owned* the means of production, but in that they *controlled* them they occupied a class position vis-à-vis the working class that was essentially similar to that between a regular bourgeoisie and proletariat. As the elites (particularly the state functionaries) realized that their distorted brand of capitalism was less efficient than regular capitalism – which was becoming ever more global and powerful – they concluded they would have to normalize economically (that is, join the mainstream). This helps to explain much of what Callinicos calls the 'authoritarian reform' of the 1980s. This realization was even more pronounced among Eastern European elites than in the Soviet Union, since the former were more dependent on the international market.

In short, 'Stalinism' had outlived itself, and was hindering the dynamism that is so much a part of Marxist historical materialism. As elites increasingly appreciated this, they themselves introduced more and more changes that set the stage for the transition to post-communism. Given both the changing views on capitalism of the East European elites, and their belief that the Soviet Union would not use force to suppress the democracy movements, it becomes easier to understand why there was relatively little reaction by 1989 to the protesting masses (in countries such as Czechoslovakia and the GDR) or resistance to the demands of the opposition forces that negotiated with the communist elites in Round Table discussions (as in Hungary and Poland). Thus one of the advantages of this approach is that it helps to explain the relative bloodlessness of the 1989–91 events (for Callinicos's explanation of the greater violence in Romania, on which he concurs with Timothy Garton Ash's interpretation, see Callinicos 1991, p. 54). It is also useful for understanding why so many former members of the party and state elites sought to become members of the nascent capitalist class following the anti-communist revolutions, rather than fight to defend the old system.

As with any interpretation, there are aspects of this approach that can be seriously questioned. For instance, many would strongly disagree that Leninism was closer to Marxism than to Stalinism, and would criticize the Bolsheviks for their excessive voluntarism in October 1917. Nevertheless, the Marxist corrective approach, as it is labelled here, does force us to question whether or not the Marxist approach to history has really been as discredited as is often maintained. If the formerly communist states are in fact now returning to the 'normal' path of capitalist development (on this see Staniszkis 1995), it could be that the communist experiment of 1917 to 1991 merely delayed and distorted the unfolding of the international process envisaged by Marx. Certainly the ramifications for the future of this approach are quite different from those implied by Fukuyama's 'end of history' thesis (see below).

Imperial Overstretch

In a recent bestselling analysis of the collapse of empires, Paul Kennedy (1987) provides a framework that can be applied to the Soviet empire – even though Kennedy himself did not appear at the time to believe that the collapse of the Soviet empire was imminent (see p. 513).

Many analysts have referred to the Soviet inner (or internal) and outer (or external) empires. By the former is meant the USSR itself, which was a collection of 15 republics and well over 100 ethnic groups. The USSR was formally established in 1922, on the basis on the previous Russian empire. While most of the republics were formally incorporated in the 1920s, four – the three Baltic states and Moldavia – did not become part of the Soviet empire until 1940. The outer empire mostly came into existence in the 1940s, in the aftermath of the Second World War. By the 1980s it was seen to comprise at least most of the communist states of Eastern Europe (excluding Yugoslavia and Albania). Beyond this, specialists disagreed. For some, all the countries of the Council for Mutual Economic Assistance (CMEA) were part of the empire; this included the countries just listed, plus Vietnam, Cuba and Mongolia. Many favoured the inclusion of Afghanistan, in whose domestic affairs the Soviet Union played a major role during the decade 1979–89. A few commentators adopted an even broader perspective and included the many African communist states under Soviet influence from the 1970s (notably Ethiopia, Mozambique and Angola).

Although there were these disputed areas, there was widespread agreement among those using the term Soviet Empire that all the Warsaw Pact countries (see chapter 11) were part of it. For such observers, the collapse of communism in these countries, and then in the Soviet internal empire, was all part of the general phenomenon of the end of empire. Kennedy's conception of 'imperial overstretch' can now be applied to the Soviet empire.

For Kennedy, the following were the four salient features of the end of empire (1987, pp. xxii–xxiv):

> there is detectable a causal relationship between the shifts which have occurred over time in the general economic and productive balances and the position occupied by individual Powers in the international system
>
> there is a very clear connection *in the long run* between an individual Great Power's economic rise and fall and its growth and decline as an important military power (or world empire)
>
> there is a noticeable 'lag time' between the trajectory of a state's relative economic strength and the trajectory of its military/territorial influence
>
> there is a very strong correlation between the eventual outcome of the *major coalition wars* for European or global mastery, and the amount of productive resources mobilized by each side.

Many of these factors can be applied to the USSR. Very crudely, all four focus on the relationship between economic performance or decline and the amount of resources devoted to the military. This would certainly help to explain the collapse of the Soviet Union, given its economic and military competition with the West. Kennedy later writes: 'What does seem incontestable . . . is that in a long-drawn-out Great Power (and usually coalition) war, victory has repeatedly gone to the side with the more flourishing productive base' (p. xxiv). This can be applied to aspects of the USSR's decline; if 'the West' is taken as being in competition with the USSR and the Soviet empire more generally, the collapse of communism can be seen as the result of the 'more flourishing productive base' in the West.

Before finishing this application of Kennedy's analysis to the USSR, it should be noted that Kennedy himself explicitly rejects 'crude economic determinism'. For him, other factors to be included in any analysis of the end of empire include geography, military organization, national morale, the alliance system, the individual folly of a leader, and battlefield competence (1987, p. xxiv). Again, readers will be able to compare each of these identified variables with their knowledge of the collapse of communism in the USSR and individual countries.

While much of Kennedy's analysis provides useful insights into the collapse of communism, it is important to note that several analysts have argued that the USSR was a peculiar kind of empire. Most empires colonize other countries and regions ultimately for reasons of vested economic interest. Indeed, as discussed in the last chapter, Lenin produced a major analysis of this, and had interpreted the First World War very much in terms of the logic of this economic imperialism. But the USSR always preached 'socialist internationalism'. On one level, and in practice, this meant that it could not too overtly exploit its 'colonies'. In fact, analyses by many Western economists hardly sympathetic to the USSR strongly suggested that the Soviet Union's imperialism actually had a negative effect on its own economy. Often, for instance, it could have sold its oil at much higher prices on the world market than it did to its CMEA partners. Rather than being an imperialist out of vested *economic* interest, the USSR can be seen to have been an imperialist for reasons of vested *political* interest – wanting to exert power over smaller countries and to convey its ideological message to those countries.

For almost three decades after 1917, the USSR and communist power hardly expanded. The only country other than the Soviet Union itself to experience a successful communist revolution in the interwar period was Mongolia. But in the aftermath of the Second World War, the USSR took advantage of the West's apparent reluctance to become too involved in the affairs of countries geographically contiguous or close to the Soviet Union. In the mid to late 1940s, communism spread to eight countries of Eastern Europe and to a number of Asian countries (Korea, Vietnam, China). Cubans under Castro overthrew the corrupt Batista regime in 1959; within three years, Castro had declared himself a Marxist-Leninist, and the country started to move into the Soviet camp. In the mid-1970s, a variety of factors – notably the West's loss of will to fight communism in Indo-China and the collapse of the Portuguese empire following the end of the Salazar–

Caetano dictatorships – led to a further swelling of communism's ranks (South Vietnam's unification with communist North Vietnam; Laos; Cambodia; Angola; Mozambique). This was in addition to the Congo and Benin, which had come under communist control in 1968 and 1972 respectively. Finally, Afghanistan came under communist control in 1978, and by the end of 1979 was very much under Soviet influence.

But the spread of communism and Soviet influence to Afghanistan in the late 1970s represented the maximum extension of the Soviet empire. The USSR had already lost its hold over Yugoslavia (from 1948), China (from about 1960) and Albania (during the 1960s); by the end of the 1980s, its grip on the rest of the external empire was released, while the USSR's own collapse in 1991 represented a quite unambiguous sign that the Soviet empire – internal and well as external – had been relegated to the history books.

To the suggestion that the Soviet Union was not a colonizer but rather a truly socialist country that was merely encouraging socialist internationalism, one need only consider the force the USSR was prepared to use to suppress ordinary working-class protesters in the GDR in 1953, Hungary in 1956 and Czechoslovakia in 1968 to realize that 'socialist internationalism' was never a society of equals. The USSR was far more powerful than any of the other members of the Soviet bloc. It also had a sense of *moral* superiority as the home of both Leninism and the first socialist revolution – a belief that it had a right and a duty to spread its own value system.

The Soviet state had tried to influence and be involved in too many countries, at the expense of its own people; by the end of the 1980s it had overstretched itself and paid the price.

Comparative Theories of Revolution

Since the First World War, a number of analysts have each studied several revolutions to see if they could detect commonalities in events as far apart temporally and physically as the English Revolution of the seventeenth century, the French Revolution of the late eighteenth century, the Russian revolutions of 1905 and 1917, the Chinese Revolution of 1911, etc. One of the more interesting propositions to have been advanced by several theorists of comparative revolution, and one which can help us to understand better the 1989–91 revolutions, is the *theory of rising expectations*. This argument is based on an idea originally elaborated in the nineteenth century by Alexis de Tocqueville in his analysis of the French Revolution and subsequently developed by Crane Brinton in a comparative study of the English, American, French and Russian revolutions first published in the 1930s; but it has been heavily modified in recent decades. Advocates of this approach point out that revolutions do not typically occur just because of widespread oppression and poverty in a given society; rather, they tend to happen when a reforming government has raised expectations but has been unable or unwilling to deliver what citizens believed it had promised.

The theory of rising expectations is but one of several theories of revolution, and it is not feasible to rehearse here the findings and hypotheses of even a few of the most celebrated comparative analysts of this century, such as Arendt (1965), Brinton (1965), Moore (1966), Gurr (1970), Dunn (1989) and Skocpol (1979); to do so even superficially would require far more space than is available. Rather, it is suggested that those interested in deepening their understanding of the 1989–91 events in Eastern Europe and the USSR compare the theories of each of the above with these anti-communist revolutions, for heuristic reasons.

Nevertheless *one* recent theory of revolution will be examined here. Since his book is one of the few that deals explicitly with the 1989–91 revolutions and is likely to be hotly debated in the coming years, it is useful to review Charles Tilly's major analysis of revolutions in Europe over the past five centuries (Tilly 1993). Tilly defines a revolution as 'a forceable transfer of power over a state in the course of which at least two distinct blocs of contenders make incompatible claims to control the state, and some significant portion of the population subject to the state's jurisdiction acquiesces in the claims of each bloc' (p. 8). He distinguishes it from 'unsuccessful rebellions, bloodless coups and top-down social transformations' (p. 9), even though all of the latter are very closely related to revolutions (on p. 15, Tilly provides some guidance for distinguishing these various phenomena).

Tilly distinguishes between a revolutionary situation and a revolutionary outcome. The former is said to entail multiple sovereignty – 'two or more blocs make effective, incompatible claims to control the state, or to be the state.' In a revolutionary situation, three proximate causes converge (p. 10):

1 the appearance of contenders, or coalitions of contenders, advancing exclusive competing claims to control of the state, or some segment of it;
2 commitment to those claims by a significant segment of the citizenry;
3 incapacity or unwillingness of rulers to suppress the alternative coalition and/or commitment to its claims.

In what Tilly calls 'larger' revolutions, there are usually a series of such revolutionary situations. As he convincingly argues, identifying the existence of the three 'proximate causes' is required if a revolutionary situation is to be recognized, although this is in itself insufficient and ultimately superficial. If the emergence of that situation is to be *understood*, then the reasons for each of the three variables in a particular case have to be analysed. Why, for instance, has a group (the 'coalition of contenders') emerged to challenge those who currently control the state?

Before considering Tilly's conception of revolutionary outcomes, it is worth noting that he applies Sidney Tarrow's (1989, cited in Tilly, p. 13) analysis of protest politics to argue that *waves* of revolutionary situations are often discernible, whereby one group of citizens is encouraged by the achievements of another, perhaps in another country.

Tilly sensibly argues that a revolutionary situation does not necessarily result in an actual revolution. A 'revolutionary outcome' is held to occur when there is a 'transfer of state power from those who held it before the start of multiple sovereignty to a new ruling coalition – which may, of course, include some elements of the old ruling coalition' (p. 14). Indeed, Tilly argues that a revolutionary situation is actually more likely to develop into a revolutionary outcome (that is, a revolution occurs) if there are many defections from the old holders of state power to the potential new ones. In this context, he stresses the importance of the military – which can defend the old order, side with a potential new order, or remain neutral. In all events, its role is crucial. In sum, Tilly identifies four proximate conditions for a revolutionary outcome (ibid.):

- defections of polity members;
- acquisition of actual force by revolutionary coalitions;
- neutralization or defection of the regime's armed force;
- control of the state apparatus by members of a revolutionary coalition.

Controversially, Tilly argues that there can be a revolutionary outcome *without* a revolutionary situation. The example he cites is of a 'top-down seizure of the state' (p. 15); while enjoying some revolutionary features, this situation does not, according to Tilly, constitute a revolution.

It is partly because of Tilly's insistence on both a revolutionary situation and a full revolutionary outcome, as he defines both, that he comes up with the polemical – and in some ways surprising – conclusion that whereas Czechoslovakia, the GDR, the USSR and Yugoslavia all had revolutions in the period 1989–92, the events constituted only 'marginal' revolutions in Albania, Bulgaria and Poland, while it is 'uncertain' whether or not Hungary had a revolution and 'doubtful' that Romania had one (pp. 234–5). This said, Tilly does accept that 'in each country the events of 1989–92 obviously had something revolutionary about them' (p. 234), and the *outcomes* were definitely revolutionary.

Part of the reason for Tilly's unconventional conclusion is his insistence that both a revolutionary situation and a revolutionary outcome must be identifiable for one to be sure a revolution has occurred. This begs the question as to whether he has correctly identified all the possible, relevant factors for recognizing a revolutionary situation. But another problem is that he appears committed to the necessity of *force* being exercised to wrest power before a phenomenon constitutes a revolution (p. 234). Why this should be a necessary condition is not clear, although it should be noted that most analysts of revolution have in the past argued that violence is a necessary and integral part of revolution (see Cohan 1975, p. 25). It would seem to follow from this position that the notion of a peaceful – a 'velvet' – revolution is an oxymoron.

Tilly's comparative approach to revolution, which stretches far beyond just Eastern Europe and the FSU, is provocative and interesting. His analyses of class conflict (for instance, vis-à-vis the Russian case, see especially p. 232) and state-led versus state-seeking nationalism (see especially pp. 46–9) provide several clues to the emergence of forces that helped to topple communist power. But like all approaches, Tilly's has its limitations. Any theoretical framework which suggests that Poland, for example, may not have had a true revolution in the late 1980s/early 1990s must be seriously questioned.

In chapter 6, we return to the question of whether or not the recent events in what was the communist world constituted a revolution. At this juncture, attention is switched to another broad analytical approach – or, more accurately, group of approaches; these focus on modernization and modernity.

Comparative Theories of Modernization and Modernity

Many modernization theorists would be surprised, perhaps horrified, to discover they have been grouped together here with theorists of modernity – and vice versa. But while there are many important differences between modernization theory and theories of modernity, there is *for our purposes* sufficient in common to warrant their bracketing in this chapter. Very often, it has been less the actual arguments than the – in some cases marked – ideological differences between modernization theorists and theorists of modernity that has led both them and outside observers to see the two groups, to the extent that they are internally homogeneous anyway, as so distinct from each other.

In the late 1950s/early 1960s, American political science in particular was dominated by the comparative approach. There were many reasons for this. One was the USA's more outward-looking approach after the Second World War. Another was that the introduction of statistical techniques into the social sciences had rendered it possible to test grand hypotheses about the connections between political phenomena in very different political contexts in a methodical way, often on the basis of hard data.

One of the most influential approaches in comparative politics was modernization theory. This was never a homogeneous body of thought. But there was just enough commonality between the methodologies and assumptions of writers such as Seymour Martin Lipset (1959), Walter Rostow (1960, 1971), Phillips Cutwright (1963), David Apter (1965), Lucian Pye (1966), and Gabriel Almond (1970) for others to identify this as a distinctive school of thought.

Two of the basic premises of modernization theory are that, first, there are marked stages in history, which progresses towards an end goal, and second, that there is *some* correlation between socioeconomic development and the type of political system a country has. For our purposes, the most important part of the argument held that, at a certain stage and level of economic and social development, systems need to move to liberal democracy.[1] It was also postulated that liberal democracy is ultimately compatible with only one kind of economic system, a predominantly marketized and privatized – capitalist – one.

This theory was subjected to considerable criticism in the 1960s and 1970s. One charge was of ethnocentrism, especially for presenting the US model as the ideal to which all countries should strive. Another was of either naivety or deception. The strongest attacks emanated from a group primarily concerned with Latin America, who identified not only ethnocentrism but also what they saw as a fundamental flaw in the argument of the modernization theorists. For these critics – the so-called dependency theorists, such as André Gunder Frank (1969), Theotonio Dos Santos (1970), Fernando Cardoso (1973), Guillermo O'Donnell (1973) and Samir Amin (1974) – not only was the correlation between democracy and socioeconomic development highly questionable, but it was also based on an unrealistic assumption. In general, they maintained that the advanced capitalist world was unwilling to permit too much economic development – for instance, product diversification – in the Third World, since this would simultaneously reduce the dependency of the less developed states on the First World countries and create competition for the latter. Moreover, far from bringing about liberal democracy, this dependency on First World capitalist states was said to encourage authoritarianism in the Third World. In short, the dependency theorists maintained that in reality it was in the interests of international capitalism to suppress both economic development and democratization in the less developed countries, not to encourage them.

Dependency theory is far more sophisticated and diverse than the skeletal argument just outlined. Some of its adherents were Marxist, others were not. But even this cursory overview begins to demonstrate why dependency theorists accused the modernization theorists of being either ingenuous or deceptive in suggesting that, sooner or later, all countries move towards a marketized, capitalist economy and the concomitant liberal democracy. According to dependency theorists, some countries would never be able to catch up with the most developed countries.

By the mid to late 1970s the dependency theorists were themselves subjected to considerable criticism, as developments in various parts of the world raised questions about their theories. For instance, it became obvious to many observers in the aftermath of the 1973 oil crisis that, in terms of dependency, the nature of the commodities which a particular underdeveloped country sold overseas was of critical importance. Countries that had large reserves of oil were held to be in a fundamentally different position from countries whose primary exports were sugar or bananas.

Another problem with the dependency approach was that the Second World – that is, the communist countries – appeared to have had very impressive growth without recourse to or dependency on that part of the international market dominated by the First World. Although Second World economic growth and development was slowing by the 1970s, many believed this might be a relatively short-lived phenomenon; in any case, First World economies had also slowed markedly in the aftermath of the oil crisis.

By the end of the 1970s the sometimes heated debate between the modernization theorists and the dependency theorists had been put on hold. Most of the arguments on both sides had been made, and the whole issue appeared to be becoming stale.

But by the mid to late 1980s what might be called 'second wave' modernization theory was again on the debating agenda. The moves towards democracy in what had been long-term dictatorships in two countries of southern Europe (Spain, Portugal) from the mid-1970s and the return of two others – Greece and Turkey – to democratic rule (in 1974 and 1983 respectively), plus the moves away from military dictatorship in several Latin American countries (including Brazil, Chile, Peru and Uruguay) during the 1980s were one reason for the rekindled interest in modernization theory. Another was the phenomenal economic success of the four little dragons/tigers. By the late 1980s these served not only to disprove once and for all the basic tenets of dependency theory, but also appeared to be taking discernible if faltering steps towards democracy. Several major works appeared during this 'second wave' of modernization theory, including O'Donnell, Schmitter and Whitehead (1986), Weiner and Huntington (1987), the four-volume edition by Diamond, Linz and Lipset (1988–9) and Rueschemeyer, Huber Stephens and Stephens (1992). In some of these, 'first wave' writers had clearly modified or refined their views in light of the developments and debates since the 1960s. Thus Samuel Huntington now argued (1987, esp. pp. 21–8) that modernization theory needed to be refined through incorporation of a more explicitly *cultural* dimension, which would allow for the apparent fact that the precise stage at which economic development tended to trigger demands for democratization varied from country to country.

As already indicated, the communist world was often cited by those who found dependency theory too simplistic. By the 1980s, limited moves there towards marketization further suggested to some that the trend towards market economics and, eventually, some form of liberal democracy was inevitable. Such views tended to be strengthened by the electoral reforms that were occurring in Hungary, Poland and even the USSR by the late 1980s. Thus it was that two pieces in particular – Francis Fukuyama's article 'The End of History?' and Zbigniew Brzezinski's book *The Grand Failure* – were published shortly *before* the revolutionary period that erupted in late 1989. Following this, Samuel Huntington's 1991 *The Third Wave* incorporated analysis of the most recent wave of moves towards democratization in the world.[2]

Few if any of the writers listed above would argue for a simple, straightforward correlation between economic development and political moves towards liberal democracy. In his 1992 book, for instance, Fukuyama argues that it is the individual's need for recognition – *thymos*, as he calls it, deriving this concept principally from Hegel – that ultimately brings about liberal democracy, which is argued to be the only political form that can ensure this. Fukuyama is also typical of many modernization theorists in being careful not to suggest too clear a sequencing and/or correlation of economic development and liberal democracy (see, for instance, pp. xiii–xv). Nevertheless, most of them maintain that, sooner or later, societies move towards a *modern* political form that is close but not identical to the American system – and that economic development, with its concomitant social effects, is the major propellant. Thus, to cite Fukuyama again (1992, p. 223), there is a 'strong correlation between advanced industrialization and democracy'. Proceeding in a somewhat different direction from Huntington, he argues that modern natural science has had uniform effects on all societies that have experienced it. One is that modern science confers *military* advantages. The other is that it:

> establishes a uniform horizon of economic production possibilities. Technology makes possible the limitless accumulation of wealth, and thus the satisfaction of an ever-expanding set of human desires. This process guarantees an increasing homogenization of all human societies regardless of their historical origins or cultural inheritances. All countries undergoing economic modernization must increasingly resemble one another: they must unify nationally on the basis of a centralized state, urbanize, replace traditional forms of social organization like tribe, sect, and family with economically rational ones based on function and efficiency . . . Moreover, the logic of modern natural science would seem to dictate a universal evolution in the direction of capitalism . . . (1992, pp. xiv–xv)

Most of the literature cited above was written *before* the collapse of communism, and many of the best-known exponents of modernization theory have not explicitly analysed this collapse in terms of their own arguments. But Fukuyama's book does. Following his own logic of economic determinism and the individual's need for recognition, he explains the collapse partly in terms of economic failure and a crisis of system legitimacy (see pp. 15, 28–31 – see next section for a fuller elaboration of the latter), and partly as occurring because communism provided a 'gravely defective form of recognition' of the individual.[3] In terms of economic failure, Fukuyama argues that communism, with its highly centralized and planned approach to economics, was sufficient for basic industrialization but incapable of progressing to the more complex stage of 'post-industrial' economics, 'in which information and technological innovation play a much larger role' (p. xv).

Those who argue that the anti-communist revolutions were *on one level* exercises in bringing communist states 'into line' with modernity are working at an even more abstract level than are the modernization theorists. This said, and as suggested above, there are important ways in which the two basic approaches overlap. Given that most readers of this book will probably have a limited interest in high levels of abstraction, the argument concerning modernity will be truncated and dramatically simplified here.

For most analysts, modernity refers to the period since the European Enlightenment, and thus dates from the seventeenth and eighteenth centuries. In theory, communists were quintessentially modern. They believed that humans could achieve almost anything, and that reason (rationality) would sooner or later provide answers and solutions to the vast majority of the world's problems. As Marxist-Leninists, they believed in a dynamic theory of history, and that history was moving towards an end goal, viz. communism. And they believed in divisions of functions (for instance, of labour) at least in the period before the achievement of true communism. All these attitudes – the very positive, optimistic and humanistic approach to the world and its future – were in line with what is sometimes called modernism (that is, belief in and support for the 'modern' project).[4] However, the communist states were atypical regarding the actual structures and processes normally associated with 'modern' states, at least in the way the latter have developed over the past century or so. Whether one considers the class structure or the political system or the economic system, the communist states were in various ways out of line with the normal pattern for Western states since about the middle of the nineteenth century. There was no real bourgeois class in the communist countries, no proper multiparty system with legalized opposition, too little tolerance of market principles, etc.

This particular argument – that the collapse of communism was a function of distorted modernity correcting itself – deserves a much fuller elaboration than is possible or, given the nature of the book, appropriate here. But the reader has at least been alerted to what is perhaps the most abstract of all the interpretations of the fall of communism (for further details of this argument see Eisenstadt 1992, Bauman 1993, L. Holmes 1993b; although writing long before the double-rejective revolution, Arendt 1965 argues that all true revolutions have occurred as a result of the pressure to move towards modernity).

Legitimation Crisis Theory

The approach the author personally finds the most satisfactory is legitimation crisis theory (others who appear to favour some version of this argument include Kontorovich 1993, esp. p. 42, di Palma 1991a, and to some extent Robinson 1995; for a critique of the approach see Pakulski 1993). Although it was originally developed primarily with reference to capitalism (see Habermas 1973 and 1976), it can be modified to provide many insights into communist systems and their demise. As with several of the approaches here, this theory can coexist with many others; indeed, in its full exposition, it incorporates at least part of many of them. Its elaboration here is reasonably full, not simply because it cannot readily be abbreviated and still make sense, but also because the issue of legitimation constitutes the underlying theme – the analytical framework – of this book. It is for this reason that legitimation crisis theory has been consciously privileged over the other approaches outlined in this chapter.

Modes of legitimation

In any political system, power is exercised primarily by two principal methods, coercion (force) and authority. In the case of the former, citizens are expected to comply with the state's demands, for fear of the consequences of not doing so. The state has various sanctions at its disposal for ensuring compliance; at its most extreme, it can use violence against the citizenry. If this violence is arbitrary, or at least appears to those affected by it to be so, then it is (state) terror.

But most political leaders appreciate that coercion is a suboptimal method of exercising power. It is brittle, and if it is the principal means by which power is exercised may well be temporary (albeit in some cases lasting for decades). This is because high levels of coercion become dysfunctional beyond a certain stage (on the reasons for this see Dallin and Breslauer 1970, esp. pp. 103–9, 130–6). Hence many leaderships seek to rule primarily on the basis of authority rather than coercion. In this situation, leaders seek the right to rule – consent – from the citizenry. The process whereby they seek to acquire authority (or legitimacy) is *legitimation* (for recent general works on this see Barker 1990, Beetham 1991).

Before legitimation *crisis* can be discussed, the various modes of legitimation need to be elaborated. The person primarily responsible for putting the issues of legitimacy and legitimation on the social scientist's agenda was Max Weber. Early in the twentieth century, he argued that there are three main ways in which political leaders of various kinds seek to legitimate themselves and the political order. These three modes are the traditional, the charismatic, and the legal-rational.

For Weber, the *traditional* mode of legitimation refers to a situation in which a leader claims the right to rule on the basis of a long-standing tradition. In most cases, the reference here is to a monarch, and such a person typically claims their right by reference to some superhuman agency. Hence the established church often plays a major role in this form of legitimation.

The *charismatic* leader, in contrast, claims the right to rule on the basis of more secular criteria. Often the leader will have successfully led a revolution and has developed authority on the basis of heroism or other exceptional qualities highly esteemed by society.

Weber maintained that the ultimate form of legitimation in the modern state is the *legal-rational*. In this case, the political order is legitimated not in terms of persons – the monarch, the revolutionary leader, etc. – but of rules and laws that are binding on everyone. One rule is that the people must have some say over who governs them. This typically manifests itself in the form of regular, free, secret and competitive elections.

Nowadays, Weber's analysis is generally held to be seminal but limited, and more complex taxonomies of legitimation have been created. For instance, T. H. Rigby (1982) argued in the early 1980s that communist states often seek to legitimate themselves in terms of what he called *goal-rational* legitimation. In this situation, those running the system seek to legitimate themselves primarily in terms of their ability to steer a given country and population to the distant end goal of communism. Such people claim they have a superior understanding of society and the world generally. In Leninist terms they constitute the 'vanguard'.

But the addition of goal-rationality still does not exhaust the list. For the purposes of this study, ten modes of legitimation – seven domestic, three external – can be identified. The domestic ones are:

1 old traditional
2 charismatic
3 goal-rational (also known as teleological)
4 eudaemonic
5 official nationalist
6 new traditional
7 legal-rational

Although the second, third and seventh of these have already been outlined, the differences between the first and the sixth, and the meaning of the fourth and fifth, need to be elaborated. It must be emphasized at this point that the above list, as well as that of external modes of legitimation, was originally constructed (see L. Holmes 1993a, pp. 13–18, 58) with particular reference to the communist world. This said, much of it can be applied to most kinds of system.

In the above taxonomy, *old traditional* refers very much to what Weber called simply 'traditional'. In the communist world, leaders did not generally claim the right to rule in terms of family tradition or divine right/ mandate of heaven (although the present North Korean leader, Kim Jong Il, might attempt something along these lines if he can maintain power long enough). However, communist leaders did sometimes attempt to enhance their own authority by reference to an earlier phase of the communist era. In the late 1980s, Gorbachev claimed on various occasions that many of his country's problems related to the fact that Lenin's successors, particularly Stalin, had distorted the original Leninist aims. Gorbachev argued that if the USSR could return to the true Leninist path, many of its difficulties would be overcome (see Smart 1990). Here, then, a contemporary communist leader was attempting to increase his regime's authority by referring back to an earlier communist leader he initially believed still commanded widespread respect. This form of legitimation can thus be called *new traditional*. Gorbachev was not the only communist leader to engage in this. The Chinese leader since the late 1970s, Deng Xiaoping, has also done it with respect to the *early* phase of Mao Zedong's leadership of communist China.

According to the *Oxford English Dictionary*, the term *eudaemonic* literally means 'conducive to happiness' or 'viewed as conducive to happiness'. In the present context, it refers to attempts by political leaders to legitimate their rule in terms of the political order's performance, especially in the economic sphere. In this situation, leaders claim the right to rule because they are, almost literally, 'delivering the goods'. In the case of communists in most of the Soviet bloc, this essentially meant that they claimed authority on the basis of impressive growth rates, better quality and more widely available consumer goods, etc.

The final term to be considered is *official nationalist*. This refers to nationalism – for now, political activism that focuses on and privileges the nation above other allegiances – that is engaged in and encouraged by the state. It is to be distinguished from the (unofficial) nationalism of particular ethnic groups in society, which may well be suppressed by the state authorities (see chapter 10). In some cases, communist leaderships who believed they were failing to legitimate their rule by other modes resorted to official nationalism.

To complete the list, the three external modes of legitimation are:

 8 formal recognition
 9 informal support
10 existence of an external role model

Two introductory remarks need to be made concerning the above. First, although the communist world has again been taken as the source of inspiration for these external modes, all can be applied in non-communist contexts. Second, these modes are held to be secondary to the domestic modes in most circumstances; this said, and as argued below, the third became critical in the final days of communist power.

The first external mode is *formal recognition* by external powers. Such external powers include not only the governments of other countries, but also international organizations such as the United Nations.

One of the features shared by the second and third external modes is that they both relate very directly to *self-legitimation* by the regime. In other words, in both cases the leaders might still believe in their own right to rule because of direct or indirect external support, even though they are aware of their unpopularity and lack of authority among their own population.

The second mode is *informal support* for a regime and its policies by external agents. One of the profound ironies of world politics by the start of the 1990s was that Gorbachev was more popular in the West than he was in his own country. Two of the many symbols of his popularity abroad were that *Time* magazine named him 'Man of the Decade' in December 1989, and that he was awarded the Nobel Prize for Peace in 1990. The relevance of this to legitimation is that Gorbachev appears to have continued to believe in what he was doing because so many outside the USSR, both politicians and ordinary citizens, had faith in him and his policies.

Finally, there is a highly abstract but critically important form of legitimation, the *existence of an external role model*. Here, leaders may well be aware of their unpopularity at home. Nevertheless, they continue to believe in their own right to rule because of their faith in the regime of another country which, to a greater or lesser extent and whether it is openly acknowledged or not, they are emulating. If this argument seems obscure, the reader should be able to follow it more readily when it is applied below to the collapse of communist power in Eastern Europe.

These ten modes of legitimation can shortly be applied to the communist world, in an endeavour better to understand the reasons for the events of 1989–91. Before finally expounding this argument, however, three assumptions need to be elaborated. The first is that there was a *dynamism* in the communist world over the decades. Readers may reject this assumption, but will then find it difficult to provide a convincing explanation of the anti-communist revolutions. Second, it is assumed that although power is exercised in any system through a mixture of coercion and legitimation, one of these always dominates. Similarly, while it is accepted that several modes of legitimation may coexist in a given system at any one time, it is maintained that one or two will usually predominate. Finally, it is assumed that there is *some* pattern to the sequence in which legitimation modes become salient in a given system, although the pattern is hazy and there are many exceptions to the general picture drawn. Thus, just as coercion tended to be replaced over time in communist systems by legitimation as the dominant form of the exercise of power, so charismatic legitimation tended to be associated with the early stages; the teleological mode was typical of the 'middle age' of communism in power; eudaemonism typically emerged later; and legal-rationality was the last form to become salient.

The reader is reminded that the following is and can only be a broad generalization, to which individual countries more or less closely approximated. While examples of the patterns described and some of the more glaring exceptions to these are provided, it is not feasible to consider each of the countries considered in this book in terms of all the stages outlined. With these caveats in mind, the following seems to be a reasonably persuasive description of the dynamism of communist power.

In the early stages of communism, regimes typically exercised power predominantly in the coercive mode. When they assumed power, most communist regimes faced resistance from sections of the population. In a country such as Poland, hostility could be found among *most* sections of the population. In Cuba and China, in contrast, there was initially far more popular support. In addition to the resistance from groups who opposed the new regime from the start, the communists often engendered more widespread hostility over time because of their desire to realize substantial change as quickly as possible – the so-called 'revolutions from above'. With the partial exceptions of Czechoslovakia and East Germany, communists took power in countries not yet ready for either socialism or communism by classical Marxist standards. Most obviously, these countries were still predominantly agrarian/rural, rather than industrial/urban, and the population typically had only relatively low levels of education. In order to reach what Marx considered to be the starting line for the transition to socialism and communism, societies had to be rapidly transformed. Economic plans were introduced, designed to bring about the rapid development of industry and to force the peasants to be more efficient by working together in cooperative (collective) farms. Although some citizens were excited by these projects, it is hardly surprising that the sheer scale and pace of change intended by the communists led many others to feel dislocated, alienated and increasingly hostile. If we add to these structural reasons for hostility the cruel and paranoid personality of Stalin, whose influence permeated not only the USSR from the late 1920s to 1953 but also all the new communist states of the 1940s, it becomes clear why terror and high levels of coercion were prominent features of the early stages of communist rule in most of these countries.

Although coercion (including widespread 'thought reform' in several of the Asian communist states) was more salient than legitimation attempts in these early stages, evidence of the latter could certainly be found. In many countries, there was charismatic legitimation around the leader. In countries in which this person had led the revolution that brought the communists to power – such as Lenin in the USSR, Mao in the People's Republic of China and Ho in North Vietnam – the charisma may have been real enough (that is, many citizens may genuinely have admired the leader for his revolutionary role). In other cases, there was a more overt attempt by the authorities to *create* charisma around a leader, in essence artificially. Such attempts were designed to encourage a 'cult of the personality', and were made explicitly around leaders such as Stalin, Kim Il Sung in North Korea and Ceausescu in Romania. Whether or not such attempts succeeded is unimportant at this point; the focus here is on regime *attempts* to acquire legitimacy, not the much thornier issue of how successful such attempts were.

Another form of legitimation often associated with the more coercive phases of communism is official nationalism. As with so many other aspects of communism in power, the trail-blazer here was the USSR with Stalin's 'socialism in one country' (see chapter 1). Similarly nationalistic forms of communism were adopted by Mao, Ho, Castro, Kim and Tito.

Official nationalist and charismatic forms of legitimation were more obvious at these relatively early stages in those countries where the communists had taken power largely or exclusively by their own efforts than in those where the communists had come to power with considerable external, usually Soviet, assistance. In the case of the latter states, Stalin and the Soviet leadership did not appreciate native communists proclaiming their own achievements (as distinct from constantly eulogizing and expressing gratitude to Stalin) and encouraging nationalism that might downplay the USSR's role in bringing communists to power in that country. Communists (such as Anton Ackermann in the GDR) who attempted in the 1940s to advocate a form of official nationalism by proclaiming the uniqueness of their own country's path to socialism fell foul of Moscow. Only where the communists owed little or nothing to the Soviets for their position were the indigenous leaderships more or less free to pursue their own nationalistic and charismatic legitimation attempts.[5]

As argued above, leaderships in most kinds of system sooner or later come to appreciate that legitimate power is more satisfactory than coercion-based power. Communist leaderships were no exception. Thus, as the dysfunctions of both terror and high levels of coercion became increasingly obvious, and as leadership teams changed, so legitimation attempts became more salient in several countries. Many new leaderships realized that both their predecessors and their predecessors' style and policies were unpopular. They therefore attempted to enhance their own legitimacy by distinguishing and distancing themselves from these. Although levels of coercion in many communist states remained relatively high in comparison with First World states, signs of liberalization were visible in most countries by the 1950s or 1960s. In addition to the most obvious of these – the dramatic reduction in arbitrary arrests, show trials and executions – early symbols of the change included Khrushchev's 'Secret Speech' of February 1956 criticizing Stalin, and the toleration of the decollectivization in Poland from the same year. Other countries had to wait longer (China's 'Democracy Wall' came in 1979–80).

With the decline of coercion, many leaderships began to place increasing emphasis on legitimation. The Soviet leadership's claim in the early 1960s that the first stages of communism would be reached by 1980 was one example. Other communist leaderships were also emphasizing that there are a number of *stages* both in the establishment of socialism and in the transition to communism, and that their societies were moving rapidly and impressively from one to the next. All this represented teleological (goal-rational) legitimation.

But this era was relatively short-lived. Many leaders appear to have realized that teleological legitimation was too abstract and distant for many citizens. Rather than 'new stages', the masses wanted better wages – or, as Michael Ellman so eloquently expressed it (1969, p. 358), not Marx and Engels but Marks and Spencer.[6] They had had enough of 'revolutions from above'; greater stability and rising living standards were now the primary aims of many citizens.

In this context, several Soviet-bloc states introduced during the 1960s what were intended to be major economic reform packages. The first of these was the GDR's New Economic System of January 1963. Other countries to introduce similar reforms included the USSR (March and September 1965); Czechoslovakia (January 1965); Bulgaria (December 1965); and Hungary (January 1968). All these were designed on one level to satisfy the consumer better. They therefore constituted a classic example of eudaemonic legitimation.

But while some were more successful than others, and several were subsequently modified, none of these reform packages resulted in as much improvement in the consumer's lot as either the leaderships or the citizens had hoped for. There were various reasons for this. One was that all the packages required a reduction of the power of central bureaucrats. Yet the main responsibility for implementing the reforms fell precisely on these people. Given that the reforms often conflicted with the bureaucrats' self-interests, it is hardly surprising that many of them did not implement the policies as enthusiastically or satisfactorily as most citizens and senior leaders would have preferred.

It was clear by the 1970s that the economic reforms were having much less impact than intended. Communist leaderships responded in a number of ways. One was to introduce modifications or new versions of the reforms. A major focus of many of these was on merging smaller enterprises into larger production units (see L. Holmes 1981, Woodall 1982).

But another response was to emphasize to citizens that if they wanted better living standards, they would have to work harder for them. In marked contrast to the more idealistic days of the high point of teleological legitimation, the prognostications of many leaderships became increasingly pragmatic and sober. This was the era of so-called '*realistic*' or '*really existing*' socialism. The decline of idealism and increasing need for realism became even more pronounced after 1973, as the world entered a recession in the aftermath of the oil crisis.

Since the economic reforms were not delivering adequately, it follows that the success of eudaemonic legitimation was also likely to be limited. In these circumstances, leaderships had to look for other modes of legitimation. In the cases of the GDR and Romania, most notably, there was a new emphasis from the mid-1970s on official nationalism. In East Germany, the authorities made much of the fact that the country had finally been recognized by the international community in the form of admission to the UN in September 1973 (the eighth legitimation mode; it should be clear from this example that modes eight and five often interact and coexist, and why). The East German leadership also emphasized the GDR's sporting achievements, especially at the Olympic Games. And it began to reassess various historical figures, now acknowledging positive features in Germans it had once roundly condemned, such as Martin Luther and Frederick the Great of Prussia. The Romanian leadership also started reassessing history (see chapter 3).

The USSR, too, could be seen to have been pursuing a form of official nationalism in the 1970s, albeit mostly of a different sort from that in Romania and the GDR. While it also emphasized its sporting achievements, the leadership made much of the country's successes in the international arena. On the one hand, the Soviet bloc was expanding, as more of Indo-China and Africa came under Soviet influence. On the other hand – and ironically, given the point just made – the Soviets could claim some credit for the marked improvement in East–West relations. The Soviet leadership was largely justified in arguing that the West now recognized their country more clearly than ever as a superpower, in some important ways (notably militarily) the equal of the USA.

But there were signs by the end of the 1970s and the early 1980s that the capacity of communist leaderships to keep switching to new forms of legitimation was limited. With the Soviet intervention in Afghanistan in December 1979, the Soviet bloc had reached its maximum size. From then on, the tide began to turn. Afghanistan itself became ever more of a problem for the USSR. The imperialist component of Soviet official nationalism was turning sour. The situation was further exacerbated by the rapidly increasing self-confidence of the West.

The USSR was by no means the only country to be experiencing problems. The Polish leadership had introduced real but short-lived improvements in incomes and living standards in the early 1970s, following riots that had brought down the Gomulka regime. These improvements were funded largely by borrowing from the West, which was much easier to do in the era of détente. In many ways, this was a classic example of attempting to legitimate the regime in terms of satisfying the population's consumerist aspirations (eudaemonic legitimation). But this proved to be only a short-term solution to the regime's problems. In the aftermath of the oil crisis, many Western countries were unwilling to grant further credits, and several wanted loans repaid more quickly than Poland had originally anticipated. By 1976, therefore, Polish citizens had come to the end of their ride. At the same time, the government could not provide longer-term hopes for improvement, since, in 'buying off' the citizenry, it had not to any significant extent invested in new plant and equipment. In this situation, and following the announcement of price rises, riots broke out in 1976. The authorities managed to contain these. But in the years following the 1976 riots, workers and intellectuals began to cooperate, in a way and on a scale unprecedented in Eastern Europe, on ways to improve their respective lots under the communist system. Dissatisfaction was building up.

The most significant result of this collaboration was the emergence of Solidarity in September 1980. This organization played a major role in highlighting the weaknesses of the communist system. The singular failure of the Polish authorities to legitimate themselves in *any* mode became very obvious on 13 December 1981, when, after failing to come to a satisfactory agreement with its own people, the Polish regime declared martial law and banned Solidarity. Poland had reverted to coercion as the principal form of power. This was a glaring example of the growing appreciation by communist leaderships that the switch to legitimation as the dominant mode of power could sometimes prove highly problematical.

Although the rise and demise of Solidarity in 1980–1 must unquestionably be seen as a watershed in the emerging crisis of communism, this crisis had still not become full-blown. Indeed, many communist leaderships apparently began to believe there was one other mode of legitimation that might save them, the legal-rational. None of the leaders would have described what they were doing in these terms; this is the jargon of the social scientist. But a growing emphasis by communist leaderships in the 1980s on the 'rule of law', broadly understood, is evidence of this new focus on legal-rationality as communist power's salvation.

Before citing evidence of the moves towards legal-rationality, some consideration of a country that had been outside the Soviet bloc since the late 1940s is appropriate. Yugoslavia is interesting precisely because it adopted a different approach from the countries of the Soviet bloc to the building of communism. Like them, however, its experiment ultimately failed.

Yugoslavia was a multi-ethnic country that had been led by the charismatic Tito since the mid-1940s. Despite various crises, Tito had managed to keep the country together until his death in 1980. He attempted to foster a pride among Yugoslavs in their unique approach to the building of communism, above all in the form of the 'self-management' system (see chapter 1). In that this was contrasted not only with capitalism but also with 'bureaucratic' approaches to the building of socialism and communism in the Soviet bloc, the ideology of self-management was *in part* a form of official nation-alist legitimation. Following Tito's death, the Yugoslav authorities at-tempted to move further towards legal-rationality, particularly in the form of regularized leadership change. Unfortunately, the economy fell into serious trouble in the 1980s, before legal-rationality had had much opportu-nity to establish itself as a long-term form of legitimation. As the economic situation worsened, so traditional ethnic rivalries came to the fore, with groups blaming each other for their deteriorating circumstances.

Legitimation attempts through legal-rationality

This is an appropriate point at which to consider concrete moves towards the rule of law (legitimation attempts through legal-rationality). The fol-lowing is the author's own listing, but its starting point is Weber's notion that what distinguishes legal-rationality from traditional and charismatic legitimation is its focus on rules rather than personal qualities. It is, in short, a depersonalized form of legitimation.

At least nine indicators of the communist states' moves towards the rule of law can be identified. Although some of these measures predated the 1980s, the whole process intensified sufficiently during that decade to justify the notion that legal-rationality was becoming a – in some cases the – dominant form of legitimation. The nine indicators were:

(a) codification of legal systems;
(b) increased control over the state's coercive agencies;
(c) increased control over leading officials;
(d) regularization and vitalization of meetings of political bodies;
(e) increasing separation of party and state, and a shift of power from party to state;
(f) changes in official attitudes towards mass participation;
(g) moves away from central directive planning;
(h) boosting of the private sector;
(i) increased overt interaction with the international market.

A full elaboration of these factors is provided in L. Holmes 1993a, pp. 274–88; here just a few points will be highlighted.

In terms of the codification of the legal system, one of the most interest-ing developments was the explicit ideological commitment to legal-rational-ity contained in concepts such as the socialist law-based state. This term was first publicly articulated by Gorbachev in April 1988, although the concept had been debated among Soviet social scientists for several years before that. Increased control over the state's coercive agencies could be seen, for example, in the measures taken to render agencies such as the Soviet KGB (Committee for State Security) less powerful and more answerable to both the government and the Communist Party. Increased control over leading officials refers, *inter alia*, to the fact that citizens in both the USSR and China were able for the first time, towards the end of the 1980s, to file suits against officials of the state. Changes in official attitudes towards mass participation refers, for example, to the changes in electoral laws that were introduced in so many communist states in the mid to late 1980s; although the practical significance of these should not be exaggerated (see chapter 7), they were of symbolic importance. The last three variables refer to what can broadly be described as an *uncoupling* of the economy. This was an interesting form of depersonalization, in that it was designed to transfer much of the control of the economy from the hands of identifiable politicians and planners to the 'invisible' hand of the market.

Contemporaneous with these moves towards legal-rational legitimation were clear indications of a move away from teleological (goal-rational) legitimation. Probably the two best examples of this were the references to 'really existing socialism', and the closely related revamping of party programmes to render them more 'realistic' than their predecessors.

Legitimation crisis

Having suggested that many communist states were attempting to move to legal-rational legitimation by the 1980s, the point has been reached at which the denouement of our story, the extreme legitimation crisis, occurred. There are several components to this explanation.

First, a distinction needs to be drawn between political *system* and *regime*, partly so as to be able to distinguish minor from major legitimation crises. By political system is meant here the totality of structures, processes and other phenomena (such as official ideology) that constitutes government in its broadest sense. A regime, on the other hand, is a particular leadership team (including its administrative wing) that runs the system at any given point in time. Thus the Soviet *system* was run by four *regimes* between 1980 and 1990 – Brezhnev's, Andropov's, Chernenko's, and Gorbachev's. With this distinction in mind, four types of legitimation crisis can be identified. The first two are relatively minor, the third is moderately serious, while the last is a major (extreme) form of legitimation crisis that typically leads to system collapse.

1 Legitimation shifts   In this scenario, a regime perceives that its attempts to legitimate the system and/or itself in terms of a particular dominant legitimation mode are becoming or have already become problematical, but it believes it will be able to overcome present difficulties by switching to another mode. Indeed, the very act of overtly recognizing the problematic nature of a given form of legitimation and more or less explicitly moving to another can in theory give a regime 'breathing space'. This can be called the *legitimating effect of legitimation shifts*.

2 Abnormal regime change   Here, a given leadership team either loses faith in itself and resigns, or is perceived by other senior politicians to have lost its way and is removed in an irregular manner (though not by violence, which would constitute more than a minor legitimation crisis). In either scenario, there is another group that still has sufficient faith in the system to take it over and maintain it. Indeed, if the citizens believe that such a change of regime will bring genuine improvements, then the overall system's legitimacy *might* increase. However, the popular legitimacy of – level of mass support for – systems and regimes is impossible to gauge with any scientifically respectable level of accuracy. This is especially so in the case of relatively closed systems, as most of the communist states were. But persuasive arguments can be made to the effect that the replacement of Ochab by Gomulka (Poland 1956), Novotny by Dubcek (Czechoslovakia 1968), and of Amin by Karmal (Afghanistan 1979) constituted examples of a new regime at least partly successfully resolving a minor legitimation crisis of this second type.

3 Reversion to coercion   A regime comes to appreciate that its attempts at legitimating itself and the system to the masses are failing to such an extent that regime and even system are endangered. The leaders are prepared to revert to coercion over the masses as the dominant mode of exercising power. This constitutes a real crisis of legitimation, since the leaders are recognizing the failure of their attempts to legitimate themselves and/or the system. But inasmuch as these leaders have not yet lost faith in themselves and their capacity to rule, it is not as extreme a version of identity and legitimation crisis as the last one to be analysed. Good examples of this form of legitimation crisis in the communist world are the 'normalization' regime in Czechoslovakia from 1969, the imposition of martial law in Poland in December 1981, and the clampdown in Beijing in June 1989. In a sense, the failed coup attempt in Moscow in August 1991 could also be interpreted in these terms, as long as it is borne in mind that only *some* leaders (that is, those who attempted to seize power at that time) believed in the possibility of this kind of action succeeding.

4 Identity crisis and general collapse of self-legitimation   If the whole, or at least most of the key elements, of the elite loses faith in what it is doing and in the very system it is supposed to maintain – if there is a near-universal collapse of self-legitimation – then the fourth form of legitimation crisis has occurred. In many ways, this concept provides one of the most important and persuasive explanations of the collapse of communism. There were basically two stages to this.

The first was the growing realization by communist leaderships that the more they attempted to transfer their systems to a legal-rational basis, the deeper they fell into a fundamental *rationality and identity crisis*. For instance, as they attempted to reduce central planning and increase the role of market mechanisms in their economies, so they began to recognize and even accept phenomena that had for decades been taboo. At the top of this list were unemployment and inflation; these represented, at a deeper level, unfamiliar fear and insecurity for the masses. These negative phenomena were not countered by marked improvements in the economies – certainly not to the extent that was necessary for citizens to accept the new, undesirable phenomena as a trade-off for rising living standards.

At the same time, although the masses were being encouraged openly to criticize officials, there were limits to this. The level of freedom to criticize politicians that most Westerners virtually take for granted was still not being secured in most communist states.

In short, the identity crisis resulted from the fact that the changes being implemented and intensified in the 1980s meant that most communist systems had all the negative features of both capitalism and communism (such as inflation, unemployment, job insecurity, growing crime; restrictions on travel, on the right to criticize and to form opposition groups) and few if any of the positive aspects of either (such as high standards of living, freedom to travel and protest; job security, heavily subsidized basics such as housing, local transport and food).

Such an identity crisis had not existed earlier. Although Stalin's policies alienated many citizens, they did represent a distinctive approach. They could not be seen as a diluted, inferior version of capitalism and liberal democracy. The same is true of the Maoist approach, including the chaotic period of the Great Proletarian Cultural Revolution (1966–76, with the most extreme stage occurring between 1966 and 1969).

Despite this identity crisis, the communist systems may have lasted a little longer had the authorities had the will to revert to coercion as the dominant mode of exercising power. But with a few exceptions, notably China, this did not occur in 1989. Instead, many communist regimes (and systems) moved to another phase of the major legitimation crisis, the collapse of faith in the external role model (number ten in the taxonomy of legitimation modes), and hence to the ultimate (second) stage, of self-delegitimation and system collapse.

One of the most significant factors contributing to the collapse of faith in the external role model emerged at the beginning of 1989, with the Soviet withdrawal from Afghanistan. The Soviet leadership not only ordered a withdrawal, but acknowledged it had made serious mistakes. It was confirming in a very tangible way its renunciation of the Brezhnev Doctrine, and thus of its right to interfere in the affairs of other countries even if communist power in those countries appeared to be under threat. At about the same time the USSR urged Vietnam to withdraw from Cambodia; this constituted further evidence of Moscow's dramatically changed position on the issue of defending international socialism.

The unambiguous rejection of the Brezhnev Doctrine meant that communist leaders beyond the USSR could no longer reasonably expect military support from the Soviets or the Warsaw Pact in the event of unrest among their own populations. Indeed, Gorbachev made it clear that such support would not be forthcoming while he was Soviet leader.

By the spring of 1989 the Soviet leadership had indicated not only that it would not militarily defend conservative communist leaderships, but also that it was tolerant – perhaps even supportive – of changes being mooted and implemented in Hungary and Poland that represented substantial moves towards political pluralism. In that there was also talk in these countries of abandoning the *nomenklatura* system (see chapter 7) and other key elements of the communist power system, it should be clear why many communist leaderships outside the USSR felt they had lost their role model.

Finally, that the Soviet leadership itself appeared to have lost its way was unquestionably a major factor in the collapse of self-legitimation among the communist leaderships of Eastern Europe. If the leaders of the home of communism could not see the way forward – had lost sight of the *telos* – where were the leaderships of other communist states to find their inspiration and support? This point is encapsulated well in the following quotation from an article by S. Kondrashov in *Izvestiya* (2 March 1990): 'We failed to provide a model of society ensuring a decent life for our own people, and we imposed this worthless model on other countries. Then, when we ourselves rejected the model . . . a swift chain reaction set in' (cited in Kramer 1993, p. 1).

It might be inferred from the above that this part of the argument is fully in line with those who argue that Gorbachev's role was all-important. While it cannot be denied that Gorbachev's role was of *major* significance, there is still one critical factor to bear in mind. If the leaderships of other communist states had continued to believe in what *they* were doing, and had managed to persuade their own coercive agencies of their legitimacy, then there was nothing to prevent them from reverting to coercion as a salient form of power, as did the Chinese leadership. Expressing this another way, it was not *only* the failure of the external role model (which can from some perspectives ultimately be attributed to Gorbachev), but *also* the internal doubts and rottenness of the systems that meant that they were in the fourth type of legitimation crisis, not the third.

At this point, it is appropriate to focus on the role of the masses. They had in general become increasingly disappointed in their governments as the 1980s proceeded, since the economic situation in so many countries meant that hopes for rapidly rising living standards faded. During the 1970s, several Western commentators identified in the USSR and many communist states of Europe what was usually called a 'social contract'. This was in essence a trade-off between the elite and the citizenry. The nub of the argument from the masses' standpoint has been summarized somewhat cynically as 'we pretend to work, and they pretend to pay us.' The basis of this largely unspoken agreement was that the masses were to be quiescent and make few political demands, in return for which they would receive the positive aspects of socialism identified earlier (subsidies, security, etc.) plus rising living standards. The elites, in turn, hoped to score some success in eudaemonic legitimation via this contract.

The deteriorating economic situation can be added to the masses' perception of the elites' growing self-doubts to explain one way in which the citizenry played a role in the collapse of communism in many states. Many theorists of legitimacy and legitimation (see, for instance, Heller 1984) have argued that for the masses to challenge their elites, they must have a vision of an alternative system they would prefer to the existing one. However, the anti-communist revolutions suggest that it is less a clear-cut alternative vision that matters than a belief that a challenge to the authorities has a reasonable chance of succeeding. This is particularly so when the masses have challenged the authorities in the past and have been put down by force, as was the case in several communist states. By 1989, with clear indications that the Soviets would not use force to suppress challenges to domestic elites within member states of the Soviet outer empire, the belief that a successful assault on the communist power structures might have become possible helps to explain why the masses were prepared to demonstrate as they did in Czechoslovakia, the GDR, Romania, etc.

There was another, less visible – but at least as important – way in which the masses played an important role in the collapse of communism. It is necessary to ask *why* leaderships ever felt the need to switch from coercion to legitimation, and from one mode of legitimation to another. Expressing this another way, if we attempt to *understand* the dynamism of communist power (as distinct from merely identifying and describing it), then it should soon become obvious that a major reason for such changes was leaders' reactions to what they perceived to be the opinion of the masses. One reason why the totalitarian approach to communist politics (see, for instance, Friedrich and Brzezinski 1965) was flawed was that it lacked a dynamic element and too readily assumed that communist leaderships had near-total control over an atomized society. The reality was always more complex than this, and communist leaderships did not live in vacuums. While some took considerably longer to recognize this than others, most leaderships eventually appreciated that they had to interact with the masses and seek to enhance system legitimacy if that system were to keep moving forward and they were to retain their position. Thus the role of the masses was always critical. It may have been more visible in the collapse of communist power in countries such as Romania and the GDR than in others (Poland, Hungary), but it would be a serious mistake to interpret the dynamism of communism, including its collapse, exclusively or even primarily in terms of the attitudes of leaders and other officers of the state.

Unfortunately for the communists, and as argued above, legal-rationality proved to be a problematical legitimation mode they could not control. One of the reasons *why* it became an uncontrollable force in the USSR was precisely because the masses appropriated it and expected more than the leadership had intended; this phenomenon was repeated to a limited extent in some of the East European countries. In the USSR, Gorbachev's conscious introduction of *glasnost* eventually backfired; the leadership had opened a Pandora's Box of mass dissatisfaction and was unable to close the lid. Inter-ethnic hostilities were perhaps the most visible and unpleasant dimension of this. Probing one level deeper, a major reason why communists cannot ultimately control legal-rationality is that, beyond a certain point, the latter cannot coexist with the communist system of power. The two phenomena are ultimately incompatible. Legal-rationality is, both as a concept and largely in practice, a highly depersonalized form of power. Marxism-Leninism is – certainly in practice, and with its focus on vanguardism to some extent in theory – a very personalized form of power.

Perhaps the clearest evidence of this is the extent to which most citizens in most communist countries believed it mattered a great deal who their leader was. If they were profoundly dissatisfied with this person, they could not normally expect to be able to remove him (it was never a her) within three to four years as most Westerners can.

A point arising from the early part of the last paragraph is that it is highly probable that most communist leaderships who ventured into legal-rational legitimation did so expecting that they would subsequently be able to withdraw, and replace legal-rationality with eudaemonism as the dominant mode of legitimation. The argument here is that the move into legal-rationality was intended to be *limited* and *relatively short-term*. For instance, it was hoped that in bringing the conservative bureaucracies to heel, the economic reforms of earlier years, albeit with substantial modifications and updating, would be more successfully implemented. Hence leaderships hoped that regimes and systems would become increasingly legitimate on the basis of (mostly economic) performance. Such an argument would help to explain how and why Gorbachev seemed to many Westerners to be genuine in his commitment to reform, especially economic, yet also continued to insist he was a (modern) communist.

Some Western analysts predicted long before 1989 that communist leaderships would attempt to remove themselves from such direct and extensive involvement in the management of their economies, precisely in order to strengthen their political grip (see, for instance, Arato 1982). However, what became ever more obvious by the late 1980s was that communists had for so long and so forcefully asserted that one of the major components of communism is the close interaction between economics and politics that the notion of the political system being 'uncoupled' from the economic system appeared contradictory, even cynical. It constituted another aspect of communism's crisis of rationality and identity.

Although the above explanation of the collapse of communist power is a complex one, it is still essentially reductionist. The intricacies of the real world can never be fully encapsulated in one argument or theory, however sophisticated. Thus some countries approximated to the model less closely and obviously than others. At first glance, for instance, the Romanian case might not appear to be readily explained in terms of the legitimation crisis approach. Even by the late 1980s, power in Romania was still being exercised primarily through the coercive mode, with the official nationalism and (highly artificial) charismatic legitimation typical of the predominantly coercive phase being secondary dimensions of the power system. In order to explain how the Romanian case is compatible with legitimation crisis theory, it is necessary to incorporate a more immediate aspect of the 1989–91 revolution, the inspirational or domino effect.

No understanding of the anti-communist revolution would be complete without reference to the role of the media in rapidly communicating information about unrest and change in one country to other countries in the region. Certainly, most Romanians were broadly aware of what was happening elsewhere in the Soviet bloc, and this must be seen as a major stimulant to both the masses and members of the state's coercive agencies. In short, many Romanians were encouraged by the developments occurring elsewhere in Eastern Europe. Since power in Romania had been exercised on a long-term coercive basis, it was brittle. It was therefore hardly surprising either that it collapsed very suddenly, or that this collapse involved more violence than in countries where coercion had been less salient. However, if it is also accepted that the regime would probably *not* have collapsed precisely when it did had it not been for the events occurring elsewhere in Eastern Europe, then legitimation crisis theory *can* be applied to Romania. It is argued here that Romania was directly affected by the *general* legitimation crisis of communist power. In a sense, there was a nice irony here for Leninists; Romania was just one of the links in the chain of communist states! Admittedly, Romania experienced some aspects of the legitimation crisis vicariously. But this does not alter the fact that the overthrow of the Ceausescu regime was an integral part of the general crisis of communism.

The reader might be wondering by now about the Asian communist states and Cuba. After all, any suggestion that communists lost power everywhere in 1989–91 is incorrect. Does this mean that the theory elaborated in the last few pages is either wrong or has only limited application? To answer this properly requires more space than is available in this chapter. The reader must therefore wait until chapter 5 for an answer to this fascinating question.

Summary and Conclusions

No fewer than nine approaches to the collapse of communism have been elaborated in this chapter. It has been emphasized that many commentators subscribe to several of these. This is appropriate, since it would be naive to suppose that a complicated phenomenon occurring in a string of culturally diverse countries had only one major cause. Although shortcomings of several of the approaches have been mentioned at various points in this chapter, it is now worth highlighting some of the weaknesses of each in turn; this more systematic method is useful in evaluating the approaches comparatively.

There can be no real doubt that *Gorbachev's policies* were a major factor in the collapse of communism. But to argue that such a collapse would not have happened without Gorbachev is unfounded. We need to ask, for instance, how and why Gorbachev both *came* to power and then *stayed* in power. Following a series of policy failures, Khrushchev had been removed by his peers in 1964; no convincing argument can be made that such a solution was not a possibility for Gorbachev's peers.

In a sense, the fact that the hardliners still did not succeed in taking power in the USSR in August 1991 endorses the notion that they did not have a convincing alternative set of policies to those of either Gorbachev or, for that matter, the recently elected president of Russia, Boris Yeltsin. While the pace and details of Soviet policy in the late 1980s may well have been largely the result of Gorbachev's own position (though it should never be overlooked that much of his wavering was a function of his attempts to compromise between different sets of views in the Soviet elite), something along the lines of Gorbachevian policy would have been introduced sooner or later whoever had come to power in the USSR in 1985. Even the man many saw by the late 1980s as the chief 'conservative' in the Soviet leadership, Yegor Ligachev, was to a limited extent a reformer.

The problems the USSR faced in 1985 were real ones, and not something Gorbachev suddenly created or imagined. The notion that the USSR could have kept 'muddling through' in the way it had under Brezhnev was simply not a realistic medium-to-long-term prospect. A major reason for Gorbachev's rise to power in the mid-1980s was that he *appeared* to have a plan for modernizing socialism without destroying it in the process. Unfortunately, the problems and contradictions were deeper than *any* Soviet leader had appreciated; nobody could have prevented the eventual collapse without reverting to coercion. This is not to say that under a different leader the collapse would have occurred when it did or in the way it did; in this sense, Gorbachev's role was unique (for a scholarly analysis of Gorbachev and his policies see A. Brown 1996). But the problems of the Soviet empire – economic, ethnic, identity, rationality, etc. – were there in 1985, whoever had taken power.

Before leaving the issue of Gorbachev's role, one further important observation needs to be made. It is ironic that many Western observers who criticized Gorbachev – referring to his failure, mistakes, etc. – were also for many years highly critical of the USSR. Such commentators appear to want to have their cake and eat it; they wanted to see an end to the communist Soviet Union, yet they criticized someone who, albeit inadvertently, brought about their objective. Whatever else, Gorbachev played a key role in bringing about the end of four decades of Cold War; in liberating the peoples of Eastern Europe; and in giving the citizens of the FSU vastly more say over their own affairs. Although the events in Lithuania in early 1991 in particular (see chapter 4) reveal that Gorbachev's hands were not entirely clean, to have achieved all the above with *relatively* little bloodshed probably represents a greater contribution to the good of the world in the second half of the twentieth century than that made by anyone else. The problems of post-communism are primarily problems of new-found freedoms, inexperience, impatience and the world economic situation. To blame Gorbachev for all this is both unfair and unrealistic (the latter, in ascribing it to one man). Western and Russian critics of Gorbachev must be careful not to create a negative personality cult.

The *economic failure* argument is important and enlightening. In isolation, however, it does not adequately explain the precise timing or nature of the collapse. As Kontorovich has noted: 'This "economic" explanation of the collapse, however, is at best, incomplete. Poor economic performance is commonplace in the world . . . [it] alone cannot directly and immediately destroy a political system' (1993, p. 35).

The argument about *opposition forces* is useful in the case of some countries, if used in conjunction with other arguments. This said, it must be noted that the masses played little overt role in countries such as Hungary, while dissidents played very little role in most of the Balkan states. As with several other explanations, it does not provide a very satisfactory interpretation of the precise *timing* of the anti-communist revolutions either.

The *competition with the West* argument has much to offer, particularly in terms of the development of self-doubt among communist political elites that constitutes such an important component of extreme legitimation crisis. But it fails to explain the Albanian case adequately. Far more significantly, it does not *per se* explain why the communist world felt it had to compete with the West, and why it could not simply have abandoned the race and focused on its own achievements and development. To find such an explanation, it is necessary to consider failures of the ideology – particularly the *dynamism* of such failures – and the economic problems.

The *Marxist corrective* argument, particularly as elaborated by Callinicos, *does* in its full version explain both the dynamism of communist power and the timing of its collapse rather well. But it is based on a number of highly controversial premises, such as the nature of class relations in the communist world, that are unacceptable not only to many non-Marxists, but even to other Marxists who have criticized the communist systems (such as Ernest Mandel) yet cannot accept the 'state capitalist' argument.

The notion of *imperial overstretch* provides many insights. But while it can explain why the Soviet empires – both the external, and to a lesser extent the internal – collapsed, it does not *per se* explain why *communism* was rejected in all these countries. It might be countered that the collapse of the Soviet system implies the collapse of its ideology in all the component parts of the empire. But this explanation would not fit with the collapse of other empires. Many of the religious and political orientations of the former colonies of the Turkish, Austro-Hungarian, British, French, Spanish and other empires survived long after the withdrawal and/or collapse of the imperial power. As a minor point, the imperial overstretch argument does not fit Albania, and requires major modification before it can be applied to Yugoslavia.

Comparative theories of revolution are necessarily broader than many other approaches. Tilly's approach provides interesting analytical tools with which to examine the 1989–91 events, and raises important questions about the categorization of the events in some countries as revolutions. But he is unduly restrictive in his definition of revolution, a point briefly addressed again in chapter 6.

Comparative theories of modernization and modernity are even more subject to the charge of non-specificity regarding the timing and nature of the collapse of communism than are most of the approaches elaborated here. On the other hand, they provide a depth and breadth – a contextualization – that some of the more specific approaches (such as Gorbachev's role) lack. They, too, have their place in any serious attempt at comprehensive analysis.

Finally, *legitimation crisis theory*, as outlined and applied here, incorporates many of the other approaches anyway. It is a broad, abstract approach; but it is also dynamic and, by *incorporating* factors such as economic crisis and *contextualizing* the Gorbachev revolution, covers much of the same ground as several of the more focused explanations. Unfortunately, it does not have the attractions of simplicity and elegance; and it has to be manipulated – the various components have to be reweighted according to the particular country to which it is being applied.

As already indicated, the preferred approach in this book is legitimation crisis theory, since it appears to have a greater explanatory value than any other. But it is also argued here that readers must be aware of the limitations of *any* general theory, which will necessarily and always have its limitations. The focus in this book is on several complex societies, and any argument to the effect that everything in all of them can be explained via one theory, however sophisticated, should be dismissed. There must be a constant search for new theories and explanations. It must be accepted that some questions will never be answered very satisfactorily at all, and that we might not even have thought of all the appropriate questions yet anyway. Certainly, any analysis of the collapse of communism must allow for what I have in another context called *the X-factor* (L. Holmes 1986a, p. 190). Basically, this is a mixture of circumstances unique to a particular case and, quite simply, fate. In connection with the latter, Myron Rush (1993) is one analyst who has referred to 'chance', 'fate' and 'bad fortune' in analysing the collapse of the Soviet Union. While neither he nor anyone else would wish to argue that the collapse of communism can be explained solely in terms of this extrahuman factor, to dismiss it altogether would be a mark of rationalist arrogance.

To argue that all theories are incomplete – and thus in some senses inadequate – is quite different from suggesting that they should be abandoned altogether. If they provide insights and new perspectives that a mere recitation of 'the facts' is unlikely to do, then they have justified their existence. It is within this *heuristic* context that the theoretical analyses provided in this chapter, and particularly the legitimation crisis theory that permeates the book, should be approached.

Ultimately, readers must decide for themselves which theories and approaches provide the most convincing explanations of the collapse of communist power. For many, a mixture of several, even all, will be optimal. Others will feel they still require more historical information before they can reach conclusions. A major objective of the next three chapters is to highlight various watersheds in the rise and demise of communist power in individual countries. If, in the process of learning about these, readers devise their own new theories and approaches, so much the better.

Notes

1 It would be quite wrong to infer that the modernization theorists argue that all states move in some linear way towards this end goal. One of their primary interests was to explain why some countries revert to authoritarianism (for one of the most recent studies of this, in which he analyses 'reverse waves' as well as democratization waves, see Huntington 1991). Nevertheless, many of these theorists assume a *long-term* trend towards liberal democracy.
2 For Huntington, the 'third wave' started in Portugal in April 1974. But he includes in his book analysis of the earliest stages of democratization in the post-communist states.
3 It should be noted that Fukuyama adds that, in the case of Eastern Europe, the 'force of local nationalism' and the fact that 'the Soviets indicated they would not intervene to prop up local elites in Eastern Europe' (1992, p. 35) must also be factored in, although these are ultimately to be seen as reflective of the system's legitimacy crisis.
4 I am indebted to Neil Robinson of the University of Essex for persuading me of the validity of distinguishing between modernism (an ideology) and modernity (a perceived reality).
5 The term 'more or less' is used here to indicate that although the USSR did not interfere in these countries in the same way it did in the GDR, Hungary, etc., it did display its wrath when Yugoslavia and China essentially asserted their independence of the Soviet camp.
6 A major British chain-store known for its high-quality consumer goods at reasonable prices.

FURTHER READING

Since each of the sections on individual approaches examined in this chapter includes references to one or more sources, it is unnecessary to repeat them here. However, readers wishing to look at another compilation of several approaches, albeit focused on the USSR, should see *The National Interest* no. 31 (Spring 1993), pp. 10–63.

Part II

Transition to Post-Communism

The Revolutions of 1989–1991

In the span of approximately two years between late 1989 and the end of 1991, all of the former communist states of Eastern Europe (Albania, Bulgaria, Czechoslovakia, the GDR, Hungary, Poland, Romania, and – with some reservations – Yugoslavia) moved to post-communism. So did several other countries, including Afghanistan, Ethiopia, Mongolia, the USSR and South Yemen. This move can be called the *first* transition, away from communism; moves towards new destinations (which are considered in chapter 12) constitute the *second* transition. Having analysed in a theoretical and comparative way both the reasons for this first transition and what post-communism might mean, the history of the collapse of communist power and the emergence of post-communism in individual countries can be examined. Before embarking on this, however, a few introductory observations are necessary.

First, since so many countries are covered in the next three chapters, the individual analyses are necessarily short. I have not attempted, mechanically and artificially, to render each subsection of equal length. Rather, what seem to me to have been the most important developments in a given country are highlighted. Short bibliographies on each country are included at the end of each chapter for the reader who wants to study particular countries in more depth.

Second, references are also included in the Further Reading section of chapter 3 on the two East European countries omitted here purely because of space limitations, Albania and the GDR.

Third, the order in which countries are analysed largely reflects my own interpretation of the sequence of events. Hungary and Poland are put first because there is little dispute that they were the trail-blazers into post-communism. The USSR's position is highly contentious, but its special role justifies the decision to devote an entire chapter to it. This said, it must be openly acknowledged that sequencing is, and can only be, to some extent subjective. The main reason is that revolutions are rarely clear-cut. Especially if most parties attempt to make a peaceful transition to a new system – as was the case in the vast majority of countries considered here – there will often be compromises and a step-by-step approach. Moreover, analysts often disagree on what should be seen as *the* watershed or turning point in the transition of a given country to post-communism.

Another problem in attempting to determine when post-communism was reached in some countries is that the leaders of the post-communist system are/were former communists; Yeltsin in Russia and Iliescu in Romania are two prime examples. Does this mean these systems are not *really* post-communist? Such a suggestion is not persuasive. If such leaders have not only rejected communism and declared themselves to be democratic – for instance in that they believe in genuinely competitive elections – but also show themselves in practice to be pluralists and committed to a largely marketized economy, to have renounced the *nomenklatura* system and all aspects of democratic centralism, etc., then it is appropriate to accept that they are no longer communists. For this reason, both Yeltsin and Iliescu are accepted as post-communist leaders. A final point to bear in mind in this context is that virtually all citizens in the post-communist world have lived under communism and were socialized by it in one way or another; thus the distinction between 'former communists' and others who lived under communism is not quite as self-evident as might initially be assumed.

For the purposes of clarity, though at the risk of oversimplification, it is assumed here that there are normally *two major steps* into post-communism (that is, in the first transition). The first is the point at which the government ceases to be numerically dominated by communists. The second is the moment when the national legislature is freely chosen by the citizenry in secret, direct, and genuinely competitive elections. If the latter result in a victory for the former communists, as happened in Mongolia in June 1992, it is still assumed here that post-communism has been reached if two criteria are met. One is that the reformed/former communists have, both in theory and practice, renounced the major features of the communist power system. The other is that the reformed/former communists appear willing to *continue* to respect the legitimacy of genuinely competitive elections (that is, continue to accept that if they lose a future election they will transfer political power to the electoral winners; the very newness of post-communism means there is little option at present but to accept stated intentions in good faith).

With the above caveats in mind, each of the following country overviews is structured according to the same basic formula. In the first part of the analysis, a *very* brief history of the country both prior to and under communism is provided. One aim of this is to highlight what appear to have been the most distinctive features of the communist era, rather than constantly repeat that each country had a politburo (or equivalent), etc. Another is to mention historical events that might help us to understand better the roots of many of the ethnic tensions in the post-communist world. Following the historical overview is an analysis of the main developments in the transition from late communism to post-communism.

3

Eastern Europe

East Central Europe

This section focuses on those countries often referred to either as East Central Europe or the Visegrad Three/Four.[1] This is justified largely in terms of the historical sequencing referred to earlier. In addition, the Visegrad Four are increasingly being treated by both Western analysts and their own politicians as a particular type of post-communist system that is in some ways distinguishable from the Balkan post-communist states. Although this distinction can be exaggerated, it does provide a second reason why the countries of East Central Europe are treated together here, and separately from Romania, etc.

HUNGARY

It is a moot point whether Poland or Hungary led the way to post-communism. The arguments in favour of the former are strong, particularly since the government there both recognized and negotiated with the un-official trade union Solidarity in 1980–1, thus setting a precedent in commu-nist Eastern Europe. But there are also valid Hungarian claims. One of these is that the Hungarian communists (formally the Hungarian Socialist Workers Party or HSWP) legalized competitive political parties earlier than did the Polish communists. The Hungarians also dropped references to the leading role of the party from the constitution before the Polish commu-nists did. And finally, since so many analysts (including J. F. Brown, Garton Ash, Glenny, Mason) attribute the honours to the Poles, the focus on the Hungarian achievement might help to redress what could be perceived to be a slight imbalance in the existing literature (though see, for instance, Bollobas 1993, p. 201)!

The various tribes that were to become the Hungarians were on the territory of today's Hungary and surrounding areas by the ninth century AD. The country was occupied by the Ottoman Turks during the sixteenth and seventeenth centuries. However, a far more powerful – Germanic – influ-ence on Hungarian culture was exercised by the Austrian Habsburg empire, which to varying degrees ruled Hungary from the end of the seventeenth century until 1918. During this time, as might be expected, there were numerous attempts by Hungarians to secure independence. Although these failed, a more equal relationship was achieved in 1867; under the Compromise reached at that time, Hungary enjoyed considerable autonomy in domestic politics, while remaining part of the Habsburg empire. Indeed, from 1867 until its collapse in 1918, the latter was also known as Austria-Hungary or, in common parlance, the Austro-Hungarian empire.

With the collapse of the Habsburg empire, Hungary became a republic and more inward looking. For much of the period between the two world wars, the country was under an essentially right-wing government appointed by the head of state, Admiral Horthy. This said, it should be noted that a soviet republic existed there for almost six months in 1919, led by Bela Kun.

Horthy's regime, which had collaborated with the Germans, collapsed in October 1944 and was succeeded by the Hungarian Nazi regime of Ferenc Szalasi. But the communists had by December made a clear bid for power with the establishment of a provisional government in the city of Debrecen. In February–March 1945, the (Soviet) Red Army marched into Budapest, removed the Nazi government, and helped relocate the Debrecen government to the Hungarian capital. Despite this, the main victors in the November 1945 elections were not the communists but the Smallholder Party. Following these elections, however, Hungary was run by a four-party coalition in which the communists became increasingly influential. They intimidated the other parties to such an extent that the Smallholder prime minister fled Hungary in June 1947; this essentially spelt the end of the Smallholders until their resurrection at the end of the 1980s. The communists secured more votes than any other party in the August 1947 elections, and in the following year merged with the Social Democrats to form the Hungarian Workers' Party. This soon proved to be a communist party in all but name; the former Social Democrats exercised negligible influence within the new organization. By 1949, Hungary was officially a People's Republic, under communist control.

As in many other countries of Europe, Hungary now underwent a highly coercive – indeed terroristic – phase, with a Moscow-oriented group of communists under Matyas Rakosi removing, often by execution, leaders of the more national-oriented communists (notably Laszlo Rajk). The country also underwent a 'revolution from above' at this stage. For instance, a major collectivization drive was begun in 1948.

Stalin died in 1953 and was eventually succeeded by the relatively more liberal Khrushchev, who condemned Stalinism in February 1956. Khrushchev also appeared to tolerate the more liberal form of socialism being pursued by Tito in Yugoslavia, and did relatively little to deal with strikes in Poland during the spring and summer of 1956. Moreover, there are clear signs that Khrushchev had been involved in the removal of Hungary's hardline leader, Rakosi, in July 1956. His replacement, Erno Gero, was hardly a liberal, but was seen as an improvement on Rakosi. All this encouraged the Hungarian masses, prompted by the liberal (by communist standards!) former prime minister Imre Nagy, to push for more radical change. Their bid emerged in October 1956.

The events of the next few weeks are too complex to relate here. Suffice it to say that Nagy was briefly returned to power, and on 1 November 1956 he declared Hungary's intention of withdrawing from the recently established Warsaw Pact. He also requested the United Nations to recognize his country's neutrality. The Soviets took major exception to Nagy's declaration, and invaded Hungary. The Hungarians resisted, and in the next few weeks, up to 20,000 people lost their lives in what French commentator Claude Lefort (1977) has called the 'first anti-totalitarian revolution'.

The Hungarian uprising was over, the protesters crushed. Nagy was replaced by Janos Kadar. Kadar, though enjoying some credibility for having been imprisoned under Rakosi for nationalist views, had taken over from a popular leader forced by the Soviets to flee (Nagy was executed in 1958), so that the Kadar era got off to a shaky start.

But over the next three decades or more, Kadar improved his public image dramatically. By the 1980s he was probably the most popular of all the East European leaders. He was responsible for the introduction of the New Economic Mechanism in 1968, a reform which, though ultimately less successful than most had hoped, was nevertheless more radical than the other East European economic reform packages.

Liberalization continued into the 1980s, in terms for instance of the right to travel abroad and to criticize the regime. But Kadar was by now an old man and had lost much of his drive. By the late 1980s leading communists such as Imre Poszgay were advocating more radical reform, consistent with legal-rational legitimation. For instance, in September 1987, Poszgay publicly argued in favour of a new constitution that would guarantee genuine freedom of expression.

In May 1988, 75-year-old Kadar was removed, relatively smoothly and painlessly, at an extraordinary party conference. He was succeeded as party leader by Karoly Grosz, who had been prime minister since mid-1987. Grosz immediately formed a politburo that included well-known radical reformists such as Poszgay, Rezso Nyers and Miklos Nemeth. The new team had its work cut out; the economy was by now in serious problems. Inflation was in double figures (approximately 16 per cent in 1988), and Hungary enjoyed the dubious honour of being more indebted per capita to the outside world than any of its East European neighbours.

Although the new leaders made serious attempts to overcome the economic problems, they could do so only by introducing unpopular measures. For instance, substantial price rises were announced in January 1989. In an atmosphere of greater political freedom and a worsening economic situation, it was not as surprising as it once would have been that unofficial political organizations critical of the HSWP began to emerge in the late 1980s. In terms of its subsequent political role, the most significant of these was the Hungarian Democratic Forum (HDF), established in September 1988. In the context of the emergence of such unofficial organizations, the

HSWP announced in November 1988 its intention to introduce legislation that would formally permit rival political parties; this promise was fulfilled in January 1989, when the Hungarian parliament passed legislation to this effect. Two months later, these – at the time radical – reforms received the official backing of the USSR, when prime minister Nemeth announced that Gorbachev had no objections to a genuine multiparty system in Hungary.

Radical change was gaining momentum in Hungary. In April 1989 the Politburo resigned; its replacement included even more reformists and fewer conservatives.

During the (northern) summer of 1989, a number of by-elections revealed that support for the recently legalized HDF was growing. The communists were at a crossroad; they could either attempt to turn back the clock by reverting to coercion, like the Polish communists in December 1981 or the Czechoslovak communists in 1969, or else move forward and accept the consequences. They opted for the latter, and participated in Round Table talks concerning Hungary's transition to democracy. These talks were concluded in September 1989. One of the first concrete outcomes was a formal name change for the country; on 23 October 1989 the People's Republic of Hungary became simply the Hungarian Republic. At much the same time, the communist party renamed itself the Hungarian Socialist Party (HSP) and formally abandoned its commitment to Marxism-Leninism.

Following an announcement to this effect in December 1989, genuinely competitive parliamentary elections were held in March and April 1990; the HDF won 164 of the 394 seats, the HSP a rather miserable 33 seats. A coalition government was formed in May 1990 by the new prime minister, Jozsef Antall.

In the Hungarian case, both the first and second steps to post-communism were taken at about the same time; by April/May 1990, Hungary had unambiguously reached post-communism. It had done so with a minimum of fuss; the whole process had been very civilized. The role of the masses had mostly been indirect; it was the perception of mass discontent that had led both to the emergence of new political groups and to the major reforms initiated by the communists, and subsequently to the decision to hold genuinely contested elections. But unlike the situation in many of the other countries of Eastern Europe, the Hungarian citizenry did not feel the need to come out on to the streets *en masse* to secure their desired changes. Indeed, the absence of major events – moments of euphoria, even hysteria – in the Hungarian transition to post-communism has led some commentators to refer to the process rather unkindly as a 'melancholic' revolution (see Simon 1993); perhaps Bruszt's (1992) term, 'the negotiated revolution', is a more suitable one.

POLAND

The modern Polish state dates only from 1918. But Poland as an identifiable country was founded by the Piast dynasty in AD 966. In the fourteenth

century, this dynasty was replaced by the Jagellonian of Lithuania and
Poland. The Lithuanian-Polish empire was the most powerful in East Central Europe during the fifteenth century and much of the sixteenth. But
following the collapse of the Jagellonian dynasty in 1572, Poland entered a
phase of weak government. This was unfortunate, since the country was
surrounded by powerful, expansionist neighbours. During the seventeenth
century, it was in almost constant conflict with the Swedes and Russians, for
instance. It more or less survived until the late eighteenth century, and had
even introduced the first codified constitution in Europe in 1791. But by
then, Austria, Prussia and Russia had resolved to carve up Poland, and had
already taken parts of the country in the First Partition (1772). Poland was
further divided up in the course of the Second and Third Partitions (1793
and 1795). The largest share was taken by the Russians; this has never been
forgotten by many Poles, and helps to explain why communism – which for
most Poles was always seen as a Russian concept – was probably less
tolerated in Poland than in any other East European state in the period
from the 1940s to the end of the 1980s.

A new Kingdom of Poland was proclaimed in November 1916. But this
was replaced by a Polish Republic in November 1918. The new republic was
led by Josef Pilsudski, one of whose first achievements was (successfully) to
resist, in August 1920, an attempt by the Russian Bolsheviks to bring
Poland once again under Russian control.

Like several other Central and East European states, the Poles experi-
mented with liberal democracy in the early interwar years. But this failed,
and Pilsudski, who had played little role in politics in the preceding two to
three years, organized a successful coup d'état in May 1926. Over the
following years, Poland became increasingly a dictatorship. Following
Pilsudski's death in 1935, there was a power struggle and near chaos in the
country. This situation was 'resolved' in 1939, when the Germans invaded
Poland. Shortly before this, the Russians and the Germans had concluded a
non-aggression treaty (the Molotov–Ribbentrop Pact); on the basis of this,
the Russians and Germans now divided up Poland once again. This was yet
another reason for Polish hatred of Russians, and of the system associated
with them, from the 1940s on.

This hatred was compounded by the fact that most Poles were devout
Catholics; given the explicit humanism and atheism of communists, it becomes even more obvious why they never achieved much popular legitimacy in Poland.

But, legitimate or not, the state of world politics after the Second World
War permitted the communists to take power in Poland. In the first years of
communist power, Poland had a hardline Stalinist leader, Boleslaw Bierut.
Bierut ordered the arrest of many communist leaders with whom he felt in
competition.

Bierut died in March 1956, shortly after Khrushchev's Secret Speech
denouncing Stalin. Following riots, strikes and an interim government in
1956, a new party leader, Wladyslaw Gomulka, was elected in October.
Like Kadar in Hungary, Gomulka enjoyed more popularity than he might
otherwise have done for having been imprisoned by the previous commu-

nist regime. This said, most commentators agree that Gomulka was more popular among Poles in 1956 than Kadar was with the Hungarians. But whereas the Hungarian leader proved over time to be more liberal and popular than many had expected, Gomulka became increasingly authoritarian and unpopular. There were various signs of discontent during the 1960s, notably student protests and demonstrations in 1968. But the most serious clash between the masses and Gomulka occurred in December 1970, shortly after Gomulka had announced major price rises. He put down the strikers by force; up to a hundred strikers were killed and more than a thousand people injured in the clashes between police and strikers.

Gomulka's increasing authoritarianism made him more unpopular not only with the masses but also with many of his colleagues, who felt he was taking ever less heed of them. Partly because of this, and partly because of their fears of the ramifications of Gomulka's violent treatment of the strikers, the Central Committee removed Gomulka and some of his leading supporters within days of the outbreak of unrest. The new leader was Edward Gierek, whose attempts to 'buy off' the masses were outlined in chapter 2. In addition to seeking legitimacy on the basis of rising living standards (that is, eudaemonism), Gierek engaged in a certain amount of official nationalist legitimation, including external legitimation in the form of wider international recognition. For instance, he played up the fact that the government was to reconstruct a building dear to many Poles' hearts that had been destroyed by the Germans in 1944, the Royal Castle in Warsaw. He also made much of the ratification of the Oder-Neisse Treaty by the West German parliament in May 1972; this constituted formal recognition by the Federal Republic of Germany of the Polish-German frontier.

The attempts at economic improvement eventually backfired, as evidenced by the mass unrest in 1976 and the strikes and establishment in 1980 of Solidarity, the first truly autonomous mass organization in communist Europe. By this stage the economy was in a very sorry state, with shortages of basics and rationing of electric power. The Polish people were further encouraged to demonstrate their dissatisfaction with the regime when a Pole (Cardinal Wojtyla) was made Pope in 1978. This apparently gave many ordinary citizens the confidence openly to criticize the authorities; the Pope had visited Poland in June 1979, and citizens saw for themselves how restrained the communists were during this visit. For some 15 months between September 1980 and late 1981, the Polish authorities recognized and negotiated with Solidarity, which was led by the increasingly charismatic Lech Walesa.

But the Polish authorities, headed since October 1981 by General Jaruzelski, eventually clamped down in December 1981 (on Solidarity see Garton Ash 1991, Pakulski 1991, pp. 125–57). This was followed in October 1982 by the formal banning of Solidarity. Although martial law was lifted in July 1983, the economy continued to be beset by problems. A referendum on economic reform was held in November 1987: the communist government was hoping to gain popular support for a short-term economic austerity package in return for promises of substantial long-term economic

improvement and immediate – if modest – political reform. But the referendum did not secure enough support to legitimate the proposed package, and
tensions between the regime and the population were rising. Following
a series of lesser strikes earlier in the year, there was a major outburst
of industrial unrest from August 1988. The strikers demanded the
relegalization of Solidarity. Following informal talks between Walesa and
the government in late 1988, formal Round Table talks between the authorities and a still technically illegal Solidarity began in February 1989
(having been delayed since the previous October). One result of these,
which lasted until April, was the relegalization of Solidarity in that month.
Another was the holding in June of what in one sense were the first 'free'
elections in Eastern Europe. However, Frentzel-Zagorska's (1989) term
'semi-free' is more appropriate, since the communists did all they could,
short of forbidding any true competition, to ensure they could retain power
where it really mattered. Thus, although they permitted genuinely free
elections to the Senate (upper house), to which Solidarity won 99 of the 100
seats, they introduced rules to ensure that they and their coalition partners
would secure 65 per cent of the seats in the Sejm (lower house).

But this was not enough to save the communists. Even though Solidarity
helped to ensure Jaruzelski the presidency of Poland in July 1989, the
communists were unable to have their own preferred candidate's suggestions for a new government accepted. Moreover, it was clear that the
communists had by now lost control of the economy; after they lifted state
controls on the prices of basics at the beginning of August, food prices
rocketed, in some cases increasing by 500 per cent. The country was clearly
in crisis. In these circumstances, Jaruzelski nominated Solidarity adviser
(and close acquaintance of Solidarity leader Walesa) Tadeusz Mazowiecki
as prime minister in late August 1989. When Mazowiecki announced his
new government in September 1989, the communists formed a minority in
it. Poland had become the first country in Eastern Europe to reach stage
one of post-communism.

Although stage two was *partly* (because of the *semi*-free elections)
reached in June 1989, the Poles had to wait longer than most of their
neighbours for normal parliamentary elections. Presidential elections were
held in November–December 1990, with former Solidarity leader Walesa
winning. But it was not until October 1991 that Poland had genuinely
competitive parliamentary elections. Turnout was low, however, at approximately 43 per cent. By this stage, many were already becoming disillusioned with their essentially post-communist system, which is one
explanation for the apparent voter apathy.

As in Hungary, the transition to post-communism was a relatively peaceful, civilized affair. As in Hungary, the communists had to respond to the
masses who, in their 1988 strikes and via their Solidarity representatives
(the membership of Solidarity had at one stage reached approximately one-
quarter of the total population, and over half the workforce), made clear
their dissatisfaction. But radical reform that led on to revolutionary change
did not emanate from the top in Poland; there was no Polish Poszgay or

Nemeth. In this sense, there were significant differences between the Hungarian and Polish paths to post-communism.

CZECHOSLOVAKIA

Czechoslovakia, as it existed until the end of 1992, was a relatively new state, having only been established as a republic in October 1918. Like many other countries considered here, the new state emerged from the collapsed Austro-Hungarian empire. Prior to this, what came to be the three main parts of Czechoslovakia – Bohemia, Moravia (often referred to jointly as the Czech Lands,[2] and constituting the Czech Republic from 1993) and Slovakia had coexisted for more than a thousand years. However, it should be noted that Bohemia and Moravia had for most of this period been much closer to each other than either had been to Slovakia. The latter had been under Hungarian control for most of this time; indeed, it was for centuries known as Upper Hungary. While Bohemia and Moravia also came under Habsburg rule in the late Middle Ages, the control was often relatively slack; in practice, much power was in the hands of the German-speaking propertied classes of Bohemia and Moravia. The descendants of these people were later known as the Sudeten Germans.

That Czechs and Slovaks had conjoined to form one state can largely be attributed to the efforts of Tomas Masaryk, helped by the Slovak astronomer Milan Stefanik. Once the new state had formalized its political arrangements, symbolized by the constitution of February 1920, Masaryk became president. He remained in that position until 1935.

One of the most significant facts about interwar Czechoslovakia was that it was the only country in Eastern Europe to have had a reasonably successful and established liberal democracy. This is not to say that there were no serious tensions within the new republic. Many Slovaks believed that power was being too centralized in Prague, and supported criticisms made to this effect by the Slovak Populist Party led by Andrej Hlinka. In the 1930s, however, tensions between Czechs and Slovaks were overshadowed by those between both of these groups and the German minority in Czechoslovakia, the Sudeten Germans. The latter had suffered proportionately more from the worldwide depression than had other groups, largely because they tended to live in the most industrialized areas, which were harder hit than the agricultural ones. Tensions increased as many – though certainly not all – Sudeten Germans supported Hitler and the Nazis, while most Czechs and Slovaks felt both threatened by and hostile to the developments to the west and north-west.

Following the annexation of Austria by the Nazis in March 1938, tensions in Czechoslovakia increased still further. By this stage, a number of Czechs and Slovaks had developed an interest in communism. The Czechoslovak government had signed a treaty with the USSR in 1935, and many citizens apparently believed that the USSR and communism would save them from the Nazi threat. Unfortunately, they were soon to learn that nobody would come to their rescue.

In September 1938, Hitler, Mussolini (the Italian fascist prime minister), Chamberlain (British prime minister), and Daladier (French prime minister) met in Munich. In one of the morally most reprehensible decisions of the twentieth century, the British and French sought to appease the Nazis and Fascists; the former were not yet prepared to attempt to halt the fascist march on Europe, and urged 'peace in our time'. One of the concrete manifestations of this policy was that the Czechoslovak government was urged to cede to Germany all those parts of Bohemia and Moravia in which the (Sudeten) Germans constituted an absolute majority of the population. The Czechoslovak president, Eduard Benes, refused to accept this ruling, and resigned. His successors did agree to the terms, however. For reasons too complex to elaborate here, the population of Czechoslovakia had by the end of 1938 declined by approximately one-third because of territorial losses, not only to Germany but also to Hungary and Poland.

But the situation deteriorated still further. The Slovak Populists, by now under Josef Tiso, concluded an agreement with the Nazis whereby the Slovaks secretly accepted a Nazi takeover of the Czech Lands in return for Slovak independence. In March 1939, one day after the Slovak parliament voted for independence, the Nazis occupied the Czech Lands and proclaimed them a protectorate of the German Third Reich.

It should be clear from the above that the Soviets did not assist the Czechoslovaks, despite the 1935 treaty. One formal reason given for this was that the treaty was to be effective only if the French were to collaborate with the Soviets. Nevertheless, many Czechs and Slovaks became more sympathetic to the Soviets and to communism in the early 1940s. One reason was that the Soviets had not actually 'sold out' the young republic in the way Britain and France had done. The second was that the Soviets, once they entered the war (1941), suffered even more than the other nations fighting the Germans; as fellow Slavs, many Czechs and Slovaks empathized with the Russians' plight.[3] There is also the fact that the communists played a major role in the expulsion of the Sudeten Germans from Czechoslovakia; much of their property was then distributed to Czechs and Slovaks. Finally, former president Benes found that, despite the sell-out in Munich, the British still took their time in demonstrating that they might have a bad conscience; although they granted Benes and his government-in-exile recognition in July 1941, this was with some reluctance and after considerable agonizing. The Soviets granted recognition in the same month, and vehemently condemned the treatment Czechoslovakia had received in recent years. Moreover, Benes visited Moscow in December 1943, where he was warmly received; he signed a 20-year treaty with the USSR at that time. All this helps to explain why the Czechoslovaks had, by the 1940s, very different attitudes towards the USSR and communism, and towards the West, from those held by most Poles.

The story of how the communists finally consolidated power in 1948 is a long and complex one; the interested reader can find useful accounts else-where (see Tigrid 1975, Kusin 1977). For now, the most important point is that Stalin and the Czechoslovak communists themselves had apparently hoped the Czechoslovak people would voluntarily choose a communist system. Certainly there were signs in the mid-1940s that this might happen. The communist party was at that time more popular in Czechoslovakia than in any other country in what was to become the Soviet bloc, having secured almost 40 per cent of the vote in the May 1946 general election. But popular attitudes changed rapidly over the next two years, and the communists did not eventually consolidate power via the ballot box. The hopes for a 'demo-cratic' path to communism in the one country in which this once seemed a possibility were dashed. The reasons are several, but one major one was that Czechoslovakia was offered a substantial reconstruction and develop-ment package by the USA as part of the Marshall Plan for Europe, which Prague then had to decline because of Soviet pressure. The growing Cold War between East and West, which led many Czechoslovaks to reassess both communism and the West, plus first-hand experience of how ruthless communists in power could be, were also important factors.

By 1948 the communists were in power in Czechoslovakia. As elsewhere, this had occurred largely by the use of intrigue, force, external (Soviet) assistance, and better organization than most other parties and political forces. Klement Gottwald (until then the communist leader) replaced Benes as president; his successor as party chief was Rudolf Slansky. A new constitution was adopted in May 1948; while this retained *some* elements of the liberal democratic constitution it replaced, it was heavily influenced by the Soviet constitution (Wolchik 1991, p. 61).

As in many other East European countries, the new government soon introduced major reforms, including nationalization of industry, collectivi-zation of agriculture and five-year plans. It also organized the arrest, and in many cases execution, of both non-communist and communist politicians – the latter usually if they were seen as being 'nationalistic' (that is, insuffi-ciently obsequious to Stalin). One of those executed during this terror phase was the erstwhile communist party leader, Slansky. Thousands of ordinary citizens were also arrested and placed in prison camps.

Gottwald died in 1953, shortly after Stalin's death. At the time of his death, he was head of both the party and the state. The new head of the party was another hardline Stalinist, Antonin Novotny. Unlike Poland and Hungary, Czechoslovakia experienced neither major unrest nor a change of leader in 1956. In the 1960s, following a period of relatively impressive economic growth in the 1950s, the Czechoslovak economy slowed down markedly. One of the most significant symbols of the economic problems was the abandonment of the third five-year plan in 1962.

Although an authoritarian leader, Novotny had ended the show trials and most of the more arbitrary aspects of state coercion in the mid-1950s. In line with developments elsewhere in the Soviet bloc and the dynamic iden-tified in chapter 2, he felt unable to return to this. Rather, he accepted the need for economic reforms, which were formally enacted from January

1965. As elsewhere, decentralization was to be a major component of the Czechoslovak reforms. However, the final package approved by Novotny was much less radical than the leading reformers, notably Ota Sik, had advocated. Probably largely because of this, they did not achieve the desired results.

By 1968, continuing economic problems, unrest among students and the cultural intelligentsia, and growing dissatisfaction among Slovak leaders about Slovakia's treatment all contributed to Novotny's removal. He was replaced by a more liberal communist – and a Slovak – Alexander Dubcek. Dubcek did not enjoy a reputation as a *particularly* radical or liberal politician at the time he assumed power. But in the following months, he permitted the introduction of one of the most radical reform programmes ever seen in the communist world. This was the era known as the 'Prague Spring'; had it been allowed to continue, this *might* have resulted in Czechoslovakia being the first country in the Soviet bloc to move to post-communism, more than two decades before the revolutions that form the focus of this chapter.

But both the Soviet and several East European leaderships (notably the Polish and the East German) became increasingly uneasy about the Czechoslovak developments. In August 1968, Warsaw Pact troops invaded Prague; although the reforms were not finally quashed until 1969, they were doomed from the time of the invasion. In the increasingly oppressive atmosphere, Dubcek was replaced as leader in April 1969 by Gustav Husak.

For many, the only positive outcome of the Prague Spring was the federalization of the country, although many Slovaks subsequently felt that even this existed much more on paper than in reality. Like Dubcek, Husak was a Slovak. Like Kadar and Gomulka in 1956, he enjoyed a certain popular credibility for having been tried and imprisoned in the early 1950s. In 1968 he had also publicly declared his support for Dubcek and the reform programme. But once in office, Husak rapidly reverted to coercion (though not actual terror) as a dominant form of exercising power; this approach was called *normalization*. In terms of the theory permeating this book, this normalization testified to a medium legitimation crisis in Czechoslovakia at the end of the 1960s.

Also in line with our theoretical framework, Husak tried to improve the situation in his country during the 1970s. He focused very much on ways to improve the economy. However, his modest tinkering did not bring the desired results, and Czechoslovakia was by the 1980s in a similar economic position to that of most Soviet bloc countries. The situation did not improve when Husak was replaced as party leader by Milos Jakes in December 1987. Although, under some pressure from Gorbachev, Jakes permitted a certain amount of reform (what the Czechs and Slovaks called *prestavba*), it was clear as late as 1989 that the leadership still had a distinctly coercive streak. One of the best indications of this was the trial and imprisonment of Czech playwright Vaclav Havel in February 1989. Havel had done no more than participate in demonstrations the previous month to commemorate the self-immolation of student protester Jan Palach exactly 20 years before. Al-

though Havel was released in May, some six months early, the imprisonment revealed just how much less liberal the Czechoslovak communist
leadership was than, notably, its Hungarian or Soviet counterparts.

Like some other communist leaderships, the Czechoslovak still hoped
that economic reforms and modest political reforms (a mixture of
eudaemonism and legal-rationality) would save them and the system. However, when in July 1989 they condemned out of hand a petition calling for
political reform and signed by more than 10,000 people, it became clear to
many citizens that their own government was much less committed to
extensive reform than was the Soviet, let alone the Hungarian or Polish.

Many Czechoslovak citizens defied the authorities and came on to the
streets in August 1989 to commemorate the twenty-first anniversary of the
Warsaw Treaty Organization invasion of their country. Despite Jakes's
claim to the Central Committee on 12 October that the situation in Czecho-
slovakia was stable, these August demonstrations were followed by far
more significant ones in late October. These were followed in turn by even
bigger protests on 17 November, which were initially led by students. At
these, the call was loud and clear not only for more radical political reform
but also that Jakes should resign. The October and mid-November demonstrations were brutally suppressed by the authorities, further inflaming an
already heated situation. Strike committees were established in Prague and
elsewhere. In this situation, the communist party's Central Committee
called for a dialogue. At about the same time (on 18 November), an umbrella political organization, Civic Forum (CF), was formed. Among its
leaders was Vaclav Havel, and one of its first acts was to call for Jakes's
resignation. On the following day, an estimated 200,000 people demonstrated in Wenceslas Square in the centre of Prague. The calls for major
political change were growing louder. The next day, Havel spoke to the
crowds who had again congregated in Wenceslas Square. Two days after
this, Dubcek addressed a huge crowd in the Slovak capital, Bratislava; he
too demanded major change.

Amid growing unrest, and with a People's Militia that could no longer be
relied on to stop mass demonstrations, Jakes and the whole of the Central
Committee resigned on 24 November. Although a new communist leader
(Karel Urbanek) replaced Jakes, it was clear to all that the communists
were in total disarray. On the same day, CF was formally registered with the
authorities. This made possible an official dialogue between the prime
minister, Ladislav Adamec, and spokespersons of CF (and other groups)
during the last week of November. Probably the most important point
discussed was the formation of a new government. By the end of the month,
parliament (the Federal Assembly) had officially revoked the article in the
Czechoslovak constitution guaranteeing the communist party its leading
role.

Despite the discussions of late November, in December Adamec attempted to form a new government in which the communists were still to be
numerically dominant. This merely led to more mass demonstrations. Some
of the Czechoslovak leaders seem to have believed that if they made con-

cessions (for instance, by reversing their former highly critical stance on the Prague Spring), they would survive the crisis. But this only reflected how out of touch they were with the mood of the masses.

By the second week of December, even the leadership was beginning to realize it had lost control. On 7 December, prime minister Adamec resigned, to be replaced by Marian Calfa. On 10 December, President Husak resigned. On the following day, Calfa announced his new government; non-communists formed a small majority in this. The first step into post-communism had been taken.

The most important events of the second half of December occurred towards the very end of the month. On 28 December, Dubcek was elected speaker of the Czechoslovak parliament. And on the following day (29th), Havel was elected president of Czechoslovakia.

As in both Poland and Hungary, so in Czechoslovakia a Round Table had been formed to discuss the transition from communist power. Early in January 1990, this Round Table resolved to hold a genuinely contested general election before July. In the event, it was held in the second week of June, and resulted in a convincing victory for CF and its Slovak counterpart, Public Against Violence (PAV); the communists secured nearly 14 per cent of the vote for both houses of parliament. Czechoslovakia had reached the second stage of the transition to post-communism.

By now it should be clear that, despite many similarities, there were also important differences between the Czechoslovak, Polish and Hungarian transitions to post-communism. Most notably, the masses played a more visible role in Czechoslovakia, demonstrating on the streets in large numbers in October and November 1989. Although Polish workers played a direct role via their 1988 strikes, most of the final stages of the transition were more in the hands of the Solidarity representatives than of the masses on the streets. If not to quite the same extent as in the other two cases considered, however, the Czechoslovak transition was *relatively* peaceful; apparently, no citizens lost their lives in the process. Yet Havel's description of the transition as 'the velvet revolution' could be misinterpreted; it should certainly be borne in mind that hundreds were injured during the 17 November demonstrations, for instance (Wheaton and Kavan 1992, p. 46). Like Poland, but unlike Hungary, the push to post-communism came from below rather than from within the ranks of the communists. However, the students played a far more important role in Czechoslovakia than in Poland, where it was above all workers' representatives who forced the pace.

The Balkan States

As indicated at the beginning of the last section, many believe that the Balkan post-communist states should be treated differently from the East Central European states. While such differences can all too easily be exaggerated, certainly regarding the transition to post-communism, it makes more sense to divide the post-communist states of eastern Europe along these lines than along any other (such as Slavic/non-Slavic) in terms of history, culture, levels of economic development, etc. Thus, despite certain reservations, this common practice is adopted here.

The present section is longer than the last, despite dealing with the same number of countries. One reason is that the transition to post-communism was more prolonged, and in many ways more complex, in the Balkan states than in the East Central European ones. Another is that an understanding of the very violent break-up of Yugoslavia, which has not so far been repeated elsewhere in eastern Europe, requires some analysis of the history of relations between at least the major ethnic groups (nations). It would be absurd to separate the emergence of post-communism from this broader question of ethnic relations, so that the Yugoslav section is longer than most.[4]

ROMANIA

By most criteria, the present Romanian state dates from 1859, although its boundaries fluctuated a great deal between then and the 1940s. Before 1859, 'Romania' comprised mainly two principalities, Wallachia and Moldavia, which had been mostly under Ottoman (Turkish) or Russian rule in recent times. But in January 1859 the assemblies of the two principalities elected a joint prince, Cuza, which meant in practice that a single state had been formed. Prince Cuza was forced to abdicate in 1866 and was replaced by Carol I, who remained king until his death in 1914. He was succeeded by his nephew, Ferdinand of Hohenzollern.

As a result of the First World War and the collapse of the Austro-Hungarian empire, Romania expanded dramatically. The major new acquisition was Transylvania to the west, although other additions included Bukovina to the north and Bessarabia to the east (Romania lost many of these gains in 1940). For most of the interwar period, political power in Romania was highly centralized. This was a source of irritation to many in the provinces, especially the newly acquired ones such as Transylvania, and was to set a pattern in Romanian politics that, in a somewhat different form, is still to be found in recent Romanian history.

King Ferdinand fell seriously ill in 1926 (he died in 1927), and supreme rule passed into the hands of a three-person Regency Council. In 1928 this Council permitted Romania's first free elections. As a result of these, a far more liberal regime came to power. One of its most popular moves, especially among Transylvanians, was to introduce a bill designed to decentralize political power.

But this more democratic phase was short-lived. Carol II became the new king in 1930 and soon reduced the powers of parliament and political parties. He initially appeared to enjoy the support of a new quasi-fascist group, the Iron Guard. However, he and the fascists grew apart during the mid-1930s, and by the late 1930s Carol II had essentially become the dictator of Romania. Many of the leaders of the Iron Guard were killed in 1938, allegedly while attempting to escape from prison, and almost certainly on the orders of the king.

With the outbreak of World War II, however, King Carol had to modify his stance, and by mid-1940 he had allowed Iron Guardists into his own National Resistance Front. But the king and the Iron Guard fell out once more, largely because the latter blamed Carol for having permitted Germany and Italy to transfer northern Transylvania from Romania to their ally Hungary (Hungary agreed to the nullification of this agreement in 1947, so that northern Transylvania reverted once again to Romanian control). Under pressure, Carol II fled in September 1940, leaving his teenage son Michael on the throne. However, real power was now in the hands of General Antonescu, who in 1941 succeeded in putting down the Iron Guard.

But mounting pressure against the Antonescu regime resulted in its overthrow in August 1944, largely by King Michael, though with the support of several political parties that had remained intact as underground organizations since the 1930s. By late August, Soviet troops were occupying Romania, and Michael included an inappropriately large (in terms of their membership and popular support) number of communists in his new administration. The communists had never been popular in Romania, but the realities of international politics dominated when Michael was forming his government.

Between 1945 and 1947 the communists assumed increasing power in Romania. They managed to do so largely by using so-called 'salami tactics', which involved removing one opposition force at a time. In December 1947, King Michael was forced to abdicate. By the following year, Romania had become a Soviet-style communist state.

As elsewhere, the communist party purged its own ranks in the late 1940s/early 1950s; leading communists such as Ana Pauker and Lucretiu Patrascanu were executed.

From the late 1940s to the early 1960s, Romania was a reasonably loyal ally of the USSR (though for a recent example of a specialist on Romania claiming that the country was already *not* part of the Soviet empire from the 1950s, see Rady 1992, p. 47). Its constitution was akin to the Soviet, and it implemented essentially similar policies to those being realized in other Soviet satellites. But in the early 1960s, under Gheorghiu-Dej, Romania began to assert itself within the Soviet bloc. By the end of the 1960s it had gained a reputation as a maverick. The principal cause initially was an attempt by the USSR and some of the other members of the Council for Mutual Economic Assistance to impose a clear division of labour on the member states. Although established in 1949, the CMEA had been relatively inactive during the 1950s. But at about the same time as the Soviets were losing influence over China (in the late 1950s/early 1960s), and being humiliated in world politics (notably during the Cuban missile crisis), they sought to integrate their East European allies more fully. Albania's reaction was the most extreme; it left the Soviet camp altogether and moved over to the Chinese. The Romanians did not go so far. However, the

Romanian leadership became aware that the emergence of the Sino-Soviet split gave them more leverage vis-à-vis Moscow, and refused to be bullied. The proposal for a division of labour was perceived by the Romanian leadership as an attempt by its powerful neighbours to keep Romania backward, since it envisaged Romania primarily as a food producer (and hence agricultural) rather than as a modern industrial state. Romania's challenge to Moscow was essentially successful: never again would it unquestioningly obey the USSR. It was the only member of the Warsaw Pact (other than Czechoslovakia itself!) to refuse to participate in the invasion of Czechoslovakia in 1968, for instance.

Following his death in 1965, Gheorghiu-Dej was replaced by Nicolae Ceausescu. In many communist states, hardline leaders were succeeded by somewhat more liberal leaders anxious to distance themselves from their predecessors; Romania was an exception. Soon Ceausescu was centralizing power and acting in as essentially dictatorial a manner as his predecessor. Over the next quarter century he cultivated the most blatant and far-reaching personality cult in Eastern Europe. He also created the most nepotistic system in the region. Indeed, some commentators have suggested that whereas Stalin introduced 'socialism in one country', Ceausescu implemented 'socialism in one family'.

Another feature of the Ceausescu era was the official nationalism that began to emerge in the early 1960s and intensified considerably in the 1970s. Until the early 1970s, the Romanian economy had been progressing relatively well. But by the mid-1970s, official growth rates notwithstanding, it was clear there were problems in the economy. In line with this book's argument about eudaemonism, the economic difficulties led the leadership to place considerably more emphasis on official nationalism. There was a major reassessment of Romanian history, and Ceausescu increasingly compared himself with various national heroes from Romania's pre-communist history – including even the notorious fifteenth-century prince Vlad the Impaler, who was the inspiration for Bram Stoker's Dracula! He also sought to enhance his popularity among ethnic Romanians by attempting to suppress the ethnic identity of the Hungarians in Transylvania; this process intensified dramatically in the mid to late 1980s.

By the late 1980s, the situation in Romania was dire. The economy was in a very poor state, and the citizens' suffering was intensified because of Ceausescu's determination to clear Romania's foreign debt. Ironically, this was yet another dimension of official nationalism: Ceausescu sought to demonstrate Romania's independence by proving it need not be indebted (in any sense) to outsiders. But the economic hardship this caused clearly outweighed any nationalist appeal. If this is an accurate reading of the situation, it would be compatible with the argument that eudaemonism is, in the medium to long term, a more powerful legitimation mode than official nationalism. Although Romania paid off its debts in April 1989, the cost to ordinary citizens was too high; there had been severe rationing of both food and energy over a prolonged period.

Thus, many citizens were by mid-1989 angry and frustrated by the economic privation. In addition, many Hungarians (and to some extent other ethnic minorities) were appalled by the regime's attempts to suppress their culture. But the relatively high levels of coercion by the Ceausescu regime meant that most citizens kept these frustrations to themselves. The secret police (the Securitate) were ubiquitous, and the average citizen was simply too frightened to rebel.

But a few Romanians *were* prepared to protest. In March 1989, for instance, six leading politicians wrote an open letter to Ceausescu criticizing much of what had been happening in recent years. They called *inter alia* for the rule of law. In the oppressive atmosphere of Romanian politics, such activity was dangerous: the six signatories were almost immediately placed under house arrest. The fact that the Letter of the Six had been written at all testified to the level of frustration among some leading Romanians, and, perhaps, to the fact that not even Romania was immune to the Gorbymania and sense of impending major change that was sweeping the Soviet bloc.

This sense of change was developing rapidly by late 1989, given events in the USSR and, even more so, in some of the communist states to the north-west of Romania. In the second and third weeks of December, this mood was transformed into action in two cities in particular. In Brasov, workers came out on strike in protest at their working and living conditions; workers in this Transylvanian city had gone on strike before (notably in November 1987), but this time their anger and determination seemed deeper and more open. If the demonstrations in Brasov reflected mainly the hostility caused by the Ceausescu government's handling of the economy, demonstrations in Timisoara (close to Transylvania) more directly reflected the Hungarian minority's anger at its treatment.

On 15 December 1989, the Romanian government issued a deportation order for Father Laszlo Tokes because of his criticism of the Romanian authorities (particularly of their treatment of Hungarians). This resulted in days of demonstrations in Timisoara, during which the city's communist party headquarters were attacked. Ceausescu responded by declaring a state of emergency in the city. The following day, crowds amassed in Bucharest to hear Ceausescu's account of what was happening in the country. Some of those present heckled the Romanian leader and found themselves fighting members of the feared and hated Securitate. Shortly after this, Ceausescu declared a national state of emergency, and called on the military to enforce this. But, in one of the most significant events of the Romanian anti-communist revolution, the military suddenly switched sides. The most commonly accepted interpretation of the reasons for this is that the military held Ceausescu responsible for the death of the defence minister (General Milea) after the latter had refused to order his troops to fire on the demonstrators. Although Romanian radio reported that Milea had committed suicide, rumours almost immediately circulated that he had been murdered by Ceausescu's personal guards, or even Ceausescu's brother Ilie (Rady 1992, p. 103), for insubordination.

Events now accelerated dramatically. Ceausescu, realizing he was in real danger if his own military establishment had turned against him, fled Bucharest by helicopter, but was soon captured. So were his wife Elena and son Nicu. For a very brief period, there were certain sections of one Romanian institution – the dreaded Securitate – that remained loyal to Ceausescu. Whether out of a sense of loyalty to their leader, or because of fears for their own future were the Ceausescu regime to be overthrown, or because of a mixture of these, some members of the secret police now launched a counterattack on the military and their own comrades. But this was short-lived, and the regime collapsed.

A new National Salvation Front (NSF), under Ion Iliescu, claimed late on 22 December that it was running the country. Three days later, on Christmas Day 1989, Nicolae and Elena Ceausescu were both tried for various crimes against the Romanian people (including genocide), found guilty and executed. The NSF formed a provisional government with Iliescu as president and Petre Roman as premier. Romania had reached the first stage of the transition to post-communism.

Two days later, some members of the Securitate made a last-ditch attempt to wrest power, but failed. Already by 29 December the military considered the situation in Romania sufficiently calm for it to withdraw from the capital's streets. The NSF announced there would be free elections the following April. They were in fact held in May, with the NSF winning an overwhelming majority. Presidential elections held at the same time saw Iliescu secure approximately 85 per cent of the vote. The second (final) stage of the transition to post-communism had been reached.

The collapse of communism in Romania was more dramatic and rapid, and involved the masses in a more direct way, than in most other countries. On one level, it could be argued that it was the struggle between two wings of the party-state apparatus, the military and sectors of the Securitate, that sealed the fate of the Romanian anti-communist revolution, rather than the role of the masses. But to do so would be to paint an incomplete picture in which these agencies are isolated from the wider context in which they operated. The army's change, and that of many Securitate officers, was deeply affected by the actions and protests of the demonstrators in Bucharest and Brasov (the influence of the Timisoara events is more difficult to assess).

It might also initially appear that the Romanian leadership was an exception to the argument about self-legitimation, since it seemed not to lose faith in itself. While there is some truth in this, the following points should be borne in mind. First, although Ceausescu himself, and perhaps a small number of people around him, appeared to retain faith in their own right to rule virtually to the end, clearly other leading politicians saw the writing on the wall and accepted what had happened. The speed with which the new regime installed itself and was accepted endorses this suggestion. Second, while Ceausescu may have remained relatively unaffected by what was happening elsewhere in the communist world, his citizens and many of his officers were not. They saw communist systems either collapsing or at least falling into increasing self-doubt all around them, and it would be absurd not to acknowledge the effect this had on morale. Certainly, the nature of the legitimation crisis was different in Romania from the other countries so far considered, as were the balances between coercion and legitimation and between internal and external modes of legitimation. Nevertheless, it is not clear that the Romanian example differs *qualitatively* from the other cases considered. Among other things, the sheer timing of the Romanian revolution indicates that it *was* part of a more general phenomenon, despite the uniqueness of aspects of its situation.

One way in which the Romanian *did* differ from the other East European anti-communist revolutions was in terms of the level of violence involved. As of late 1989, some Western estimates of numbers killed in the Romanian revolution went as high as 60,000 (Rady 1992, p. 116). Official figures released in 1990 and 1991, by authorities with no vested interest in playing this down, were between 689 and 1033 deaths (ibid., p. 120). To a large extent, the violence was indicative of the more repressive nature of the communist regime, and of the higher level of public hostility to that regime. It may also have related to the violence many observers have claimed is entrenched in Romanian culture. In all events, Ceausescu's rule provides strong evidence for the argument made in chapter 2 that, over time, highly coercive regimes become increasingly brittle – especially if they mismanage the economy.

BULGARIA

Bulgaria's history can be traced back at least to the fifth century AD, when there was the first reference to Bulgars. But most historians see modern Bulgarian history as dating from 1878 when, after almost five centuries under Ottoman (Turkish) rule, Bulgaria became a principality. Initially, this occurred largely as a result of Russian successes in the Russo-Turkish war of 1877–8. However, an agreement between Russia and Bulgaria under the terms of the Treaty of San Stefano was soon challenged by Britain and Austria-Hungary, and the greater Bulgaria that had been established by the San Stefano document was considerably reduced under the Treaty of Berlin (also 1878). Nevertheless, even this smaller Bulgaria enjoyed considerable autonomy, although the area was initially under heavy Russian, and still some Turkish, influence.

Over the next three decades, the Bulgarian princes (Alexander, then Ferdinand) sought even greater autonomy. In 1908, Ferdinand proclaimed himself king of an independent Bulgaria; the declaration of independence was widely recognized by foreign powers in 1909.

Bulgaria increased in size in 1885, and again after the First Balkan War (1912–13), but lost most of its gains as a result of the Second Balkan War (1913) and the First World War, ceding territory to Greece, Romania and the newly established Yugoslavia. It remained a monarchy in the interwar period under Boris III, who succeeded his father Ferdinand in October 1918. A peasant-oriented government under Stamboliiski was overthrown in 1923 and replaced by a right-wing coalition. This was in turn replaced by a more liberal government in 1926. Thus in the late 1920s and early 1930s there was a brief period of what came close to being liberal democracy as Westerners would understand this.

But Bulgaria, like the other countries of Europe, suffered the effects of the October 1929 Wall Street crash and the subsequent depression, and authoritarian forces developed rapidly. The most visible result of this was the military coup of May 1934. However, the officers behind this were inexperienced as politicians. Having removed the elected liberal government, they soon had to permit King Boris to become a virtual dictator. All political parties were banned, and the role of parliament declined markedly.

During the Second World War, traditional Balkan rivalries led Bulgaria to adopt a peculiar policy, under which it initially sought not to have to condemn or commit fully to either the German or Soviet positions. When Germany invaded the USSR in 1941, the Bulgarians preferred not to endorse German policy, since it was anxious not to upset the Soviets. It therefore declared war on the UK and the USA, but not on the USSR. But this did not save the Bulgarians from Soviet wrath, and, with the tide turning in favour of the Soviets, the USSR started to penetrate the Balkans. They entered Romania in August 1944, and declared war on Bulgaria at the beginning of September.

By this stage, Bulgaria was being governed by a three-person Regency Council, since Tsar Boris had died in 1943 and been succeeded by a minor. The new head of this Regency Council tried to placate the Soviets by declaring Bulgaria's neutrality, and subsequently that it was at war with Germany. But it was too late. The Soviets entered Bulgaria on 8 September 1944. By the following day, Bulgaria had experienced a coup d'état: the existing order was overthrown and replaced by the Soviet-backed Fatherland Front. This was a coalition of various anti-fascist parties, including the communists. One of its first actions was to mount a witch-hunt against politicians who either had or were alleged to have worked closely with the Nazis. Many of these were imprisoned or executed.

Although the communists were represented in the new Fatherland Front government, they were not numerically dominant in the early stages. Moreover, there was an allied control commission in Bulgaria between 1944 and 1947; although headed by a Soviet, this included British and American representatives. Nevertheless, the Soviet military presence in Bulgaria provided a psychological fillip to the Bulgarian communists, who soon began pressuring their coalition partners, particularly the popular Agrarian Party. This pressure, and the communists' self-confidence, increased with Georgi Dimitrov's return to Bulgaria in March 1945. He had been head of the international organization of communist parties, Comintern (which existed between 1919 and 1943), and enjoyed a considerable reputation both at home and abroad.

Given the Soviet military presence, declining Western interest in Bulgaria (the Western allies vacated the country in 1947), and the return of leading communist politicians, it is not surprising that Bulgaria came increasingly under communist influence. Following a referendum, the country formally became a republic in September 1946. In 1947 a major clamp-down on other political parties was initiated by the communists; this resulted in Bulgaria becoming a *de facto* one-party communist state by 1948. The country's first economic plan was adopted in April 1947 and a major collectivization drive was launched at the end of 1948.

Once firmly in power, the communists began to purge both their own ranks and the various agencies of the state (including the military). For example, leading communist Traicho Kostov was removed from his post of deputy premier in 1949 and subsequently executed. To the extent that a pattern was discernible, it appeared that the Muscovite communists were purging the leading domestic ('national') communists.

This terror phase lasted well into the 1950s. A slight improvement could be perceived by the mid-1950s, particularly once Todor Zhivkov became head of the party (1954) and in the aftermath of Khrushchev's Secret Speech. But the level of liberalization should not be exaggerated. For instance, there was a clampdown following the Hungarian events of late 1956. There was also a renewed collectivization drive in the countryside, as a result of which over 90 per cent of arable land was being collectively farmed by mid-1958. The Bulgarian 'revolution from above', like so many others, resulted in major structural changes, but did not guarantee sustained high-level economic growth.

Economic problems became very visible in 1962, with the announcement of major price rises. This led to a limited debate on how best to overcome these difficulties through restructuring and, in December 1965, an economic reform package. But this was less successful than many had hoped; by 1968, important aspects of the reforms were being modified or discarded. Further structural changes occurred in the 1970s, such as the creation of agro-industrial complexes, but they too had limited success (on all these reforms see Vogel 1975).

Despite the reforms of the 1960s and 1970s, the Bulgarian economy faced essentially similar problems to those of its Soviet-bloc neighbours. The leadership therefore sought legitimacy through modes other than eudaemonism from the mid-1970s on. For instance, there was a new emphasis on official nationalism (see Glenny 1990, p. 168), and teleologism; the best example of the latter was the announcement in 1976 that communism would be achieved by 1990.

But these legitimation modes also appeared to have limited effect. By the mid-1980s, Zhivkov reluctantly opted for the legal-rational mode Gorbachev was increasingly emphasizing. He introduced a policy of restructuring (*preustroistvo*) that closely resembled the Soviet concept of *perestroika*, and urged more *glasnost*. New electoral laws adopted in December 1987 *required* multicandidate elections in future and gave ordinary citizens the possibility of nominating candidates (though still subject to the approval of the authorities). As in the USSR, however, it soon became obvious that these moves into legal-rationality might be getting out of hand. At a conference of the Bulgarian Communist Party (BCP) held in January 1988, senior leaders advocated a more cautious approach to *preustroistvo* – even as they emphasized that the changes it involved were necessary. These statements were made just weeks after four senior academics in Sofia had been dismissed for expressing doubts about the feasibility of the leadership's policy of, and commitment to, restructuring; these dismissals led to student demonstrations. Then, in July 1988, two of Bulgaria's leading reformers were dismissed from senior party posts, apparently for wanting to maintain the pressure for change.

The leadership appeared increasingly uncertain about the way forward. Nevertheless, the January 1988 BCP conference had appeared to encourage unofficial citizens' associations. It was in this climate that communist Bulgaria's first significant organized opposition groups emerged in 1988. Until then, there had been very little evidence of political opposition; most analysts refer only to a May 1953 strike in the tobacco-growing region around Plovdiv, and a failed coup attempt by a small group of (mostly military) officials in April 1965. But in early 1988 two citizens' groups were established – the Independent Association for the Defence of Human Rights in Bulgaria and the Rusé Defence Committee respectively. The latter, an environment-oriented group, emerged at the time of demonstrations in the Bulgarian town of Rusé against chemical clouds that regularly floated over the border (across the Danube) from the Romanian town of Giurgiu. Then, in November, approximately 80 of Bulgaria's leading intellectuals established the Club for the Support of *Glasnost* and *Preustroistvo* in Bulgaria; like the two expelled politicians mentioned earlier, these people were concerned that the Zhivkov leadership team was in reality less enthusiastic for change than it claimed and needed to be.

Zhivkov's responses to all this further revealed confusion. In December 1988, at a meeting of the Central Committee, he urged better implementation of *preustroistvo* and appeared to criticize the lower levels of the bureaucracy for their resistance to change. But at the very same meeting, the two reformist politicians who had lost their posts as Central Committee secretaries in July were expelled from the Central Committee altogether.

The clampdown was directed not only against senior members of the BCP. Already in early 1988 several leaders of the unofficial human rights organization mentioned above had been harassed, and one of them was sentenced to two years' internal exile. In January 1989 there was another clamp-down on the organization. And in September, when the environmental group Ecoglasnost, which had been established in March 1989 on the basis of the Rusé Defence Committee, made a formal application to register, it was rejected by the authorities.

Party reformists and dissident intellectuals were not the only ones to suffer under the Zhivkov regime in the late 1980s. Many ordinary citizens were suffering from the mismanagement of the economy, as evidenced by food shortages as early as the winter of 1987–8. In addition, the Turkish minority was feeling particularly aggrieved. The authorities had hounded the Turks before. But there were particularly serious clashes between Turks and the police in May 1989. As a result of these, over 250 Turks were deported. This encouraged large numbers of Bulgarian Turks (well over 300,000 by August 1989) to leave Bulgaria for Turkey. Many of these had played a significant role in Bulgarian industry and agriculture, and their departure had a serious, immediate impact on the labour force. Eventually, Turkey closed the border again to stem the tide. However, the damage was already done. By July 1989 the Bulgarian authorities had lengthened the working week for Bulgarian workers as a way of compensating for the loss of labour. Understandably, this was very unpopular.

But it was the environmental issue, rather than the ethnic issue, which resulted in the biggest unofficial demonstration to take place in Bulgaria since the communists had come to power. On 3 November 1989, thousands demonstrated outside the National Assembly building in Sofia. The Conference on Security and Cooperation in Europe had been holding a meeting on the environment in the Bulgarian capital since 16 October. While this was in progress, three of the major opposition groups had publicly defied the Bulgarian authorities in one way or another. In Ecoglasnost's case, this was mainly by organizing a huge petition calling for a better environment and more openness. This petition was paraded through the streets of Sofia on the last day of the CSCE conference, 3 November. By the time they reached the National Assembly the demonstrators were making general political demands for more genuine reform and human rights (on Ecoglasnost see Crampton 1990).

One of Zhivkov's closest allies, Politburo member and foreign minister Petur Mladenov, had become increasingly uneasy during 1989 about his leader's handling of various issues, including the treatment of the Bulgarian Turks. On 24 October, Mladenov sought to distance himself publicly from Zhivkov by attempting to resign as foreign minster; he had become embarrassed at having to defend Bulgaria's actions against its minorities to the outside world. Zhivkov refused to accept Mladenov's resignation. A few days later, Mladenov stopped off in Moscow on his way home from an official visit to China. It seems that here he received the go-ahead to oust Zhivkov (Glenny 1990, p. 172). Exactly one week after the huge demonstrations in Sofia, which suggested how out of touch Zhivkov was with the mood of the masses, the man who had headed the BCP since 1954 was forced to resign at a meeting of the party's Central Committee. Zhivkov was replaced as party leader by Mladenov (for details of Zhivkov's removal see J. F. Brown 1991, pp. 196–7). One week later, Zhivkov's removal was completed when Mladenov replaced him as president. Within weeks, there had been a (non-violent) purge of the upper ranks of the BCP, with many of Zhivkov's closest allies being removed.

Most Bulgarians considered Mladenov an improvement on the hated Zhivkov. But he was still a communist, and even his more liberal brand of communism appeared outdated. Many Bulgarians now felt confident enough to keep up the pressure on the BCP leadership to ensure none of the backsliding that had typified the last two years of Zhivkov's rule. In this climate, nine of the leading opposition groups (including Ecoglasnost) banded together in December 1989 to form an umbrella organization, the Union of Democratic Forces (UDF). Just days after its establishment, Mladenov called for free elections, to be held in June 1990.

By the middle of December, the UDF, under its leader Zhelyu Zhelev, was organizing large rallies in many towns. Mladenov tried to address one of these in Sofia on 14 December and was heckled. Many citizens considered that the authorities, despite their new openness, were still too close to the old ways. Large numbers of Turks, for instance, joined the demonstrations, demanding the right to revert to their Islamic names (over 800,000 Turks had been forced to 'Bulgarianize' their names since 1984 as part of the government's assimilation programme) and to be allowed to practise their religion freely.

In this strained atmosphere, the Politburo announced its willingness to start Round Table talks with the UDF. By the end of 1989, the authorities had also publicly condemned the forced assimilation policy and announced that Turks would henceforth be permitted to use their Muslim names.

The Round Table talks started in the middle of January 1990 and lasted until April. They did not invariably proceed smoothly. Nevertheless, it was eventually agreed that the elections proposed for June 1990 would be held. The UDF agreed reluctantly, since they believed that they and other new organizations would have insufficient time to prepare.

Two other developments in the first half of 1990 need to be mentioned. The first was an interesting change of government. Georgi Atanasov and his team resigned at the beginning of February. The new premier was Andrei Lukanov; when he announced his government on 8 February it comprised *only* BCP members. Ironically, this was the first time ever that the government had been exclusively communist; hitherto, it had always included members of the one other party that had been permitted throughout the communist era, the Bulgarian Agrarian National Union (BANU). Although always subservient to the BCP and never an opposition party, the BANU did at least have a separate organizational structure from the BCP's and, in a very limited sense, a separate identity. In the new era of Bulgarian politics, however, it wanted to keep its distance more clearly from the BCP. Second, the BCP renamed itself the Bulgarian Socialist Party (BSP) in early April.

Despite some confusion because of the complex voting system, the BSP were the clear winners of the June elections, securing some 47 per cent of the vote and 211 of the 400 seats in the National Assembly. The UDF gained approximately 38 per cent of the vote and 144 seats. In that this was a contested election, and the BSP had rejected many of the basic principles of a communist party, it could be argued that this represented the second stage of the transition to post-communism. Conversely, the first stage (a government in which communists either constitute a minority or are not represented at all) had not yet been reached, and many still saw the BSP as a revamped BCP. Moreover, there was evidence to suggest BSP manipulation of the electoral results. Given this ambiguity, the story of the Bulgarian transition to post-communism is not yet complete.

Following the elections, Lukanov stayed on as prime minister, and his government continued in office for some months. But it resigned in August, some two months after the election, and Lukanov took approximately a month to form a new one. Both delays – in the old government resigning, and the new one being sworn in – were largely the result of political squabbling between, primarily, the BSP and the UDF. The latter continued to complain that they had not fought the BSP on equal terms and were dissatisfied with the electoral result. Largely because of this, they refused to participate in a coalition government. Therefore, when Lukanov announced his new government on 20 September 1990, the UDF were not represented in it; the vast majority of members were BSP.

Meanwhile, there were interesting developments in the presidency. Although Mladenov had been a reasonably popular president, certainly in comparison with his predecessor Zhivkov, a scandal led to his resignation in July. In December 1989 he had been videotaped arguing that mass demonstrations by citizens opposed to the BCP/BSP should be dealt with by military force; this obviously raised doubts about the sincerity of his renunciation of the traditional hardline communist method of governing. Although Lukanov initially claimed that the video was a fake, his party refused to support him, and eventually he had to step down. The BSP itself, particularly the reformists within it, had played a major role in removing Lukanov; nevertheless, it was tarnished by the affair, to the advantage of the UDF. The latter openly suggested that Mladenov's views revealed that the BSP's commitment to democracy was still in question. It was therefore not so surprising that the leader of the UDF, Zhelev, was elected President of Bulgaria at the beginning of August – though only after protracted voting in the BSP-dominated National Assembly.

In October 1990 the government formally proposed major economic reforms, including a much greater commitment to marketization; these proposals were debated by parliament in October and November. At about the same time, rationing of several basics was introduced. The economy was clearly in trouble, and many ordinary citizens were concerned about their own future under the proposed changes. It is thus understandable why there were major demonstrations (many again led by students) against the government, and then a general strike in November. In late November, the opposition parties started a boycott of the National Assembly. Against this background of unrest, the Lukanov government resigned at the end of November. After approximately three weeks of wrangling, a new government was formed by the new prime minister, Dimitur Popov. Not only was Popov himself not a BSP member (he was an independent), but the BSP had only eight out of the 18 seats in the new government. The first stage of the transition to post-communism had now definitely been reached.

Economic reforms proceeded at a reasonable pace in 1991. Their implementation was greatly assisted by the fact that the trade unions and employers had agreed a 'social peace' plan in January 1991, which committed the unions to a prolonged no-strike period. With this guarantee, the government was able to remove subsidies on many basics in February, following which further aspects of economic reform, such as land restitution, were legislated.

In October 1991, parliamentary elections originally scheduled for September were held. By this stage, some of the kudos the UDF had acquired in 1990 through the Lukanov affair had worn thin, the harsh realities of the new economic order having negatively affected most ordinary citizens. Nevertheless there was still sufficient residual support for the UDF to win the election by a very narrow margin (34.4 per cent of votes to 33.1 per cent for the BSP). Such a narrow victory meant that a third party, the Turkish-oriented and non-communist Movement for Rights and Freedoms, held the balance of power in parliament. Bulgaria had now unequivocally passed through the second stage of transition; it was a post-communist state.

The transition was slightly more prolonged in Bulgaria than in many of the other East European states. Nevertheless, it was *relatively* swift; two years is not long in the grand order of things. It was also for the most part peaceful, although some UDF supporters were reported killed during the campaign for the June 1990 elections; it was certainly far less violent than the Romanian transition. It was also similar to the Czechoslovak and East German cases in the sense that the masses, especially through their visibility at demonstrations, played a significant role in maintaining the pressure for change. In the final stages, however, the masses were largely excluded, especially given the 'social peace' accord of January 1991.

YUGOSLAVIA

Yugoslavia and the country to be analysed in the next chapter, the USSR, had much in common. Both were multi-ethnic federal systems, with one group, the Serbs and the Russians respectively, seen by many members of the other ethnic groups to have dominated the system. In both cases, it is not merely the system that has collapsed, but also the political unit (that is, the country). And in both cases, part of the reason for the collapse of the prevailing political configuration was that different component parts moved to post-communism at different rates; this is clearer in the Yugoslav case than the Soviet, however.

Like so many other countries considered in this book, Yugoslavia as it existed until 1991 was a relatively new state, having been created shortly after the end of the First World War. It was formed partly as a result of the collapse of both the Habsburg and Ottoman empires. In December 1918, Serbia, Croatia, Bosnia, Hercegovina, Slovenia and Montenegro were united under the Serbian king Peter (who was succeeded by his son Alexander in 1921) to form what was at that time known as the Kingdom of Serbs, Croats and Slovenes; it was renamed Yugoslavia, meaning land of the southern Slavs, in October 1929.

The new unit made a great deal of sense. In the light of what has been happening in the former Yugoslavia in the 1990s – the historical claims and counterclaims of nationalists of various kinds – it is worth briefly examining the ethnicity and history of some of the major groups. The story is extremely complex, with changing boundaries and allegiances over the centuries. All that can be done here is to highlight some of the most important landmarks and developments.

The largest group is the *Serbs*, who constituted nearly 40 per cent of the population of the former Yugoslavia. The first references to them as a group date from the ninth century AD. Until the late fourteenth century, they were very much under Byzantine (Christian) influence. But in 1389 the Serbs were attacked in Kosovo by the Turks; despite brave attempts to resist the Ottoman empire over the next 70 years, they came under Turkish occupation in the middle of the fifteenth century, and Serbia became part of the Ottoman empire for almost 350 years. The Turks essentially obliterated the Serb aristocracy, partly because of the latter's attempts to retain its Christian ways. But in Bosnia, which had been linked to Serbia for some of the Byzantine period, the dominant Serb aristocracy managed to save their lands and lives by adopting Islam. Thus most of the members of the elite that accepted the Muslim way in Bosnia were ethnically Serbs. Unfortunately, many other Serbs have come to believe that the Bosnian Serb elite had 'sold out'; this is part of the historical background to the bloody fighting between Bosnian Muslims and Serbs in the 1990s.

In the eighteenth century, Habsburg armies began invading the Ottoman empire, and many Serbs (as well as Croats) fought on the side of the Habsburgs. One reason for this was that most Serbs felt a greater affinity for the Christian culture of Austria than for the Islamic culture of Turkey. During the nineteenth century the Habsburg empire became stronger, while the Ottoman empire was weakened. Given this, Serbia came increasingly under Austro-Hungarian influence in the late 19th century.

But tensions between Serbia and the Habsburgs increased in the early twentieth century, to no small extent because the latter resisted attempts by the former to link up with the Serbs of Bosnia. This tension was part of the reason for the assassination of the Austrian Archduke Ferdinand by a Bosnian Serb in the Bosnian capital, Sarajevo, in June 1914. This event is usually cited as the trigger for the First World War.

The recorded history of the *Croats* is longer than that of the Serbs. The Croats migrated in the sixth century AD from what is now part of Ukraine, and in the following century converted to Christianity. In the early ninth century, some parts of what is now Croatia were under Byzantine rule, whereas others were part of the Frankish empire. Following a relatively short period of independence, much of Croatia came under Hungarian rule at the beginning of the twelfth century and remained under Hungarian influence – although the level varied over time – for the next eight centuries; while parts of it were under Ottoman domination for a brief period from the sixteenth century, the country was never as dominated by Turkish values as Serbia was.

During the nineteenth century, tensions between the Croats and the Habsburg empire increased. Eventually, in 1868, the Croats reached an agreement with the Hungarian side of the empire whereby Croatia was granted greater autonomy while remaining part of the Hungarian kingdom.

This was an early example of success by autonomist nationalists. However, it was not enough for some Croats, an increasing number of whom wanted full independence. But their successes were limited, and the formal agreement between Hungary and Croatia remained valid until 1918.

In the years before the First World War, a Croatian-Serbian coalition was established in Croatia, which performed well in elections. This indicated how closely Serbs and Croats – whose language was essentially the same, though written in different alphabets – could cooperate. This is worth bearing in mind, given the subsequent history of Serb–Croat relations.

It seems that most Croats initially welcomed the formation of the new Kingdom of Serbs, Croats and Slovenes in 1918. Before long, however, some began to complain that the Serbs were centralizing too much power in Belgrade, and demanded a reorganization of the political unit along federal lines. Before substantial moves in this direction could be made, the Croat leading this autonomist movement, S. Radic, was assassinated in parliament (1928). Largely as a result of this, the experiment with liberal democracy under a monarchy that had typified the first years of the new state came to an end in 1929, when King Alexander became the virtual dictator of Yugoslavia. Members of the Croatian Ustasha movement (see below) in turn assassinated King Alexander in 1934;[5] tensions between the Croats and the Yugoslav state were increasing.

Croatian demands for greater autonomy did not cease in the 1930s. In 1939, Croatia linked up with parts of Bosnia-Hercegovina (and Dalmatia) to form a far more autonomous political unit within Yugoslavia. But even this was insufficient for Croatian secessionist nationalists, who wanted a totally independent state. Following the occupation of Yugoslavia by the Axis powers, a group of nationalists proclaimed an independent Croatian state in April 1941. This was almost immediately recognized by the Axis powers. However, the latter wanted Croatia to be under German control; when the leader of the dominant Croatian Peasant Party refused to accept this, the Germans installed the leader of the pro-Nazi Croatian nationalist group, the Ustashi. The new Croatian leader, Ante Pavelic, soon proved to be a brutal dictator, and particularly hostile to the Serbs. His regime collapsed in May 1945, shortly after Germany had surrendered to the Allies, and Pavelic fled abroad. Croatia was once again integrated into Yugoslavia. But Serbs would not forget the appalling atrocities committed against many of their number by the Ustashi.

The history of *Bosnia-Hercegovina* is in some ways even more complex than those of Serbia and Croatia. It has over the centuries been united with Serbia; under both Ottoman and Habsburg control; and independent. Although it was largely under Austro-Hungarian rule by the late nineteenth century, its culture has been more influenced by Turkish/Islamic values than by Austro-Hungarian/Catholic ones. Even here though, it is in some ways unique. For instance, while its Serbian aristocracy largely adopted Islam, they never accepted all of its tenets; polygamy, for instance, was rejected.

In 1908, Bosnia-Hercegovina was formally annexed to the Austro-

Hungarian empire, to the dismay of many Bosnians. Feeling a far greater affinity with Serbia than with Austro-Hungary, many Bosnians were delighted at the collapse of the Habsburg empire and seemed content to join the new Kingdom of Serbs, Croats and Slovenes in 1918.

Ideally, one would also consider here the history of the Slovenes, the Yugoslav Macedonians, and the Montenegrins – as well as the Albanians in Kosovo and the Hungarians in Vojvodina (the latter two political units were still part of Serbia at the time of writing, though their future looked uncertain). However, space constraints necessitate selectivity; the interested reader can obtain histories of all ethnic groups in the Balkans in Wolff 1956 (esp. chs 3–6). For now, the formation and history of communist Yugoslavia can be examined.

As indicated, there were serious tensions between Croats and Serbs in the interwar period, and Croatia was an independent state under the fascist Ustashi between 1941 and 1945. There was also a quasi-military movement in Serbia – the Chetniks – during the Second World War. They too were right-wing, with some members being fascist. This latter point is important to note in attempting to understand why the Western Allies eventually supported a communist movement in Yugoslavia. The story warrants unpacking.

Initially, the Chetniks were anti-Nazi, so that there was little reason for them to be at odds with the Western Allies. From the start, however, many in the West made clear their preference for a united Yugoslavia, so that movements which could be seen as divisive (in that they were primarily based on one ethnic group) were not supported as enthusiastically as they might otherwise have been. Once it became clear, in 1943, that many of the Chetniks were collaborating with the Germans, the Allies switched their support to Tito and his communist partisans.

The communists already had one major point in their favour – they did not represent any particular ethnic group, and instead made clear their commitment to a unified Yugoslavia. In addition, Tito was soon making strenuous efforts not to appear to be too hardline a communist, preferring an image of leader of a moderate, conciliatory movement. When communists in Montenegro and Hercegovina emphasized the revolutionary aspects of their movement in the early 1940s, they were formally censured by the party's Central Committee. Not only did Tito seek to portray his movement as a relatively moderate left-wing one, but it also gained credit with the Allies for its organizational and administrative skills. Following a brief period of collaboration with the Chetniks to 1941, the communists opted to work alone, and established National Liberation Committees in whichever parts of Yugoslavia they were able to take power. By 1942 they had even established a *national* government. While they did not push for recognition of this – there was after all a government-in-exile recognized by the West – it did mean that the communists were able to provide evidence both of their pan-Yugoslavism and of their ability to administer and govern, within limits, in very difficult circumstances.

Once the Allies decided to switch allegiance from the Chetniks to the communists, they *de facto* recognized the Tito government for the time being. However, they preferred not to abandon the government-in-exile altogether, and therefore urged the two sides to form a coalition. This materialized in March 1945, when a Provisional Government was established. However, the collaboration did not proceed smoothly, and by mid-1945 it was clear the communists were harassing the non-communist members of the government. Many of the latter fled, and by the end of 1945 Yugoslavia was under communist control. This was formalized with the adoption of a new constitution in January 1946.

From the start, the Yugoslav communist authorities decided to recognize ethnic differences within the state by organizing it along federal lines. They distinguished between *nations* (groups whose traditional territory lay wholly within Yugoslavia) and *nationalities* or *national minorities* (groups that were part of a larger nation, most members of which still lived beyond Yugoslavia's borders). Each of the five major Slavic nations was granted a republic (Serbia, Croatia, Slovenia, Montenegro, Macedonia), while a mixed republic, designed partly to cater for the Bosnian Muslims, became the sixth republic. The two major nationalities, the Albanians in Kosovo and the Hungarians in Vojvodina, were granted their own administrative units (an autonomous region and an autonomous province respectively) within the republic of Serbia. To endorse the notion of ethnic representation at the federal level, the legislature included an upper house, the Council of Nationalities. However, all these elaborate arrangements proved in retrospect to be a two-edged sword, and there were various ethnic tensions during communist Yugoslavia's 45-year existence.

Initially, Yugoslavia was a loyal member of the Soviet bloc, even though the USSR had played very little role in the Yugoslav communists' accession to power. But in 1948, relations between Tito and Stalin rapidly deteriorated, to such an extent that Yugoslavia was expelled from the Soviet-dominated Cominform (see chapter 11). Among the many reasons for this dispute was the fact that Stalin had lost his earlier enthusiasm for the notion of a federalized Balkan union of communist states; personality clashes between Tito and Stalin; and Tito's belief that Moscow was attempting to impose excessive uniformity on the member states of Cominform, something he considered to be at odds with socialist internationalism. Moreover, given Tito's special status among East European leaders (in owing so little of his success to Moscow), he was less deferential than his peers towards Stalin. The megalomaniacal Stalin found this quite intolerable. Indeed, it was almost certainly the relative independence of Tito and the Yugoslav leadership that, more than any other factor, led Stalin to want to expel them from 'his' Cominform (on the break see Rusinow 1977, pp. 22–31).

In all events, Yugoslavia went very much its own way within the communist world from the late 1940s. Whereas the other East European countries joined the Soviet-dominated economic and military blocs (Comecon and the Warsaw Pact respectively), Yugoslavia did not formally join any economic grouping and became a prominent member of the Non-Aligned Movement. Moreover, as mentioned in chapter 1, it pursued a radically different approach to the building of socialism and communism from that of any of its East European neighbours. By the early 1950s, the Yugoslav conception of self-management had begun to take shape; it developed significantly during the 1950s and 1960s (in addition to the sources cited in chapter 1, see Zukin 1975, pp. 48–75).

Another key (and related) component of the Yugoslav model was the delegate system. This concept explicitly rejected the notion of representative democracy, largely on the grounds that the latter often results in elected representatives voting either in line with views from above or their own opinion. Instead of this, the Yugoslav communists wanted a system in which elected representatives would be encouraged by the people who elected them to vote in a particular way on a given issue. Although in practice the delegate system proved to contain several inherent problems, it did represent a serious attempt by the Yugoslav communists to create a system radically different from what they saw as the essentially top-down bureaucratic system of the USSR and most East European states.

Despite these efforts to create a more genuinely democratic socialism than existed elsewhere in the communist world, Yugoslavia experienced severe political conflicts of various kinds during the communist era. Most of these reflected ethnic tensions.

The first really serious manifestation occurred at the beginning of the 1970s, following a period of liberalization by the central (federal) authorities after 1966. In 1971, Croatian nationalists in particular came into conflict with Belgrade over the issue of hard currency. Several leading Croats resented the fact that such a high proportion of the foreign currency earned by their republic was being transferred to and redistributed by the central Yugoslav authorities. They therefore sought an arrangement under which Croatia would retain most or even all of its hard currency earnings for its own investment and redistribution purposes. But the federal authorities reacted negatively to such demands. This rejection of Croatian demands resulted in major demonstrations in the Croatian capital (Zagreb) in November 1971, and the dismissal of several high-ranking Croatian politicians. Over the next few years the Yugoslav authorities resolved to deal more firmly with nationalists. Fifteen Croatian nationalists received long prison sentences in 1975, for example. This coercive policy kept unofficial nationalism and ethnic politics largely under control for the rest of the 1970s.

But with the death of Tito – himself part Croat, part Slovene – in 1980, one of the most powerful integrating forces in Yugoslav politics disappeared. Tito had introduced measures in the 1970s designed to ensure a relatively harmonious arrangement after his departure. Thus a complex system of regular and frequent leadership changes for the topmost party and state positions, designed to give each republic and province a representative at the summit for a year every few years, became operational on Tito's death.

Unfortunately, this elaborate and sensitive attempt to ensure harmonious relations was not very successful. Less than a year after Tito's death, nationalist demonstrations erupted in Kosovo. This had long been the poorest part of Yugoslavia and still did not enjoy republic status. Many Albanians considered the federal authorities were being insufficiently sensitive to their needs and demanded either greater autonomy within Yugoslavia or else that Kosovo be allowed to secede from Yugoslavia and become part of Albania (different groups made different demands). Although there had been minor outbreaks of Kosovar nationalist protest on various occasions since at least 1968, the March–May 1981 riots were more serious. According to official announcements in June of that year, nine people had been killed and 257 wounded in the few weeks of demonstrations.

Although the 1981 Kosovo riots were brought under control, and despite the more hardline approach towards nationalists following them, nationalist and ethnic politics in Yugoslavia continued to simmer throughout the 1980s. Early in 1989, for instance, Serbian moves to bring Kosovo under greater Serbian control led to further riots in Kosovo, in which more than 20 people were killed.

By the end of the 1980s, the Yugoslav authorities had more than just the Kosovars to deal with. There were already signs that some of the constituent republics might want to break away. The first clear indication of this came in September 1989, when the Slovene parliament proclaimed Slovenia's right to secede. This declaration brought many Serbs and Montenegrins (the latter have traditionally almost always sided with the Serbs) on to the streets in protest. It is partly in this context that the landslide victory of the Serbian nationalist Slobodan Milosevic in the Serbian presidential elections of November 1989 is to be understood. Milosevic had been head of the Serbian communist party until early 1989, but in May had been elected (by parliament) to the presidency. He was endorsed in this position by almost 90 per cent of the 75 per cent of Serbian voters who went to the first direct, contested presidential election later that year. Although a communist, he was – and at the time of writing still is – above all a charismatic nationalist leader, who argued strongly for a unified Yugoslavia. In practice, this was to be dominated by his own Serbs. Many Serbs, including in the Serb-dominated officer corps of the military, were keen to hold Yugoslavia together, and were prepared to support someone who would resist secessionist moves by Slovenes or any other group.

In the month following Milosevic's victory, the Serbs mounted a commercial boycott of Slovenia, after Slovene authorities had forbidden a demonstration by Serbian nationalists. The Croats, who have often had common interests with the Slovenes, supported them against the Serbs.

By December 1989, Yugoslavs were as aware of what was happening elsewhere in Eastern Europe as was the rest of the world. In this context, and perhaps seeing the writing on the wall, the Croatian and Slovene communist parties promised genuinely free and competitive elections in 1990. By now the economic crisis that was so important to the collapse of communism elsewhere was highly visible in Yugoslavia. One clear sign was an annual inflation rate in excess of 1,200 per cent.

The rising economic and nationalist tensions were manifest at the congress of the Yugoslav communist party (the League of Communists of Yugoslavia – LCY) in January 1990, where Serbian and Slovene communists mounted strong verbal attacks on each other. The Slovenes eventually walked out of the congress, claiming that the other republics were implementing political reform too cautiously. Shortly afterwards they withdrew from the LCY altogether. The congress itself broke up in disarray soon after the Slovene departure, though not before it had voted to abolish its own constitutionally guaranteed leading role in the state and society. Although there were two further attempts to make a success of the congress, in March and May 1990, it was clear to almost everybody that the federal communist party was finished. A new organization, the League of Communists-Movement for Yugoslavia, was established in November 1990 and seen by some as a revamped LCY; but the dominance of Serbs, particularly military officers, in the new party severely limited its credibility as an integrative pan-Yugoslav communist organization. It was all but still-born.

The real focus by early 1990 had in fact shifted away from Yugoslavia as a whole and towards the individual republics. Elections were held in Slovenia in April and Croatia in April-May; in both cases, non-communist – essentially nationalist – groups won. This trend was repeated in two other republics, Macedonia and Bosnia-Hercegovina, in November–December. However, in Serbia and Montenegro, 'former communists' won; inverted commas are used here primarily to indicate that although the Serbian communist party had merged with the Socialist Alliance in July 1990 to form the new Socialist Party of Serbia, this was still headed by Milosevic and retained many of the policies and approaches of the former communist party. Moreover, an attempt by Yugoslav prime minister Ante Markovic to pull Yugoslavs together under a new pan-Yugoslav party, the Alliance of Reform Forces, failed miserably; his party did not win in any of the six republics.

Thus, by the end of 1990, four republics had moved to post-communism, whereas two, including the dominant Serbia, had returned leaders who were only marginally reformed communists. While some of the leaders in other republics had also been communists, such as Franjo Tudjman in Croatia, they appeared to be more genuinely committed to a post-communist system than did Milosevic. This is important, and should not be overlooked when attempting to understand the disintegration of Yugoslavia. It was not *only* traditional ethnic rivalries that brought this about, but also the fact that different groups were at different stages in the transition to post-communism. It is at least conceivable that the break-up would have been much more peaceful, *possibly* even avoidable, had the Serbs chosen in 1990 to move unambiguously to post-communism.

But this was not to be. There were numerous signs of growing ethnic conflict in 1990, such as between Serbs and Croats in Knin (Croatia) from August, and between Serbs and Muslims in Bosnia-Hercegovina from September. In November, Yugoslav prime minister Markovic criticized the Serbian, Croatian and Slovene leaderships for their divisive policies. This came shortly after Yugoslav president Borisav Jovic had also criticized

Serbs and Croats for fighting each other. By February 1991 tensions were so high that Slovenia called for a dissolution of Yugoslavia, albeit by peaceful negotiation. Both the federal authorities and the Serbian leadership rejected such calls and attempted to hold the federation together. But it was already too late. In June 1991 both Slovenia and Croatia declared their independence. This led to war between the federal army and both Croats and Slovenes in the second half of 1991. The federal army withdrew from Slovenia by late 1991, but continued to fight in Croatia.

On 15 October 1991, exactly one month after Macedonia had proclaimed its independence, Bosnia-Hercegovina declared its sovereignty. [6] Some five months later, Bosnian president Alija Izetbegovic declared Bosnia-Hercegovina's independence. Within weeks his country had become the site of the bloodiest fighting of all during the break-up of Yugoslavia, as Muslims, Serbs and Croats sought to control various parts of the former republic.

Although, as of mid 1996, there was still a rump left – consisting of a still *de facto* largely communist-run Serbia and Montenegro, and perhaps to include Serbian-dominated parts of Bosnia-Hercegovina in the future – Yugoslavia as the world had known it since 1918 was no more. One of the most persuasive symbols of this came in December 1991, when the then Yugoslav president Stepan Mesic resigned on the grounds that Yugoslavia no longer existed. The path to post-communism, still not fully trodden by all republics, had been a very difficult and bloody one.

Notes

1 That is, Hungary, Poland and what was Czecho-Slovakia but is now Czechia and Slovakia. The term derives from a February 1991 meeting held in Visegrad (Hungary), at which the Polish and Czecho-Slovak presidents and the Hungarian prime minister discussed mutual cooperation. This was followed in October 1991 by the signing of a cooperation agreement in Krakow (Poland), and in December 1992 by the establishment of CEFTA (Central European Free Trade Agreement).

   Although the GDR was excluded from this chapter primarily because of space, this decision can be partly justified on the grounds that it is now part of another state that was never under communist rule.
2 Southern Silesia is also part of the Czech Lands; but the Silesians constituted only 0.4% of the population of the Czech Lands at the time of the 1991 census.
3 This point about 'fellow Slavs' should not be exaggerated: Poles are also Slavs, and have not traditionally been warm towards the Russians.
4 Given its unique history in the communist era and the high levels of ethnic tension and violence there in the 1990s, Yugoslavia could justifiably be treated separately from the other Balkan states. However, there are a number of long-term historical commonalities that counterweigh such differences. Because of these, and for purely practical reasons, Yugoslavia is included in this chapter.
5 Some historians (see e.g. McAdams 1992, p. 25) claim that the king was assassinated by a member of the Macedonian Revolutionary Organization, Vlada Gheorghieff. But even many of those who believe the actual assassination was carried out by a Macedonian accept that he was working under orders from the Croatian Ustashi.
6 For the distinction between sovereignty and independence see p. 302.

FURTHER READING

A valuable overview of the collapse of communist power in Eastern Europe (excluding Albania) that makes considerable use of interview data is Stokes 1993. For further analyses of the collapse in the six countries considered in this chapter see J. F. Brown 1991, chs 3, 4 and 6–9 (the last of these includes Albania, while chapter 6 analyses the GDR); Glenny 1990, chs 1–5 and 7 (chapter 6 covers Albania). Batt 1991 (esp. ch. 2) is good on East Central Europe. For a useful reference source on all the countries see East 1992.

For detailed studies of the collapse of communist power and/or early post-communism in individual countries see Wheaton and Kavan 1992 on Czechoslovakia; Bozoki, Korosenyi and Schopflin 1992 on Hungary; Hancock and Welsh 1994 on the GDR; Kaminski 1991, Staar 1993 and Millard 1994 on Poland; Rady 1992 on Romania; Glenny 1993 and L. Cohen 1995 on Yugoslavia.

For the pre-communist and/or communist histories of the individual countries see Pano 1968 and Prifti 1978 (on Albania); Crampton 1987 and McIntyre 1988 (on Bulgaria); Wolchik 1991 (on Czechoslovakia) and Kirschbaum 1995 (on Slovakia alone); Dennis 1988 (on Germany and the GDR); Heinrich 1986 (on Hungary); Kolankiewicz and Lewis 1988 (on Poland); Shafir 1985 (on Romania); and Singleton 1985 (on Yugoslavia). A comparative historical and contemporary overview of the Balkan states is provided in Cviic 1991, while two excellent overview histories for this chapter are Held 1992 and Crampton 1994.

4

The USSR

The story of how the FSU (Former Soviet Union) moved to post-communism warrants at least a book; in fact, the Soviet Union comprised 15 republics – the history of *each* of which deserves consideration in its own right. Unfortunately, this is not possible in a book of this scale and nature, and only a very generalized historical overview can be provided here (a useful starting point for a recent analysis of each of the former republics is Bremmer and Taras 1993).

History and Politics

The USSR was formally established in 1922, just a few years after the Bolshevik Revolution of October 1917. It was formed largely on the basis of the former Tsarist Russian empire. This was originally established in 1721, and by 1917 included countries such as Ukraine, Lithuania, Estonia and Georgia.

Russia was far and away the largest unit in the USSR, comprising approximately three-quarters of its total area, and extending across 11 time-zones. Territorially, it is the world's largest country. The identifiable history of both it and Ukraine date back to the establishment of Kievan Rus in the ninth century, although the first federation of eastern Slavonic tribes can be traced back to the third century AD. Russia converted to Christianity in the ninth century; during the tenth, under Byzantine influence, this became the official state religion.

Kievan Rus collapsed in 1240 as a result of the Mongol invasion, and the component parts became more insular for the next two to three centuries. By about the fourteenth century, new subdivisions of the Russian people began to emerge, notably the Belorussians. The three main centres of this disparate entity were Halicz, Novgorod and Moscow; by the early Middle Ages, the Grand Prince of Moscow was claiming also to be the Grand Prince 'of all Russia'.

Perhaps the most famous of the Grand Princes of Moscow and of all Russia was Ivan III, who expanded Russia considerably in the latter half of the fifteenth century. He raised claims against Lithuania, as part of a general Russian advance to the Baltic in search of outlets to the sea.

With the fall of the Byzantine empire in the middle of the fifteenth century, Moscow was widely recognized to have assumed the religious role Constantinople had played and became the centre of the Orthodox Church. In the early sixteenth century, Russia expanded further still, at the expense *inter alia* of Lithuania, when it incorporated Smolensk.

During the second half of the sixteenth century, Russia was dominated by Ivan IV (the Terrible), who centralized the administration of the sprawling area known as Russia. Russia was crystallizing into a strong state. In 1547, Ivan had himself crowned the first Tsar (from 'Caesar') of Russia.

Although there are many justifiable reasons for contemporary Poles to be indignant about Russia's role in their history since at least the late eighteenth century, the Poles themselves invaded Russia in the early seventeenth century. It was in the aftermath of this that Russia's last royal family, the Romanovs, founded their dynasty in 1613. Initially, the Romanovs made a number of territorial concessions to Poland. But with the collapse of the Polish system in the middle of the seventeenth century, Russia reversed roles and went on the offensive. Consequently it acquired Kiev (nowadays the capital of Ukraine). This expansionism continued for centuries. Already by the time of Peter the Great (who reigned jointly with his brother from 1682 to 1696, and alone from 1696 to 1725), Russia was a huge, multi-ethnic unit. Peter had this recognized in 1721, with the formal establishment of the Russian empire. It was under Peter that, following Russia's victory over Sweden, Estonia was incorporated into the empire. Over the following century and a half, the Russian empire acquired parts of Poland, Finland, the Transcaucasus and what was in the Soviet era known as Central Asia. Thus the Bolsheviks inherited an enormous empire from the Romanov dynasty.

Although established in 1922, the USSR did not initially include the 15 republics it comprised by the 1940s. Thus the Baltic states (Estonia, Latvia and Lithuania), for example, were sovereign states from the early 1920s to 1940; they were annexed by the Soviet Union in 1940 as a result of an agreement made between Nazi Germany and the USSR in mid-1939 (the Molotov–Ribbentrop Pact). Similarly, Moldavia (now Moldova) was incorporated in 1940 – having earlier been part of the Russian empire – when Germany permitted the USSR to annex it from Romania.

As already indicated, it is not feasible to examine the history of each component part of the union here; instead, the point having been made that different parts of the USSR 'joined' (in most cases reluctantly and under threat of force) the federation at different times between the early 1920s and 1940 the history of Soviet communism, the transition to post-communism, and the break-up of the USSR can be considered.

The Russian empire was in a revolutionary situation by the early twentieth century. The clearest indication of this was the mass unrest of 1905 and the resultant political reforms introduced by Tsar Nicholas II; many refer to the 1905 events as the first Russian Revolution. But the Romanov dynasty managed to survive until February 1917, when it was overthrown and replaced by a fledgling liberal democracy. The provisional government that took office following the February revolution was weak and divided, however, and in October 1917 Lenin and the Bolsheviks (eventually to become the Communist Party of the Soviet Union) seized power from it.

With the Bolshevik victory, the Russian empire became the first country in the world to proclaim a socialist revolution. Within months, the Bolsheviks were at war with various anti-Bolshevik forces; civil war engulfed the empire from 1918 to 1920. Although the Bolsheviks retained power, they considered there was sufficient hostility to their ideas and rule to necessitate a relatively coercive regime. Thus a secret police force, at that time known as the Cheka, was established in 1919. In its various guises, most recently as the KGB, this body was to be an important component of Soviet life for more than seven decades, although its powers were substantially reduced in the later years of communist power.

Lenin died in January 1924. In the absence of a regularized method for replacing leaders, there followed a power struggle, in which Stalin eventually emerged the victor by 1928–9. He remained in power until his death in March 1953. During his rule, at least three aspects of communist rule crystallized.

First, central planning and direction became a key feature of Soviet life. Although Lenin had favoured the concept of central planning, relatively little had been done to introduce it during his lifetime. Indeed, it was under Lenin that, in 1921, the so-called 'New Economic Policy' had been introduced. This has been seen by commentators such as Carr (1966, p. 276) as a return to capitalism; this is an exaggeration, but private enterprise and trade were certainly encouraged under this policy. Moreover, although a central planning organization (Gosplan) had been created in 1921, it played little role in the economy in Lenin's time.

The situation changed dramatically in the late 1920s. The USSR's first five-year plan came into effect in October 1928. Over the next four to five years, Stalin directed both an enormous industrialization drive and the forced collectivization of the peasantry. Lenin had wanted peasants to work together to farm the land, both because of greater efficiency and to develop a more collective (socialist) consciousness among a group he believed was inherently conservative. But his preferred method for collectivization was to establish *model* collective farms, so as to show peasants their advantages. In short, he favoured collectivization by example rather than coercion. But Stalin was impatient, and the vast majority of peasants who joined collective farms in 1929–30 did so because of coercion rather than their own convictions. All this was part of Stalin's 'revolution from above' – the rapid transformation of the economy and society from a predominantly agricultural and rural arrangement to an industrial and urbanized one.

By 1953 the economy had indeed been transformed. The USSR had developed a modern industrial base sufficient for it to begin competing with the USA as a military power and to be recognized by the world as a superpower. On the other hand, the development was lop-sided ('skewed'). Although heavy industry had developed very well, light industry – especially the consumer durables industry – had progressed far less impressively. Moreover, much of the agricultural sector was in a worse situation at the time of Stalin's death than in 1928 (Nove 1992, pp. 186, 343). The successes of 'the revolution from above' had thus been patchy. The economy was distorted, and bringing it into better balance was to be a challenge for every Soviet leadership team from now on.

Second, the coercion Lenin had considered necessary for the consolidation of Soviet power in its early days intensified and became far more systematic under Stalin. By the mid-1930s the high levels of coercion had become terror. This terror reached its apogee in the late 1930s. Although it declined somewhat during and after the Second World War, terror was from now on to be seen as a key feature of Stalinism.

Third, the internationalism both Lenin and Trotsky had so passionately espoused was replaced under Stalin by a form of communist nationalism, 'socialism in one country' (see chapter 1). The concept appeared to be a very practical one; by suggesting it was possible to promote economic development and modernization through domestic (internal) generation of investment, it seemed the USSR could be economically modernized without either indigenous capitalists or foreign investment, of both of which there was a marked shortage.

In sum, the USSR did develop, in some ways impressively, under Stalin; but the development was uneven, and had been extremely costly in human terms.

Following Stalin's death, there was again a power struggle. The eventual winner – by 1957 – was Khrushchev. Although it would be misleading to describe him as a liberal as most Westerners would understand this term, he did introduce major changes to the Soviet system, some of which represented a renunciation of aspects of Stalinism. For instance, he renounced terror; although the Soviet system always relied on coercion to a much greater degree than do Western systems, there was a perceptible change of political atmosphere in the USSR during the mid-1950s. In his so-called Secret Speech of February 1956, Khrushchev denounced Stalin's *errors*; by 1961 the party leader was prepared to go further and condemn Stalin for his *crimes* against the Soviet people.

Khrushchev introduced numerous changes to other aspects of both domestic and foreign policy. In the former, for instance, he sought to give the consumer a better deal, particularly in terms of non-durables. Thus he launched a major agricultural programme, the Virgin Lands campaign, whereby he attempted to improve the food situation by dramatically increasing the amount of land under cultivation (extensive development). He also tried to improve the administration of the economy by decentralizing from the largely Moscow-based ministries (most of which he abolished) to local agencies in 1957. A further move in this direction was the involvement of the party directly in the management of the economy with his 'bifurcation' policy of 1962 (see Tatu 1970, pp. 249–52).

In foreign affairs, he sought in the mid-1950s to end the rift with Yugoslavia, with some success. Conversely, relations with the Chinese deteriorated markedly as, among other differences, the latter became increasingly critical of Khrushchev's de-Stalinization campaign. Relations with the West improved substantially; whereas Stalin had discouraged interaction with 'the enemy', Khrushchev encouraged Soviets to learn from the West, mainly in the scientific field, and pursued a policy of 'peaceful coexistence'.

Although Khrushchev was far more liberal than Stalin, he was still a hardline communist in some areas. For instance, he was relatively tolerant of critical literature (particularly if this accorded with his own criticisms of Stalin, such as Solzhenitsyn's short novel *One Day in the Life of Ivan Denisovich*), yet highly intolerant of modern art. He was particularly harsh in his dealings with the church.

Khrushchev was a wilful and self-centred leader, which greatly contributed to his downfall. He was removed from office by the Central Committee of the CPSU in October 1964. While his ever more autocratic manner was one reason for his downfall, another was the relative failure of several of his policies. In foreign affairs, for instance, many of Khrushchev's colleagues had become increasingly uneasy about the rift with China, while the USSR's international humiliation during the 1962 Cuban missile crisis had angered many senior politicians. Perhaps even more significantly, the promise of major economic improvement had not been fulfilled. Indeed, following a marked improvement in the mid to late 1950s, agricultural output had slumped in the early 1960s. This was hardly a good omen for the future; after all, Khrushchev (via the CPSU Party Programme) had in 1961 promised the Soviet people that communism would 'in the main' be reached in the USSR by 1980.

One of the first tasks of the new leadership team that assumed office in October 1964, the Brezhnev–Kosygin regime, was to reform the economy. Within months, major reforms were announced, first of agriculture (March 1965), then of industry and the economy more generally (September 1965). Some aspects of the reform looked very much like a return to the pre-1957 situation, notably the return of central ministries for the economy. Others, however, appeared to represent significant change and reflected the relatively progressive ideas of an economist (Liberman) whose proposals had been the subject of much debate ever since their publication in the party newspaper *Pravda* in 1962. The USSR was attempting to move towards eudaemonic legitimation.

But the 1965 Soviet economic reforms did not bring the desired improvements. Further reforms were introduced in 1973 and 1979, but to little avail. One major reason for the relative failure was that many of the bureaucrats charged with implementing reforms either did not fully understand them, or else were hostile to them since they were intended to reduce the powers of the central ministries and boost those of the managers of enterprises (and, later, groups of enterprises known as associations). Whereas the position of officials could be a dangerous one during the Stalin era – proportionately, they were targeted by the terror machine far more than were ordinary citizens – by the time the Brezhnev team took power, the central leadership had apparently decided that the system would not function properly unless there was a reasonably secure and content bureaucracy to run it. It was in this context that the Brezhnev regime introduced a policy of 'stability of cadres'; unfortunately, many cadres felt so secure in their jobs that they were prepared to block their superiors' policies if it suited them. Although there was a partial resurrection of Stalin in the Brezhnev era – novelists and poets were now actively discouraged from criticizing the Stalin period – the position of party and state officials was a clear indication of just how much the situation in the USSR had changed since the Stalin era.

Brezhnev died in November 1982. For the next two-and-a-half years, the Soviet Union was led by what many foreign observers described as 'care-taker' general secretaries of the party. Such a label is somewhat unfair to the immediate successor, Yurii Andropov, since he did attempt substantial change during his very limited tenure (he died in February 1984). For example, he instituted a major anti-corruption campaign almost as soon as he came to office, which was intended on one level to weaken the strangle-hold of the bureaucracy. On the other hand, there was little innovation under Andropov's successor, Konstantin Chernenko (in power from February 1984 to March 1985).

During the period 1982–5, it appears that many members of the Soviet senior leadership were searching for a new long-term leader with innovatory and imaginative ideas, someone who would restore dynamism to the Soviet system after the stagnation of the later Brezhnev era. The person most of them eventually chose was certainly dynamic. Mikhail Sergeevich Gorbachev did not merely change the Soviet Union – he played a major role in its collapse, the collapse of communist power in Eastern Europe and the end of the Cold War.

On assuming office, Gorbachev sought to continue many of the policies started but not followed through by Andropov. He revitalized the anti-corruption campaign, for example. He also soon launched an anti-alcoholism drive, believing that one of the main reasons for low productivity in Soviet industry was the high level of alcoholism and alcohol-related absenteeism.

In the early days of his rule, Gorbachev appeared to be more concerned with *economic* reform than with political. Thus *perestroika* (restructuring) started life primarily as a policy of economic change. Only as it became increasingly clear that economic reform would necessitate significant political reform was the concept of *perestroika* broadened, while the concepts of *glasnost* (public openness) and *demokratisatsiya* (democratization) increasingly became part of everyday Soviet life. Since these terms and their ramifications have been so closely associated with both Gorbachev and the collapse of communist power, a brief examination of each is warranted.

The word *perestroika* is somewhat ambiguous in Russian, since it can refer to both 'restructuring' and 'reconstruction'. The former implies less radical change than the latter; in a sense, this very ambiguity summarizes well the ambivalence in Gorbachev's own mind, as well as the fact that he had to steer a difficult path between what came to be known as 'conservatives' (hardline, orthodox communists) and 'radicals' or 'progressives' (those who believed the USSR would have to become much more like the West if it were to survive and prosper). The term was not new when Gorbachev started using it. However, within months of his taking office, the key shorthand terms for Gorbachev's policies were *perestroika* and *uskorenie* (acceleration). Both referred primarily to the need to overhaul, modernize and make more efficient the sluggish Soviet economy (for evidence that *perestroika* was essentially about the economy in the early days see Gorbachev's speech to the Twenty-Seventh Congress of the CPSU in *Pravda*, 26 February 1986). This said, it must be emphasized that Gorbachev never had a very coherent or strategic conception of *perestroika*. In a manner not dissimilar from Lenin's with his New Economic Policy of the early 1920s, Gorbachev had a reasonably clear idea of what he was rejecting, but a much hazier idea of where he was heading. In terms of the legitimation crisis theory permeating this book, one important ramification of this is that the concept of *perestroika* was inadequate to become a new goal or *telos*, and therefore could not form the basis of a new form of teleological legitimation.

Although Gorbachev appreciated that the Soviet economy required revitalization and intensification, and while he also accepted that there would soon have to be changes in policy, the new General Secretary also seems to have understood from the start *why* so many of his predecessors' reform policies had not succeeded. He grasped that it was of little use introducing radical new policies if those charged with implementing them were simply going to block them. Thus, to the extent that *perestroika* involved *political* change in the early days of Gorbachev's rule, it was mainly in the sense that the new General Secretary initiated major personnel changes. As Sakwa (1990, p. 13) points out, within one year of his accession to power, Gorbachev had replaced two-thirds of the top elite – including eight of the 11 members of the Central Committee Secretariat, approximately one-third of the republican and regional leaders and 48 out of 134 central ministers.

But this was not enough. As Sakwa further argues (ibid.), many of the newcomers differed little from those they replaced. And in any case, it was necessary to attack the *middle-level* bureaucracy as well as the upper echelons; this Gorbachev did not – could not? – yet do to the requisite extent.

It was largely in this context that a concept he had first referred to in December 1984 – and to which he again referred in his first speech as CPSU General Secretary (*Pravda*, 12 March 1985) – but on which he had placed little emphasis in his early rule, *glasnost*, rapidly became a major feature of the Gorbachev approach from about mid-1986.

As with most phenomena, it would be misleading to suggest that the new emphasis on *glasnost* can be explained in terms of just one variable. Part of the reason was that Gorbachev had come to realize that, for it to succeed, economic reform would need the support and enthusiasm of the masses. Closely connected with this, he believed that greater openness by the authorities would not only enhance their legitimacy in the eyes of the masses, but could also be used to mobilize the masses against conservative and corrupt officials who were hindering reform. A third factor was the international one. Gorbachev well understood that a major reason for the USSR's problems was its competition with the West. If he could reduce the tensions in East–West relations, and if the USSR could benefit (in the sense of learning) through greater interaction with the wealthier and technologically more advanced West, then this would almost certainly have positive spin-offs for the Soviet economy and hence the legitimacy of both the Soviet system and his own rule. He did make a good start with the West: shortly before he assumed office, in December 1984, no less a hardline anti-communist than British prime minister Margaret Thatcher claimed she could 'do business' with Gorbachev.

It was against this backcloth that the Chernobyl disaster was such an important trigger in the development of *glasnost*. Until then, the Soviets had had a reputation for suppressing news of major disasters. But in April 1986 a huge explosion at the Chernobyl nuclear reactor in Ukraine released vast amounts of radioactive material into the atmosphere. For several days the Soviet authorities maintained a silence on this, as was their wont. But when the West began detecting the atmospheric pollution, the Soviet authorities had to admit to the disaster. Once they did, it was claimed this was part of the new *glasnost*. However, for the West to take this claim seriously after so many days' silence by the USSR, the Soviet authorities were going to have to follow this up with more open reporting of all kinds of disasters. While they still did not report quite as openly in the following years as the West is used to, there is no question that the limits to *glasnost* were dramatically extended as a result of the Chernobyl experience.

Like *perestroika*, *glasnost* started as a relatively narrow concept but then broadened out. Initially, it focused on the problems of the Stalinist past; people could now much more openly discuss and criticize Soviet history. But by late 1986/early 1987, this was beginning to expand to include contemporary problems. By the end of the 1980s, *glasnost* was out of control from the perspective of Gorbachev and the CPSU, as people openly criticized Lenin, the role of the party, Soviet imperialism and various other topics that had for decades been taboo.

In sum, the first year or so of Gorbachev's rule focused on calls to improve the economy and changes to the elite. This period was followed by far more open discussion of what had gone wrong in Soviet society and why. By 1988, Gorbachev appeared to have reached the conclusion that what the USSR needed now was its own version of the legal-rational state. The reader is alerted to the wording here: Gorbachev was not calling for a *full* legal-rational system as most Western theorists would understand this, but rather a *socialist* legal (or law-based) state. His first known public reference to this was in April 1988; at its Nineteenth Conference in June–July 1988, the CPSU formally adopted the concept. In practical terms, this meant *inter alia* that the decades-long confusion between party and state would have to be ended, and that the role of the popularly elected part of the political system would have to be enhanced.

Already in January 1987, at a key plenum of the Central Committee, Gorbachev had argued that democratization (as well as *glasnost*) was a vital part of *perestroika*. At that stage, there was much talk of democratization – including of the need to have secret, genuinely competitive elections to local soviets (councils) – but relatively little substantive change. Admittedly, during local soviet elections in June 1987, voters in a tiny number (just over 1 per cent – see White 1991, p. 29) of revamped constituencies did have some real choice of candidates. But this was all very limited. With the adoption of the concept of a socialist law-based state by the Nineteenth Party Conference, democratization began to develop into something far more meaningful.

A major symbol of this was the adoption by the Supreme Soviet (the legislature) in December 1988 of a series of constitutional amendments that both substantially restructured the major legislative and executive bodies of the state, and altered the method of electing the membership of these; these changes were broadly in line with those proposed by Gorbachev at the Nineteenth Party Conference a few months earlier. Thus the 1,500-member Supreme Soviet was to be significantly reduced in size to 542 deputies, and the frequency of its meetings dramatically increased. At the same time, a new body – the Congress of People's Deputies – was established, partly to ensure wider representation than the Supreme Soviet alone would be able to provide, and partly to act as a watch-dog on the smaller, upgraded Soviet.

The USSR's first national multicandidate elections were held in March 1989. While voters were able to demonstrate their dissatisfaction with the conservative hardliners, the elections were still limited by Western standards. Who could nominate and be nominated, for instance, was narrowly defined. Moreover, the elections were to the Congress of People's Deputies, not the Supreme Soviet; the latter was to be elected *indirectly*, by the Congress. Inasmuch as the Congress had little if any more power than the former weak Supreme Soviet, it becomes clear why the 'democratization' inherent in the many changes to the political institutions has to be kept in perspective.

In May 1989 the new Congress of People's Deputies met and elected the new Supreme Soviet and its president, Mikhail Gorbachev. The powers of the president were substantially increased – to such an extent that some, such as the erstwhile nuclear physicist and dissident Andrei Sakharov, warned against the excessive concentration of power in the hands of one person. Eventually, in March 1990, Gorbachev was elected to the newly created post of President of the USSR (as distinct from Chairperson of the Supreme Soviet). For the first time, the USSR formally had a president. Although the fact that the president's tenure was to be limited (to a maximum of two terms/ten years) represented a move in the direction of the legal-rational state, Gorbachev and the other reformers did not yet have sufficient faith in the masses to permit the Soviet electorate to choose a president; this was to be the prerogative of the new Congress. In some senses, the significance of this should not be exaggerated. After all, the masses play no role in determining the head of state in many countries, including the UK and Australia. That a monarch is head of state in such cases is partly a function of tradition. But it must also be seen in the context that the role of such heads of state is largely ceremonial, so that even radical democrats have until recently rarely complained strongly about this situation. In contrast, the Soviet president was to be a powerful head of state, and should more appropriately be compared with the American or French president; in both the USA and France, the mass electorate *does* have a real say in who is to fill this post. Nevertheless, the USSR was making progress.

Social Forces

The focus so far has been on the political elite, particularly its policies and restructurings. But any understanding of the transition to post-communism in the USSR and of the latter's collapse must incorporate an analysis of the role of social forces. As already indicated, the central authorities rapidly lost control of *glasnost* in the late 1980s. One of Gorbachev's 'mistakes', to the extent that *any* communist politician could have maintained control and retained office in the circumstances, was that he did not keep pace with the changing mood in the USSR. The events were even more complex in the Soviet Union than in the other countries analysed in this book, partly because of the more complex ethnicity and sheer scale of the country. Hence the analysis must be even more superficial; the focus will be primarily on ethnically based movements and on the emergence of unofficial political organizations akin to parties – part of the phenomenon Russians call 'informals'.

As Soviet citizens began to accept that Gorbachev's liberalism and reforms might be genuine, so increasing numbers of them began to air their various grievances. In August 1987, for instance, nationalist demonstrations were held in various parts of the Baltic states to protest against the forced annexation of these countries in 1940, while Crimean Tartars demonstrated in Moscow's Red Square about their treatment under Stalin and since.

By 1988 there were the first signs that local elites might side with ordinary citizens – or indeed *lead* their populations – against Moscow. Perhaps the clearest example was in an area of Azerbaijan at that time hardly known to the outside world, Nagorno-Karabakh. This was populated mainly (about 70 per cent by the late 1980s – Hunter 1993, p. 246) by Armenians, but had been fully incorporated into Azerbaijan in 1921 on Stalin's orders. In addition to this historical reason for the Armenians of Nagorno-Karabakh to resent being part of Azerbaijan, there were also fundamental cultural differences between Armenians and Azeris. Most obviously, the former are Christians, the latter Muslims. In February 1988 the Supreme Soviet of Nagorno-Karabakh voted to secede from Azerbaijan and reunify with Armenia. Many Azeris resented this irredentist nationalism (see chapter 10), and 30 Armenians were massacred in the Azeri city of Sumgait a week after the Nagorno-Karabakh parliament's declaration. The first steps towards what in January 1990 became a war between Armenia and Azerbaijan had been taken.

Secessionist demands also became more open. By late 1988, 'Popular

Fronts' aimed at taking Estonia, Latvia and Lithuania out of the USSR had been established in all three Baltic states. In the Lithuanian case, the coalition of local elites and citizenry that had emerged in the case of Nagorno-Karabakh was repeated, to such an extent that the Lithuanian Communist Party 'seceded' from the CPSU in December 1989. The Lithuanians thus beat the Slovenes in Yugoslavia by almost two months, and set a precedent for both the Soviet Union and Yugoslavia.

The development of open nationalism against Moscow was accompanied by the development of nascent opposition parties in the USSR. Already by late 1987 some 30,000 groups of 'informals' (so called because of their refusal to register formally with the authorities, as they should have done according to a 1986 law on associations) had emerged in the new climate of *glasnost*. A large proportion of these were not political in any meaningful sense, being, instead, bodies concerned with the *independent* (of the state) pursuit of hobbies, sports, etc. However, a *few* were overtly political and they formed the basis of the 500 or so political parties that were to emerge by 1990 (see Tolz 1990). One of the most important early developments was the so-called 'meeting-dialogue' held in Moscow from 20 to 23 August 1987. This was the first organized conference of informals, and was attended by more than 50 groups from 12 cities. It involved some of the best-known left-wing informal groups, including Klub Perestroika and the Club for Social Initiatives. Although significant differences soon emerged between some of these groups, the conference did result in the consolidation of a number of relatively small groups into larger ones. Some of these, such as the Federation of Socialist Clubs, were to play an important role in Russian politics over the next few years (for details of the early development of the informals see Hosking 1992b).

Events of 1990–1991

By March 1990 the USSR had undergone substantial political change. In terms of formal organizations, power had shifted from the CPSU to the state, and the USSR had a presidency that was more akin to the US presidency than to the traditional conception of a Soviet general secretary. But power was also shifting away from the centre altogether – sometimes to local elites and sometimes to groups of ordinary citizens, who were becoming increasingly organized.

In May–June 1990, what was to prove to be the most serious threat yet to the federal authorities emerged with the election of Boris Yeltsin as *de facto* president of Russia (the RSFSR) by the Russian Supreme Soviet. Having earlier been allies, Yeltsin and Gorbachev had by now become adversaries; even though both men attempted to compromise on various occasions, the scene was being set for the final collapse of both Soviet and communist power.

Even before Yeltsin's election, there had been a clear sign that the latter might happen with the abandonment of Article 6 of the Soviet Constitution in March 1990; this article had until then formally ensured the leading role of the CPSU within the Soviet state and society. Another sign came in July 1990, when the CPSU held its Twenty-Eighth Congress; this proved to be its last. At the congress, Yeltsin dramatically resigned from the CPSU. He was soon followed by the charismatic mayors of both Moscow and Leningrad (now St Petersburg), Gavriil Popov and Anatolii Sobchak respectively. The resignations of arguably the three most important Russian politicians testified to the crumbling of Soviet communist authority. Another sign was the sheer confusion at the congress: very little agreement was reached on the way forward. With communist power already dead or dying in most of the countries of Eastern Europe, Soviet communism looked distinctly fragile.

By late 1990 the Soviet system appeared to be entering its terminal phase. The three Baltic states had, in different ways, unilaterally announced either their independence or their intention to become independent (Lithuania and Estonia in March, Latvia in May). Other republics had declared sovereignty, including Ukraine and even Russia itself (in July and June 1990 respectively). The Russian declaration on one level revealed that the Russian elite was no longer prepared to wait for the federal authorities to devise a solution to their country's economic problems.

It was in this context of impatience that, in September 1990, the Russian Supreme Soviet adopted the Yavlinskii–Shatalin '500-Day' programme for reforming the Russian economy. This action was in marked contrast to the federal Supreme Soviet, which kept voting to defer any final decision on how best to reform the economy. In one sense, these delays reflected the deep divisions within the federal body, between those who believed in a 'shock therapy' approach to the economy, those who wanted to retain much of the old system, and the many confused deputies who adopted various positions somewhere between these two extremes. In another sense, though, it looked very much as if the federal Soviet authorities were fiddling while Moscow, Kiev, Alma Ata, etc., burned. Gorbachev's efforts to look like a strong leader – for instance, by having the USSR Supreme Soviet grant him emergency presidential powers in September 1990 (for details see White et al. 1993, pp. 73–8) – appeared increasingly ridiculous and irrelevant.

But the system's death was a lingering one, and the centre was not yet prepared to concede defeat. Early in 1991 there were clear indications of a medium legitimation crisis. Following the declarations of independence the previous year, and an impasse between Baltic and federal Soviet leaders in terms of negotiating the properly recognized secession of the Baltic states, Soviet military intervention in Lithuania in January revealed that the centre was prepared to use force (coercion) if deemed necessary; at least 14 people were killed in clashes between peaceful protesters and Soviet troops. Paratroopers were also ordered into several other Soviet republics (Armenia, Georgia, Moldova and Ukraine) to enforce conscription.

In March the federal authorities organized a referendum on whether or not the USSR should be preserved. Six of the 15 republics boycotted this, despite the fact that the referendum sought to grant constituent republics not only considerably more rights than they had enjoyed until about 1990, but even more than envisaged in the November 1990 draft Union Treaty. Partly because of the boycott by six republics (the three Baltic states plus Armenia, Georgia and Moldova), it is not possible to measure precisely the level of support for the retention of the (radically revamped) USSR. But however the results are measured, it was clear that a majority of Soviet citizens – at least 56 per cent of all electors – supported the notion of preserving the Soviet Union in some form. Given the high levels of *glasnost* in Soviet society by this stage, such a high percentage 'yes' vote demonstrates how strongly committed to the notion of a federal USSR many Soviet citizens remained even by early 1991.

Following this referendum, and talks between Gorbachev and the leaders of the nine republics that had not boycotted it, a pact – usually called either the Novo-Ugarevo agreement, after the country house near Moscow where the talks had been held, or the '9 + 1' (that is, nine republics plus the federal authorities) agreement – was signed in April 1991. It looked as if much of the USSR might hold together after all.

But the situation was still highly unstable. For instance, Gorbachev and Yeltsin had appeared to relate better to each other at the Novo-Ugarevo talks than they had done for months. But Yeltsin's election as Russian president in June 1991 following *direct* elections (those a year before had been indirect) gave the Russian leader greater self-confidence, and the gap between him and Gorbachev widened again. The *political* (as distinct from personal) differences between Gorbachev and Yeltsin were still not as great, however, as those between the two of them and some of the hardliners; after all, both men were in their different ways reformers.

In August 1991 the tensions that had been building up over the previous months and years between the reformers and the conservatives finally reached a climax. On 19 August there was an attempted coup d'état by a small group formally headed by the Vice-President of the USSR, Gennadii Yanaev, and including the Soviet prime minister (V. Pavlov), the Minister of Defence (Marshal D. Yazov), the Deputy Chair of the Defence Council (O. Baklanov), the Minister of Internal Affairs (B. Pugo) and the head of the KGB (V. Kryuchkov). This alliance of heads of some of the most powerful coercive organizations in the USSR initially looked as if it might be able to consolidate power very quickly. The group, calling itself the State Emergency Committee, declared that Gorbachev was unable to perform his presidential duties for reasons of ill-health, and declared a six-month state of emergency to deal with 'the profound crisis, political, ethnic and civil strife, chaos and anarchy that threatened the lives and security of the citizens of the Soviet Union'. The Committee also emphasized the need to preserve the 'unity of the fatherland'. As Vice-President, Yanaev claimed the right to presidential power, given Gorbachev's alleged incapacity.

The wording of the State Committee's declaration was revealing. On one level, it testified to what many Western observers (for instance, White 1979) have seen as a widespread Russian fear of chaos and anarchy. On another, the references to ethnic and civil strife, and to the unity of the fatherland, reflected the plotters' fear that Gorbachev and the federal authorities were about to permit the *de facto* dissolution of the USSR. Indeed, the *timing* of the attempted coup is best understood in terms of wanting to seize and centralize power before Gorbachev and the various republic leaders could sign a document that might well have meant in practice the end of the Soviet Union.

But the coup failed miserably, in two senses. First, there was the more immediately obvious fact that its leaders had failed in their bid for power. It became clear within a couple of days that the plotters had planned their attempt poorly. In fact, the whole incident looked increasingly farcical, as it transpired that the highest members of the military and the security police had not ascertained whether or not their own troops and officers would support them. Many soldiers sided with President Yeltsin, who defied the coup plotters. In a bold move, he climbed atop a military tank in Moscow and encouraged the masses to resist the 'traitors' who were, he claimed, attempting to turn back the clock by seeking to rescind the citizens' newly granted freedoms and return the USSR to authoritarianism. The attempted coup lasted a mere three days. Following its collapse, Gorbachev returned to Moscow (he had been in Crimea at the time the plotters made their bid) and resumed his position as Soviet President. The plotters were arrested; Pugo committed suicide.

The second and more significant way in which the attempted coup failed was in terms of its objectives. In a very real sense, the attempted coup resulted in outcomes diametrically opposed to those intended. Far from preventing the break-up of the USSR, the attempt can be seen to have accelerated and extended the process of disintegration. And far from restoring authoritarian communist power, the communist party collapsed. Both events require elaboration.

Within days of the coup, Yeltsin had confirmed Russia's recognition of the independence of the Baltic states. In doing so before the federal Soviet authorities did, Yeltsin was further marginalizing the latter. Nevertheless, over the next few months most of the republics appeared ready to accept an arrangement on economic cooperation that would, in practice, have bound them together in a very real sense. This suggested there might still be a role for a federal authority. The high point of this collaboration was the Alma Ata agreement of early October 1991, when all 12 republics still more or less remaining part of the USSR initialled an agreement to such an economic package. However, all this soon broke down, as Azerbaijan, Georgia, Moldova and Ukraine declared their unwillingness to participate in the economic arrangement after all. Similarly, an agreement reached in November 1991 between nine of the former republics to form a new 'Union of Sovereign States' came to naught.

Following these various failures to agree on a revamping of the USSR, on 8 December Yeltsin – together with presidents Kravchuk of Ukraine and Shushkevich of Belarus – declared the USSR dissolved. At the same time, it was announced that Russia, Ukraine and Belarus were forming themselves into a new unit, the Commonwealth of Independent States (CIS). The three initial members were joined within days by eight other 'states' (that is, former Soviet republics); the Baltic states and Georgia opted to stay outside the CIS.[1]

The collapse of the CPSU happened even more quickly than the disintegration of the USSR. Gorbachev's actions and statements during and immediately following the attempted coup revealed either confusion or, to be charitable, a rapidly changing consciousness. On 22 August 1991 he announced that he would struggle vigorously for a renewal and moral upgrading of the CPSU; by any criteria, this implied that Gorbachev envisaged the continued existence of the party for the foreseeable future. But he resigned as General Secretary (*de facto* head of the CPSU) just two days later, and argued that the party should dissolve itself. The change of mind, he explained, had occurred because of new evidence that the CPSU's Central Committee had been ambivalent during the coup, whereas Gorbachev was firmly of the opinion that it should have immediately condemned the plotters and made public its support for him.

The resignation of the leader of the party, and his argument in favour of its dissolution, represented a severe body blow to the CPSU. Another was the forced suspension of CPSU activities in late August 1991 and the seizure of its property (Yeltsin's government had already banned the CPSU from Russian workplaces in July 1991). Finally, on 6 November 1991, Yeltsin signed a decree banning the CPSU within Russia; this constituted a fatal attack on the party. Although the constitutionality of this act was subsequently challenged, the fact is that the communist party, in Russia and several other republics, was now in essence disbanded.

As might be expected, the transition to post-communism in the USSR was somewhat different from those in Eastern Europe. It was more prolonged, for instance, although this should not be exaggerated, since the difference was marginal in the grand scale of history. Moreover, the simple two-stage model of transition (see chapter 6 for a more sophisticated model) proposed in this book does not fit Soviet developments as closely as it does most of the East European countries. As with Yugoslavia, different parts of the FSU moved to post-communism at different paces. Indeed, Russia itself did not reach the second stage of the transition (properly contested elections for parliament) until December 1993. This said, the fact that the CPSU had been suspended and then banned in 1991 – and even allowing for its partial return, for instance in the form of various Russian communist parties – must be taken as an alternative version of the more usual passage to post-communism.

Note

1 Georgia subsequently applied for membership of the CIS in October 1993, and was formally admitted in December.

FURTHER READING

On Russian history generally see Dukes 1990. On the period before the Russian revolutions of 1917, see Florinsky 1969; Pipes 1974; Riasanovsky 1984. On the Soviet period, see Hosking 1992b; McAuley 1992; Nove 1992 – while Sakwa 1990, White 1991 and A. Brown 1996 provide detailed analyses of the Gorbachev era. On the collapse of the Soviet Union see J. Miller 1993; Walker 1993; White, Gill and Slider 1993. More specifically on the disintegration of the CPSU see Gill 1994. For analyses of Russian politics in the 1990s see Sakwa 1993; White, Pravda and Gitelman 1994; Lowenhardt 1995. On the various countries that used to be the republics of the USSR see Bremmer and Taras 1993. And on Russian political culture see White 1979. Finally, an invaluable reference book is Brown, Kaser and Smith 1994.

5

The Survivors

By 1993 it was clear that the anti-communist momentum of 1989–91 had dissipated before it had removed the existing power-holders in all 23 states still communist at the beginning of 1989. In fact, five of the 23 – China, Cuba, Laos, North Korea and Vietnam – were still under communist control. In this chapter, the focus is on two of these 'survivors', China and Cuba (space precludes an examination of the others). Following a historical overview of both, the principal question to be addressed is how and why the communist elites in these countries were able to avoid the fate of their comrades elsewhere.

China

For some observers, particularly many Sinologists, China has long been seen as radically different from most of the European communist states and the USSR. For some, its Asian traditions mean it was always likely to have a quite different development path from the European states. This argument is not entirely persuasive, for at least two reasons. First, three other Asian states – Cambodia, Mongolia and South Yemen – *were* affected by the anti-communist mood, and moved to post-communism at much the same time as the other formerly communist states. Second, if a longer historical perspective is adopted, the fact that China overthrew a basically monarchical system and became a republic at much the same time as many other countries – in 1912, just five years before the Russian empire and six years before Germany – must raise doubts about its alleged uniqueness. In addition, it became communist – thereby adopting a basically European theory and ideology – in 1949, at almost the same time as the countries of Eastern Europe.

This said, the People's Republic of China (PRC) *is*, like all other communist and formerly communist states, in some important ways unique, despite its commonalities with those states at least until the late 1980s. The main question to be addressed here is why the PRC is still, as of late 1995, under communist control. Were its differences more significant than its similarities with the rest of the formerly communist world? Does China disprove the legitimation crisis theory that permeates this book? Will China remain under communist rule for the foreseeable future? Before attempting to answer these questions, China's traditions and history can be briefly surveyed, as a starting point for understanding its unusual situation.

China has one of the oldest civilizations in the world, with a recorded history reaching back almost four millennia. For much of this period, it was a very inward-looking (its own name for itself, *Zhongguo*, means 'central country' or 'central nation') and hierarchical society ruled by dynasties. Unlike most countries, China never had a dominant religion as such. Rather, its values were strongly influenced by *Confucianism*, named after the Chinese philosopher and political theorist Confucius (551–479 BC).

In the second century AD, during the Han dynasty, Confucianism was officially adopted as the state's orthodoxy. Like so many value systems and ideologies, there are significant contradictions – or, perhaps, creative tensions – in Confucianism (see Gray 1977). Nevertheless, it has several widely accepted basic tenets that need to be grasped in any attempt at understanding traditional (and even contemporary) Chinese political culture. One is respect for scholars in the political process: education generally has been highly revered in Chinese culture, and meritocracy rather than plutocracy was a salient feature from early on. Another, closely connected with the first, is the notion that society should be led by the wisest and most virtuous. Indeed, what is sometimes seen as the Chinese counterpart to the European concept of the divine right of monarchs, the mandate of heaven, differs from the European idea in at least one very significant way. In the traditional version of the latter, the masses are expected to obey the monarch largely because he or she has been granted the right to rule by God. The populace is not meant to question this. In the Chinese approach, in contrast, the emperor or empress enjoyed the right to rule primarily on the basis of virtue; any sign that the monarch might be exercising powers more because of love of privilege or lust for power was considered improper. Indeed, according to the so-called 'second sage' of Confucianism, Mencius, the people have a right to challenge and remove a ruler who is exercising power in the 'wrong' way or for the wrong reasons. This notion is essentially absent in Western conceptions of divine right.

A second special feature of China is that, unlike many Asian countries, it was never truly colonized. In a very real sense, this point can be made of the communist period too; although the People's Republic of China was close to the USSR in the early period following the communist revolution, the two giants of the communist world were by the late 1950s rapidly growing apart. By the late 1960s, tensions had become so great that there were even border skirmishes between Soviet and Chinese troops in 1969 (for a brief summary and analysis of the dispute see L. Holmes 1986a, pp. 369–76). In short, the PRC was never really part of the Soviet empire, or of any other. In this sense, had China experienced an anti-communist revolution in the period 1989–91, it would have been only a single-rejective one.

With these general observations in mind, a brief politico-historical overview is appropriate. The centuries-old traditional Chinese way of life was by the nineteenth century clearly being disturbed. One important reason was that external forces, primarily European imperialist powers, were becoming increasingly interested in China. Europeans had been fascinated by China for centuries, as witnessed by the interest in Marco Polo's accounts of his prolonged stay there in the late thirteenth century; but by the nineteenth century, various major powers were becoming more aggressive towards China. This was particularly true of Britain, which fought opium wars against the Chinese in the 1840s and 1850s. But during the latter half of the nineteenth century, China was also involved in conflicts with France, Japan, Russia, the USA and other powers.

By the end of the nineteenth century, many Chinese had decided that the Qing (or Manchu) dynasty that had ruled since 1644 was not defending China sufficiently against foreign intervention. Indeed, there was a perception in some quarters that the monarchy was becoming too subservient to foreign interests. One clear sign of these xenophobic emotions was the anti-foreigner and initially anti-imperial Boxer rebellion of 1900 (the Boxers subsequently became more supportive of the imperial dynasty). Moreover, a tiny capitalist class had begun to emerge in China, many members of which believed that their interests were being insufficiently protected against foreign investors.

At the beginning of the twentieth century, the government of the Empress dowager (Ci Xi) acknowledged that China required economic modernization, but it was also sensitive to the political dangers of being seen to be overly compliant with the wishes of foreign capitalists. It looked overseas for development models, and was particularly impressed by Japan: since the so-called Meiji restoration beginning in 1868, Japan had succeeded in modernizing economically while retaining its traditional culture largely intact. Between 1906 and 1910 the imperial government introduced important political changes, rather as the Russian Tsar had done in 1905. Notably, there was a new constitution, the establishment of 21 new provincial assemblies, and the holding of China's first-ever elections – albeit with a very limited suffrage – to the newly created parliament (National Assembly).

But many Chinese intellectuals considered the changes inadequate and became increasingly critical. Moreover, just as the Russian Tsar had overruled the new Russian parliament (Duma) whenever it attempted to adopt major policies of which he did not approve, so the Chinese Emperor (by now the boy Pu Yi – Ci Xi had died in November 1908) and his father (the Regent, Prince Chun) overrode the national Assembly if they disapproved of its decisions. The most important example of this related to the construction of railways; on this issue, the Emperor wanted a policy that would encourage foreign investment. Given the widespread unease over the previous decades at growing foreign involvement in China, the Qing dynasty lost considerable favour by pursuing its policy.

In line with traditional Confucian values, the masses had in a sense a right to protest against such actions. After all, the Emperor appeared to others to be placing his own vested interests above those of the Chinese people, and was thus losing legitimacy. In October 1911 an uprising that started in the city of Wuchang rapidly spread to other parts of China. Of the

21 provincial assemblies established in 1909, 15 now declared their independence of the centre. In November 1911 two rival regimes – one in Beijing under Yuan Shikai, the other in Nanjing under Sun Yat-sen – were established. With Pu Yi's abdication in February 1912, China had overthrown its dynastic rule and, like Russia for several months before October 1917, had 'dual power'.

Whereas the gap between the collapse of the monarchy and the establishment of communist power was a mere eight months in the Russian empire, it was almost 38 years in the Chinese case. Following the period of 'dual power', and a further period during which much of China was run by local warlords, the later years were dominated by a struggle between the Nationalists (Guomindang) under Sun's successor, Chiang Kai-shek, and the Communists. This interim period did not witness the development of either a large bourgeoisie or a substantial urban proletariat; indeed, at the time of the final communist victory over the Nationalists in October 1949, China was even more of a peasant society than Russia had been in 1917. Yet again, communists had taken power in conditions Marx would have considered quite inappropriate.

From the time the communists took power until his death in September 1976, China was very much under the influence of the person attributed with having led the communist victory over the Nationalists, Mao Zedong. Although Mao's position was weakened on occasions, notably in the early 1960s, it was he who oversaw the enormous political, economic and social changes that engulfed China from the 1950s to the 1970s.

In the last ten years or so of Mao's rule, the Chinese population was subjected to a relatively coercive and arbitrary period known as the Great Proletarian Cultural Revolution. Although it would be quite wrong to exaggerate the similarities between this and Stalin's terror of the 1930s, the Cultural Revolution did have a highly destabilizing effect on the Chinese bureaucracy (as well as the ordinary citizenry). With Mao's death, it became clear that his successors wanted to stabilize the country after the recent chaos and near anarchy.

But as in other communist states, the absence of a regularized leadership succession arrangement meant there was a struggle for power in the years following Mao's death. The eventual victor was someone who had been in and out of favour during Mao's time, Deng Xiaoping. Although many analysts of Chinese politics argue that it was not until 1982 that Deng finally consolidated power, there is little doubt that his ideas for reforming China were already the main inspiration for policy, especially in the economic sphere, by the late 1970s. Admittedly, the main reform package – the Four Modernizations Programme (focusing on industry, agriculture, defence, and science and technology) – was based on an idea first mooted by the then prime minister, Zhou Enlai, in 1975. But this had been neither elaborated nor adopted while Zhou was alive (he died in the same year as Mao), and it fell to Deng and his colleagues to turn it into reality. One of the many reasons they were able to do so reasonably successfully was precisely because, as a result of the Cultural Revolution, they did not have as confident and obstructive a bureaucracy to deal with as did the Soviet and many East European leaderships in the 1960s and 1970s.

By now, there can be little doubt that Deng's approach to and successes with economic policy was a major reason why the Chinese communist system did not collapse when so many others did. In the aftermath of the Cultural Revolution, the new Chinese leadership sought to move away from coercion and towards a more stable system in which eudaemonism would be a – perhaps the – salient mode of legitimation. The first stage of the reform programme focused on the largest section of the population, the peasants. They were granted far more autonomy and responsibility than they had enjoyed in the later Mao era, and agricultural production increased significantly. Subsequently, industry also underwent a radical transformation, with an increasing amount of privatization and foreign investment, and ever less central control.

During the 1980s the Chinese economy performed much better than the economies of the European communist states. The problems that arose related more to its success – there were difficulties with overheating, for instance – than to its failures. On one level, eudaemonism appeared to be working.

But it would be wrong to infer that there were no serious problems in China. Like other communist states, China was experiencing an identity crisis. As Deng continued to stress that 'it does not matter whether the cat is black or white, as long as it catches mice' (a phrase he first used publicly in the 1960s, but which became very much part of his approach once in power), he was adopting a form of pragmatism that testified to the abandonment of teleologism. By the late 1980s, the Chinese economic reforms had gone so far that many observers argued that China was rapidly becoming a capitalist country (see, for instance, Chossudovsky 1986). In fact, it is an irony that by the early 1990s there was a higher proportion of manufacturing output emanating from the private sector in 'communist' China than in any of the new 'post-communist' states.

In short, there *were* serious contradictions in the Chinese system by the late 1980s. The economy looked increasingly capitalistic and post-communist, whereas the political system was still clearly communist. Admittedly, the latter underwent some reform. The legislature (the National People's Congress) began to look more like a debating chamber in the period 1987–9, for instance, and the Chinese had their own weak version of *glasnost*, in the form of 'transparency' (*toumingdu*). Nevertheless, there was a growing contradiction between the alleged commitment to communist principles and what was actually being encouraged and happening in the economy.

These tensions became very visible in the period April–June 1989, when there were mass demonstrations in Beijing in favour of greater democracy. Although it might be true, as some outside observers have argued, that whatever the Chinese demonstrators were advocating it was not democracy as many Westerners would understand this term, this is ultimately of marginal relevance. What matters is that thousands of ordinary citizens were protesting against the communist political system. When Chinese troops were used to suppress the Beijing demonstrators in June 1989, it became clear that the communists could no longer rule primarily on the basis of legitimation, but instead had to revert to coercion. The PRC had undergone a medium-level legitimation crisis.

Despite this, the system survived; the medium-level crisis did not develop into an extreme legitimation crisis. In the 1990s, the Chinese economy has continued to prosper, and eudaemonic legitimation has returned as a salient feature of Chinese communist rule. This is one reason why communist power *might* be less endangered than some anti-communists might prefer.

Another is that the numerous and in many cases severe problems of the post-communist states, particularly the FSU, may have helped to bolster the communist regime in Beijing. Various Sinologists (see, for instance, Hinton 1978, p. 7) have argued that the Chinese are traditionally fearful of chaos, confusion and anarchy (Confucianism advocates harmony and strong government), which might suggest that they would prefer their rather authoritarian communist system to the insecurities of early post-communism.

A third – alluded to above, in the reference to the single-rejective revolution – is that the Chinese have not felt dominated by an external power in the way so many East Europeans and even non-Russian Soviets evidently did. This means there is one major source of oppression and alienation less among them.

Does all this mean that communist power will survive in China? Despite the three points just elaborated, it is argued here that it is unlikely to survive much longer, since the identity crisis that emerged in the 1980s has not disappeared; in many ways, it is even greater in the 1990s. One major component of the Chinese system, namely the economy, is by now largely post-communist anyway; attempts by the central authorities in 1994 and 1995 to assert greater control over the economy only highlighted the contradictoriness of their policies. There is increasing unease at the growing stratification between regions and between social groups. And there is considerable dissatisfaction at the rampant corruption and elitism within the system. One sign of this dissatisfaction was the peasant unrest in Sichuan in June 1993; another was the demonstrations by miners against Politburo member Li Ruihan in May 1994. Such incidents are likely to increase as the disparities within China widen and as corruption spreads still further. In a real sense, there is already much of the ideological and moral vacuum in China that was identified in chapter 1 as a salient feature of *post-communism*. In this context, it is interesting to note that the General Secretary of the Chinese Communist Party (and President of China) himself, Jiang Zemin, stated publicly in August 1993 that corruption was now undermining the very foundations of communist rule in his country (see *Beijing Review*, vol. 36, no. 36, p. 5). This was a clear acknowledgement by the leadership of elements of crisis in the system.

In sum, there are already many elements of post-communism in China (for elaboration of this argument see Pei 1994). Too many factors are unknown to permit a confident prediction of just when the Chinese communist political system will collapse. But several signs of crisis have been identified here. Chinese history suggests that the death of the paramount leader (Deng) could lead to a high level of instability; given the general crisis of communist power, this might in turn lead to the collapse of the system. But this is speculation. What is interesting to note is the confluence of traditional Chinese culture, comparative analysis, and legitimation crisis theory – *all* of which suggest that communist power is currently far more fragile than many Western politicians and businesspeople wish to acknowledge. They could be in for as big a shock as the whole world was in the period 1989–91 (for conflicting views on whether or not Chinese communist power is likely to collapse, see Nathan 1990, esp. ch. 11; Huang 1995; Goldstein 1995).

Given that so much of the Chinese economy is already privatized and operating according to market principles, the early stages of full-blooded post-communism *might* be less traumatic in China than in many countries, since the transition would be less comprehensive. However, ethnic conflict and at least partial dissolution of the country could well be features of post-communist China, as ethnic minorities such as the Tibetans seek independence from the Chinese, and as wealthier regions strive to distance themselves from poorer ones. Partly in their endeavours to avoid such conflict, the post-communist leaders are at least as likely to be authoritarian as they are to be democratic.

Cuba

Given the very sorry state of its economy in recent years, plus the fact that it was in many ways part of the Soviet empire, it is initially surprising that communist power in Cuba has not yet collapsed. Does this mean that legitimation crisis theory is wrong, or that Cuba is an exception that proves the rule? This is a major issue to be addressed in this section.

Being an island, Cuba has not experienced the frequent boundary changes many of the European and Asian states have. From this perspective, it might appear that Cuba has fewer grounds for fearing its own territorial integrity than many of the formerly communist states. But the reality is not so simple. Cuba lies only 90 miles off the coast of the mighty USA, and this has been a very important factor in Cuban history and political culture. Indeed, it is vital not to underestimate the significance of this fact in any attempt at understanding why communist power in Cuba did not collapse in 1989–91.

Like most of South and Central America, Cuba had been colonized by the Spanish in the sixteenth century, and was subject to Spanish colonial influence for centuries. But following US victory in its war with Spain at the end of the nineteenth century, Cuba was occupied until 1902 by the Americans. In that year, Cuba was formally granted what initially appeared to be a relatively high level of autonomy. However, shortly before the granting of this status, the US Congress passed the Platt Amendment, under which the

USA claimed the right to intervene in Cuba if the political system there appeared to be under serious threat; this amendment was formally included in the Cuban Constitution of 1901. Between 1902 and 1934, when it was deleted, the USA invoked the Platt Amendment on several occasions as an excuse for interfering in Cuban domestic affairs. Thus were sown the seeds of anti-US resentment that helped Fidel Castro come to power in January 1959 and to keep him there ever since.

Cuba was ruled mostly by dictators in the period 1902–59: despite various short-lived attempts at introducing democracy, it had not developed a democratic political culture by the time of the communist takeover. Like so many other countries considered in this volume, Cuba was also primarily an agricultural (though not peasant) country at the time of the communist revolution. However, unlike most East European countries, Cuba's path to communist power did not involve Soviet 'assistance'; Castro and his supporters took power from the corrupt Batista regime without external support of any significance.

Indeed, one of the most interesting points about the Cuban revolution is that Castro did not even claim to be a communist at the time he took power. It was not until December 1961, nearly three years after he had assumed office, that Castro declared himself a Marxist-Leninist.

At the time of taking power, Castro was certainly left-wing, and determined not to permit the USA to interfere in Cuban affairs. He immediately set about attempting to redistribute wealth. Cuba was at that time a *relatively* wealthy country, at least by Latin American standards. But there was an enormous, and in Castro's view unacceptable, gap between rich and poor. The new Cuban leader soon encountered substantial resistance to his redistributive policies, however; this reaction only radicalized him still further.

Whether justifiably or not, Castro increasingly associated what he saw as unfair attitudes towards the distribution of wealth with the USA. In July 1959 he dismissed the President and various senior ministers, all of whom he had himself appointed, for what he claimed was their excessive sympathy towards American attitudes on wealth creation and distribution. He then asserted his power over the USA in what was probably the only realistic way he could in 1960: he nationalized American enterprises in Cuba. Castro appears to have decided that nationalization (what Marxists often call socialization) was a desirable policy *per se*, and was soon nationalizing most of the large indigenously owned enterprises. In doing so, he believed he had the ultimate trump-card over those wealthy capitalist Cubans who had been resisting his attempts to redistribute wealth.

As relations with the USA rapidly deteriorated, those with the USSR developed. A Soviet deputy prime minister visited Havana in February 1960 and promised modest amounts of Soviet aid. After an abortive attempt by Cubans living in the USA to invade Cuba and overthrow Castro (the Bay of Pigs incident, April 1961), Castro sought even closer relations with Moscow; diplomatic relations were established, and Castro proclaimed a socialist revolution in Cuba. In December, Castro went further still and proclaimed himself a Marxist-Leninist – although he also publicly acknowledged that he had read very little of either Marx or Lenin.

Castro's adherence to communist ideas and ideals was in fact based less on deep study and analysis than on emotion; he explicitly described himself and his followers as 'sentimental Marxists, emotional Marxists' (Gonzalez 1974, p. 146). One indication of his unconventional approach to Marxism-Leninism was that there was no truly Marxist-Leninist party in Castro's Cuba until 1965; even when it was established, it played a minor role until the 1970s.

All this endorses the notion that Castro was above all a Cuban nationalist, who was increasingly attracted to communism because of its alleged commitment to greater equality and justice, and because it was total anathema to the Americans.

The USA became ever more concerned about developments in Cuba. This concern reached its peak in October 1962, when, for a few days, it looked as if nuclear war might break out between the USA and the USSR. For reasons too complex to analyse here, the Soviet leadership decided to install ballistic missiles with nuclear warheads in Cuba, targeted on the USA. American President John F. Kennedy soon made it abundantly clear to Khrushchev that the USA would not tolerate such an overtly aggressive and threatening act. The USSR backed down; the missiles were dismantled and returned to the Soviet Union. Both the USSR and Cuba had been humiliated by the Americans, although it must be acknowledged they had largely brought this on themselves.

Cuba was now clearly in the Soviet camp. However, Castro was not yet prepared to be overly obsequious towards Moscow, and on several occasions during the early and mid 1960s openly disagreed with the Kremlin leadership. The most common cause for such conflict was differences over policy towards revolutionary activity in the Third World. The Cubans were frequently more radical and supportive in their attitudes than were the Soviets, partly because the latter were determined to be taken more seriously by the First World after the humiliation of the Cuban missile crisis.

But following the Soviet-led invasion of Czechoslovakia in 1968, Cuban and Soviet perceptions and policies became more closely aligned. The reasons for this are not of concern here; suffice it to say that the Soviets were now increasingly assertive in the world, including in the Third World. Thus Cuba and the USSR tended to adopt essentially similar positions on international issues such as the Angola crisis that erupted in 1974. The closer relationship manifested itself in various ways. One was that Cuba joined the Soviet-dominated economic bloc Comecon in 1972. Another was that Soviet and Cuban troops and advisers worked together in various hotspots, notably Angola and Ethiopia.

By the late 1970s, Cuba had moved so close to the USSR that its independence within the Non-Aligned Movement (NAM) was being questioned. The NAM had emerged after the Second World War and was meant to promote and defend the interests primarily of Third World states that were outside the major military blocs. Cuba had been one of the 25 states represented at the first NAM summit conference held in Belgrade in 1961, and for many years had been seen as more closely aligned to the developing countries of Asia, Africa and Latin America than to the Soviet bloc. But by the time of the 1979 summit in Havana, some member states of the NAM clearly believed that the Cubans had moved too far into the Soviet camp to qualify still as non-aligned. This belief was only endorsed by the Cubans' initial statements at the summit, in which they argued there was a 'natural alliance' between the NAM and the communist world. Although Cuba eventually compromised on this and emphasized its commitment to revolutionary movements above loyalty to the communist bloc, many NAM countries considered the Cubans were becoming too sycophantic towards the USSR.

The situation began to change again by the mid-1980s. Like so many other communist states, if later than most, Cuba had begun to liberalize in the economic sphere by the beginning of the 1980s. This was seen, for instance, in the legalization of private farmers' markets at the beginning of the decade. But at precisely the time when so many communist states in Europe (including the USSR) were intensifying the moves towards market economics, Castro announced that his government was concerned at the negative effects private markets were having on socialist morality in Cuba, and shut them down (1986). As Gorbachev adopted ever more measures that Castro interpreted as endangering socialism, so the Cuban leader distanced himself and his country from the USSR. Of course, there were limits to how far he could go, since his country was by now virtually dependent on the Soviets economically. Nevertheless, whereas so many European communist states moved rapidly into an identity crisis, Castro took concrete steps to avoid this by, in essence, turning back the clock.

But comparative historiography suggests that clocks can be held steady or turned back only on a temporary basis. One of the effects of the forced closure of the farmers' markets was a deterioration in the supply of agricultural produce. Moreover, even before the collapse of so much of the communist world, the USSR had insisted on a much more businesslike approach to trade within Comecon, which had negative implications for Cuba; these problems were greatly exacerbated for the Caribbean island following the total collapse of the CMEA in 1991.

Thus, by the early 1990s, Cuba had avoided much of the identity crisis that had led to a legitimation crisis in so many other communist states, but was in the kind and level of economic crisis that often leads to other kinds of crisis and collapse. By 1993 – the year described by Castro early in 1994 as the toughest ever since the 1959 revolution – this economic crisis was forcing Cuba back on to the contradictory path its leadership had attempted to steer it off in 1986. Foreign investment and various other aspects of capitalism were now being encouraged. Very moderate political reform, primarily in the form of direct (though non-competitive) elections to the legislature, was also introduced. But history suggests this will give the communists in Cuba only a temporary respite; Cuba is likely to experience revolutionary change in the not-too-distant future.

Certain special features of the Cuban case need to be highlighted. One is that the country is still – as of late 1995 – being led by the leader of the revolution. Castro continues to enjoy a certain amount of charismatic legitimacy because of this, in a way that no Soviet or European communist leader could have done by the late 1980s; interestingly, one of the only other remaining communist states, North Korea, was also still being led by the man that led the communist revolution (Kim Il Sung) until his death in July 1994. Second, Cuba's geographical position, and the implications of this for legitimacy, cannot be overlooked. One aspect of this is that its sheer distance from Europe made the extraordinary events of 1989–91 rather remote; if it is further borne in mind that Cuban communications are underdeveloped in comparison with many countries, this point becomes more convincing than it might initially be to a First World reader. The other point is that the USA factor was still highly relevant in Cuba by the time of the anti-communist revolutions; Castro's regime was being legitimized to no small extent through 'anti-Yankee' official nationalism.

The above argument helps to explain why the Cuban communist system did not collapse when so many others did. However, it has also been argued that the economic crisis that was so important a part of the delegitimation of other countries is currently seriously affecting Cuba. Ironically, the USA's intransigence and hostility towards Castro's regime, notably in the form of applying sanctions against the small island-state, is almost certainly a major factor why that regime's collapse has been and continues to be delayed. One point to have been endorsed by recent events in the communist and post-communist worlds is that regimes can bolster themselves in times of extreme economic privation and/or social unrest by playing on the nationalistic and xenophobic values of the citizens. Once again, the close but complex relationship between external legitimation and official nationalist legitimation comes into focus. This said, such official nationalism is rarely an adequate and reliable source of system legitimation in the long term, while charismatic legitimation can disappear overnight with the death of a revolutionary leader.

FURTHER READING

On China before communist power see Bianco (1971); Chesneaux, Bastid and Bergere (1976); Chesneaux, Le Barbier and Bergere (1977). On China since 1949 see Chesneaux 1979; Liu 1986; Ogden 1989; Wang 1992; Dreyer 1993; Brugger and Reglar 1994. On Cuban history see Perez 1988, while useful overviews of the Castro period include Gonzalez 1974; Dominguez 1982; Azicri 1988; Rabkin 1991.

6

A Comparative Overview

Now that so many examples of transition have been considered, it is possible to highlight commonalities. This short chapter uses the information provided in earlier ones to create a model of transition, following which is a brief discussion of the concept of revolution.

A Model of the Transition to Post-Communism

Earlier, a simple two-stage model of the transition to post-communism was suggested, primarily as a method for identifying when a particular country had reached post-communism in the political sphere; it is now appropriate to produce a more sophisticated model. This is offered not only as a way of summarizing some of the considerable detail provided in chapters 3 and 4, but also as a checklist for analysing the potential significance of future developments in those countries in which the communists are still in power (for another model, albeit one focused exclusively on eastern Europe, see Jasiewicz 1993, esp. pp. 131–3).

As with all models, this one has its limitations; *not all countries experienced all stages of the transition, and the sequence varied somewhat from case to case*. Moreover, it is difficult to be consistent in the cases of formerly communist states that have subsequently divided into two or more smaller countries; although the general guideline here has been to provide details only on the original state, occasional examples from the successor states to the USSR, the Socialist Federal Republic of Yugoslavia and Czechoslovakia are included where this seems appropriate. Despite these numerous caveats, the model was devised after careful comparison of all the European post-communist states and the FSU, and does provide a useful shorthand analysis of the transitional processes for heuristic purposes.

Comparative analysis suggests at least the following eight discernible stages in the transition from communist power to post-communism.

Leadership crisis   In several countries, there were clear signs of a leadership crisis in the run-up to the overt collapse of communist power. The person generally considered to have been *the* leader, and who in many cases had been in office as first or general secretary of the party for many years, either resigned under pressure or was removed. Examples include Kadar in Hungary (May 1988 – in power since 1956), Jaruzelski in Poland (July 1989 – in power since 1981), Honecker in the GDR (October 1989 – in power since 1971), Zhivkov in Bulgaria (November 1989 – in power since 1954), Jakes in Czechoslovakia (November 1989 – in power only since December 1987), Ceausescu in Romania (December 1989 – in power since 1965) and Alia in Albania (April 1991 – in power since 1985). Gorbachev's case in the USSR is slightly different, in that he remained Soviet President even after the banning of the communist party. However, the gap here was only a few months, during which Gorbachev was in any case almost powerless; in this sense, this 'exception' is only marginally so. Moreover, closer scrutiny reveals that Jaruzelski's position in Polish politics after July 1989 and Alia's in Albania after April 1991 were in *some* ways similar to Gorbachev's position by about 1990 or 1991. One glaring exception to this general pattern was Yugoslavia, which had no dominant leader after Tito's death in 1980; but the rapid rotation of leaders there itself constituted a serious leadership problem.

Round Table talks   Although many countries did not have these, any comparative model should refer to the fact that Round Table talks were held between the authorities and opposition forces in several East European countries. In the case of Poland, these were held at a relatively early stage of the transition (February–April 1989), before the long-term leader stepped down; in the cases of Hungary, the GDR and Bulgaria, in contrast, they were held at a slightly later stage (June–September 1989, December 1989 to March 1990 and January–April 1990 respectively).

The party loses its 'leading role'   In most countries, constitutional references to the leading role of the communist party in the state and society were dropped in the early stages of the collapse of communist power. This is true of, *inter alia*, Hungary (February 1989), Czechoslovakia (November 1989), Poland and Lithuania (December 1989), Bulgaria and Yugoslavia (January 1990), the USSR (March 1990), and Albania (November–December 1990).

Legalization of opposition parties   Often at about the same time as the previous stage occurred, communist governments formally acknowledged the right of other political parties both to exist and to challenge the communist party in elections. This happened in Hungary in January 1989, in Poland (with limitations) in April 1989, in the GDR in November 1989, in Bulgaria and Romania in December 1989, in the USSR in October 1990, and in Albania in November 1990.

Significant changes to the communist party   In many countries, the communist party changed its name, to symbolize both its abandonment of Marxism-Leninism and its commitment to a more moderate and democratic form of socialism or social democracy. In some cases, the membership of the former communist party was unable to agree on how radical a change was wanted, and in which direction; this resulted in the splitting of the former communist party into two. Countries to which one or the other of the above scenarios pertains include Hungary (October 1989), the GDR (December 1989), Poland (January 1990), Romania and Yugoslavia (November 1990), Albania (June 1991). The most notable exception to this general pattern was Czecho-Slovakia: despite signs earlier in the year that it was likely to follow the example of many other former communist parties in eastern Europe, the CPCS eventually decided in November 1990 *not* to change its name.

Holding of competitive parliamentary elections   Having legalized other parties, and in most cases renamed itself, the communist party permitted genuinely competitive parliamentary elections. Often the communist or former communist party performed *relatively* poorly in such elections. This is true of Poland (though with major reservations – see chapter 3) in June 1989, the GDR in March 1990, Hungary in March–April 1990, Croatia in April–May 1990, and Czecho-Slovakia in June 1990, In other countries, the communists or former communists performed well, but there were questions concerning the fairness of the elections: examples are Bulgaria in June 1990 and Albania in March–April 1991. In such cases, fresh elections were held relatively soon afterwards (in October 1991 and March 1992 respectively). Russia held properly contested elections in December 1993, but this was long after the communist party had lost most of its direct influence over Russian politics.

The name of the state is changed   Although it might appear to an outsider to be a very subtle change, the significance to their own citizens of the name changes of most post-communist states should not be underestimated. The new names are important symbols of a rejection of the past and the start of a new era. Typically, the new name drops any reference to 'socialist' or 'people's', since both terms are associated with the communist era. Countries that introduced such changes to the name of the state include Hungary (September 1989), Poland and Romania (December 1989), Czechoslovakia (April 1990), Bulgaria (November 1990), Albania (April 1991), the USSR (December 1991; but this is a special case – see chapter 4).

In addition, a few states changed the name of the country. The principal reason was to symbolize a move away from a name perceived to have been imposed by an external force and/or to link the present with the pre-communist past. Thus Moldavia became Moldova in June 1990 (Fane 1993, pp. 149–50), while Kirgizia eventually became Kyrgyzstan in December 1990 (Huskey 1993, pp. 407, 416).

Adoption of a new or highly modified constitution   The final stage is reached when a brand new constitution is adopted (as in Bulgaria, July

1991; Republic of Macedonia, November 1991; Romania and Slovenia, December 1991; Turkmenistan, May 1992; Estonia, June 1992; Lithuania, October 1992; the Czech Republic, December 1992; Kyrgyzstan, May 1993; Russia, December 1993; Belarus, March 1994). In some countries, including two of those just listed, the adoption of a new constitution is preceded either by the partial or total resurrection of a *pre-communist* constitution (Lithuania, March 1990; Estonia, May 1990; Latvia, May 1990 and July 1993), or by the adoption of wide-ranging amendments to the existing (communist-era) constitution (Hungary, from October 1989; Poland, December 1989 and September 1990), or by new interim constitutional arrangements (as in Bulgaria, April 1990; Albania, April 1991; Poland and Georgia, November 1992), pending the adoption of a new constitution.

On Revolution

It was pointed out in chapter 2 that the substantial comparative literature on revolution reveals a lack of consensus on what exactly constitutes a revolution. It was further pointed out that one recent comparative analysis (Tilly 1993) concluded that some of the formerly communist states did experience revolutions in the period 1989–91, others probably did not, while there is confusion over a third group.

Tilly is by no means the only analyst to have experienced difficulties in classifying recent events. A major reason some observers have been hesitant about describing developments in certain countries as revolutions is that radical changes were initiated from the top, by communist leaderships themselves. In one of the more enterprising attempts to distinguish such scenarios from others in which change has originated from below, Timothy Garton Ash (1989, p. 276), focusing on developments in Poland and Hungary in the late 1980s, coined the term *refolution*. One advantage of this term is that it captures well the fact that, in some countries, communists introduced radical reform which then went out of control and resulted in revolutionary change. However, the term ultimately *does* connote revolution: rather than being an alternative concept to revolution, it describes a particular type.

That many of the transformations were initiated from above is not the only reason for debate. Another is that many argue that revolutions are necessarily violent. By this criterion, the transitions to post-communism in several countries could not have been revolutions since they were basically peaceful. Others maintain that violence is *not* a necessary condition of revolutions, merely a feature of many.

Ultimately, there can be no definitive answer as to whether or not Eastern Europe and the USSR underwent revolutions in the period 1989–91. The answer depends both on the definition of revolution used, and the particular countries being considered. This said, the frequent references in the last few chapters to the double-rejective revolution, the anti-communist revolutions, etc., will make it obvious to the reader that it is this observer's clear opinion that the 1989–91 events *did* constitute revolutions.

The *Oxford English Dictionary* provides two definitions of revolution relevant here: 'complete change' and 'fundamental reconstruction'. All of the countries examined in chapters 3 and 4 were essentially one-party systems with basically command economies in the mid-1980s, and almost all were by the early to mid 1990s genuinely multiparty systems (rare exceptions to this were Turkmenistan and arguably Tajikistan), with increasingly privatized and marketized economies. The state ideology had in all cases been dismantled. By any definition, all this represented a *rapid and fundamental change of system*, which is surely the most basic and universal definition of what most people understand by revolution. Whether a system disappears with a whimper or a bang, and whether the process starts from above or below, means simply that there are different kinds of revolution, not that only bottom-up violent transformations constitute 'true' revolutions (for another plea to redefine revolution in light of the 1989–91 events see Bauman 1994).

Conclusions

The ways in which and reasons why the East European states and the USSR overthrew communist power and moved to post-communism have now been analysed, as have some of the reasons why a few communist states survive. Factors affecting both collapse and survival include geographical location; the level of penetration by Western media; the extent to which there was a sense of external domination; the level of coercion; the presence or not of a charismatic, revolutionary leader; and economic performance. None of these individual variables would be sufficient in itself to explain why a given country did or did not experience revolutionary change in the period 1989 to 1994. Equally, the particular balance of variables is unique to each country. Nevertheless, this list can serve as a starting point for any discussion of the reasons why some communist systems collapsed and others did not.

It is also argued here that the few remaining communist states will not be so for much longer. The reasons have already been given in the cases of China and Cuba; readers interested in the arguments about the other three countries, as well as further points about China and Cuba, can find these in L. Holmes 1993a, pp. 295–302. But one factor that might delay the collapse of communism in these last few states is the problematic nature of early post-communism in eastern Europe and the FSU. The rest of this book considers both the problems and the achievements of the post-communist states, as well as possible future developments. This said, and as indicated in chapter 1, the double-rejection theme of this book means that each chapter starts with a brief overview of the communist period, as a way of beginning to understand why certain options rather than others have been adopted in the post-communist era.

FURTHER READING

For interesting arguments about various aspects of the collapse of communist power and its implications for the left generally, and the West, see Chirot 1991; Jowitt 1992 (esp. chs 7–9); Lemke and Marks 1992; Mestrovic 1994.

Part III

Early Post-Communism

7

Institutional Politics

Understandably, many of the political institutions of post-communism have been established in such a way as to distinguish them clearly from the institutions of communism; most of this chapter will be devoted to contrasting the party and state structures, and the nature of institutional politics, of both late communism and early post-communism. Another underlying theme is the extent to which the recent commitment to democracy sometimes conflicts with the need for strong and efficient government in a time of major transition. As will become obvious, many of the most serious political conflicts and problems of post-communism reflect this tension.

The Communist Era

The *communist party* can be seen as the real locus of power in any communist system. Such systems have therefore sometimes been described as partocracies (Avtorkhanov 1967). In several of them (such as Bulgaria, the GDR, Poland), there were *formally* biparty or multiparty systems. But the minor parties very rarely challenged the position or policies of the communist party. If they had their own newspaper, this was censored and often even more directly controlled by the communists. And the number of seats such parties had in the legislature was not merely so low that they could never have mounted any serious challenge, but were often determined by the communists anyway. The Polish minor parties and legislative factions had relatively the most autonomy. But even in Poland it was common knowledge that such parties were subject to ongoing communist control, albeit of varying levels over time, so that their autonomy was severely circumscribed. They could not challenge the communists for the right to run the country. Nor was the notion of a loyal opposition ever legitimated in the communist world.

Although it is an accepted convention to refer to the communist parties of what was Eastern Europe and the Soviet Union, several did not feature the word 'communist' in their formal titles. The Hungarian party, for instance, was called the Hungarian Socialist Workers' Party, while the East German was the Socialist Unity Party. The main reason for this was that many communist parties merged with other left-wing (usually socialist) parties in the 1940s and adopted names that reflected this. In all cases, communist principles and practices soon came to dominate the 'new' parties, so that it is appropriate to call them communist, whatever their formal title.

The basic organizational principle of all communist parties is *democratic centralism* (for a detailed analysis see Waller 1981). This concept was originally devised in the 1840s, but was later developed by Lenin and the Bolsheviks in the early twentieth century. It was based on the assumption that decision-making should be centralized but subject to some control by the membership of the party. At the same time, decisions were to be binding on all members, who were not to question such decisions once made. A typical elaboration of democratic centralism can be found in the rules of the CPSU adopted by the Twenty-Seventh Congress in March 1986:

(a) electivity of all leading party organs, from the lowest to the highest;
(b) periodic reports of party organs to the party organizations and to higher organs;
(c) strict party discipline and subordination of the minority to the majority;
(d) the binding nature of the decisions of higher organs on lower organs;
(e) collectivity in the work of all organizations and leading party organs, and the personal responsibility of every communist for the fulfilment of their duties and party assignments.

Although democratic centralism initially applied only to the party, it gradually became the organizational principle for most political institutions in communist countries. This was just one of the many ways in which the communist party came to dominate virtually all politics in these systems. Interestingly, however, it was in most cases not until the 1960s or 1970s that the constitutions of communist states formally reflected the long-established reality that the communist party dominated everything: the new or amended constitutions of that period referred for the first time to the 'leading role' of the party in the state and society.

Probably the most significant way in which communist parties exercised their hegemonic role was via the so-called *nomenklatura* system. Communists were highly secretive about this system, and it was only through clandestine methods that Westerners, or ordinary citizens in the communist world, were able to obtain information on the arrangements; for obvious reasons, details have become more readily available in recent years. The *nomenklatura* system basically meant that the communist party was involved in the appointment of people to all the most senior posts in society – not merely within the party itself, but also in the state administration, the police, the military, the judiciary, education, the economy (including managers of enterprises), women's organizations, trade unions, etc. Since it was such a powerful weapon in the armory of any communist party, it warrants examination.

At every level of the party, the secretariat would have two lists: one was of the most important posts at that level (the level of a republic, or a city, for example), the other of individuals (cadres) who might be eligible to fill those posts or who were already occupying them. The aim was to ensure an optimum correlation between the positions and those occupying them. The criteria for filling a particular position varied according to the post and the political climate. In essence, a balance had to be struck between expertise and 'redness' (the desired ideological qualities and political experience). Sometimes the party would place more emphasis on a person's technical qualifications, at other times on their political qualities. The details of how the party was involved in hiring and firing to and from *nomenklatura* posts varied according to the post and the particular country. In some cases, the person could not be appointed without the direct involvement and approval of the communist party. At other times, usually for the less important posts at a given level, the party would merely insist on being informed of any appointments or dismissals, to enable it to keep tabs on the career patterns of individuals it was considering for higher office in the future.

Although it might initially appear that the *nomenklatura* system assured communist parties of total control over appointments, certain realities should not be overlooked. As in any system, communist states could only ever choose from a limited pool of candidates with the appropriate qualities, and sometimes had to compromise in the balance between redness and expertise. Many of the leading scientific and technological personnel were not as politically aware or active as the party would have preferred, but had the best technical qualifications for the particular position. In such circumstances, communist parties would often choose them, rather than the politically soundest applicants. This said, the *nomenklatura* system meant that the party was able to penetrate and influence all the most important sections of society. All editorships of leading newspapers, for instance, were on the *nomenklatura* list, so that the party was able to influence in a very direct way the manner in which news and views in the media were selected and disseminated. Similarly, its role in appointing rectors of universities and principals of schools meant that the communist party had enormous powers for influencing the socialization process of young people (on the *nomenklatura* system see Harasymiw 1969, Rigby 1988).

In addition to selecting personnel and socializing the population, communist parties were responsible for determining the future direction of society (goal setting) and for ensuring that society kept to the planned path (goal attainment). These functions will become clearer through an analysis of the structure of the party and the role of the various bodies within it at the different levels.

The structure of communist parties was similar throughout the communist world. Parties were organized on an essentially pyramidal principle, with a large number of party cells (the 'primary' or 'base' party organizations) in workplaces and, sometimes, places of residence, above which was an ever-decreasing number of organizations as the level ascended (village or town, county, district, province or republic, centre). At each level, there would be a mass meeting, usually called an assembly or congress (the 'organizations' referred to above in the description of democratic centralism). This would generally meet infrequently, but would 'elect', subject to direction, officers to perform the various day-to-day tasks of the party at that level. Assuming the party organization at the given level was sufficiently large, it would 'elect' a committee, which in turn would 'elect' a bureau and/or a secretariat. The people who staffed these bureaus and secretariats were usually – at least above the base/primary party organization level – full-time professional party officials, and were generally referred to as *apparatchiki* (that is, people working in the party apparatus). They staffed the smaller, operational bodies of the party, the 'organs' referred to in the analysis of democratic centralism. Though formally elected, the *apparatchiki* were subject to the *nomenklatura* system.

At the centre, the mass assembly was called a party congress. It usually met once every five years, to discuss and approve both the previous five years' work of the party and the coming five years' work. It would also 'elect' a central committee. This normally met two to three times per year in most communist states, and was to make decisions between congresses. Whereas the number of members of the congress often ran into four figures, the central committee in most cases numbered between one and three hundred members. Usually, the central committee would concentrate on one major theme at each of its meetings (called a plenum), such as the economy, foreign policy or education. Another of its tasks was to 'elect' what in practice were usually the most powerful organs in the communist political system, the central committee secretariat and politburo. The terminology in some cases varied slightly from this; thus the (extended) politburo in Romania was known as the Political Executive Committee.

In addition to operating the top layer of the *nomenklatura* system (personnel policy), a major task of the central secretariat was to decide what information was to reach the top decision-making body, the politburo, and which items should be included on its agenda. Thus, in exercising a major influence over both what the politburo discussed and what information was available to it for discussion, the secretariat was highly influential.

The politburo was a relatively small body, averaging 10 to 25 members (both full members, who had voting rights, and candidates, who did not). Typically, it met between one and four times per fortnight, and decided on all major issues. The extent to which it was genuinely collective, as it was supposed to be, varied according to time and country. Nevertheless, the first or general (the terms are essentially interchangeable) secretary was in practice *the* leader in communist systems: although not formally the head of the politburo, in practice he – the first/general secretaryship was never occupied by a woman – tended to dominate its proceedings.

In addition to the other central bodies, communist parties would sometimes convene party conferences. These were not to be confused with congresses. Whereas the latter met on an increasingly regular basis, the conferences were typically convened at short notice, at any time, to discuss a particular problem. Perhaps the best known in the late communist era was the CPSU's Nineteenth Conference, held in June–July 1988. Its main task was to discuss the future of *perestroika*, and various ramifications of that policy.

A common misperception among Westerners who knew little about communist politics was that all or most citizens were communists. In fact, membership of the party as a percentage of the total population varied in the countries under consideration from a low of 4.7 per cent and 5.8 per cent in Albania and Poland to a high of 14.0 per cent and 16.1 per cent in the GDR and Romania (figures refer to 1988, and have been calculated by the author on the basis of Staar 1989, p. 60).[1] Not only was the overwhelming majority of the population in these countries not in any formal sense communist, but even many members of the party were so more because of opportunistic reasons or perceived necessity than genuine ideological commitment and fervour. Thus, if one sought promotion in many professions, it was necessary to be a party member. This is one of several reasons why care must be exercised in interpreting data on party membership.

What was the role of the main *organs of the state*, and the division of labour between the party and the state? Given communists' commitment to being involved in all areas of life, and particularly their emphasis on state ownership of the means of production and central planning, the state apparatuses of the communist countries were comparatively large. Communist capital cities housed many ministries or similar bodies (such as state committees for planning, supplies, statistics, etc.) that would either have no equivalent in the West or else would be far larger and more numerous than in the capitalist world. Many of these were responsible for managing branches or sectors of the economy. In addition, there were ministries that did have approximate equivalents in other societies, such as for foreign affairs, defence, etc. The most senior ministers and heads of state committees were members of the chief executive body of the state, usually called the Council of Ministers; this would often have an inner core, the Presidium of the Council of Ministers. The head of the latter was the Chairperson of the Presidium of the Council of Ministers, who was frequently referred to in Western literature as the premier or prime minister of the given country. Like many of the top state officials, the prime minister was usually also a member of the politburo. Certainly, the vast majority of senior state officials were members of the communist party.

As might be expected, there were also state administrative officers at the various local levels, although these were usually under relatively high levels of control from central state bodies, as well as supervision from the party organs at their level.

The focus so far has been on state bodies whose primary task was to implement policies, the executive and administrative organs. But another important function of the state was to pass legislation. While it was almost always the top party bodies that laid down general policy directives, the legislatures and their committees were responsible for their detailed elaboration and formal promulgation as laws. Since discussion in the law-making bodies was usually very limited and controlled, it is more appropriate to call them legislatures than parliaments. The latter implies real discussion before a law is adopted, and this was not the usual practice in communist legislatures. Among the better known were the Supreme Soviet in the USSR (at least until 1989, when the Soviet legislative arrangements became more complex – see chapter 4) and the Polish Sejm; most of the other legislatures were called the National or People's Assembly.

In any society, the state not only passes and implements laws but also interprets and enforces them. Communist states were no exception, although the manner in which the judicial and police agencies were organized differed somewhat from the typical Western pattern. For instance, professional judges were in many communist countries formally 'elected', though subject to the party's *nomenklatura* system. In addition to professional judges, most communist states allowed for participation by lay (people's) assessors in many hearings and trials.

Police officers were mostly full-time professionals, although ordinary citizens were in some cases permitted to play a role in policing minor misdemeanours, such as parking offences. The police organs were divided into the regular police and the security (or secret) police. The latter were invariably professionals, and usually constituted one of the most feared and hated agencies of the state – whether it be the KGB in the USSR, the Stasi in the GDR, or the Securitate in Romania. Although the officers of such bodies were professionals, they would not have been able to permeate society as well as they clearly did had it not been for a wide network of informers in many countries. These were typically ordinary citizens who helped the security police spy on other citizens. The reasons informers engaged in such unsavoury activity varied, from material incentive to the fact that they themselves might be subject to blackmail by the secret police.

Finally, the state was also responsible for defence. In most cases, the military was clearly under the control of the communist party. But the relationship was on occasions more overtly a two-way one. Thus, in the increasingly confused political situation of Poland in 1981, it was a military leader, General Jaruzelski, who eventually came to head the party and then to impose martial law. Very occasionally, the role of the military was clearly destructive for party rule. Thus, during the Romanian revolution of December 1989, the military's turn against Ceausescu was a major reason for the tyrant's fall.

Very crudely, the division of labour between the party and state was that the party set general guidelines for society's development, which were then elaborated and implemented by the state; the party was then reponsible for checking on implementation. If the party's control of the state through the *nomenklatura* system is added to this, the reader will have a basic grasp of what the respective roles of party and state were supposed to have been. In practice, however, there was often overlap and confusion between them.

One of the most revealing aspects of the nature of communist power was the fact that *the masses* had remarkably little control over their political elites – certainly far less, even, than ordinary citizens have in the West. Although the situation was beginning to improve by the late 1980s, the fact is that communist political systems were in practice barely answerable to the masses in whose name they putatively ruled. This led some to argue that what should have been a dictatorship *of* the proletariat was in fact a dictatorship *over* the proletariat in all communist systems.

Certainly, one way in which ordinary citizens in liberal democracies exercise some control over the state and the political elite, via regular, direct, secret and competitive elections, was not a salient feature of Eastern Europe and the Soviet Union. Although elections were in most cases held fairly regularly, and while many were direct, ballots were not usually secret in the sense most Westerners would understand this term, nor was there competition between parties (or even, in many cases, candidates – for further details and explanations see Pravda 1986). Their primary function was not to enable the electorate to exercise choice, but rather to appear to give popular legitimacy to the decisions and rule of the political elites. They were also a method for educating ordinary citizens about the political system and its leaders.

The situation regarding choice in elections improved slightly in some countries, notably Hungary and Poland, during the 1980s. Nevertheless, elections still had far less significance in communist states than they do in liberal democracies. One reason is that they were for *state* bodies whereas it was common knowledge that real power resided at the top of the *party*. Again, some change was beginning to occur on this front in the late 1980s. Most notably, Gorbachev's attempts to shift power from the party to the state symbolized a modest upgrading of the role of the Soviet masses within the political system. But, as had by 1991 become all too obvious, such moves were too little, too late.

The Post-Communist Era

The events of 1989–91 have been described in this book as the double-rejective revolution. It has been argued that neither the peoples nor the elites of the post-communist world had clear ideas either of what they wanted following the overthrow of communist power, or of how to achieve this. However, they did reject partocracy and had a general commitment to 'democracy'; though vague, the latter included concepts such as a multiparty system, some form of separation or division of powers, and constitutionalism. In short, it represented concrete moves towards legal-rationality. Their achievements and problems to date can now be examined.

This section is divided into six parts. The first focuses on political parties, the nature, number and role of which have all changed dramatically since the late 1980s. This is followed by an examination of the various electoral systems and the results of elections. The third part outlines the formal legislative and executive structures of the new political systems. In the fourth, the relationships between presidents, prime ministers and parliaments are taken both as examples of recent significant change in the politics of the region, and as reflecting the tension between the desire for democracy and the need for strong leadership. This is followed by a brief overview of other state organs, such as the police and the military. The sixth part is devoted to an analysis of constitutions and constitutionalism. Following all this are some general conclusions.

POLITICAL PARTIES

One of the most visible changes between the communist and post-communist eras is the substantial increase in the number of political parties in the latter. While truly autonomous political parties were beginning to emerge in some countries even *before* the collapse of communist power, change has accelerated in the 1990s. Moreover, there is good reason to assume that multiparty arrangements are here to stay in most parts of the post-communist world (there are doubts about some parts of Transcaucasia and Central Asia), which was not *clearly* so in late communism.

In the USSR, 'alternative' parties began to develop in the late 1980s. Following the emergence of left-oriented parties by 1988, a mass of new parties, covering virtually the whole spectrum of ideological perspectives, had been established by 1990. But these were at that stage all outside the legislature. In many ways more significant was the crystallization of identifiable groupings *within* the ultimate legislature, the All-Union Congress of People's Deputies. By 1990 the two most obvious groupings were the Interregional Group of Deputies and Soyuz (Union). The former was established in July 1989 by approximately 400 of the more progressive deputies to the Congress, and had as its aim an acceleration and deepening of the reform process. The latter was a more conservative group of deputies. With the collapse of the USSR, its all-union groups disappeared too. But a precedent of open debate and competition within the legislature had been set.

In several countries, the very newness of post-communism and the fact that political tendencies need time to gestate and crystallize is one major reason for the relatively large number of political parties that have been contesting elections. But the electoral systems, which are explored later in the chapter, have largely determined whether or not these high numbers have been reflected in the final composition of parliaments. For instance, 23 parties and blocs contested the 1993 Latvian elections, of which only eight secured seats in parliament.

Few of the major parties of the early post-communist world included the word party in their formal titles; examples include Civic Forum (CF – in the Czech Lands) and Public Against Violence (PAV – in Slovakia) in Czecho-Slovakia; the Hungarian Democratic Forum (HDF) and the Alliance Of Free Democrats (AFD) in Hungary; the National Salvation Front (NSF) in

Romania; and the Union of Democratic Forces (UDF) in Bulgaria. There are several reasons for this, depending on the particular group; in some cases, more than one of the following explanations pertain.

First, some organizations were established during the late communist era, when it was still illegal to form parties. Such organizations therefore often opted for a title that would give the communist authorities less justification for clamping down on them than would have been the case had they called themselves parties. A good example is Slovenia, in which 'independent organizations' began to be legalized as relatively early as 1987, whereas organizations explicitly defining themselves as political parties could not be legally recognized until 1990. This said, and unlike the situation in several other post-communist states, many Slovenes did opt to call their organizations parties as soon as this was permitted (McMahon 1992, pp. 68–70). Elsewhere, many organizations decided to retain their original name even when it became legal to form political parties, since they had already begun to develop a positive image under its banner.

The second reason is that many 'parties' were in fact coalitions (blocs) of several small organizations. Thus, at the time of the June 1990 elections in Bulgaria, the UDF comprised no fewer than 17 political parties and groups (Garber 1992, pp. 138–9).

Third, several groups avoided the use of the term party because this word was linked in people's minds specifically with the *communist* party. Thus, writing on Czecho-Slovakia, Carnahan and Corley note: 'One campaign poster partly demonstrated how thoroughly the Communist Party had tainted the word "party" by declaring: "Parties are for Party members. Civic Forum is for everybody"' (1992, p. 123). For obvious reasons, many political leaders were reluctant to permit anything that would link their organizations with the communists.

Although many new organizations were initially loath to call themselves parties, electoral laws in some post-communist states have stipulated that *only* political parties (or blocs of these) or individuals may compete in elections. This has been done partly to avoid a situation in which well-established organizations linked in the past to the communists, such as some trade unions, could compete against the fragile new political parties.

In a few cases, post-communist governments have banned particular kinds of party (in addition to communist parties). Thus the Albanian electoral law of 1992 stipulated not only that only parties or individuals could compete in elections, but also that political parties were not to be formed on the basis of religion, ethnicity or region. Whereas some Albanians defended this on the grounds that the law was intended to reduce divisiveness and racism in society, others perceived it as an attempt to limit the rights of minorities. In particular, members of the Greek minority had established a party, Omonia, in 1991, and objected to this rule. Eventually, under pressure from various international organizations – the rule contravened CSCE provisions, for instance – the Albanian authorities permitted the establishment of a 'Party for the Defence of Human Rights', which in practice was a substitute for Omonia. One major difference, however, was that ethnic

Albanians could also join the new party if they wished. The outcome was thus a compromise and, by most criteria, more democratic than the original situation.[2]

In sum, despite the reluctance of many organizations to call themselves parties, there has been pressure on them in some countries to do so. Yet many 'parties' would barely qualify as such from a West European political scientist's viewpoint. For the latter, a political party should have some formal organization (such as a party statute defining the structure of the party, what is expected of members, etc.); either an ideology or, at least, a clear set of commitments and objectives across a full range of issues; and open membership (see Duverger 1954, Blondel 1990, pp. 114–15). Many of the entities called parties in the earliest post-communist era were so new, led by such inexperienced people and focused on such specific issues that even such minimum requirements were not met. On the other hand, these organizations represented the political views of particular groups, and were in most cases explicitly intended to compete in elections. In this sense, the use of the term party is as appropriate as any; it must simply be remembered that the word may connote something much less structured in the early post-communist states than it normally would in an established liberal democracy of Western Europe (though not in the USA, where the major parties are also loosely organized, relatively undisciplined and have vague objectives).

Most of the political parties that sprang up like mushrooms in the late 1980s and early 1990s were brand new. Some, however, were old parties that had existed in the pre-communist period and were re-established or revitalized. For example, the Latvian Social Democratic Workers' Party was revived in December 1989, but had been established in 1904 and operated abroad during the communist period (Bungs 1993, p. 45).

In addition to new and revitalized organizations, there were well-established parties that had coexisted with the communists in those communist states that had *de jure* tolerated other political parties, but which distanced themselves from the communists as soon as this was politically feasible (usually the late 1980s). Examples include the Bulgarian Agrarian National Union, and the Christian Democratic Union in the GDR. Conversely, some parties that coexisted with the communists during the communist era have retained close links to the communists' successors. A good example is the Polish Peasant Party (formerly the United Peasant Party).

Finally, there were the communist parties themselves. As demonstrated in part II, many of these changed their names and their approach to politics in the late 1980s and early 1990s – the Communist Party of Czecho-Slovakia being a rare exception. This applied even in some Soviet successor states. Thus the Estonian Communist Party voted to change its name to the Estonian Democratic Labour Party in November 1992, at which time it also discussed a new statute and party programme. Most of these name and image changes were self-initiated. But in countries such as Albania the process was encouraged by new electoral laws that forbade communist-style parties; in Russia and several of the FSU states, the communist parties were rapidly banned in the aftermath of the August 1991 attempted coup. Even where communist parties were not banned, in some countries many of their assets were confiscated (as in Czecho-Slovakia, November 1990), so that they were less privileged in resource terms over other parties.

On one level, the banning or pecuniary emasculation of the highly organized and experienced communist parties has been advantageous to other parties. However, this advantage has been partly eroded in some countries, as communist parties have either re-formed under another name in response to a ban, or else, following challenges, have been deemed legal by courts that have overturned the rulings of presidents and/or parliaments. With qualifications, the latter point applies to Russia. Shortly after a November 1992 ruling by the Russian constitutional court (see p. 191), in February 1993, a 'new' Communist Party of the Russian Federation (CPRF) held its first congress; many of its members were former members of the CPSU. The CPRF claimed a membership of 600,000, making it the largest party in Russia (Tolz et al. 1993, p. 20). It was also the most popular party in the December 1995 elections.

Although a few – mostly the successors to former communist parties – are relatively large, most political parties in the post-communist world have small memberships, and many are poorly equipped for fighting elections. The latter fact is often a function of the former; parties with only a handful of members could not be expected to have the resources to publish their own national newspapers, for instance. The small size of political parties is partly explained by the very multitude of organizations that have sprung up. Often a party will have been established in one city and have views similar to those of a party in another, but each will have been unaware of the other. This is understandable given the still inadequate communication networks in some post-communist states. But as time passes, a mixture of greater mutual awareness, the centripetal forces of threshold rules for parliamentary representation, and in some cases growing inertia after the initial enthusiasm generated by the rapid legalization of opposition parties, is likely to result in what can already be seen in several states – coalitions of parties under umbrella organizations crystallizing into far fewer but bigger and better organized political parties. This is based on the assumption, considered briefly in chapter 12, that new forms of authoritarianism do not replace the currently fragile democratic saplings.

While the *general* trend for political parties and other political organizations is likely to be centripetal, there have already been important examples of centrifugal forces at work. Not only do countrywide parties almost necessarily have to divide when post-communist states disintegrate, as has so far happened in three cases (USSR, Yugoslavia, Czecho-Slovakia), but some significant parties have also split because of ideological and/or policy and/or personality differences. Whereas hostility to a common enemy overrode many of the differences within these groupings when they were in opposition, disagreements surfaced and often exerted a destructive influence once the group was either itself in power and had to adopt actual policies, or, more modestly, no longer had the goal of defeating the com-

mon enemy to hold it together. Perhaps the best known example of such a
split is Civic Forum in Czechia, in which two rival factions agreed to what
has been described as an 'amicable divorce' (East 1992, p. 59) in February
1991. This eventually resulted in the emergence of two new parties, the
Civic Democratic Party under Vaclav Klaus and the Civic Movement under
Jiri Dienstbier. Somewhat similar splits have occurred in parties and coalitions in Russia (numerous), Slovenia (DEMOS, December 1991), Romania
(NSF, March 1992), Croatia (HDZ, April 1994) and elsewhere.

Electoral laws in the post-communist states have mostly exerted centripetal pressure on parties; but occasionally they have the opposite effect.
Thus, one (unnamed) analyst has argued that the November 1993 Ukrainian electoral law, with its complicated requirements for running as a party
candidate, discouraged party formation and encouraged most candidates to
run as unaffiliated individuals (*EECR*, Spring 1994, pp. 26–7; see too Arel
and Wilson 1994, pp. 6, 9–10). In this particular case, the law was almost
certainly designed to advantage the well-organized and experienced communists. If so, the results of the March-April 1994 elections (which in fact
required several further rounds in *some* constituencies throughout 1994)
might suggest that the law met its framers' objectives.

In sum, both centripetal and centrifugal forces currently coexist in the
post-communist world, even if a comparative analysis over time of political
trends around the democratic world suggests there will be an overt process
of consolidation and simplification in most post-communist states in the
next few years.

With the exception of the ban on communist and some ethnically oriented parties in a few post-communist states, there is a reasonably full
political spectrum of parties in these countries. But even before the fall of
communism, the application of terms like right and left, or conservative and
progressive, to parties in these states was often misleading or confusing.
With the collapse of communism, this confusion has grown. Most notably,
communist parties – which were usually described as extreme left-wing in
Western societies – have in recent years frequently been described as conservative in the case of the post-communist states. This is because many
communists are reluctant to change too much of the system and policies
they have known for decades – hence conservative. Conversely, those advocating radical privatization, as little state interference in the economy as
possible and a minimal welfare state are often seen as progressives (which
in turn is often described as left-wing in Western systems) in post-
communist states, whereas the same views in the West would probably be
described as dry ultraconservatism or right-wingism. Thus the problem of
political labelling has recently become even more acute than it already was.

However, if some impression of the political positioning and range of
parties in the post-communist states is to be formed, general labels are
necessary; without them, it would be difficult to highlight similarities between parties and groupings in different states. Solely for this reason, the
terms reformist and conservative (which are marginally less troublesome
than the terms left and right), and the relatively uncontroversial centrist,

are used here. For the purposes of the following analysis of current Russian political parties, reformist implies that a party seeks substantial change from the communist period, which in turn suggests a very laissez-faire approach in economics and politics. As a corollary of this, it implies an outward-looking approach, in which a given country is seen as part of the larger world and global economy. Conservative, in contrast, implies here that a group believes in high levels of state involvement in economics and politics. It also often implies a relatively high level of nationalism.

So many parties have been created in Russia since the late 1980s (for listings see Tolz 1990; Hosking et al. 1992, pp. 216–18; Pribylovskii 1992) that it is well beyond the scope of this book even to list, let alone analyse, them all. Rather, it makes sense to focus on those that had by late 1995 developed sufficiently to be able to run in the December 1995 parliamentary elections. No fewer than 43 parties and blocs competed; although 28 of these secured representation in the new Duma, most of them did so only through winning a very small number of seats in single-member constituencies. A mere four parties (the CPRF; the LDPR; Our Home is Russia; and Yabloko) cleared the 5 per cent hurdle for representation through the party lists.

At the reformist end of the spectrum were groupings such as Russia's Democratic Choice-United Democrats (RDC) and Yabloko. The first of these was led by the radical economist and former prime minister Yegor Gaidar; another prominent member was the man many have seen as the intellectual force behind *perestroika*, Alexander Yakovlev. Yeltsin himself had at one time informally supported the predecessor to RDC, Russia's Choice, which had performed relatively well in the December 1993 election (see table 7.2 on p. 164); but by 1995 he had moved to a more centrist position. Yabloko was named after its three leaders, Yavlinskii, Boldyrev and Lukin. It was less radically reformist than RDC, though still clearly in the pro-privatization, pro-marketization and pro-West camp.

At the opposite end of the political spectrum were the conservatives. This included groups that might initially appear to be odd bedfellows, some hankering after the old communist system, others being very much nationalists. But one point these groups had in common was a disdain for excessive emulation of, let alone what they saw as sycophancy towards, the West. Closely connected with this was a common abhorrence of Boris Yeltsin and his policies. Many communists saw him as a hypocrite, in that he fared very well for much of his career as a communist official and then rejected virtually everything the party stood for – even banning it. At the same time, many believed that Yeltsin not only permitted the break-up of the USSR, but had even been allowing the *de facto* dismemberment of Russia itself.[3] Among the best-known parties in this group were the CPRF, led by Gennadii Zyuganov; the Agrarian Party, basically opposing privatization of agriculture, led by Mikhail Lapshin; and, at the extreme nationalist end, the misleadingly titled Liberal Democratic Party, which was neither liberal nor democratic. The LDPR sought to reconstitute much of the former USSR (though not Transcaucasia, which it saw as responsible for much of the dramatic increase in criminality in Russia), but as an enlarged Russia. It is often and appropriately described as a neo-fascist party. Its leader, Vladimir Zhirinovskii, secured almost 8 per cent of the vote in the June 1991 Russian presidential elections, coming third out of six behind Yeltsin and former Soviet prime minister Nikolai Ryzhkov. He is openly anti-semitic and often anti-Western. But he is also very much an opportunist and can change his position suddenly and dramatically (on the Liberal Democrats and Zhirinovskii see Lentini and McGrath 1994, Morrison 1994, Frazer and Lancelle 1994).

Perhaps reflecting the polarization in Russia in the early 1990s, the centrists had at that time been the least organized of the three groupings. Yet they had included, or had enjoyed the apparent support of, some of Russia's most skilful, experienced and influential politicians. Among these were former vice-president Alexander Rutskoi; former speaker of the Russian parliament, Ruslan Khasbulatov; Russian prime minister Viktor Chernomyrdin; and former Soviet leader Mikhail Gorbachev. Once again, this was a disparate group that included a range of opinions. But in general, the centrists disagreed with Yeltsin's radical approach to economic reform during the early 1990s. They preferred both to slow it down and to alter the sequence of stages (see chapter 8). They also advocated a greater role for the state in the economy than Yeltsin had once done. Many of them had considered the president too sycophantic towards the West. While they were generally much less chauvinistic than the conservatives, several of them regretted the break-up of the USSR. In general, they favoured the CIS, which for them was better than the total break-up of the former Soviet Union. Although at one time critical of Yeltsin, most of the centrists were basically democratic and believed in constitutionalism. But they also believed that, as true democrats, they had the right and duty to criticize the president if they considered him or his policies wrong or inappropriate.

By 1995, Yeltsin had moved towards the centre anyway and was close to the main centrist party to fight the 1995 election, Our Home is Russia. This party was headed by prime minister Viktor Chernomyrdin and was established only in May 1995.

Finally, Women of Russia – formed in October 1993 and led by Ekaterina Lakhova – has been seen by some as centrist (see Slater 1994a, p. 14; Halligan and Mozdoukhov 1995, p. 22), though the close ties of its predecessor organizations to the communists have led others to place it in the conservative camp.[4]

Given that the Russian pattern is more or less repeated in so many other post-communist states – albeit usually in a somewhat less fractured form – it is not possible to provide even an outline of the parties, parliamentary factions, etc., in other countries. As with so many phenomena in this book, the interested reader will have to use the sources in the bibliography to obtain further details on individual countries. This said, there *is* one significant difference between the political spectrum in Russia and some other post-communist countries. Thus, not every post-communist state has had clearly centrist parties. Some analysts made this observation vis-à-vis the

1992 Czecho-Slovak elections (see, for instance, Obrman 1992, p. 12) and the 1993 Latvian elections (Bungs 1993, p. 47); by 1994, some observers were even referring to the decline of centrist parties in Russia (see Slater 1994a).[5] The significance of this will be considered at the end of this chapter.

For now, this section can be concluded by reiterating that the post-communist states are still very much in flux, which is reflected in the constant forming, re-forming and disbanding of political parties. A prolonged continuation of this will be dysfunctional to post-communism; but for now, it can still be seen as a basically healthy sign of early democratization. The plethora of parties in so many countries will probably decline sharply in the coming years – assuming democracy itself is not overthrown – as some become better organized and have better leaders than others; as communications improve; as groups realize their commonalities and the advantages of amalgamating; as the impact of electoral rules takes a firmer hold (on the impact of electoral systems on parties and parliaments, see McGregor 1993 and next section); and so on. There are certainly precedents for the number of parties to decline dramatically, and for a party *system* to emerge fairly quickly, in countries that have only recently democratized. As Roskin (1993, p. 49) points out, 161 parties competed in the 1977 elections that followed the end of the Franco dictatorship in Spain, but by the 1980s, Spain had a party system similar to many in Western Europe.

But as yet, and despite brave attempts by some to identify them (for an early threefold classification of post-communist east European countries into 'dominant non-authoritarian', 'dominant authoritarian' and 'competitive multiparty' see Korosenyi 1991), it is still too early to talk of proper party systems in any of these countries. Nevertheless, assuming extremists do not take power, such systems should be identifiable in several of the post-communist states within a decade or even sooner. By then, many of the social cleavages that have been the norm in the West, and that are still partly reflected in voting behaviour, may well have emerged in the post-communist world. A new bourgeoisie should largely have crystallized by then. This in turn *could* render workers more aware of commonalities among themselves, resulting in more solidly class-based or socially identifiable parties. Admittedly, such cleavages and social bases have long been withering in the West, as many parties seek increasingly to become 'catch-all' (on this concept see Kirchheimer 1966, Dittrich 1983). But even such a development implies a party *system*, in which politics are on one level dominated by a small number of reasonably distinct, well-organized, basically predictable parties that have policies on all major issues, and that all work more or less to the same rules of political conduct within an essentially stable political system.

Whether there is a move to the class-based politics of an earlier stage of liberal democracy, or to the more catch-all stage of more recent Western politics, party systems as just defined could undoubtedly emerge, despite the apparent polarization in some recent elections. Since the issue of economic reform still appears to be dominant at present in all post-communist states (as to the speed, direction and sequencing of reforms, and more or less state intervention), and since economic policy and its social ramifications are often the primary feature in distinguishing between modern Western parties, many of the post-communist systems might move directly to their own versions of an issue-oriented political system, rather than a class-based, socially cleavaged one. This said, it should be noted that there is no *necessary* division between class-based and issue-oriented party systems; *a priori*, it is quite conceivable that the working class will tend to favour more statism and cautious reform, the new entrepreneurial class less statism and more radical reform (for an argument that the socio-economic position of voters is likely to be the main determinant in post-communist voting patterns see Kitschelt 1992). Just because systems took decades to emerge in many West European societies does not mean they will take as long in the post-communist states. The latter can learn vicariously and rapidly from others' mistakes and experiences. However, it is likely that stable party systems will in future be more typical in countries in which perceived ethnic differences do not play a major role than where they do – though Switzerland and Belgium, for instance, demonstrate that *relatively* stable systems *can* sometimes be achieved even in ethnically and linguistically diverse states (via so-called consociational democracy; for an analysis of the likely future bases of party allegiance and competition in much of the communist world, which incorporates ethnic and other factors as well as socio-economic cleavages, see Evans and Whitefield 1993).

ELECTIONS

A basic tenet of both liberal democracy and legal-rationality is that the masses should be able to exercise some control over their leaders. One way in which this can occur is via contested elections, in which those seeking high public office compete against each other for popular support. As indicated, there was little electoral competition in the communist world; in line with the argument here about the double-rejective revolution, therefore, there should be real competition in post-communist elections.

What other qualities should be expected of such elections? First, suffrage should be universal. Normally, this is interpreted to mean that all citizens other than criminals and perhaps the insane should have the right to vote.

Second, elections should be equal. This is usually taken to mean, as a minimum, that each citizen has only one vote. Some believe it should also imply that each person's vote should have approximately the same 'weight' within the overall elections. But even in Western states it is often difficult to ensure this; in the real world, the fact that one voter lives in a safe seat and another in a marginal one often means that the latter's vote is perceived to be more important. Given this problem, expectations of electoral 'equality' in the post-communist world should be realistic.

Third, balloting should be genuinely secret. In most communist states, many citizens feared the consequences of formally exercising their right to enter an election booth.

Fourth, elections should be conducted fairly. For instance, there should be no intimidation or vote rigging. More controversially, it can be argued that there should be no undue privileging of some parties over others. This can be a difficult factor to interpret and determine. Is it fair that some political parties have far greater resources than others, perhaps because they make more effort to raise funds, which they can use to mount more impressive electoral campaigns? No Western democracy has been able to reach total consensus on this issue, and we should be wary of passing judgement too quickly if post-communist states cannot reach agreement on the optimal arrangement.

A fifth aspect is even more controversial. For some observers, all elections should be direct – that is, voters should be able to vote directly for their representatives and leaders, as distinct from a situation in which voters elect representatives, who in turn choose the highest level legislatures and leaders (indirect elections). In many countries, such as the UK and Australia, neither the head of state (who is not elected at all) nor the head of the government is directly elected by the masses. Even in the USA, the president is *formally* elected by the Electoral College; as textbooks on American politics usually point out, it is theoretically possible that the Electoral College would elect a president who was not the electorate's first preference, even though this has not happened since the nineteenth century. In sum, requirements about direct elections should also be realistic.

Finally, there is the question of whether voting should be compulsory or not. In the communist world, citizens were not *formally* required to vote. In practice, they were usually under considerable pressure to do so, since the authorities wanted to be able to boast high levels of turnout and support. Voting is not compulsory in most Western countries – Belgium and Australia being rare exceptions; it is widely accepted that it should be a basic right, but not a duty, of citizens formally to express political preferences.

Bearing all the above in mind, electoral arrangements in the post-communist states can be considered. Following this is a brief survey of the results of such elections.

There are at least three kinds of elections in the post-communist world – parliamentary, presidential and local. Given space constraints, the third group will not be considered at all;[6] the first two will be analysed in the order just given.

In almost every post-communist state that had by late 1995 held parliamentary elections (see tables 7.1 and 7.2 on pp. 157–65), the electorate had been offered a genuine choice of parties; Turkmenistan was the only exception to this. However, a slight majority of post-communist states had by then introduced electoral rules to ensure that extremely small parties are not represented in parliament. One way of doing this has been to ensure that they cannot even field candidates. For instance, for parties to have qualified to compete in the 1995 Russian elections, they were required to have obtained at least 200,000 signatures, from supporters in several constituencies. But there are also hurdles even for those parties that *do* qualify to compete, via party lists in elections. By 1995, the electoral laws in most post-communist states with a proportional representation component required parties to achieve a minimum percentage of votes before they could be represented in parliament. The threshold for representation ranged from 3 per cent in Croatia and Romania to 11 per cent for large blocs (coalitions of parties) in the Czech Republic (see tables 7.1 and 7.2).

The general direction has thus been to encourage competition while also seeking to reduce the likelihood of producing highly fragmented, and hence ineffectual, parliaments. Moves to limit the number of parties represented in parliaments should be interpreted in this light, rather than as anti-democratic.

Despite increasing standardization in terms of threshold rules, actual voting systems vary widely across the post-communist world. In general, the new regimes have sought to devise systems that are fair yet workable. But there is no agreement on electoral rules. Some attempts have resulted in extraordinarily complicated systems. Probably the best example is that used in the 1990 and 1994 Hungarian elections. This involved no fewer than three methods for selecting the 386 members of the unicameral legislature. Of these, 176 were to be elected on an absolute majority basis in single-member constituencies, with a provision for run-offs. Up to a further 152 deputies were to be elected on the basis of party lists in 20 multimember constituencies; only parties securing 4 per cent of the vote nationally could be allocated seats under this arrangement. In addition to these first two methods, at least 58 seats were to be allocated on the basis of *national* party lists, 'proportionally allocated from "unused" votes not needed to win a seat in a constituency or from a county list' (Melia 1992, p. 53). Although there were thus three ways in which deputies were elected, the individual voter cast only two ballots – one each for the local constituency and the multimember county list. If neither of these votes was needed, because candidates and/or parties already had sufficient support to warrant a seat, then that voter's choices were added to the national party lists.

Although the above arrangements, and others such as those for the June 1990 Bulgarian election (see Garber 1992), were complicated, there were good reasons for them. One was that there was a conscious attempt in several countries to counter the natural advantages enjoyed by the communists or their successors, in terms of organizational experience, funds, etc. Another was that some countries were consciously learning from their own pre-communist traditions. Third, electoral laws were often the result of heated debate and compromise, and thus a sign of more open politics. Finally, many east Europeans were impressed by the Federal Republic of Germany's electoral system (which also reflected attempts to learn from the past) and wanted more or less to emulate it, subject to local modifications.

The German system initially appears complicated but, once mastered, has various advantages. Electors have two ballots; without elaborating the system (for details see Deutsch and Smith 1987, pp. 194–6), suffice it to note that it is designed to allow voters both to choose *individuals* they find impressive, and to express a more general *party* preference. The system probably comes as close to meeting this criterion as is practically possible.

The Germans learnt from their own experiences during the Weimar Republic (1919–1933) and early Bonn Republic (since 1949) that, while this might
on one level seem more democratic, there can be serious drawbacks to any
system that allows many small parties in the national parliament. It can
result in indecision or suboptimal decisions, and many have seen the weaknesses of the Weimar parliamentary system as a major reason for Hitler's
takeover of power in 1933. After the Second World War, the Germans
studied the Weimar era, and in 1953 the FRG introduced minimum thresholds for representation (in their case, the threshold is 5 per cent or at least
three constituency seats).

As part of their endeavours to avoid the fractiousness common in systems in which the legislature comprises many small parties, those who
drafted *inter alia* the Hungarian, Bulgarian and Czecho-Slovak electoral
laws in early post-communism studied the German experience and system.
One intended advantage of the percentage threshold was that it would force
small parties that were in many cases very similar to each other to consider
joining with other like-minded parties to form more viable coalitions,
thereby securing parliamentary representation. In many cases, this is precisely what happened. In Bulgaria, for instance, 40 parties and blocs competed in the October 1991 elections to the National Assembly, yet only
three secured representation. Of these, two clearly dominated – the 17-
party coalition that constituted the UDF, which secured just over 34 per
cent of the vote, and the successors to the communists (the BSP), with just
over 33 per cent (see McLean and Garber 1992, pp. 55, 103–4).

Not all countries took heed of the German experience. Poland had its
first truly free parliamentary elections in decades in October 1991. Without
a minimum threshold for representation, the Polish parliament (Sejm)
finished up with no fewer than 29 parties (out of 62 that contested the
election). The two most popular, the Democratic Union and the Democratic Left Alliance, secured only some 12 per cent of the vote each (Roskin
1993, p. 49, has calculated that, if Poland had had a 4 per cent national
threshold for the 1991 election, only nine parties would have been represented in the Sejm). It should be noted, however, that Poland soon fell into
line, introducing minimum thresholds in its April 1993 electoral law. Under
this, no party with less than 5 per cent of the vote, and no coalition with less
than 8 per cent, may be represented in the Sejm. Largely because of this
law, the number of parties and coalitions in the Polish parliament declined
dramatically, from 29 to six, following the September 1993 elections. Like
Poland in the earliest post-communist phase, Romania consciously sought
to create a system in which small parties would be represented in the
legislature, believing this to be more democratic (see Carothers 1992, pp.
80–1); but it, too, soon changed this and conformed to the predominant east
European arrangement.

If some of the east European systems reflect German influence, several
have also learnt from French experience. Thus the two-round run-off system, used by the French for both presidential and legislative elections, is
seen as another way of combining democracy and efficiency; there can be

large numbers of candidates/parties running in the first round, but this is narrowed down to the front-runners in the second, to ensure a clear-cut result.

Before finishing this consideration of electoral arrangements, it is worth pointing out that several of the CIS states have opted for absolute majority systems with run-off and minimum turnout[7] provisions. In practice, this has led to difficulties in filling all the parliamentary seats in states such as Belarus, Kyrgyzstan and Ukraine. Given these problems, there are likely to be new electoral laws in several countries. Even if the absolute majority provisions are retained, the minimum turnout requirements may well be reduced, perhaps to as low as the 25 per cent stipulated in the June 1995 law on elections to the Russian Duma (lower house – on the 1995 Russian electoral laws see Orttung 1995a).

In almost all post-communist states, all sane non-criminal citizens have the right to vote from the age of 18; in some of the states of the former Yugoslavia, the minimum voting age is 16 for those in full-time employment, while the minimum age for everyone in Slovakia is 21.

Regarding equality – it should already be clear from the extraordinarily complicated arrangements adopted in some post-communist states that many politicians and state officials are making serious efforts to ensure voters have a proper say. The fact that multimember constituencies can vary so much in size (between 2 and 14 members per constituency for the upper house in Romania, for example – Nadais 1992, p. 195; between 3 and 26 in Bulgaria – Garber 1992, p. 140) could be seen as very unequal. On the other hand, these differences reflect differences in population, and it could be argued that since citizens do not space themselves out equally over a given political unit, it would be highly artificial to create subdivisions of similar size in population terms but enormously different in terms of territorial size. There are very few examples of more than one person per vote in the post-communist world proper. In the 1990 Slovene elections, however, only employed citizens could vote for one of the three chambers that existed at that time, the Chamber of Associated Labour; this arrangement was heavily criticized, however, and both the privileging and the chamber itself disappeared by the time of the 1992 elections.

Secrecy at the polling–station is almost bound to be a necessary condition where elections are genuinely contested. Citizens no longer merely drop the ballot form into a box without marking it, as so frequently happened in the communist era. Instead, they now express preferences. Foreign observers have by and large been satisfied with this dimension of post-communist elections. This said, it should be noted that there have been charges of inadequate secrecy in some post-communist elections. Some Bulgarian voters complained during the 1990 elections that the voting booths were made of such thin cotton that they could be seen inside (Garber 1992, p. 150); while this may have been true, it seems unlikely that people outside the booths would have been able to see how individuals voted. Another problem related to secrecy was the relative transparency of the ballot papers and/or envelopes in both the May 1990 Romanian and the June 1990 Bulgarian elections (Carothers 1992, p. 90; Garber 1992, p. 150).

One area in which there has in many countries been a *reversal* of the notion of secrecy from the communist period is in the counting and checking of votes. These processes were opened up to both domestic and external observers, to an extent almost unknown in established democracies. This may well prove to be a feature only of early post-communism, however, as new parties and politicians seek both to distance themselves from the communist era, and to establish their own and the new system's legitimacy; once such legitimacy has been established, the need for such external scrutiny will almost certainly diminish sharply (on the issue of secrecy from a comparative perspective see Nadais 1992, pp. 200–2). Expressed differently, once the rule of law is reasonably firmly established in these countries – assuming this occurs – there will be less pressure on post-communist authorities to prove their commitment to 'normal' democratic political methods.

There have been *relatively* few allegations of physical intimidation or vote-rigging in post-communist elections; most have related to individual constituencies, and have usually been satisfactorily resolved. The Romanian election of May 1990 was something of an exception, with several very nasty incidents reported during the campaign. On the other hand, some external observers, as well as domestic politicians, have argued that elections in some states have been very unfair, in the sense of some parties or coalitions enjoying enormous advantages over others. Romania again provides one of the best examples of this. Carothers writes the following of the 1990 election:

> The campaign was systematically unfair. The Front [NSF] enjoyed all the advantages of having assumed the reins of an absolutist state and exploited these advantages to the maximum. The opposition suffered from a lack of every possible resource, including experienced personnel, funds, materials and equipment ... Access to electronic media was another major area of inequity ... In addition, opposition parties provided evidence of systematic government intimidation designed to discourage publication and limit the range of expression. (1992, pp. 83–4)

Somewhat similar, if less trenchant, criticisms were raised about, for instance, the 1993 upper house elections in Croatia (Bicanic and Dominis 1993, p. 19), the 1994 Ukrainian parliamentary elections (see *KRWE 1994*, p. 39971) and the 1994 Kazakh elections (Nourzhanov 1994, p. 3).[8] While it would be unrealistic to expect all parties, especially in *early* post-communism, to be more or less equal in terms of 'experienced personnel', a genuine commitment to what most liberal democracies would understand as basic democratic principles would bring an end to many of the above injustices perpetrated by the NSF and by other parties in other countries.

The situation regarding the directness of post-communist elections is reasonably clear. As of mid-1994, the vast majority of parliamentary elections in the post-communist states have been direct, especially for unicameral parliaments. One exception was Kazakhstan, where 42 of the parliament's 177 deputies to the 1994 parliament were nominated by the president, ostensibly on the basis of recommendations from national and regional government officials. In the rare cases where elections are indirect, as in Russian elections to the Federation Council until 1995 and in Kazakhstan from 1995, these are to the upper house only; Croatian regulations permit the president to nominate up to five of the nearly 70 members of the upper house.

Finally, post-communist states have not introduced compulsory voting, for at least two reasons. First, most are seeking to learn from – while not blindly emulating – the experience of established liberal democracies. Second, this can be interpreted as yet another part of the double-rejective revolution; since so many communist states *de facto* required their citizens to vote, most post-communist politicians do not wish to appear to be following this practice. This said, some states, including Lithuania and Romania, have minimum turnout requirements for validating elections.

Turnout has varied considerably so far in the post-communist world. At one end of the spectrum are countries with figures above 85 or even 90 per cent, such as Czecho-Slovakia (June 1990), the GDR (March 1990), Albania (March 1991 and March 1992), Bulgaria (June 1990); Turkmen figures are *so* high as to raise doubts about their reliability. At the other extreme is Poland, where there was a mere 26 per cent turnout in the second round of the June 1989 election (62 per cent in the first round) and just over 43 per cent in the October 1991 election. Hungary has also had relatively low turnouts (approximately 46 per cent in the second round of the 1990 election and 55 per cent in the second round of the 1994 election).

No single explanation for low voter turnouts can be provided. However, one reason in some cases is voter confusion caused by the sheer number and range of parties and blocs competing in the elections; this has led many citizens to feel unqualified to participate. In countries such as Belarus, this problem has been exacerbated by poor media coverage of the electoral campaigns. Other reasons for low turnout include a perception of a surfeit of elections, which is exacerbated by run-off arrangements (this helps to explain the 'second round' phenomenon just hinted at – although the 1994 Macedonian elections reveal that this explanation is not universally applicable); a perception of less difference in some countries than in others between late communism and early post-communism, so that voters are not as excited about exercising new political rights as they would be in countries in which late communism was still relatively repressive; and disillusionment with *all* parties and blocs, as voters perceive no alternative to severe deprivation and insecurity in early post-communism, but prefer not to legitimize the (necessary) bringers of pain. Finally, it should not be overlooked that turnout is often relatively low in many Western countries too!

It is not possible to analyse comparatively the results of so many elections; the individual outcomes are summarized in tables 7.1 and 7.2. This said, one feature common to many post-communist states in their earliest

Table 7.1 Legislative elections in the east European successor states (1989 to December 1995)

Country	Date	Electoral system[a]	Minimum threshold for party/bloc representation	Turnout (%)[b]	Results[c] Parties	% of votes	Seats
Albania	Mar–Apr 1991	Single-member, absolute majority constituencies with run-off provision	None	96.9	*Party of Labor of Albania*	67.6	169
					Democratic Party	30.0	75
					Others	2.4	6
	Mar 1992	Mixed (2 systems – single-member, absolute majority constituencies with run-off provision; nationwide multimember constituencies filled by p.r.)	4%	90.3	Democratic Party	62.1	92
					Socialist Party	25.7	38
					Social Democrats	4.4	7
					Others	7.8	3
Bosnia-Hercegovina	(Scheduled for May 1996)						
	Nov–Dec 1990	Mixed (2 systems – single-member, absolute majority constituencies, with run-off provision; multimember constituencies, filled by p.r.)			Party of Democratic Action	33.8	43
					Serbian Democratic Party	29.6	34
					Croatian Democratic Alliance	18.3	21
					Socialist Democratic Party	8.0	15
					Others		17
Bulgaria	June 1990	Mixed (2 systems – single-member, absolute majority constituencies, with run-off provision; multimember constituencies, filled by p.r.)	4%	90.7; 84.1	*Bulgarian Socialist Party*	47.1	211
					Union of Democratic Forces	36.2	144
					Movement for Rights and Freedom	6.0	23
					Bulgarian Agrarian National Union	8.3	16
					Others	1.0	6
	Oct 1991	Mixed (Multimember local constituencies, filled by mixture of p.r. [for parties] and quota [for independent candidates])	4%	83.9	Union of Democratic Forces	34.4	110
					Bulgarian Socialist Party coalition	33.1	106
					Movement for Rights and Freedom	7.5	24
	Dec 1994	As in 1991	4%	74.0	*Bulgarian Socialist Party* coalition (inc. Ekoglasnost)	43.5	125
					Union of Democratic Forces	24.2	69
					People's Union	6.5	18

Table 7.1 cont.

Country	Date	Electoral system[a]	Minimum threshold for party/bloc representation	Turnout (%)[b]	Results[c]		
					Parties	% of votes	Seats
					Movement for Rights and Freedom	5.4	15
					Bulgarian Business Bloc	4.7	13
Croatia	Apr–May 1990				Croatian Democratic Alliance	27.0	84
					League of Communists		36
					Others		30
	Aug 1992	Mixed (2 systems – single-member, simple majority constituencies; nationwide multimember constituency filled by p.r.)	3%	c.75	Croatian Democratic Alliance	41.5	85
					Croatian Social-Liberal Party	18.3	14
					Party of Democratic Changes	5.8	11
					Others	33.9	28
	Oct 1995		5%		Croatian Democratic Alliance	45.2	75
					Peasant Party Coalition	18.3	16
					Croatian Social-Liberal Party	11.6	12
					Social Democratic Party	8.9	10
					Other	16.0	14
Czechia	(Scheduled for May–June 1996)	Mixed (2 systems – multimember local constituencies filled by p.r.; nationwide multimember constituency, filled by p.r.)	5% for single parties; 7–11% for blocs, depending on number of constituent parties				
Czecho-Slovakia	June 1990	Multimember local constituencies, filled by p.r.	5%	96.0	Civic Forum/Public Against Violence		87
					Communist Party		23
					Christian Democratic Movement		20
					Others		20
	June 1992	As in 1990	5%	84.8	Civic Democratic Alliance	24	48
					Movement for a Democratic Slovakia	11	24
					Left Bloc	10	19
					Party of the Democratic Left	5	10
					Others	45	39

Country	Date	Electoral system	Threshold	Turnout (%)	Party	% vote	Seats
GDR	Mar 1990	Multimember local constituencies, filled by p.r.	None	93.4	Alliance for Germany (inc. Christian Democratic Union)	48.1 (40.9)	192 (163)
					Social Democratic Party of Germany	21.9	88
					Party of Democratic Socialism	16.4	66
					Others	13.4	54
Hungary	Mar–Apr 1990	Mixed (3 systems – single-member, absolute majority constituencies with run-off provision; multimember local constituencies filled by p.r.; nationwide multimember constituency filled by p.r.)	4%	63.2; 45.9	Hungarian Democratic Forum	24.7	165
					Alliance of Free Democrats	21.4	91
					Independent Smallholders Party	11.7	44
					Hungarian Socialist Party	10.9	33
					Others	31.3	53
	May 1994	As in 1990	4%	68.9; 55.1	*Hungarian Socialist Party*	54.2	209
					Alliance of Free Democrats	18.1	70
					Hungarian Democratic Forum	9.6	37
					Independent Smallholders' Party	6.7	26
					Others	11.5	44
Rep. of Macedonia	Nov–Dec 1990	Single-member, absolute majority constituencies with run-off provision		c.80	Internal Macedonian Revolutionary Organization – Democratic Party for Macedonian National Unity		38
					League of Communists of Macedonia		31
					Party of Democratic Prosperity		17
					Others		23
	Oct–Nov 1994	As in 1990		c.55; c.55; 77.8	Alliance for Macedonia		95
					Party of Democratic Prosperity		10
					Democratic People's Party		4
					Others		11
Poland	June 1989	Multimember constituencies, absolute majority, with run-off provision – but only 161 of 460 seats contested (rest were allocated under Communist direction)	None	62.1; 25.9	(Communist Bloc)		276
					(Catholic Bloc)		23
					Solidarity		161

Table 7.1 cont.

Country	Date	Electoral system[a]	Minimum threshold for party/bloc representation	Turnout (%)[b]	Parties	Results[c] % of votes	Seats
	Oct 1991	Mixed (2 systems – multimember local constituencies filled by p.r.; nationwide multimember constituency filled by p.r.)	None	43.1	Democratic Union	12.3	62
					Democratic Left Alliance	12.0	60
					Polish Peasant Party	8.7	48
					Catholic Electoral Action	8.7	49
					Confederation for an Independent Poland	7.5	46
					Others		193
	Sept 1993	As in 1991	5% for parties; 8% for blocs	52.1	Democratic Left Alliance	20.4	171
					Polish Peasant Party	15.4	132
					Democratic Union	10.6	74
					Labour Union	7.3	41
					Others	44.6	42
Romania	May 1990	Multimember local constituencies filled by p.r.	None	86+	National Salvation Front	66.3	263
					Hungarian Democratic Union	7.2	29
					National Liberal Party	6.4	29
					National Peasants' Party	2.6	12
					Ecological Movement	2.6	12
					Others	14.9	51
	Sept 1992	Mixed (2 systems – multimember local constituencies filled by p.r.; nationwide multimember constituency filled by p.r.)	3% for single parties; up to 8% for blocs, depending on number of constituent parties	76.3	Democratic National Salvation Front	27.8	117
					Democratic Convention of Romania	20.0	82
					National Salvation Front		
					Romanian National Unity Party	10.2	43
					Hungarian Democratic Union	7.7	30
					Others	7.5	27
						27.0	42
Slovakia	Sept–Oct 1994	Multimember local constituencies filled by p.r.	5% for single parties; up to 10% for blocs, depending on number of constituent parties	75.6	Movement for a Democratic Slovakia and Peasant Party	35.0	61
					Common Choice	10.4	18
					Hungarian Coalition	10.2	17
					Christian Democratic Movement	10.1	17

Country	Date	Electoral system	Threshold	Turnout	Party	% vote	Seats
Slovenia	Apr 1990	Single-member, absolute majority constituencies with run-off provision		80+	Democratic Union	8.6	15
					Others	25.7	22
					Democratic Opposition of Slovenia Bloc (DEMOS)	54.8	47
					Party for Democratic Renewal	17.3	14
					Liberal Party	14.5	12
					Others	7.8	7
	Dec 1992	Mixed (2 systems – multimember local constituencies filled by p.r.; nationwide multimember constituency filled by p.r.)	3%	76	Liberal Democratic Party	23.7	22
					Christian Democratic Party	14.5	15
					United List of Social Democrats	13.6	14
					Slovene National Party	9.9	12
					Slovene People's Party	8.8	10
					Others	29.5	17
Yugoslavia (Serbia-Montenegro)	May–June 1992	Mixed (2 systems – single-member, absolute majority constituencies; multimember local constituencies filled by p.r.)	None		*Socialist Party of Serbia*	61.0	73
					Serbian Radical Party		33
					Democratic Party of Socialists of Montenegro		23
					Others		9
	Dec 1992				*Socialist Party of Serbia*	31.4	47
					Serbian Radical Party	22.4	34
					DEPOS Bloc (Serbian Democratic Movement)	17.2	20
					Democratic Party of Socialists of Montenegro		20
					Democratic Party	2.8	17
						6.0	5
					Others	7.3	15

[a] All countries have detailed further provisions concerning elections, but it is beyond the scope of this comparative review to include them.

[b] Where two or more figures are supplied, the election was in two or more rounds.

[c] Parties often described as 'former communist', as well as actual communist parties and parties very closely aligned to the communists, are italicized. In bicameral legislatures, details are for the lower house. In cases of mixed electoral systems, the percentages cited usually refer only to the p.r. component.

Sources: Sword 1990; Batt 1991; East 1992; Garber and Bjornland 1992; Cohen 1995; Lucky 1994; Szajkowski 1994; Staff of the US Commission CSCE, Washington D.C.: *RFE/RL Research Reports; KRWE; EIU Country Reports; Transition; Britannica Book of the Year.*

Table 7.2 Legislative elections in the successor states of the FSU (1991 to December 1995)

Country	Date	Electoral system[a]	Minimum threshold for party/bloc representation	Turnout (%)[b]	Results[c]		
					Parties	% of votes	Seats
Armenia	July 1995	Mixed (2 systems – 150 members in single-member, absolute majority constituencies with run-off provision; nationwide multimember constituency filled by p.r.)	5%	54.9	Republican Bloc	42.7	119
					Shamiram (Women's Organization)	16.9	8
					Communist Party	12.1	7
					Democratic Union	7.5	5
					Others		51
Azerbaijan	Nov 1995	Mixed (2 systems – 100 members in single-member absolute majority constituencies with run-off provision; nationwide multimember constituency filled by p.r.)		79.8	New Azerbaijan		
					Azerbaijani Popular Front		
					National Independence Party		
Belarus	May 1995[d]	Single-member, absolute majority constituencies with run-off provision and 50% turnout requirement		64.7; 56.0	Agrarian Party		31
					Communists		27
					Other parties		55
					Independents		
Estonia	Sept 1992	Mixed (3 systems – multimember local constituencies, filled by either simple quota or p.r.; nationwide multimember constituency filled by p.r.)	5%	67.4	Pro Patria	22.0	29
					Secure Home Alliance	13.6	17
					Popular Front	12.2	15
					Moderates	9.7	12
					Estonian National Independence Party	8.7	10
					Others		18
	Mar 1995	As in 1992	5%	68.9	Coalition Party/Rural Union Coalition	32.3	41
					Estonia Reform Party/Liberal Coalition	16.2	19
					Estonian Center Party	14.2	16

Country	Date	Threshold	Electoral system	Turnout	Party	% vote	Seats
					Pro Patria/ESRP Union	7.9	8
					Moderates	6.0	6
					Others	23.4	11
Georgia	Oct 1992		Mixed (2 systems – single-member, simple majority constituencies; multimember constituencies filled by p.r.)		Mshvidoba (Peace) Bloc		29
					October 11 Bloc		18
					Unity Bloc		14
					National Democratic Party		12
					Greens		11
					Others		151
	Nov 1995	5%	Mixed (2 systems – single-member, absolute majority constituencies with run-off provision; multimember constituencies filled by p.r.)	64.0	Union of Citizens of Georgia	23.7	109
					National Democratic Party	7.9	34
					All-Georgia Union for Revival	6.8	31
					Others		61
Kazakhstan	Mar 1994[e]		Mixed (135 members in single-member, simple majority constituencies; 42 from list presented by president)	73.5	Congress of National Unity of Kazakhstan		30
					Trades Union Federation		11
					People's Congress of Kazakhstan		9
					Socialist Party		8
					Others		119
	Dec 1995		Single-member, absolute majority constituencies with run-off provision	78.0	Party of National Unity of Kazakhstan		
					Democratic Party		
Kyrgyzstan	Feb 1995		Single-member absolute majority constituencies with run-off provision and 50% turnout requirement	62.0: 61.1	Ata Meken		
					Social Democratic Party		
					Communist Party		
					Party of Kyrgyzstan Unity		
					Others		
Latvia	June 1993	4%	Multimember local constituencies, filled by p.r.	80.4	Latvia's Way	32.4	36
					National Independence Movement of Latvia	13.3	15
					Concord for Latvia	12.0	13
					Latvian Farmers' Union	10.6	12
					Others		24

Table 7.2 cont.

Country	Date	Electoral system[a]	Minimum threshold for party/bloc representation	Turnout (%)[b]	Results[c] Parties	% of votes	Seats
	Sept–Oct 1995	Similar to 1993, but with higher threshold	5%		Saimnieks ('In Charge')	15.3	18
					Latvia's Way	14.7	17
					Popular Movement for Latvia	15.1	16
					For the Fatherland and Freedom	11.6	14
					Latvian Unity Party	7.2	8
					Latvian National Conservative Party	6.2	8
					Latvian Farmers' Union	6.1	8
					Others		11
Lithuania	Oct–Nov 1992	Mixed (2 systems – single-member, absolute majority constituencies; nationwide multimember constituency filled by p.r.)	4%	c.75	*Lithuanian Democratic Labour Party*	42.6	73
					Sajudis	20.5	30
					Lithuanian Christian Democratic Coalition	12.2	18
					Social Democrats	5.9	8
					Others		12
Moldova	Feb 1994	Single nationwide multimember constituency filled by p.r.	4%	79.3	*Agrarian Democratic Party*	43.2	56
					Socialist Party and Unity Movement Bloc	22.0	28
					Peasants' and Intellectuals' Bloc	9.2	11
					Christian Democratic Popular Front Alliance	7.5	9
Russia	Dec 1993	Mixed (2 systems – single-member constituencies, simple majority with 25% turnout requirement; nationwide multimember constituency filled by p.r.)	5%	54.8	Russia's Choice	15.4	70
					Liberal Democratic Party	22.8	64
					Communist Party	12.4	48
					Agrarian Party	7.9	33
					Women of Russia	8.1	23
					Yabloko Bloc	7.8	23
					Others (inc. independents)		183

Country	Date	Electoral system	Threshold	Turnout	Party	%	Seats
	Dec 1995	As in 1993	5%	64.4	*Communist Party*	22.3	157
					Our Home is Russia	10.1	55
					Liberal Democratic Party	11.2	51
					Yabloko	6.9	45
					Others (inc. independents)		142
Tajikistan	Feb–Mar 1995			c.84	*Communist Party*		60
Turkmenistan	Nov–Dec 1992	Single-member constituencies		99.5	*Turkmen Democratic Party*		
	Dec 1994	Single-member constituencies		99.8	*Turkmen Democratic Party*		
					(No other party permitted)		
					Independent candidates		
Ukraine	Mar–Apr 1994[d]	Single-member, absolute majority constituencies with run-off provision and 50% turnout requirement		74.7; 66.9	Left Bloc		118
					(of which *Communists*)		(86)
					National Democratic Bloc		33
					Liberal Bloc		9
					Rational Nationalist Bloc		7
					Independents		171
Uzbekistan	Dec 1994–Jan 1995	Single-member, absolute majority constituencies with run-off provision		93.6	*People's Democratic Party*		69
					Fatherland Progress Party		14
					Local nominees (inc. 120 PDP members)		167

[a] All countries have detailed further provisions concerning elections, but it is beyond the scope of this comparative overview to include them.

[b] When two figures are supplied, the election was in at least two rounds.

[c] Parties described as 'former communist', as well as actual communist parties and parties very closely aligned to the communists, are italicized. In bicameral legislatures, details are for the lower house. In cases of mixed electoral systems, the percentages cited usually refer only to the p.r. component.

[d] Many seats remained unfilled even after the run-off election – figures presented here refer to the post-second-round situation.

[e] These elections were declared invalid in March 1995.

Sources: RFE/RL Research Reports; East European Constitutional Review; Transition; KRWE; EIU Country Reports; OMRI Daily Digest.

days was widespread support for relatively nationalistic parties/blocs. This is in line with the reasons for and dynamic of post-communism elaborated in chapter 1. As some countries have moved on to their second or even third elections under post-communism, however, there have been signs that many voters have become nostalgic for *some* aspects of the communist period, notably the greater security. This development – the rise of parties often referred to as former communist – is analysed in chapter 12, in a discussion of what some media commentators have called a 'pink revolution'. At this point, it can be noted that former communist parties that incorporated a strong nationalist orientation performed well even in the first post-communist elections in countries such as Albania, Bulgaria and Ukraine; but, as indicated in chapter 6, there were allegations in many of these cases of unfair play by the former communists.

Turning to presidential elections – as part of the anti-communist revolutions, some post-communist countries have striven to move away from the situation under communism in which the *de facto* head of the party (the general/first secretary) and leader of the country was not only not elected by the mass electorate, but was only very indirectly elected even by the membership of the communist party itself. Given that the president in most post-communist states is intending to play a relatively active political role, it is seen as particularly important in some countries that the office of the presidency be popularly legitimated. This said, several post-communist states have opted to have the president elected by parliament.

As demonstrated in tables 7.3 and 7.4, as of late 1995 the president (or equivalent) of six east European countries (Bulgaria, Croatia, Republic of Macedonia, Poland, Romania and Slovenia) had been directly elected. The other countries have opted for indirect elections. In the case of Hungary, citizens were asked in a November 1989 referendum if they would prefer to elect their president directly; by a small margin, the voters opted to leave parliament (the National Assembly) to choose the head of state. In July 1990 the Hungarian electorate was again asked to vote on this issue in a referendum; only 13.8 per cent of the electorate bothered to vote, so that the National Assembly again elected the president (Goncz), in August 1990. Interestingly, all of the successor states of the FSU except Latvia have opted for direct elections.

In several of the post-communist states of eastern Europe and the FSU, citizens have had a choice of candidates in presidential elections. For instance, Lech Walesa stood against six candidates in the first round of the Polish presidential elections in November 1990 (and against 12 in 1995). Most observers were expecting Polish premier Tadeusz Mazowiecki to be the main competitor for Walesa in 1990. In fact, it was a Polish immigrant recently returned from Canada, Stanislaw Tyminski, who came second in the first round (with 23.1 per cent of the vote to Walesa's 39.9 per cent). It was therefore Tyminski who competed directly against Walesa in the second, run-off election in December. In the second round, Walesa secured almost 75 per cent of the vote, despite (or perhaps because of) Tyminski's

Table 7.3 Presidents (or equivalent) of the east European successor states (December 1995)

Country	President (or equivalent)	Date first took office	Date of most recent election	Method of selection	Contested	Term of office (years)
Albania	S. Berisha	April 1992	April 1992	Indirect	No	5
Bosnia-Hercegovina	A. Izetbegovic	December 1990	December 1990	Indirect (but direct elections to collective presidency)	Yes (in that elections to collective presidency were contested)	
Bulgaria	Z. Zhelev	August 1990	January 1992	Direct, run-off provision	Yes	5
Croatia	F. Tudjman	May 1990	August 1992	Direct	Yes	5
Czechia	V. Havel	December 1989 (at that time, for all Czecho-Slovakia)	January 1993	Indirect	Yes	5
Hungary	A. Goncz	May 1990	June 1995	Indirect	Yes	5
Rep. of Macedonia	K. Gligorov	January 1991	October 1994	Direct	Yes	5
Poland	A. Kwasniewski	December 1995	November 1995	Direct, run-off provision	Yes	5
Romania	I. Iliescu	December 1989	Sept.–Oct. 1992	Direct, run-off provision	Yes	4
Slovakia	M. Kovac	February 1993	February 1993	Indirect, run-off provision	Yes	5
Slovenia	M. Kucan	April 1990	December 1992	Direct, run-off provision	Yes	5
Yugoslavia (Rump – Serbia and Montenegro)	Z. Lilic	June 1993	June 1993	Indirect	Yes	4

Sources: The World Factbook 1993–94; RFE/RL Research Reports; KRWE; McGregor 1994; OMRI Daily Digest.

Table 7.4 Presidents (or equivalent) of the successor states of the FSU (December 1995)

Country	President (or equivalent)	Date first took office	Date of most recent election	Method of selection	Contested	Term of office (years)
Armenia	L. Ter-Petrossyan	October 1991	October 1991	Direct	Yes	
Azerbaijan	G. Aliev	June 1993	October 1993	Direct	No	5
Belarus	A. Lukashenka	July 1994	July 1994	Direct, run-off provision	Yes	
Estonia	L. Meri	October 1992	October 1992	Direct in principle, but actually elected by parliament in 1992	Yes	5
Georgia	E. Shevardnadze	March 1992	November 1995	Direct	Yes	3
Kazakhstan	N. Nazarbayev	April 1990	December 1991	Direct	No	5[a]
Kyrgyzstan	A. Akayev	October 1990	December 1995	Direct	Yes	5
Latvia	G. Ulmanis	July 1993	July 1993	Indirect, run-off provision	Yes	3
Lithuania	A. Brazauskas	February 1993	February 1993	Direct	Yes	5
Moldova	M. Snegur	September 1990	December 1991	Direct	No	5
Russia	B. Yeltsin	May 1990	June 1991	Direct, run-off provision	Yes	5 (4 from 1996)
Tajikistan	I. Rakhmonov	September 1991	November 1994	Direct	Yes	
Turkmenistan	S. Niyazov	June 1992	June 1992	Direct (but parliament nominates who electorate can vote for)	No	5[b]
Ukraine	L. Kuchma	July 1994	July 1994	Direct – run-off provision	Yes	5
Uzbekistan	I. Karimov	March 1990	December 1991	Direct	Yes	5[c]

[a] Following a referendum in April 1995, term of office extended to December 2000.
[b] Following a referendum in February 1994, term of office extended to 1999.
[c] Following a referendum in December 1994, term of office extended to 2000.

Sources: The World Factbook 1993–94; RFE/RL Research Reports; Staff of CSCE; Joeste 1991; *East European Constitutional Review;* OMRI *Daily Digest.*

somewhat unrealistic claims that he would be able to take Poland to a thriving market economy with very little pain for the population.[9]

One of the potential drawbacks of having presidents popularly elected is that this can give them a strong sense of popular legitimacy, which may in turn render them more willing to fight parliaments – even if this increases political instability and fragility – than might otherwise be the case. This is probably a major reason why some post-communist parliaments have opted for indirect elections, even though these may appear less democratic. In the next but one section, examples of such power struggles will be considered, since they have become a salient feature of post-communist politics. At this point, however, a brief overview of the new legislative and executive arrangements is appropriate.

But before finishing this section, it should be noted that the *referendum* has been widely used in the post-communist world. While there were also referenda in the communist era, they have in the 1990s been used more frequently. Citizens have been consulted on new constitutions; on economic and other policies; on voting systems – and sometimes fairly obviously as a means for defeating opponents. In addition to those already cited, examples will be given below (on referenda see White and Hill 1996).

LEGISLATURES AND EXECUTIVES

Much of the basic information on the legislatures of the post-communist world can be found in tables 7.5 and 7.6; this is mostly self-explanatory, but a few observations are in order.

First, there is no consensus on whether legislatures should have one chamber or two. Not even historical precedent is a fail-safe indicator. Thus Czechoslovakia had a bicameral assembly from 1969; when the country divided, Czechia formally opted for a bicameral arrangement (although it is not intending to introduce an upper house until late 1996), whereas Slovakia chose a single-chamber one, thereby breaking an agreement made in the last days of the Czecho-Slovak state. In those communist states that have adopted bicameral arrangements, it appears that this is mostly in broad emulation of typical Western practices, and is seen as another dimension of the division of powers. By having an upper house, there is another check on the activities of the lower. In the communist era, the bicameral arrangements in the three federal states – the USSR, Yugoslavia and Czechoslovakia – were designed to provide ethnic representation; despite the break-up of these multi-ethnic states, this concept has been partly retained in both Russia (see below) and the rump of Yugoslavia, Serbia-Montenegro. It should be noted that although the CIS does not yet have a multistate legislature, it has established a body to bring together delegates of the new legislatures, the Inter-parliamentary Assembly. It is possible that a CIS legislature will be created in the future, perhaps along the lines of the EU's European Parliament. At the time of writing, however, tensions between some of the members of the CIS mean that such a development

Table 7.5 Legislatures of the east European successor states (December 1995)

Country	Name of legislature	Unicameral/Bicameral[a]	No. of seats	Max. term of office (years)
Albania	People's Assembly	U	140	4
Bosnia-Hercegovina	Assembly	B Chamber of Communes	110	4
		Chamber of Citizens	130	4
Bulgaria	National Assembly	U	240	4
Croatia	Assembly	B House of Municipalities	68	4
		House of Representatives	127	4
Czechia		B Senate[b]	81	6
		House of Representatives	200	4
Hungary	National Assembly	U	386	4
Rep. of Macedonia	National Assembly	U	120	4
Poland	National Assembly	B Senate	100	4
		Sejm	460	4
Romania	Parliament	B Senate	143	4
		Chamber of Deputies	341	4
Slovakia	National Council	U	150	4
Slovenia	National Assembly	B State Council	40	5
		Chamber of Deputies	90	4
Yugoslavia (Rump –	Federal Assembly	B Chamber of Republics	40	4
Serbia, Montenegro)		Chamber of Citizens	138	4

[a] For bicameral legislatures, the name of the upper chamber is given, then that of the lower.
[b] Had not been established by late 1995, although formation agreed in September 1995.

Sources: RFE/RL Research Reports; World Factbook 1993–94; Cohen 1995; KRWE; The Europa World Year Book 1993; Inter-Parliamentary Union 1995; OMRI Daily Digest.

Table 7.6 Legislatures of the successor states of the FSU (December 1995)

Country	Name of legislature	Unicameral/Bicameral[a]	No. of seats	Max. term of office (years)
Armenia	National Assembly	U	190	4
Azerbaijan	National Assembly	U	125	5
Belarus	Supreme Council	U	260	5
Estonia	State Assembly	U	101	4
Georgia	Parliament	U	235	3
Kazakhstan	Supreme Council	B Senate	47	5
		People's Assembly	67	5
Kyrgyzstan	Supreme Council	B Legislative Assembly	35	5
		People's Assembly	70	5
Latvia	Saiema	U	100	3
Lithuania	Seimas	U	141	4
Moldova	Parliament	U	104	5
Russia	Federal Assembly	B Federation Council	178	4
		State Duma	450	4
Tajikistan	Supreme Council	U	181	5
Turkmenistan	People's Council	U	50	5
Ukraine	Supreme Council	U	450	5
Uzbekistan	Supreme Council	U	250	5

[a] For bicameral legislatures, the name of the upper chamber is given, then that of the lower.

Sources: *RFE/RL Research Reports*; *World Factbook 1993–94*; *KRWE*; *The Europa World Year Book 1993*; EIU *Country Reports*; *Transition*; *Pravda*; Inter-Parliamentary Union 1995; OMRI *Daily Digest*.

seems unlikely in the short term. Indeed, it is not clear that the still fragile CIS will hold together in its current configuration.

The arrangements in Russia in the early 1990s – with what some have called a 'superparliament' in the form of the Congress of People's Deputies, and a smaller parliament, the Supreme Soviet – always appeared unlikely to last. In fact, that system collapsed with Yeltsin's closure of parliament in September 1993. By January 1994, Russia had a new bicameral Federal Assembly, comprising the Federation Council and the State Duma. The former represents the 89 republics (largely ethnically based administrative units) and regions of Russia, each of which has two deputies in the Council. The latter comprises 450 deputies, half of whom are elected on a proportional representation basis via nationwide party lists with a 5 per cent threshold, the other half of whom are elected in single-member constituencies on a simple majority basis.

The principal task of the legislatures of the post-communist states is, like most legislatures, to produce laws. They are also supposed to monitor the activities of and interact with the executives. Many of the post-communist legislatures have already become far more like their Western counterparts than were their communist predecessors. In several cases, they are now open debating chambers, where there are heated arguments, overt criticisms, and divided votes. In short, many have become genuine *parliaments* (that is, places for speaking and debate; for detailed analyses of the politics of new parliaments in Czecho-Slovakia, Hungary, Russia and Ukraine see Remington 1994a).

The term 'executive' is used here to include both the head of state and the government. As in the West, there is no single pattern to the conception of the role of head of state in the post-communist world. In most post-communist states (including Croatia, Kazakhstan, Poland, Romania, Russia, Turkmenistan and Ukraine), the president is clearly playing a major political role and is far more powerful and influential than the prime minister. In just a few (such as Czechia, Hungary, Slovakia, Slovenia, rump Yugoslavia), the president *appears* to play a less explicitly political, more ceremonial role – although McGregor (1994) questions the accuracy of this perception, especially regarding Hungary, where the president has a considerable range of powers. Certainly, the president is currently fulfilling a more overtly political function even in these states than does the head of state in the UK or Japan, for instance. Nevertheless, the prime ministers in these countries appear to be more powerful than their peers in more president-oriented post-communist systems.

Most commonly, the head of the government (the prime minister) is formally nominated by the president, ratified by parliament, then appointed by the president. The prime minister then nominates his or her ministers (government) – usually having to bear in mind coalition partners (most post-communist governments are coalitions) or other aspects of political balance between the dominant parties in parliament – who are then formally appointed by the president; one exception to this is Slovenia where, formally, the parliament appoints and dismisses ministers.

With this brief description of the *formal* institutions of the executive and legislative wings in mind, the relations between these two in the *practice* of early post-communism can be considered. In the next section, the focus gradually moves away from constitutional and abstract description and towards an analysis of real politics.

PRESIDENTS, PRIME MINISTERS AND PARLIAMENTS

One reason why the balance of power between presidents and prime ministers varies across the post-communist world is that in creating their political systems many post-communist politicians looked to Western arrangements as potential role models – only to discover that Western democratic systems and constitutional arrangements differ, sometimes considerably. This said, most democracies tend towards one of *three* possible models in terms of where most power in the system lies: presidentialism, semi-presidentialism and parliamentarism (for a more nuanced approach, identifying five configurations, see Shugart 1993).

Fairly obviously, the first of these concentrates power in the office of the head of state, who acts in a real sense as the chief executive. The president is more or less directly elected by the citizenry for a fixed term, and typically cannot be removed by parliament. In this arrangement, the government is under far greater presidential control than parliamentary control (for instance, the president rather than parliament appoints the government, and he or she also actually heads it). Only one First World country, the USA, has such an arrangement, although it has also been a popular model in Latin America.

The parliamentary approach focuses on the legislature, although it must be emphasized that there are a number of differing parliamentary models in the West. Typically, and within a range that varies, the head of the government (the prime minister) has considerably more powers in such a system than does any other individual. It might therefore appear that there is in practical terms little difference between a presidential system and a parliamentary one in which the prime minister has wide-ranging powers. But the difference *is* more than just the semantic one of 'the' leader being the head of state or head of the government. In the parliamentary case, 'the' leader and chief executive officer is still very much part of the legislature: he or she participates in parliamentary debates, and is directly and regularly answerable to other parliamentarians. The leader in such a system is controlled and legitimated primarily by parliament rather than by the electorate or the head of state. In this type of system, heads of state are typically either elected by the legislature or bodies answerable to it, or else, in the case of constitutional monarchies, occupy their position on the basis of tradition and heredity. Normally, the role of the head of state in such systems is largely ceremonial. Such systems do not have as clear-cut a separation of powers between the legislative and executive wings as does the American. Countries having variants of this model include the UK (the 'Westminster model') and Germany (where the prime minister – called the chancellor – has far more power than does the president).

The term semi-presidential is generally attributed to Maurice Duverger, who coined it in the 1970s; his first major analysis of the concept in English was published in 1980. It refers to systems in which there is a popularly elected president with considerable powers, rather than a largely ceremonial role, but who faces a prime minister and government that require some parliamentary support (Duverger 1980). In short, the president is less powerful than in a presidential system, yet more powerful than in a parliamentary system. Several other terms have been used to describe such an arrangement, such as quasi-presidentialism and semi-parliamentarism; this reflects the fact that, as with the other systems, there are in the real world several versions of the basic model. A semi-presidential system was first adopted in the Weimar Republic (Germany) after the First World War, where it was not a resounding success. But many analysts accept that contemporary France, Finland and Portugal demonstrate that semi-presidential systems can be both stable and efficient.

As indicated, only one major Western country has a presidential system, and several observers (see Riggs 1988, Linz 1994) have questioned its appropriateness for the contemporary USA. Many maintain that such an arrangement either encourages dictatorship or, in countries where there is a deeply entrenched liberal democratic culture, increases the likelihood of delayed or overly compromised decision-making. Many in the post-communist world feel they cannot afford delayed or overly compromised decision-making, yet fear the possibility of dictatorship; consequently, the presidential model has in many countries enjoyed relatively little overt support. On the other hand, parliamentary systems appear to work well only if there is a well-developed party system and a relatively high level of party discipline. Since post-communist systems have neither, the parliamentary model would at present also appear to be inappropriate.

By a process of elimination, therefore, it might seem that post-communist states should at this stage opt for semi-presidential systems; indeed, although many *claim* to be primarily parliamentary, several appear in practice to have done so. One necessary if insufficient indicator of this is that so many countries have introduced direct elections for the presidency. Another is that many new constitutions stipulate that governments are answerable – albeit in different ways and to varying degrees – to both the head of state and parliament.

Semi-presidential systems are often seen as particularly appropriate for transitional societies, of which the post-communist states are prime examples. But this model has its disadvantages, too. Since the government is more or less equally answerable to both the president and parliament, it can be caught in the crossfire between the two if there is a major conflict, which in turn can result in policy-making stalemate. Indeed, as Baylis (1996) points out, in many post-communist countries presidents have – at least at the time of their election – reasonably high levels of popular legitimacy but few real powers, whereas many prime ministers have considerable power but little legitimacy; this means there are structural factors tending to increase the likelihood of conflict. Moreover, as in any system, the personalities of the incumbents of senior offices can dramatically affect the efficacy of a particular arrangement, no matter how carefully the designers of that arrangement – the constitutional architects – attempt to overcome or limit the impact of individuals. Other things being equal, there is likely to be less conflict and fewer delays in decision-making where there is a president with a strong personality and clear policy preferences working with a weak prime minister who has a relatively underdeveloped personal agenda; and, conversely, more conflict and delays where *both* the president and the prime minister have strong personalities and clearly defined – and different – policy preferences. Given this and other drawbacks, some analysts (such as Stepan and Skach 1993) have argued that parliamentarism is in fact a better arrangement for consolidating democracy than is semi-presidentialism or presidentialism. Certainly, attempts to create a proper parliamentary system can help to strengthen party systems in a way presidential, and to a lesser extent semi-presidential, systems do not. Considered from a slightly different perspective, parties cannot be certain of their role and status until it is clear which of the three basic models has been adopted (Hill 1994, pp. 103–4).

At the start of this discussion of models of elite politics, it was argued that *democracies* tend towards one or other of the three. Ultimately, there are advantages and drawbacks to all three: how well one of them works relative to other possibilities depends largely on the particular political culture and set of circumstances. Where a political culture does not include a well-established tradition of compromise and mutual respect for 'the rules of the game', *none* of the three models will function as well as where such a tradition exists. Similarly, any arrangement will be more troubled where there is an economic crisis, for instance, than where the economy is performing well.

In no post-communist state are the traditions of either compromise or rule of law well established, even though some states have so far made better headway in developing these than have others. Once again, the very fluidity of early post-communism means that different political actors have different views both on what type of system would be optimal at this juncture and on what type should be sought in the longer term. These differences – cultural, politico-structural and personal (including personality clashes between politicians) – help to explain why, despite the professed preference of many post-communist politicians for the parliamentary or semi-presidential models, in practice examples of all three models can be found in the contemporary post-communist world. Thus, in his classification of 25 early post-communist states (plus the Czech and Slovak republics prior to 1993), Remington (1994b, pp. 13–15) identifies seven (Azerbaijan, Georgia, Kazakhstan, Kyrgyzstan, Russia, Turkmenistan and Uzbekistan) as presidential, nine (Albania, Belarus, Bulgaria, Czecho-Slovakia, the GDR, Hungary, Latvia, Slovenia and Tajikistan) as parliamentary and nine (Armenia, Croatia, Estonia, Lithuania, Moldova, Poland, Romania, Ukraine and rump Yugoslavia) as semi-presidential. Not only do recent constitutional changes, and likely future ones, in some of these countries suggest the need for reclassification, but there is also often a gap between formal descriptions of what *should* exist and perceived reality. Moreover, much is still in flux. Hence, while it is useful to consider abstract models as possible end goals, it is also important in any serious attempt at understanding post-communist institutional politics to study actual examples of elite political conflict.

During most of the communist period, analysts typically had to speculate about much of what was happening at the top of the political system (for a fine example of such 'Kremlinology' see Tatu 1970). In marked contrast, elite politics in most post-communist states is often highly visible. Tensions between presidents, prime ministers and parliaments are in many cases openly reported and analysed in both domestic and foreign media. An examination of the history of relations between the executive and the legislature in Russia and Poland will provide concrete examples of the kinds of problems that have arisen.

Boris Yeltsin was elected *de facto* president by the Russian legislature in May 1990. In June 1991 he became the first-ever directly elected President of Russia. In much of the subsequent debate between Yeltsin and the two-tiered legislature as it existed until September 1993, the president played on the fact that he was elected in properly contested elections, whereas elections to the legislature had been held at a time when Russia (and the USSR more generally) was still very much under communist influence. Moreover, the more powerful chamber of the legislature, the Supreme Soviet, had not been directly elected. In short, Yeltsin claimed greater popular legitimacy.

It will be recalled from chapter 4 that in August 1991 it was Yeltsin more than anyone who publicly challenged those attempting to take power via a coup d'état. Particularly given that the plot failed, Yeltsin was for a time seen as a national hero, almost as someone who had led a new revolution. In short, he briefly enjoyed a high level of charismatic legitimacy.

For much of the rest of 1991, Yeltsin's primary political struggle was with Gorbachev, who did not resign as Soviet leader until Christmas Day 1991. But with Gorbachev gone, Yeltsin discovered that many of his own former supporters had begun to turn against him.

In a sense, the rot started in November 1991, when Yeltsin announced that Russia was to move to a fully marketized system, and that he was to be prime minister as well as president. At the time, the Congress of People's Deputies *appeared* to support him; the president was still far too popular for them to do otherwise, and the economy was in such dire straits that many conceded there might be a real need for a radical approach. The Congress therefore granted Yeltsin special powers for one year, and permitted him – via his first deputy prime minister, Gaidar – to introduce radical reforms in January 1992. They did this even though the speaker of parliament, Ruslan Khasbulatov, had already expressed misgivings about such a concentration of power into Yeltsin's hands.

By April 1992 it was clear that many members of the Congress had serious reservations about developments in their country. At the sixth session of the Congress held that month, major differences emerged between Yeltsin and the legislature. Under pressure, the president agreed to deconcentrate power by transferring the premiership and much of his control over the economy to Gaidar. But he soon *increased* his hold over security matters, foreign affairs and defence, when he established a new Security Council in June 1992. It was also at about this time that he started calling for a referendum, to allow the Russian people to decide for themselves the kind of political system they wanted.

By mid-1992, parliament was increasingly forming into discernible groups. Despite these divisions within the legislature, there was enough commonality of view for the Congress to constitute a relatively solid bloc of opposition to Yeltsin. By December, Congress was sufficiently hostile to the president that it both refused to extend his special powers and, initially, to grant his request for a referendum. Eventually, it *did* concede to a referendum, but on different issues from those Yeltsin wanted. The president also made concessions, notably in sacrificing his radical acting prime minister Gaidar in December 1992 and replacing him with the more cautious Viktor Chernomyrdin. When Chernomyrdin claimed that Russia needed 'a market, not a bazaar', he was widely interpreted to be saying that he intended to keep the reins on the marketization process in Russia. However, when he announced his government in late December, the new prime minister retained many of the same people Gaidar had had in his government, so that it was unclear how much of a slowdown or reversal of policy Russians could expect.

In its early stages, the conflict between the Russian president and parliament was conducted primarily in terms of policy differences, particularly concerning the economy. Many parliamentarians considered that Yeltsin was forging ahead too rapidly with reform, and that he was pursuing the wrong *sequence* in the reforms (see next chapter). But by late 1992 at the latest, it had become obvious that personality clashes were also an important aspect of Russian elite politics. By then, one of the harshest critics of the president was Arkadii Volskii, who, together with Alexander Rutskoi, spearheaded the parliamentary group most challenging to Yeltsin, Civic Union.

By early 1993 two leading politicians who had once been very close to Yeltsin, Rutskoi and Khasbulatov, had become his most outspoken and influential critics. On various occasions, both men repeated charges that had often been made since 1991 that Yeltsin was becoming increasingly dictatorial. Rutskoi, in particular, also claimed that several members of the Yeltsin team were corrupt, although he stopped short of making such claims about the president himself.

By March 1993, tensions between Yeltsin and much of the rest of the political elite had reached boiling point. The president attempted to impose special rule. This only confirmed the suspicions of those who had been arguing that he had a proclivity towards dictatorship.

After a vicious and open debate between Yeltsin and parliament in the early part of 1993, the president was eventually able to take the elite struggle to the masses in the form of a referendum. It will be recalled that this had been proposed by Yeltsin as early as mid-1992 (with a very overt call in December), but could take place only with the formal approval of the Congress. The referendum contained four questions, and related very much to the balance of power between the president and the legislature. The first question asked voters if they had confidence in the president. Approximately 59 per cent of the nearly 65 per cent of the electorate who participated in the referendum indicated they did. To the surprise of many both in Russia and the West, a majority (53 per cent) of those who voted also indicated general support for Yeltsin's economic package, despite the inflation and generally very poor economic situation in Russia. Over 67 per cent of the voters favoured early parliamentary elections, and slightly less than half favoured early presidential elections. Overall, and for reasons too complex to elaborate here, a majority of those who had exercised their right to vote had supported the president rather than the parliament.

But the referendum did not represent a complete victory for Yeltsin. Under rules adopted by Congress before the referendum and endorsed by the Constitutional Court after Yeltsin supporters had tried to overturn them, at least 50 per cent of the *total* electorate would have had to have supported the notion of early parliamentary elections for the vote to have been binding (on the April 1993 referendum see Tolz and Wishnevsky 1993,

Corning 1993). Yeltsin thus failed to achieve the required level of support for his demand for such elections.

Despite criticisms of, and ambiguities in, various aspects of the referendum, Yeltsin claimed the electorate had shown he was the only legitimate authority in Russia. Anyone unaware of the essential unpredictability of the current Russian president could be mistaken for assuming that this would have encouraged him to forge ahead with the radical economic reforms he was at that time seeking. But shortly after the referendum, Yeltsin appointed two new deputy premiers known to be cautious about economic reform, Oleg Lobov and Oleg Soskovets. This was possibly because Yeltsin was prepared to be magnanimous in (near) victory. Certainly, several of his former opponents became more positively disposed towards Yeltsin following the referendum (one important exception being Khasbulatov), so that he may simply have decided it was better to compromise and work on a consensual basis than to continue to delay Russia's recovery while he and the parliament squabbled.

While it is possible to produce a sympathetic reading of Yeltsin's actions after the April referendum, there is also a more critical one. According to this, Yeltsin's actions constituted another example of the unpredictability that made some members of the legislature so wary of him. Another example of this inconsistency was the president's attitude towards a new constitution. Two days before the April 1993 referendum, Yeltsin announced the major features of a new draft Russian constitution. This was not the first such draft, but in that it emanated from the presidency, it was treated by some as more serious than earlier versions. Many observers, both within Russia and in the West, noted that the arrangements proposed in the Yeltsin constitution of April 1993 would have given the president dramatically enhanced powers over parliament. But another draft – prepared by the executive secretary of the Constitutional Commission, Oleg Rumyantsev – was published at the end of April 1993. This version envisaged more extensive powers for parliament, and far fewer for the president; predictably, it appeared to enjoy the support of Khasbulatov. The great irony was that Yeltsin himself had formally chaired the commission that produced the 'Rumyantsev draft', as critics such as Rutskoi were quick to point out. Both drafts were eventually superseded anyway in November 1993, by yet another Yeltsin version.

This new constitution was adopted following the December 1993 referendum, and enhanced the formal powers of the president. The point made earlier about *interpreting* such a document still pertains, however. It is never possible, or indeed desirable, to specify too precisely the relationship between a president and a parliament. There must always be room for new interpretations in the light of changing situations. This said, there should also always be built-in safeguards to ensure that no one individual concentrates so much power that he or she can totally disregard the other agencies of a democracy. Many considered that the new constitution too clearly increased presidential powers at the expense of parliament, and contained insufficient safeguards. Even those critics who believed that Yeltsin himself was unlikely to attempt to become a dictator feared that a successor would be able to establish a *de facto* dictatorship on the basis of the new document's provisions.

Despite these concerns, the level of tension between the Russian president and parliament was *lower* for most of 1994 than it had been in 1993. In order to understand this general improvement, it is necessary to start by considering the extraordinary events in Moscow in late 1993. In September the relationship between Yeltsin and parliament became so strained that the president shut down the legislature. Most commentators agree that Yeltsin's move was unconstitutional; indeed, the Russian Constitutional Court subsequently declared it so (see Reid 1995). It was therefore perhaps not surprising that several parliamentarians refused to move from the parliamentary building (Moscow's White House). They were soon joined by other rebels, including paramilitary forces, opposed to the president. These rebels then attacked the offices of the mayor of Moscow, as well as Russia's principal television station, killing many in the process. At that point (October 1993), Yeltsin ordered troops to fire on the White House. Many more were killed, and the leaders of the anti-Yeltsin camp, including both Rutskoi and Khasbulatov, were arrested. So ended the conflict between Yeltsin and parliament.

Yeltsin could almost certainly have imposed a dictatorship in late 1993 had he chosen to do so. He did not. Instead, he organized parliamentary elections for December. Some of Yeltsin's actions during the pre-election period, such as shutting down several newspapers, deserve to be criticized. Nevertheless, the facts are that the elections were held, and conducted *reasonably* properly; that Yeltsin accepted the results of these elections; and that a new, popularly mandated parliament was established as a result. Initially, it appeared that since the new parliament enjoyed greater popular legitimacy than its predecessor, it might therefore be even more willing to challenge the president, resulting in yet greater conflict. But there were at least two more powerful countervailing forces operating, which help to explain why, despite numerous relatively minor conflicts between the president and parliament during 1994, the relationship was overall *less* strained than it had been in late 1992 and 1993.

First, parliamentarians had seen for themselves that Yeltsin would, given sufficient provocation, use force and even violence against a difficult legislature. Few were prepared to risk a repeat of the October 1993 bloodshed.

Second, the results of the December 1993 elections revealed that a substantial minority of Russians were willing to support extremists: Zhirinovskii's Liberal Democrats and the resurrected communist party had between them secured over 35 per cent of the party list votes to the lower house (State Duma), and 112 of its 450 seats. Given that Yeltsin had not only held elections, but also accepted the results of these, many now began to look at him in a more favourable light. There appeared to be less danger of a true dictatorship emerging under Yeltsin than there would were Zhirinovskii or one of the other extremist leaders somehow to assume power. This fear of a far more dictatorial system – the so-called Zhirinovskii factor – was a major reason for the improved relationship between the president and most parliamentarians following the 1993 elections.

Other factors also helped to improve the atmosphere in Russian elite politics during 1994. For instance, parliament declared an amnesty in February for those imprisoned for their role in the events of August 1991 and September–October 1993; as a result, Rutskoi and Khasbulatov, among others, were released from prison. Yeltsin accepted this, albeit reluctantly. Another positive development was the growing reputation of and faith in Yeltsin's prime minister, Chernomyrdin. His image as a sensible and reliable politician who could steer a steady centrist course through heated debates enhanced both his standing and that of the president who had chosen him. In fact, Chernomyrdin's image improved so much that some believed by mid-1994 that he might have been in a position to challenge Yeltsin; he certainly appeared to have become more assertive towards his president. But a rouble crisis in October 1994, for which the prime minister received much of the blame, temporarily marred Chernomyrdin's image and reduced the likelihood that he would mount a serious challenge to the president – at least in the short term.

Unfortunately, tensions at the top of the Russian political system had begun to increase again by the end of 1994 and early 1995. Two major factors were Yeltsin's decision to use high levels of military force in Chechnya (see next section) – which was strongly criticized even by long-term allies such as Gaidar – and the president's increasing tendency to appear in public in a highly inebriated condition. The latter annoyed both parliamentarians and citizens, especially when Yeltsin appeared drunk overseas (notably in Ireland and Germany in late 1994); many felt the president was humiliating not only himself but also Russia. Particularly for a country that had just lost an empire and was experiencing an identity crisis, such behaviour was unacceptable. Given this, it seemed as of late 1995 unlikely that Yeltsin would win the presidential election scheduled for June and July 1996. But Russian politics remained too volatile to permit confident predictions, and by May 1996, opinion polls suggested Yeltsin was rapidly gaining ground on his main opponent, communist leader Gennadii Zyuganov. Yeltsin did in fact win the 1996 election.

Aspects of the Russian debate and developments can be found in other post-communist states. In many cases, leaders who once were popular heroes and claimed to be committed to democracy have subsequently been accused of having dictatorial tendencies. When such charges have been made, a typical response is for the accused to refer to their own popular legitimacy and/or to test this; it has already been demonstrated how Yeltsin did this in April 1993 via a referendum. But another response is for presidents to assert themselves, testing the limits of their powers and hence, indirectly, their level of legitimacy. This was the path taken by Lech Walesa in Poland in May 1993. The story warrants recounting.

Lech Walesa first became known to both the majority of Poles and the outside world in the autumn of 1980. As Solidarity's role in Polish society increased, so did the profile of its leader. So when Walesa was elected (directly) President in December 1990, his fellow Poles were showing support for and confidence in someone who had stood up to communist power at least as much as they were opting for a democrat.

Virtually from the time of his election in December 1990, relations between President Walesa and parliament, especially the lower house (the Sejm), were almost constantly strained. In the early stages, until the genuinely free parliamentary elections of October 1991, Walesa and his supporters could claim that such tensions were a result of the political complexion of the lower house (it will be recalled from chapter 3 that the communists had allowed genuinely free elections to the Senate in June 1989, but had ensured their own continued dominance of the Sejm). Like Yeltsin in Russia from June 1991, the new Polish president could with some justification claim he was *more* legitimate than the (lower house of) parliament.

There was a major dispute between the Sejm and Walesa in 1991 over the forthcoming parliamentary elections. Part of the dispute centred on the *timing* of these; the Sejm won that argument. Then there were disagreements over the electoral *procedures*, with Walesa claiming that the Sejm's proposals were too complicated for most citizens to understand properly. This particular dispute resulted in an almost farcical – if it were not so serious – situation in July 1991: Walesa finally signed the new electoral law (which was much closer to the Sejm's wishes than his own) at the beginning of the month, and then three days later submitted his own revised version to the Sejm. The latter promptly, and not unexpectedly, rejected it.

In September 1991, with Walesa's support, the government attempted to increase its own powers by proposing rule by governmental decree on all major economic matters. This was rejected by the Sejm. In the following month, the Sejm also rejected the government's bill on a new Polish constitution, arguing that this would have excessively increased the powers of the executive at the expense of the legislature. Tensions between the two major wings of the political system were high.

Following the indecisive result of the October 1991 elections, Walesa proposed himself as prime minister. This suggestion was not popular with the new, and by most criteria legitimate, parliament. After weeks of bickering and attempts at compromise, Walesa reluctantly accepted that Jan Olszewski should be the new prime minister. But in the middle of December 1991, less than a fortnight after the president had formally nominated him as premier, Olszewski attempted to resign, following Walesa's criticisms of his cautious economic programme. The parliament refused to accept Olszewski's resignation, however, and he formed a government a few days later. At about the same time, Walesa withdrew proposals he had earlier made for constitutional change, after the Sejm had attempted to dilute them. The Polish president was losing the battle with his parliament.

But Walesa was unwilling to concede defeat and throughout 1992 continued to fight parliament. Despite an attempt by his opponents from June 1992 to discredit him (by suggesting he had been an informer during the communist era), Walesa scored some successes. He appeared to be in the ascendancy by the middle of the year, when Olszewski was obliged to resign and was eventually replaced by Poland's first female prime minister – and far more radical economic reformer – Hanna Suchocka. Following tensions between the Suchocka government and parliament, in January 1993 the government once again attempted to secure the right to issue its own legally binding decrees on economic matters. This was rejected. Suchocka presented a very tough budget and in February, following her threat to resign and Walesa's threat to dissolve parliament if the latter were not to adopt it, she managed to have it accepted by the legislature.

Opposition to the president continued to grow, however, particularly within Walesa's original power base, Solidarity. The latter considered the measures being taken to transform the economy too draconian, and believed they were placing an unduly heavy burden on ordinary working Poles. Eventually, in May, and following a three-week widespread strike in Poland, Solidarity instructed its deputies to the Sejm to table a no-confidence vote in Suchocka's government. Given his strong support for Suchocka, the vote had to be seen as a criticism of Walesa as much as of Suchocka herself. Moreover, the fact that Solidarity raised the issue testified to the level of estrangement that had arisen between the Polish president and his former power base. Although Solidarity had apparently not intended matters to go so far, the no-confidence motion was passed, by a mere one vote (223 for, 198 against, 24 abstentions).

This was too much for Walesa, who dissolved parliament. He also persuaded Suchocka to stay on as caretaker prime minister. As of mid-1993, therefore, Walesa had won the battle with his difficult and fragmented parliament. There was a great irony in this, as what must surely be seen as the most significant outcome of the May 1993 debacle was precisely what parliament had for so long been attempting to avoid – an excessive concentration of power in the president's hands (on all this see Vinton 1993a).

But Walesa did not become a dictator. Like Yeltsin, he held new parliamentary elections relatively quickly, in September 1993, and basically accepted the outcome of these. Walesa unquestionably displayed authoritarian leanings. For instance, it was well known even at the time of his election that he was a great admirer of the Polish dictator of the interwar years, Marshal Pilsudski, with whose situation he compared his own. Even some of those once close to him criticized Walesa for his authoritarian manner; in mid-1990 the former dissident Adam Michnik accused him of acting 'like a Caesar'. Yet it is important to distinguish between strong leaders and dictators. As long as the former continue to show respect for the ballot box and the constitution, for instance, they are not dictators. Walesa was replaced as president by Alexander Kwasniewski in December 1995 by democratic, constitutional means. Although he protested about irregularities in the presidential election, Walesa ultimately accepted its outcome.

Numerous further examples of political struggle between presidents and parliament in the post-communist world could be cited. Major power struggles have occurred between both the past president of Ukraine, Kravchuk, and his successor, Kuchma, and their parliaments (see next subsection).

President Havel had several clashes with the Czecho-Slovak parliament, and has had differences with the new Czech legislature. President Berisha was less fortunate than Yeltsin when he put a proposal for increased powers to the Albanian electorate via a referendum in November 1994: more than 60 per cent of the voters opposed his suggested constitutional amendments, thus supporting the parliament over the president. Conversely, the Belarusian citizenry supported President Lukashenka against his parliament in a May 1995 referendum; this took place shortly after the president had ordered police to remove from parliament some 20 opposition deputies who had been staging a hunger strike in protest at his plans to hold the referendum. In April 1993, the president of Kyrgyzstan, Akayev, strongly criticized the parliament that had been trying to remove some of his powers – and, in an interesting example of role reversal, accused parliament of becoming dictatorial (*FBIS-Sov-93-072*, 16 April 1993, p. 38). Evidence of differences – not only of policy, but also of principle (who is responsible for what, for example) – can be found in most other post-communist states.

Although the focus in this section has justifiably been on the relationships and tensions between heads of state and parliaments, the relationship between both of these and the head of government can also be troublesome. This is to be expected particularly in countries tending towards semi-presidentialism or where the system has still not properly crystallized. Examples have already been alluded to in the references to differences between Yeltsin and Chernomyrdin in Russia, Walesa and Olszewski in Poland, and the Sejm and Suchocka in Poland. Numerous further instances of both – tensions between the president and the prime minister, and between the prime minister and the parliament – could be cited.

An example of the first was the ongoing conflict throughout 1993 between the Estonian president (Meri), on the one hand, and his prime minister (Laar) and parliament, on the other, partly relating to differences over policy on citizenship (see chapter 10). This reached a peak in January 1994, when parliament began discussing a draft law on the presidency, on the grounds that the formal position of the president in the constitution was too vague. Both the prime minister and the parliament made it clear they considered Estonia to be a parliamentary system rather than a presidential one, and made proposals in the draft law designed to limit presidential powers.

The most significant conflicts between prime ministers and parliament tend to occur in countries orienting themselves more towards parliamentarism, where the premiership is a powerful position. A good example is Slovakia, which experienced political problems within days of becoming fully independent. In January 1993, prime minister Vladimar Meciar failed to have his preferred candidate, Roman Kovac, elected president of the new state by parliament, and in the following month had to accept Michal Kovac (no relation to Roman). This was both a setback and a humiliation for the man who likes to think he led his people to freedom from Czech domination. Tensions became so great that Meciar was removed from office (formally by the president) in March 1994. But Meciar made a comeback in the September–October 1994 parliamentary elections, and has taken on both the president and hostile elements within the new parliament.

The significance of all these conflicts is considered in the conclusions. Before this, however, it is necessary briefly to analyse state bodies other than the topmost legislative and executive bodies, and the issue of constitutionalism in the post-communist world.

OTHER STATE ORGANS

It is not possible here to elaborate and analyse all the new state organs in the post-communist world. In any case, much is still in flux and has yet to be properly researched. This section will therefore merely list the major branches that need to be considered, and make a few somewhat random observations, based mostly on what appear, from both the literature and interviews, to be the most important issues.

Any modern state requires a large administration, often somewhat pejoratively called the state bureaucracy, to implement its policies. Since communist states were far more interventionist than any liberal democratic state, they might be expected to have had much larger bureaucracies than the new post-communist states, given the conscious efforts of the latter substantially to reduce the state's role in the economy. The early evidence suggests this is not necessarily the case. Thus, according to the director of the Institute of Socio-Political Research of the Russian Academy of Sciences, the state apparatus in Russia alone was, by the end of 1992, larger than the *combined* central state and party apparatus of the former USSR and RSFSR, while some of Yeltsin's opponents claimed early in 1993 that the staff of Yeltsin's Council of Ministers (government) was approximately two-and-a-half to three times *larger* than its Soviet equivalent had been under former Soviet prime ministers Ryzhkov and Pavlov (in Yasmann 1993a, p. 18).

But should such figures be surprising? On one level, an increase at a time of serious power struggle might be expected, as the major contenders each seek to build up as large and powerful a support staff as possible. Even dismissing this essentially Machiavellian explanation, the post-communist states are implementing new 'revolutions from above'; although the end goal of so many governments is allegedly much less state intervention in the economy and society, the *process* of reaching that end goal takes time and effort.

In the next two chapters, some of the many new tasks for the post-communist states will be analysed. All these processes require staffs. Thus, while the state might be seeking to be less involved in planning and price-setting, it has a major role to play in devising and administering privatization schemes, such as issuing coupons, determining the best ways to sell off factories, etc. While many states are less involved than they were in running child-care facilities, they now administer unemployment benefits schemes, monitor citizen payment of income tax (to which there has been strong resistance in several countries), etc. And many post-communist states are having to address the problems of environmental degradation more seriously than did their communist predecessors.

Some of these tasks should in principle be relatively short term, such as the process of uncoupling the economy; this should eventually lead to a downsizing of the state administrative organs. Thus the GDR set up the *Treuhandanstalt* in 1990 specifically to sell off East German enterprises. This organization employed a large number of administrators, but it was downsized by early 1994, and shut altogether at the end of that year. Other tasks, on the other hand, will be ongoing (such as new forms of welfarism). Hence, while a reduction in the size and scope of post-communist state bureaucracies in the future is likely, the difference in scale compared with the communist period might be less than initially anticipated. This difference will vary from country to country, depending partly on whether the governments tend to be more market oriented or more social democratic (*ceteris paribus*, the latter would be expected to have larger state bureaucracies). But even in well-established market-oriented systems in the West, demands for consumer protection, a better environment, etc., often result in the growth of bureaucracies.

In the communist world, the most hated wing of the state in many countries was the security (secret) police. One of the professed aims of many post-communist governments has been to dismantle these agencies; certainly, many have been disbanded since 1989. There has also been an opening up of these agencies' files to public scrutiny in several countries, partly as a result of which some of the most popular politicians of earliest post-communism (such as Lothar de Maiziere of the Christian Democratic Union, in what was the GDR) either have been obliged, or have felt a personal need, to resign.

However, the break with the past has been slower and less decisive in some countries than it might have been. Although the KGB was disbanded in Russia shortly after the August 1991 attempted coup, it was in essence soon replaced by a Ministry of Security, which many saw as a *de facto* replacement for the KGB (see Yasmann 1993b); not until late 1993 did Yeltsin, believing the loyalty of the security forces to have been in question during the September–October crisis, disband the Ministry of Security and engage in a radical restructuring of Russia's security organs (for details see Yasmann 1994; Yasmann 1993d argues convincingly that the security forces were in fact divided over the September–October events). In the case of Romania, a disturbing development emerged in early 1993. Several former Securitate officers banded together under the leadership of Gheorghe Ivascu and declared themselves ready to restore order and honour to Romania, if needed. They voiced serious misgivings about the new democratic order in Romania, in a way that should and did concern many people committed to the consolidation of democracy there.

In light of this Romanian example, the unambiguous role of certain senior members of the KGB in the attempted coup in Russia in August

1991, and the doubts raised in Russia in late 1993 (for instance, because of the anti-Yeltsin role played by Deputy Minister of Internal Affairs Andrei Dunaev), the potential of the security police to pose a threat to any political system – especially fragile fledgling democracies such as the post-communist states – should not be underestimated. But at least as great a potential danger is posed by the military. Since it would be of greater significance to the whole world, not just domestically, if the former Soviet military were to assert itself politically than if any other in the post-communist world were to do so (partly because of sheer numbers, partly because some of the member states of the CIS were as of 1995 still nuclear powers), a focus on the formerly Soviet army in the 1990s is warranted.

While it still existed, the USSR had the world's second largest army (after the People's Republic of China). In the 1980s this had been deployed over much of the Soviet empire, including the 'northern tier' states (Czechoslovakia, GDR, Hungary and Poland) of Eastern Europe and Afghanistan. It withdrew from the latter at the beginning of 1989. As many of the countries of the 'external' empire in Europe moved to post-communism, followed by the countries of the 'internal' empire (the former Soviet republics), so the new governments demanded the withdrawal of Soviet troops from their sovereign territory. This led to numerous problems for the Soviet military. One was the practical issue that approximately half a million troops stationed in the East European part of the Soviet empire had no or inadequate accommodation or jobs to return to within Russia, which assumed responsibility for looking after the returning troops. Another problem was essentially psychological, and is considered below; at this point, it is sufficient to note that this psychological factor must be included in any attempt at understanding the potential danger from the military.

Since the collapse of the Soviet Union, the former Soviet army has undergone important changes; at times it has perceived itself to be a cake to be divided up against its will between the member states of the CIS. Already at the first CIS summits, serious disagreements were visible between the member states over the dividing up of the military and its assets. Following the August 1991 attempted coup, Yeltsin had instituted a major personnel shake-up and had brought in a person known to be – by military standards – a progressive to head the Soviet defence establishment, Marshal Yevgenii Shaposhnikov. Shaposhnikov had originally hoped the defence arrangements for the CIS would be similar to those of the former USSR. But by late December 1991 he had acknowledged this was a vain aspiration. By the end of the month, the right of three countries – Ukraine, Moldova and Azerbaijan – to create their own armies had been recognized by the CIS. The splintering was in many ways finally confirmed in May 1992, when Russia established its own independent army.

Not only were several of the member states of the new CIS establishing their own armies, but major disputes between the defence establishments in, notably, Russia and Ukraine revealed serious tensions between these countries. These related above all to the division of military assets in the post-Soviet period. By mid-1992, Ukraine and Russia had reached agreement on conventional troops and tactical nuclear weapons. But they continued to bicker throughout 1992 over the Black Sea fleet, and – more seriously from the point of view of the outside world – over strategic nuclear weapons. By mid-1993 the Ukrainian president appeared close to an agreement with Yeltsin over both nuclear weapons and the Black Sea fleet. However, Kravchuk came under serious attack from Ukrainian parliamentarians for having made what they considered to be overly generous proposals to Moscow (while Yeltsin was similarly criticized by the Russian parliament), and neither issue had been fully resolved by the time Kravchuk was replaced as president by Leonid Kuchma in July 1994.

The disputes between Russia and Ukraine were not the only signs that the CIS was experiencing difficulties in developing an integrated, pan-CIS defence establishment. Throughout 1992, CIS forces were deployed in various parts of the FSU where fighting had already broken out, or where situations threatened to worsen. In fact, these 'CIS' forces were often heavily Russian dominated, and many of the non-Russian states felt that Russia was reverting to its traditional 'big brother' role. This appeared to render it more unlikely that the CIS would be able to develop a truly multinational, integrated defence force. Given this, and opposition to the notion of a unified CIS force even from within the Russian Ministry of Defence (Slider 1994, p. 279), the joint military command was abolished in June 1993, and Shaposhnikov resigned.

Thus the early years of post-communism have not been good ones for the once-mighty Soviet army; it (that is, its putative replacement) reached its nadir by 1993. Its largest successor component, the Russian army, has also experienced numerous problems. In late 1994, for instance, it looked as if the Russian army might be about to regain some of its credibility when it was called on to suppress rebellious forces in the Russian republic of Chechnya. In the event, the Chechen rebels proved far more difficult to suppress than the Russian defence minister, Pavel Grachev, had publicly stated would be the case, which reflected badly on the Russian military. Early in 1995, Yeltsin criticized the military for its bad handling of the Chechnya affair (which had still not been resolved by early 1996), but had also claimed there would soon be major reforms to improve the military. Only time will tell if these materialize and are successful. But given the marked deterioration in both the military and the economy in the 1990s, it is unlikely that the lot of the former will improve significantly in the foreseeable future.

In general, the psychological variable mentioned earlier – which gives significant cause for concern – relates to attitudes in the armies (especially the Russian) which succeeded the Soviet military. Various developments in recent years have made some officers and soldiers despondent, others angry: these include the dramatic warming of the relationship with communism's erstwhile enemies, culminating in Russia's declaration of its intention to join NATO's Partnership for Peace programme in June 1994 (even though this decision was then not ratified – see chapter 11); the SDI affair ('Star Wars' – see chapter 2); major cuts in the defence budget;

humiliation caused by the withdrawal from Afghanistan, Eastern Europe
and the Baltic states, as part of the collapse of the Soviet empire; Soviet
toleration of the unification of Germany; the very limited success in retaining some of the FSU in the form of the CIS; the humiliation and criticism of
some parts of the military because of the failed August 1991 coup and the
unimpressive performance in Chechnya from late 1994; and non-payment
of wages.

Some Western analysts have argued there is little or no danger of an
attempted military coup (see Mendeloff 1994, Herspring 1995), largely
because the military *is* so despondent and disorganized. This may prove to
be correct. On the other hand, the argument of those who dismiss the
possibility of such a coup attempt on the grounds that there is no tradition
of self-initiated military involvement is fallacious. In 1917, General
Kornilov rebelled against the Russian provisional government of Kerensky,
while the August 1991 events certainly involved leading military figures. In
any case, even if those arguing against a military threat cite past precedent
(erroneously), this is not necessarily a useful guide to future actions. One
major reason why there may have been a significant change in attitudes
during the 1990s is that the military could for decades look to the CPSU as
a tightly structured organization that controlled society: many military personnel identified with its policies, hierarchy and discipline. With the collapse of the party, it is far from clear that most members of the military are
content either with their lot, or with the direction in which their country is
heading.

Thus, even were there *no* historical precedents, it should not be assumed
too readily that the military will not play a direct role in politics in Russia
and other CIS countries in the future. Indeed, the Russian Fourteenth
Army was by 1993 perceived to be playing a significant *political* role in the
conflict between the Moldovan authorities and a group of mostly Russian
separatists on the eastern banks of the River Dnestr. This army was led by
Lt Gen. Alexander Lebed, whom the Moldovan government accused
of playing too great a role in their republic's affairs. While Russia and
Moldova finally agreed in October 1994 on the withdrawal of all Russian
troops from Moldova within three years, Lebed himself has developed a
strong following among sections of the Russian population; he resigned
from the military in June 1995 to enter politics, and did well in the Russian
presidential elections of June 1996 (for an insight into Lebed's thinking see
the interview with him in *Time*, 17 February 1995, pp. 28–9, and Orttung
1995b). Given all this, it is hardly surprising that leading Russian politicians,
such as Yegor Gaidar in January 1995, have warned of the danger of a
military coup – although it appears that *some* military officers might prefer
to exert their influence through political parties or as civilian politicians.

It seems reasonable to infer that many armies *outside* the CIS now feel
more liberated and content than they did, since they are no longer under
the influence of the Warsaw Treaty Organization (see chapter 11) or the
USSR. Moreover, some enjoy a very good reputation with their own
populations. Opinion surveys conducted in 1991 and 1992, for instance,

suggested that the military was held in higher esteem in Romania and Bulgaria (Chin 1993, p. 40) than were most civilian institutions, while a 1994 Russian survey yielded a similar result (Rose and Haerpfer 1994b, pp. 31–3). While this might on one level reflect well on the military (for instance, in that they are seen by many as less corrupt than many civilian bodies), it also means that some military leaders could interpret this as a sign of popular support for a military takeover if civilian politicians appear incapable of running the post-communist countries properly. As with the FSU, therefore, the future of democracy in some post-communist states could be endangered by the military. Although the latter can sometimes play a pro-democratic role, in the sense of removing a dictatorship and permitting the installation of a democratic system (as happened in Portugal during and after 1974), the fact that there are – albeit shaky – democracies in most of the countries considered here suggests that military intervention in their politics is unlikely to be interpreted as a progressive move.

The final branch of the state to consider is the judiciary. Important changes to note here include the removal of communist party influence from the work of the judiciary, and the enhancement of the role of defence lawyers. One subdivision of the judiciary that requires elaboration, given this book's focus on legal-rationality in late communism and early post-communism, is the emergence or vitalization of constitutional courts; their role is considered in the next subsection.

CONSTITUTIONS AND CONSTITUTIONALISM

Most countries in the world (the UK and Israel are exceptions) sooner or later adopt a formal written document that, *inter alia*, specifies the nature and responsibilities of the country's political bodies. This document, the constitution, is in some cases long and detailed, in others relatively short. In some countries, such as the USA, the document is an enduring one subject to relatively few amendments; in others, constitutions are short-lived or frequently amended.

During the communist era, most constitutions were highly political, designed to lay down future goals, legitimize existing arrangements, etc. Generally, they did not in any meaningful sense limit politicians or political agencies. In contrast, most post-communist constitutions (or amendments to old constitutions) have been designed on one level to act as a foundation for democracy, in which politicians will be under much greater control than they were under communism.

Despite the relative newness of post-communism, several states have already adopted brand new constitutions. As a stopgap measure, others have either substantially revised existing constitutions (from the communist era) or else revitalized parts of the *pre-communist* constitution, in both cases pending agreement on new constitutions (for example of both new and modified constitutions, see chapter 6).

Considering the unstable political situation in all post-communist states in their early stages, the sheer speed at which constitutions have been produced in so many *might* suggest they will be either short-lived or marginalized (that is, not taken seriously). The latter would be a particularly unwelcome development, suggesting that a given post-communist state was moving away from legal-rationality. In a model legal-rational state, the constitution should occupy a central role and be above party politics.

One country where within months the new constitution was already being somewhat marginalized was Czechia. According to the 1992 constitution, Czechia should have an upper house of parliament (Senate). But this is not to be established until late 1996 at the earliest, largely because of political wrangling over the optimal arrangements. One aspect of this argument, concerning electoral arrangements to the Senate, did not directly relate to the constitution. But some parliamentarians and others opposed the very idea of an upper chamber, which was clearly an anti-constitutional stance.

While it is possible that constitutions will be marginalized, the speed at which they were produced in so many cases should not *per se* give rise for concern (though for a thought-provoking argument *against* the rapid adoption of new constitutions by post-communist countries see S. Holmes 1995). It could be objected that the USA's Founding Fathers took some 11 years to produce the durable American constitution of 1787. However, several of the *principles* contained in that document have by now become widely accepted as basic tenets of any democratic system. Thus the framers of the new constitutions of the post-communist states did not have to reinvent the wheel; they were able to learn vicariously from the constitutions of countries such as the USA, the FRG and France.

For a constitution to be relatively durable, it should not be overly detailed or specific. If it were, it might be too inflexible to cope with changed circumstances in a given country, and thus be either irrelevant or a conservative block on change. Constitutions therefore have to be interpreted in particular and changed contexts. Sometimes this is done by parliaments. But if members of parliament disagree among themselves, or a president interprets the constitution in one way while parliament interprets it in another, there is a need for a third party to arbitrate. Similarly, the legislature might pass or be intending to pass a piece of legislation some citizens consider unconstitutional; since it is parliament that has done or is suggesting this, it would be unrealistic to expect *it* to be able to consider objectively the citizens' claims. It was largely with the aim of formalizing the role of arbitrator in these and other kinds of conflict that countries such as the FRG established constitutional courts. It is true that a few communist states – Czechoslovakia, Poland and Yugoslavia – also established constitutional courts, while communist Hungary established an essentially similar body, the Constitutional Law Council. However, the role of these bodies was relatively insignificant; certainly, they never seriously challenged the real centres of power.

In contrast, *some* of the new constitutional courts in those post-communist states that had established them by 1995 are already playing a significant role (the states include Albania, Belarus, Bulgaria, Czechia, Hungary, Kazakhstan, Lithuania, Republic of Macedonia, Poland (which is a continuation of one established in 1985), Romania, Russia, Slovakia and Slovenia – while Estonia and Ukraine, to name but two, had announced their intention to establish such bodies and in some cases had begun the process of doing so). The new Russian court, which was formally established in July 1991 and commenced work in December,[10] was already by 1993 being described as a 'third branch of government' (Wishnevsky 1993, p. 1). This is despite initial suspicions that it would be of 'purely symbolic' significance (ibid.). For several influential Russian observers, the constitutional count was seen as *the* most successful development in Russian politics during 1992.

The court played a highly controversial role during its first two years. Its very first act was to nullify a decree from President Yeltsin that merged the KGB successor bodies with the Ministry of Internal Affairs (on this see Schwartz 1993a, pp. 178–82). Then in November 1992, after seven months of deliberation, the court produced a complex ruling on whether or not Yeltsin's government had been within its rights to ban the CPSU almost exactly one year earlier, and on whether the CPSU had been an unconstitutional body; the Russian government had made the latter charge on the grounds that the CPSU had not recognized the right of other parties to exist or to oppose it. On the first question, it resolved (by 11 to 2) that it *had* been appropriate to ban the higher organs of the CPSU (including the Central Committee and Politburo), from which some of the August 1991 plotters and support for them had emanated. However, it also ruled that it had been unconstitutional to ban the rank-and-file organization. On the latter question, it argued that it was not entitled to make any ruling, since the CPSU was an all-union (that is, Soviet) body rather than a Russian one. Moreover, it concluded that the CPSU had not technically been a political party but a 'state within a state'; this implicitly endorsed the views of Western observers such as T. H. Rigby (1990), who had long maintained that the Soviet political system was essentially 'mono-organizational'. Finally, it added that the CPSU no longer existed, implying there was little point in passing retrospective judgements (on all this see Wishnevsky 1993, pp. 5–6).

If feelings were mixed over its ruling on the CPSU, there was widespread praise for the constitutional court – particularly for its Chair, Valerii Zorkin – over its role during the constitutional crisis of December 1992. This arose out of the overt clash between the president and parliament. The court played a major role in bringing about a compromise solution. According to one Russian source (*Novoe Vremya*, cited in Wishnevsky 1993, p. 1), up to 70 per cent of Russian deputies named Zorkin the hero of the Seventh Congress of People's Deputies (December 1992).

Of the other post-communist constitutional courts, only the Hungarian appeared by mid-1992 to be playing a significant role (Schwartz 1993a, pp. 176–7). One example of its activity relates to an attempt (via a petition) by Hungarian citizens to have the Hungarian parliament organize a referendum on whether or not to call an early parliamentary election. In January 1993 the Hungarian constitutional court ruled that it would be unconstitutional to hold such a plebiscite. But it went further than this, recommending that the existing law on referenda be amended, since it allowed citizens to make formal demands for new elections. Although the reason for such a recommendation was that the law was in conflict with the resolution, it is possible to interpret all this as an example of the Hungarian constitutional court attempting to limit civil rights.

Whereas most constitutional courts in the post-communist world were either not yet operational or else only barely so in early 1992, it is a testimony to the speed at which political change has been occurring in this part of the world that *several* were by 1993 playing a significant role in their respective polities (see Schwartz 1993b). But these courts, like most political institutions in these states, are still relatively new and their role is still crystallizing. There have been allegations of courts being too 'political' and demands that they limit themselves to legal arguments. However, such allegations have often been made by high-ranking officials against whose interests the courts have ruled; they should therefore be treated cautiously. In any case, it would be absurd not to acknowledge that constitutional courts are *necessarily* political, in the sense of playing a direct role in the power balance. This is true of constitutional courts everywhere in the world. What they must strenuously seek to avoid, rather, is a reputation for consistently favouring one branch of government or political grouping over another. In short, they must strive to ensure that they are as non-partisan as possible if they are to become respected pillars of the legal-rational state.

Zorkin was well aware of this danger of partisanship and on numerous occasions publicly committed himself to the rule of law above all. When the Russian constitutional court placed a temporary ban on President Yeltsin's proposed merger of the KGB successor bodies and the Ministry of Internal Affairs, Zorkin is reported to have said: 'The Russian President's decree on organizing a Russian Ministry of Security and Internal Affairs is contrary to the principle of organizing a state based on the rule of law' (in Schwartz 1993a, p. 179). Zorkin's record and that of his court to about mid-1993 suggested that the court was acting primarily on legal rather than partisan grounds. However, as the struggle between Yeltsin and the Russian parliament intensified in mid-1993, Zorkin was seen to move fairly overtly into the parliamentarian camp. This was certainly how Yeltsin perceived Zorkin's position and why the Russian President forced the resignation of the head of the Russian constitutional court in October 1993. This act, plus the fact that there were several threats made against various members of the Russian constitutional court in 1992 and 1993, and even physical attacks on them, revealed that the path towards the legal-rational state in Russia would be a stony one.

For almost a year following October 1993 the Russian constitutional court was essentially dead. But President Yeltsin signed a new law in July 1994 and the reconstituted court became operational in February 1995. It soon proved to be controversial (see *EECR*, vol. 4, no. 3, pp. 23–5), suggesting it might once again become a force in Russian politics. Nevertheless, that it had been shut down once before when it appeared to be overly critical of the president is likely to act as a constraint on it in the future.

The constitutional courts elsewhere are likely to share the same uncertain status as their Russian counterpart, since the *culture* of legal-rationality cannot be created overnight. Some post-communist states are moving slowly and falteringly towards a situation in which the constitution is likely to become a higher power than any individual organization or political actor, and in this sense they are on the way towards constitutionalism. But some of these countries may yet fall by the wayside, and *all* still have a long way to go.

Conclusions

So many details have been included in this chapter that it is not feasible to summarize them all. But an attempt can be made to distinguish the wood – to the extent that there is one – from the trees and to provide an initial evaluation of the current state of institutional politics in the post-communist world (the argument is further developed in chapter 12).

First, much of the confusion caused by the duplication of institutions – the existence of the party-state complex – during the communist period has now all but disappeared. During the earlier era, not only was there a head of state, a head of government, a government and a legislature, but also more or less equivalent party officers and organs, such as a general secretary, a central committee secretariat, a politburo, a central committee and a congress. Attempting to ascertain who was actually responsible for what, or even who was *supposed* to be responsible for what, during that period was often difficult. From this perspective, the situation has improved.

At the same time, it has from another angle become *more* confused. In an era of far more open political debate, major differences over both the path to democracy and the optimal end goal (in terms of the three models identified in this chapter) have been highly visible to all in most post-communist states.

These differences have been explained partly in terms of clashes of personality and different basic values. But another important reason, closely related to the latter point, is the varying emphases placed by individuals and groups on the various components of Offe's 'triple transition' (see chapter 1). Those for whom the top priority is political distancing from the communist power structure will usually tend towards a more parliamentary system. Conversely, many of those for whom the economic transition is the most important task at this stage will veer towards presidentialism, in the belief that there is presently a need for strong leadership and efficient decision-making. Those who see these first two transitions as inseparable, and who reject the notion that a choice has to be made between democracy and effective decision-making, are often attracted to the semi-presidential model. Offe's third transition makes the picture even more complex. The more open political atmosphere, added to the contexts in which post-communism emerged, has sometimes resulted in demands for the redrawing of boundaries and the dissolution of existing political units. Those who oppose such changes – sometimes for ethically defensible reasons, such as an aversion to measures that further divide people into 'them' and 'us' – may conclude that strong leadership is necessary to avoid either total disintegration or, less radically, increasing autonomism. They therefore opt for a strong presidency, despite their more general inclination towards the parliamentary model.

Some confusion, or at least flexibility, in the precise role and relationships of various offices and institutions is normal in stable democracies, as are real differences of opinion and ambitiousness among politicians. In many ways, such fuzziness is even desirable. Certainly, it would be absurd to expect a totally clear-cut division of political labour – especially between the president, the government and the legislature (and between the two houses in a bicameral legislature) – *ever* to emerge in such systems. The American system, for instance, operates largely according to a code adopted more than two centuries ago, yet the relationship between the president and Congress is still a dynamic one. In this sense, it might be argued that the significance of confusion and tensions in the post-communist world should not be exaggerated.

However, it must again be emphasized that there are typically more firmly established and widely accepted democratic conventions in Western states than in the transitional post-communist ones, and that these help to limit the divisive effects of clashes of interest and opinion. The near absence of such long-established rules in the post-communist world renders elite clashes potentially more dangerous, and the overall political situation more fragile. Presidentialism can all too easily deteriorate from strong leadership into dictatorship. Extreme polarization, of parties and in parliaments, is also more dangerous than in more solidly established systems. It is in this context that the absence of clearly centrist parties in some countries is cause for concern. Where such parties are absent or very weak, there is a greater likelihood of a reversion to authoritarian politics. Only goodwill, common sense and, above all, *time* can bring about the solid framework of conventions – the 'rules of the game' – that are the essence of genuine constitutionalism and legal-rationality,[11] which in turn will help to ensure that countries do not become dictatorships.[12] At this point, the long-term significance of the current struggles between so many presidents, prime ministers and parliaments is not clear; the jury is still out.

The fragilities and uncertainties just outlined do not mean *per se* that the future of post-communism in the short to medium term (the next 5–15 years) is *necessarily* bleak. The existence at present of real, open politics in the vast majority of post-communist states is a healthy sign. So are the commitments to *some* conception of separation or division of powers; to constitutions that will be taken more seriously than were their communist predecessors; and to judicial review (via the constitutional courts). And it is encouraging that constitutional courts are apparently prepared to defy presidents and parliaments, both the latter being – so far – *mostly* prepared to accept the rulings of such courts. Many of the tensions and conflicts highlighted in this chapter should thus be seen as growing pains.

Of course, there is also a need to be realistic. Post-communism was in its honeymoon period during the early 1990s. There may have been more tolerance then than there will be in the future, especially as memories of the worst aspects of the communist era, and hence the bonding aspects of the rejection of communist power, fade. It would therefore be unjustified to be overly sanguine about current and future developments in institutional politics.

Nevertheless, there must be recognition of the extraordinary advances that have been made in such a very short time-span. On balance, there are still more optimistic than pessimistic dimensions to post-communist institutional politics. Considering the enormity of the tasks facing them, the sorry state of the international economy at the time of the anti-communist revolutions, and the political traditions inherited by the post-communist countries, the fact that politics have so far developed as *relatively* well as they have in most countries can only be wondered at and admired.

Notes

1 The percentages are higher, by up to half as much again in some cases, if membership is taken as a proportion of the *adult* population only. While such figures would in some ways be more meaningful, since only adults could join the communist party, many communist states did not disaggregate population data in a way that would make it possible to calculate the proportion of adults only. Even if this were possible, the basic point being made here – that the vast majority of citizens were not party members – would still hold.
2 It is worth noting that a somewhat similar situation occurred in Bulgaria, where the constitution formally prohibits parties which are explicitly based on ethnicity and religion. Following an April 1992 ruling by the constitutional court, the Movement for Rights and Freedom – which in practice exists primarily to represent the Turkish minority – has been allowed to continue and to compete in elections. But it has to be careful not to appear to represent ethnic interests too overtly. Turkmenistan also forbids parties based on ethnicity and religion; but since only one party, the (pro-President Niyazov) Turkmen Democratic Party, is permitted anyway, the significance of this ban should not be exaggerated.
3 See the quotation from *Sovetskaya Rossiya* cited in Dunlop 1993, p. 56. In fact, many Soviet republics declared independence very soon after the attempted coup of August 1991, seeking to ensure this while it still seemed possible. It is far from clear that Yeltsin is personally to blame for the disintegration. Indeed, it could be argued that it was more the incompetence of the conservative plotters that accelerated and made certain this process.
4 While some have seen Women of Russia as quasi-feminist, the majority view is that they represent traditional family values. This would help to explain why so many men voted for them in both December 1993 and December 1995.
5 Slater herself identified the decline in reference to the 1993 elections, but believed the centre could make a comeback; the 1995 elections proved her correct.
6 This is unfortunate, for various reasons. For example, countries such as Poland have explicitly sought to boost the significance and role of local politics, precisely

as a way of countering the centralism that typified communism (Latynsky 1992, p. 108). On local governments in eastern Europe and parts of the FSU see Coulson 1995.

7 In most cases, at least 50% of the electorate in a given constituency must vote for the election to be valid.

8 So serious were the criticisms of the last of these that the Kazakh constitutional court in March 1995 declared them invalid. After some wavering, President Nazarbayev used the court's ruling as an excuse to dissolve parliament. But the parliamentary elections of December 1995 were *also* subject to widespread and serious criticism, and Kazakhstan is still a long way from democracy.

9 It is interesting to note in parenthesis that there have been several 'returned immigrants' running for the presidency in various post-communist states. Examples include Campeanu and Ratiu in Romania (May 1990), Lozoraitis in Lithuania (February 1993), and Meierovics in Latvia (July 1993). None of these candidates performed particularly well.

10 The USSR established a Committee on Constitutional Supervision in January 1990. Although this did nullify some of Gorbachev's decrees, the general view is that it was not as powerful a body as it needed to be. It was disbanded in December 1991.

11 A brief but enlightening definition of constitutionalism, provided by Claus Offe at a March 1996 seminar held in Melbourne, is that it is an arrangement in which a political system is sufficiently consolidated that its major decisions are made *according to* rules rather than *about* rules.

12 One or two post-communist states – notably Turkmenistan – could already be described as dictatorships. Even if this is accepted, however, they have not *become* dictatorships *after* having seriously attempted to move towards democracy. Rather, they have yet to take bold steps along the democratization path.

FURTHER READING

The literature on this topic is enormous and this introductory list focuses on up-to-date, accessible and comparative sources. For the communist period, see White, Gardner and Schopflin 1987, esp. chs 3 and 4; Holmes 1986a, esp. chs 6–9; Szajkowski 1981. For the post-communist period, general introductions to most aspects of politics covered here include White, Batt and Lewis 1993 (on eastern Europe); Michta 1994 (on eastern Europe and the clearly European parts of the FSU); Sakwa 1993 and White, Pravda and Gitelman 1994 (on Russia and the CIS). Among the most useful reference sources on the earliest stages of post-communism are Sword 1990 and East 1992 – and for institutions Whitefield 1993. For a comprehensive collection on parties see Szajkowski 1994; a much shorter comparative analysis of the east European parties is Lewis, Lomax and Wightman 1994, while Cotta 1994 provides a more theoretical analysis and Pridham and Lewis (1996) compare parties and party systems in eastern Europe with those in Southern Europe. On post-communist elections and electoral systems, see Garber and Bjornlund 1992, McGregor 1993 and the various articles and tables in *East European Constitutional Review*, vol. 3, no. 2 (Spring 1994), pp. 39–77; a more general comparative analysis of electoral systems is Grofman and Lijphart 1986, while an extremely brief but valuable overview can be found in the *Economist*, 1 May 1993, pp. 17–19. An interesting comparative analysis of post-communist constitutions, constitution-making and constitutional courts is Howard 1993; on these topics and the rule of law more generally see too the various articles in *East European Constitutional Review*, vol. 2, no. 2 (Spring 1993), pp. 28–53, and the whole issue of *RFE/RL Research Report*, vol. 1, no. 27 (3 July 1992). On the new parliaments, see Agh 1994, Remington 1994a, Agh 1995, Agh and Ilonsaki 19 (pt 4) and *EECR*, vol. 4, no. 2 (Spring 1995), pp. 56–90. On relations between post-communist presidents, prime ministers and parliaments see Shugart 1993, McGregor 1994, Colton and Tucker 1995 and Baylis 1996, while readers interested in the more general debates on presidentialism, semi-presidentialism and parliamentarism are advised to read Lijphart 1992 and Linz and Valenzuela 1994. On post-Soviet armies see the whole issue of *RFE/RL Research Report*, vol. 2, no. 25 (18 June 1993); further analyses of individual armies include Obrman 1993, Girnius 1993a, Reisch 1993a, Herspring 1995. On security police agencies see Yasmann 1993b, Yasmann 1993d, Engelbrekt 1993 and J. M. Waller 1994.

Given the rapidly changing developments in this area, readers may want to know that useful sources for up-to-date information include the bi-weekly *Transition*, which in essence replaced the invaluable *RFE/RL Research Reports* in January 1995; the quarterly *East European Constitutional Review*, which includes material on the FSU as well as eastern Europe; and the bi-monthly *Problems of Post-Communism*.

8

The Economies

Real-world economics cannot be understood without a knowledge of politics – and vice versa. Hence, although this book is directed primarily at the student of politics, it is vital that one chapter be dedicated to the *modus operandi*, problems and prospects of post-communist economies. As with the other chapters in part III, the first part of this one focuses on the communist era. This is followed by a longer section on post-communist economies, after which is a short section on the environment.

The Economy under Communism

Although there were differences, some of them significant, between the various communist economies of Eastern Europe and the USSR, there were also sufficient commonalities to warrant a broad, comparative analysis.

For many communist economists themselves, the key difference between a capitalist and a communist economy was not the issue of ownership of the means of production (factories, farmland, etc.), but the organization of the economy. Whereas many such economists used to describe as 'anarchic' the system of production, distribution and exchange that is now generally called the market, they classified their own systems as planned. Not only were communist economies planned, but most of the important planning was undertaken in central institutions rather than at the level of the production unit. For this reason, communist economies have often been described as centrally planned economies, or CPEs. Given the high level of centralized direction and involvement, another term used to describe them is command economies. The key elements of such systems can now be elaborated.

Communists often argued that market (or equilibrium) economies tend to favour the stronger in society, and that it takes conscious intervention to redress this tendency of the abstract forces of the market. They further maintained that if an economy is to develop as rapidly and efficiently as possible, it needs to be consciously directed according to priorities and policies agreed and set in advance. For this reason, the first *central planning* organization in the communist world, Gosplan (from the Russian acronym for State Planning Committee), was established in Russia in 1921 under Lenin. However, this played a rather insignificant role in Lenin's time and it was not until October 1928 that the communist world's first five-year plan was adopted. The USSR had set a precedent that was eventually to be emulated, in various guises, in all of the communist states.

The plan enabled the centre to set priorities in the economy, and to ensure their implementation at all levels by having a reasonably clear blueprint of what each production unit was to achieve during the next five years. A draft plan would be produced by the state planning agency on the basis both of general directives from the central party and state bodies and detailed information from the actual production units. Once the draft five-year plan had been agreed on by the legislature, it would become law. At this point, the state planning agency would collaborate with the various economic ministries (for agriculture, electrical engineering, etc.) to ensure its implementation. The ministries played a major role in disaggregating the plan for their branches in order to determine what each unit would have to achieve to ensure that the plan as a whole for that branch would be at least fulfilled, if not *over*fulfilled.

There were several major problems with the centralized (or command) approach to planning. As the years passed, so the boldness and ideological commitment of the early planners – for instance, in terms of converting a predominantly rural society into an urbanized one through prioritization of industrial investment – came to be replaced by a far more incremental and instrumental approach. The plan became more of a bargaining arena, in which both sides sought to gain as much as possible, without daring to overstep certain limits. If an enterprise overfulfilled the plan by 5 per cent, for example, its staff might appear to be energetic and efficient; if it overfulfilled by 10 per cent, they ran the risk of appearing to have deliberately understated its potential at an earlier stage, which could be interpreted as either duplicity or incompetence.

The whole system thus increasingly encouraged improvement at the margins, rather than bold new initiatives. Indeed, central planners feared such initiatives from the politicians since, in an economy in which every part is supposed to be consciously related to every other part, one large and radical alteration could have enormous knock-on effects and require major new calculations. This innate conservatism of the planning process in practice is one of the reasons the economies became ever less responsive, and is just one of innumerable factors helping to explain the slow-down of communist economies that contributed to the downfall of communist power.

In recent decades, most communist leaderships attempted to streamline and modernize the central planning mechanism. The number of plan indicators was reduced, and suppliers and users were encouraged to conclude contracts directly with each other rather than communicate indirectly via central ministries. While this represented a gesture towards market economics, it was ultimately tokenistic and often resulted in the worst of all worlds rather than the best. It was in this context that moves towards *real* marketization were taken in so many countries in the late communist era.

A final problem of planning was that it required a level of information and processing that was in practice beyond the capacity of communist planners to gather and implement properly: the sheer scale and complexity of national economies were such that it became ever more difficult to coordinate all the component parts.

Another aspect of the command economy was *centrally determined prices* and heavy *subsidization* of many goods and services. Unlike the situation in a pure market economy, where prices emerge and change according to supply and demand, the CPEs were highly insensitive to variations in demand. The communists' ideological and political aversion to market pricing was one of the factors that led to the distortion of so many communist economies. Although it might be argued to be more compassionate to set prices according to what socialist planners perceived to be ordinary people's priorities (low prices for basics, with big profits being made more on 'luxury' items), empirical evidence suggests that, eventually, most prices are best allowed to find their own level in accordance with supply and demand. Many communist leaders appear to have accepted this by the 1980s.

The economy in communist states was *organized on a hierarchical basis*. At the bottom were the individual production and service units – industrial enterprises, farms, stores, etc. At the centre, above these, were the economic ministries, which were responsible for distributing plans, checking on plan fulfilment, coordinating different units and liaising with central party and state bodies (including the central planning agencies). In between were often intermediate bodies, variously called combines, associations, amalgamations, etc.

According to classical Marxism, private *ownership* of the means of production is the principal reason for the existence of antagonistic class relationships. Leninists basically agreed with this precept, so that communist states typically sought to socialize the means of production. Typically, this was done rapidly and rather crudely, without adequate compensation to former owners, within a decade of so of the communists coming to power.

Although socialization of the means of production most frequently meant that the state owned most of the important assets in society, there were always other types of ownership in the communist world. One was collective (or cooperative) ownership, which mostly pertained in agriculture. Here, several farmers jointly owned the buildings, equipment, animals and produce of large farms (though the land itself usually belonged to the state) and worked these farms.

In all communist states, many farmers also had the right to a small *private* plot, a form of individual or family ownership. Once again, the land itself was state property, but in most cases anything the farmers and their families reared or cultivated on their plot could be sold privately (in Albania, the private plot was for personal consumption purposes only until the late 1980s). Although such plots were typically very small (usually a quarter to half a hectare in the USSR), they were also often the most productive part of a farm. In 1980, for instance, approximately 0.02 per cent of the total Soviet cultivated area was being worked privately, yet this accounted for about 6 per cent of eggs, 6 per cent of milk, 14 per cent of meat, 15 per cent of vegetables, and 49 per cent of the potatoes sold in Soviet markets (Lane 1985, pp. 12–13). Bearing in mind that many peasants fed themselves from the private plots before taking surpluses to markets, the significant role played by the private plots in feeding the Soviet population becomes clear. Similarly, the private sector accounted for only 3 per cent of the arable land in Czechoslovakia by 1985, yet produced 40 per cent of eggs, 40 per cent of vegetables and 60 per cent of fruit (Wolchik 1991, p. 230).

Perhaps the high level of productivity on the private plots should have made clear to the communists the benefits of private ownership in the countryside. But most communist leaderships were ideologically committed to collective and state ownership, and resisted pressures for further privatization in the countryside. The notable exceptions to this were Yugoslavia and Poland, which, albeit reluctantly, permitted decollectivization – and private farms – from 1951 and 1956 respectively.

The *priorities* of communist systems also proved to be problematic. Among the numerous factors contributing to the collapse of communism was the defence burden on the USSR. Soviet competition with the West clearly involved a military dimension. Following the Cuban missile crisis of 1962, the USSR devoted huge sums to the development and expansion of its military arsenal. In some senses, this was one of the great success stories of the Soviet era, inasmuch as the West came to perceive the USSR as a military peer, and in some areas even as superior.

But military expenditure, including on the space research programme, was an enormous drain on the Soviet economy. This had knock-on effects for the other countries of the Soviet bloc. For instance, shortages of Soviet non-military products meant that the USSR's Comecon partners had either to attempt to make up the shortfall via externally sourced supplies from third countries or else go without. Both options were problematical. The first often required making payments in hard currency, of which most communist states had relatively little. The second resulted in shortages and a limited range of goods, with all the negative implications for eudaemonic legitimation.

A second ramification was that Moscow often pressured the other members of the Warsaw Treaty Organization to increase their contributions to the communist military alliance. This was particularly so in the late 1970s, when member states of the WTO were expected to increase defence expenditure by some 3 per cent per annum. Some countries, such as Romania, claimed they could not afford to do this, and simply refused. Nevertheless, the WTO and CMEA countries did find that the Soviets' priorities had tangible effects on their own economies.

The defence burden was only part of a larger prioritization issue. The privileging of heavy industry over other sectors under Stalin resulted in a serious *skewing* problem (that is, an imbalance between sectors) that was never fully solved by his successors. As with all economic issues, political considerations had to be included in the equation. Thus, decades of privileging had created a powerful lobby – the so-called 'steel-eaters' – that was unwilling to allow its position to be undermined. The military was very much part of this group, and communist leaders were always aware of the potential danger from this quarter if the military's interests were to be blatantly disregarded. Conversely, the long-term underprivileging of other sectors meant there were few powerful voices with a vested interest in promoting those sectors.

The above problem pertains more to the Soviet economy than to the East European ones, where the influence of Stalin and his priorities lasted for a shorter time and was less direct. Nevertheless, as with the military competition issue, the sheer size and dominance of the Soviet economy within the CMEA meant that all the member states were affected by the ramifications of this skewing problem, albeit to varying degrees.

A final issue relating to prioritization in the USSR and most of Eastern Europe is that the communist emphasis on collective goods was another reason why consumer goods industries – which are oriented towards the individual – were generally underdeveloped in the communist world. It is tempting to think of durable consumer goods as luxuries. But the lot of the homemaker – particularly, in practice, women labouring under the 'dual (or triple) burden' (see next chapter) – was considerably more difficult than it might have been because of the shortages and poor quality of many electrical items that can help to lighten domestic chores.

Many of the above issues also applied to a greater or lesser extent to the East European countries that were *not* part of the Soviet 'external empire', namely Yugoslavia and Albania. But certain aspects of these two economies need to be examined discretely, in order to show why they too were less successful than they might have been. In the case of Yugoslavia, conflicts over the distribution of funds between republics were an ongoing problem. Very crudely, the wealthier republics – Slovenia and Croatia – often indicated their resentment at having to subsidize the poorer regions and republics (notably Kosovo and Macedonia). With Tito's death in 1980, the main integrative force in Yugoslavia disappeared. Tensions between the component parts of the federation increased, with all the negative economic effects of this.

Albania's almost complete isolationism by the end of the 1970s meant that significant prospects for a major injection of external funds or preferential trading agreements disappeared. Given that the economy was underdeveloped anyway – and hence could not internally supply all the major items even most East Europeans had come to take for granted – it is not surprising that, by the time of the collapse of communism there, Albania had the lowest standard of living in Europe.

Numerous analysts of the collapse of communist power have stressed the relative failure of the economic systems as a major contributory factor. Indeed, the underlying theoretical framework of this book emphasizes the failure of eudaemonism, itself closely related to *economic performance*. This is an appropriate point at which to assess this performance in more detail.

One method for analysing it is to consider economic growth rates over time. This was always a difficult task in the case of the communist states, for two main reasons. One was that communist states tended to use a different method for calculating growth than do most Western states; the latter usually focus on either GDP (Gross Domestic Product, which excludes income generated abroad) or GNP (Gross National Product – GDP plus income generated abroad), whereas communist states often presented an aggregate picture of their economies in terms of NMP (Net Material Product, which focuses on national income). In general, NMP figures tended to make communist-type economies appear to be performing better than they would have done measured by GNP or GDP.

The second problem was the reliability of the data themselves. There is abundant evidence that many of the data published in the communist world were highly questionable.

The reasons for this varied. In some cases, the communist authorities consciously manipulated – even invented – data in order to present a better picture of the state of the economy than was appropriate. This is revealed in the following quotations (cited in Secretariat of the Economic Commission for Europe 1990, p. 82). The first is from a 1990 Soviet article by the head of the Soviet Statistical Office, V. Kirichenko:

> In truth, for decades the prevailing stance has been to demonstrate successes and advantages, to keep silent about difficulties and negative features in the development of the country and its regions. Statistics, as well as theory, were assigned a perverted ideological function of forming the illusion of the well-being and infallibility of the command-administrative system.

This article goes on to point out that 'in actuality, NMP produced did not rise by 3.5 per cent in 1985 but only by 1.6 per cent, and in 1986 not by 4.1 per cent but by 2.3 per cent.' The second quotation is from a November 1989 editorial in the BCP Central Committee's daily newspaper *Rabotnichesko Delo*:

> Real data on the situation in the country have been carefully hidden from the broad public and the mass media, covered by a veil of secrecy . . . it was in the interest of the peace and quiet of that very system that the population was so generously supplied with calming reports . . .

In other cases, unreliable data were less a reflection of conspiracy than incompetency. The sheer scale and complexity of the economies noted above, plus the frequently suboptimal availability of techniques and equipment for gathering and processing information, sometimes resulted in the production of aggregate data that were based on incomplete and unreliable data sources.

There is no way that either aspect of the second problem of unreliable data can be adequately overcome. The first problem of the method of calculation of growth rates is less serious. On the one hand, it means that it is not always possible directly to compare economic growth in communist countries with that of non-communist countries. On the other hand, if the principal interest is in the economy over time within one communist country, there is no major problem in using NMP other than the fact that one is not considering the whole economy. At least an internally consistent picture can be produced of how well or badly a substantial part of the economy performed over a number of years.

Bearing all these problems in mind – and thus acknowledging that the following figures *cannot* be treated as definitive – Soviet and East European economic performance can be examined. One of the most illuminating ways of doing this is to consider economic growth rates for five-year periods since the 1960s.

It is obvious from table 8.1 that *even though* economic statistics were sometimes manipulated by the communist authorities, they still did not hide the fact that growth slowed down markedly in most countries over the decades. The most dramatic decline was in Yugoslavia following Tito's death. But it was also obvious in the majority of countries listed. Interestingly, Poland constituted an exception, since its growth improved quite strongly in the mid to late 1980s in comparison with the early part of the decade. However, it is important to bear in mind the dramatic effect on production of the first Solidarity era (1980–1) – when the country was in a semi-revolutionary situation – and the period following this, when it was initially difficult to motivate the workforce despite (or because of) the imposition of martial law. Even allowing for the marked improvement in the mid-1980s, the annual average growth rate in Poland in the second half of the decade was still well below that of the 1960s or early 1970s.

Table 8.1 Average annual growth rates of Net Material Product (produced) per quinquennium in communist states, 1961–5 to 1986–9 (per cent)

	1961–5[a]	1966–70[a]	1971–5	1976–80	1981–5	1986–9	(1986–90 plan)
Albania[b]	5.7	8.8					
Bulgaria	6.7	8.6	7.9	6.1	3.7	3.1	(5.4)
Czechoslovakia	1.9	6.8	5.7	3.7	1.8	2.1	(3.4)
GDR	3.5	5.2	5.4	4.1	4.5	3.1	(4.6)
Hungary	4.7	6.8	6.2	2.8	1.4	0.8	(3.0)[c]
Poland	6.2	6.0	9.7	1.2	−0.8	2.9	(3.3)[c]
Romania	9.1	7.7	11.2	7.2	4.4	5.1[d]	(10.3)
USSR	6.5	7.6	5.7	4.3	3.2	2.7	(4.2)
Yugoslavia[e]	7.0		5.9	5.6	0.7	0.4	

[a] Growth rates on national income produced.
[b] Fuller details not available from source used.
[c] Averaged out, between the lower and higher plan estimates.
[d] 1986–8 only; it is highly probable that inclusion of the 1989 figure would reduce this average.
[e] Data for Yugoslavia are calculated by a different method from the CMEA data, and are for GMP (Gross Material Product).

Sources: All information from the Secretariat of the Economic Commission for Europe, *Economic Survey of Europe* (New York: United Nations, various years).

The other point to note from the table is that none of the countries was on target to fulfil its own plan targets for the latter half of the 1980s at the time of the anti-communist revolutions. In Poland, the shortfall was not too serious, while in others – notably Hungary and Romania – the level of underperformance was significant.

Since the figures in table 8.1 are based on official statistics, and therefore represent the *best* possible scenario, it becomes obvious why many citizens in these countries were so disappointed at their regimes' performances. The communists had long claimed they would rapidly bring high standards of living for all, and in some cases that they would overtake the West (see Hardt 1977, p. xi). While it should not be forgotten that many Western economies had slow-downs in this period too, they were from a much higher base and standard of living. Overall, many communist economies were not merely not catching up and surpassing their capitalist counterparts, but were not even keeping pace with them.

But there were other ways in which ordinary citizens knew the econo- mies were performing poorly, with all the negative implications of this for eudaemonic legitimation. Two major problems were the *quality* and the *availability* of consumer goods, both durable and non-durable; many citi- zens were aware that both the quality and availability of goods were far superior in the West.

One of the few forms of relief for many citizens in this otherwise rather bleak picture was the black (semi-legal or illegal) market. On one level, the existence of this took some of the pressure off the authorities, since many citizens were able to improve their access to scarce – and often better quality – goods via this channel. On the other hand, the very existence and success of the black market was concrete evidence of the inadequacy of the official economy and thus helped to undermine whatever legitimacy the communist system had.

Many citizens might have been more supportive, or at least tolerant, of the communist system had the authorities given them reason to believe the situation would improve. But, as argued in chapter 2, with the moves away from the grand schemes of teleological communism towards the mundane and almost defeatist images of 'really existing socialism' from the 1970s on, the *prospects* for improvement withered. The communists were failing to deliver and were unable to persuade either the masses or themselves that this situation was likely to improve much. Eventually, most of them appear to have decided that marketization was the only way forward. One problem with this was that it was ultimately incompatible with basic tenets of com- munist ideology and hence undermined communist legitimacy and power.

The Economy under Post-Communism

For the sake of clarity, this chapter has been divided into the communist and post-communist periods. By this stage of the book, however, the reader will be aware that – dramatic events such as the overthrow and execution of the Ceausescus notwithstanding – there was no overnight change from communism to post-communism. Indeed, the transition has in many ways been more prolonged and complex in the economy than in the polity, at least in terms of structures. It is important to remember that many of the features popularly associated with post-communism were in fact being introduced during the late communist period, since this was a major component of the identity and rationality crisis that led to the collapse of communist power.

A second introductory point about the transition to post-communist economies is that nothing quite like what has occurred in eastern Europe and the FSU in recent years has been tried before. There are no role models for attempting such a rapid, total transition from a predominantly planned and state-owned to a predominantly marketized and privatized economy. As Michael Kaser (1993, p. 386) points out, Chile under General Pinochet is often taken as an example of a country which undertook a rapid economic transition, yet it privatized only 470 enterprises and organizations in the 16-year period of 1973–89; many of the post-communist states have been attempting to privatize *thousands* of enterprises in about one-third or less of this time.

One ramification of this is that there have been very different views on how to achieve the most effective transition. Not only do Western economists disagree on this, but the actual practitioners – the politicians who have to choose one policy and approach rather than another – also often find it difficult to concur. This is not merely a technical issue: the potential political and social implications of a particular choice have been enormous in all the post-communist states, and it is not fanciful to suggest that the citizenry of these countries will tolerate only so much unsuccessful implementation. Considered from a different angle, the fact that politicians can and do openly disagree with each other in the post-communist world in a manner virtually unknown until the late 1980s means that the overall leader sometimes feels compelled to forge a compromise between radically different proposals and factions. Many of the problems faced by Gorbachev from about 1989 on, or to some extent by Yeltsin since 1991, can be understood in terms of their attempts to steer a middle course or reach a compromise. But it should also be borne in mind that the disputes have overwhelmingly been between people committed to radical change; it is the pace and details, rather than fundamentals, that cause such heated debate.

At the risk of oversimplification, the debates on how best to handle the economic transition can be summarized under two headings: 'shock therapy' (also known as the 'big bang' approach) and gradualism. By and large, those countries that have been heavily influenced by Western radical rationalists such as Harvard economist Jeffrey Sachs have tended towards the 'shock therapy' approach, whereas others – usually those which have been more ambivalent about the communist period, and which do not necessarily want to reject everything from it – have been more gradualist.

Thus post-communist Poland, initially under the influence of deputy premier Leszek Balcerowicz, opted for several elements of the 'shock therapy' approach. (Balcerowicz himself has made it clear he does not favour the use of the term shock therapy to refer to his and his successors' policies; but others still often describe them as such.) This was to be introduced in two stages. The first, implemented from January 1990, involved making the Polish currency far more convertible, lifting most price controls, and ending most subsidies; further details on the whole approach will emerge in the following sections. Russia, too, eventually opted for a 'shock therapy' approach in the area of pricing, essentially allowing most prices to find their own level from January 1992 (although it back-tracked on this in early 1993, under the new prime minister Chernomyrdin). And as Vaclav Klaus's influence in Czecho-Slovakia/the Czech republic grew – initially as finance minister, subsequently as prime minister – so that country has also tended towards the radical approach.

In contrast, both Hungary and Romania have tended to opt for a more gradualist approach, albeit largely for different reasons. In the case of Hungary under the late premier Antall, there was a sense that the economy had been transforming itself satisfactorily anyway, even in the later years of communism, and the more extreme approach was neither justified nor necessarily advisable. The Romanian government under Petre Roman (prime minister from December 1989 to September 1991) tended to favour a more radical approach; however, although his immediate successor (Theodor Stolojan) was also of a fairly radical persuasion, he believed that too rapid and wide-ranging a transition would have had an excessively destabilizing effect on the economy and society, so that the transition slowed down.

While the 'shock therapy' versus 'gradualism' dichotomy is useful as a shorthand summary of the approaches of different leadership teams, a closer analysis reveals that a given leadership can appear more or less radical as different components of the transition are considered, and that the implementation of certain policies has sometimes required politicians to modify them. Thus a 'big bang' country can become more gradualist, or vice versa, because of changed circumstances (including a change of government) and perceptions. Partly for this reason, it is useful to consider several of the major components of the transitional economies. After that, as with the section on the communist era, an assessment is given of the performance of the early post-communist economies.

MARKETIZATION

Many mistakenly believe that marketization and privatization are essentially synonyms. While the two often overlap in practice, they are discrete concepts, and one does not necessarily imply the other. Very crudely, marketization should be seen as the opposite of planning, since it allows supply and demand to balance themselves out via abstract forces – Adam

Smith's 'invisible hand' of the market – rather than through conscious intervention in the economy. It relates very much to *pricing* and *competition*.

Post-communist leaderships have all committed themselves to a far greater role for the market in the economy than was the case in even the most liberal communist state. The area in which this is most visible is pricing. The new governments have, to a greater or lesser extent, ended the practice of price-setting by central planners and have allowed more and more prices to find their own levels. This has required an ending not merely of the direct involvement of central authorities in pricing itself, but also, as a corollary, of state subsidies.

Most governments considered it appropriate to end subsidies on what were held to be luxuries soon after coming to power. Thus the Roman government formed in Romania in June 1990 unfroze prices on many items in November, and the Bufi government that was appointed in Albania in June 1991 lifted price controls on a wide range of goods five months later.

But there have been significant differences between post-communist states on how rapidly to remove subsidies and price controls on basics such as housing and foodstuffs. In Poland from 1990 and Czecho-Slovakia from the beginning of 1991 the approach was to remove as many subsidies as quickly as possible. It was believed that the sooner the economy was marketized, the better: since change had to occur anyway, it was preferable to take the plunge and be done with it. Such an approach can be seen as taking advantage of the honeymoon period of post-communism, implementing the toughest changes first and quickly, while citizens still demand the opposite of the communist approach. The ministers who implemented this – notably Balcerowicz (initially) and Suchocka in Poland, Klaus in the Czech Republic, Gaidar in Russia – knew that the changes would hurt, particularly in terms of short-term inflation (a tight control of the money supply was expected to keep inflation under control in the longer term) and perhaps unemployment. But they maintained that there was no feasible alternative: the step-by-step approach preferred by Hungary or, by late 1991, Romania, was considered likely to prolong instability, with the possibility that the citizens' patience with the new post-communist government would run out. As they saw it, this in turn increased the danger of a return to a command economy and an authoritarian political system.

The Hungarian leadership clearly believed otherwise. This largely reflected the different transition in that country, in which change came mostly from above, incrementally and peacefully. Since this pattern had worked so well in the late 1980s, there was less perceived need to make major changes quickly, before citizens had time to become disillusioned and start reassessing the past more favourably.

Russia has been the scene of a protracted and vicious political struggle over the issue of marketization and the sequencing of reforms (see Aslund 1993, pp. 27–8). Following his election as president of Russia in 1991, Yeltsin attempted to introduce a radical marketization policy. As mentioned earlier, the clearest indication of this came with the wide-scale freeing of prices in January 1992. This move put Russia clearly into the 'shock therapy' category, since it was implemented instantly, unlike the privatization policy of July 1991.

But the 1992 price liberalization meant Russia had finally opted for price rises *before* demonopolization had proceeded very far. The policy thus represented only partial marketization. It was also very different from the '500-day' transition programme (1990) devised by economists Grigorii Yavlinskii and Stanislav Shatalin, which had proposed Russia adopt a more incremental and differently sequenced approach. Yeltsin and his acting prime minister of 1992, Gaidar, were heavily criticized by the Russian parliament for this price reform policy. Even Yeltsin's own vice-president, Rutskoi, condemned many aspects of it.

There were several reasons for the criticisms, but five main ones. First, some of the more radical politicians considered the reforms would fail because the various components were being introduced in the wrong order. Second, many believed that radical price liberalization and moves towards marketization can encourage negative phenomena such as rising inflation, unemployment and crime rates. Third, some of the more conservative and nationalistic politicians found it difficult to accept Russia's new post-imperial and post-communist role. For them, excessive enthusiasm for the market system was seen as kowtowing to the West (that is, an external agent) and hence humiliating. Fourth, some parliamentarians were still genuinely committed to a more socialist-type economy, in which the state subsidizes many items for the welfare of most of the citizenry. Finally, some feared their power would be eroded the more that price-setting was transferred from the state to the abstract forces of the market.

By the end of 1995, the more conservative views had become dominant within the Russian parliament; while Yeltsin had still not accepted them, his approach towards marketization and economic reform more generally was far more cautious than it had been in the early 1990s.

Attempts to promote *competition*, which is an essential part of marketization, have taken many forms in the post-communist world. The ending or severe reduction of subsidies was intended *inter alia* to make enterprises more price-conscious and efficient. But another way of achieving this is to subject production units to more competition through domestic demonopolization and greater exposure to the *international* market. Largely to achieve the latter, most post-communist governments have made their currencies increasingly *convertible*. In the communist era, exchange rates were mostly set by governments, at levels that artificially boosted the value of currencies relative to Western currencies. The communist governments also had a near monopoly over exchange, generally not permitting ordinary citizens to exchange currencies freely.

The pace of moving towards convertibility has varied from country to country. In some, such as Russia, the government decided to introduce convertibility in a piecemeal manner, initially putting only some economic transactions on a true market basis in terms of exchange rates. In others, notably Poland, the government opted to switch suddenly to a convertible currency arrangement virtually across the board, although no post-communist state had by 1994 introduced *full* convertibility.

PRIVATIZATION

One reason bureaucrats in communist systems were so powerful was precisely because the state owned the means of production. Early in the twentieth century, Weber had argued that one of the most effective limitations on the powers of the capitalist state is a substantial business class to counter state bureaucracies (see Gerth and Wright Mills 1970, p. 235). The virtual absence of such a class in the communist states thus helps to explain the higher concentration of power in the hands of the *nomenklatura*.

Partly to overcome this (as part of the commitment to greater democracy), and partly because many post-communist politicians believed that a predominantly privately owned economy would perform better than a state-owned one, the post-communist states have all pursued policies of privatization. They have done so via a number of methods (see below), and at differing paces. But privatization has been a difficult process for all of them, whether they are committed in principle to a rapid or to a more incremental approach.

A major reason for this is that there did not exist a sufficiently large group of citizens in any of these countries with both the funds required to buy major enterprises off the state, and the necessary initiative, entrepreneurial skills and experience either to *want* to buy these enterprises or to make them operate efficiently once purchased. Many states – including Poland, and Czecho-Slovakia in its earliest post-communist phase – were anxious not to sell off too many of their country's assets to foreign companies, yet found it difficult to raise sufficient domestic capital for a major privatization drive (Hungary once again adopted a different position and strongly encouraged foreign investment).

Before analysing the various privatization methods, one point needs to be emphasized for an understanding of the complexities of privatization and to avoid inappropriate comparisons when discussing it. As J. F. Brown (1994, p. 147) has sensibly highlighted, two kinds of privatization have been under way in the early post-communist states. One is small in scale – of shops, restaurants, trade services (such as plumbing) and other small businesses employing only a very limited number of people. The privatization of such businesses had already begun during the communist era in several countries, and has in general been very successful in recent years. The other is large-scale privatization – of manufacturing and processing plants, extractive companies, airlines, etc. In most of the literature on post-communist privatization, and in *most* of the following analysis, the focus is on this large-scale privatization.

In endeavouring to find solutions to the problem of privatization, post-communist states have both adopted methods tried elsewhere and devised a number of new ones. For the sake of analysis, most of these can be divided

into two main groups: mass privatization programmes and foreign investment. However, the distinction between these is sometimes hazy, particularly as some countries (including two of the Baltic states) have invited
foreign companies to administer investment programmes so as to boost
privatization.

Mass privatization programmes

Two principal methods for implementing this approach have been used.
Common to both is a belief that making ordinary citizens shareholders
(either directly in enterprises, or more indirectly via investment funds),
thereby giving them a stake in the country's future, will enhance both
economic performance and the legitimacy of the post-communist system.

Citizen voucher schemes   There have been two main types of citizen
voucher schemes in the post-communist world. In the first, citizens are
allocated complimentary vouchers by the state entitling them to acquire
shares in enterprises or investment funds. Following a presidential decree in
April, such a system was introduced in Russia in late 1992; the value of the
voucher given to each citizen was 10,000 roubles. Citizens can, if they
prefer, sell their entitlement vouchers (for a detailed early analysis of the
Russian voucher programme, see Boycko and Shleifer 1993; see also Djelic
and Tsukanova 1993).

   This kind of voucher system costs the state very little, yet encourages the
development of a property-owning mentality. According to privatization
minister Anatoly Chubais, by late 1994 there were some 40 million shareholders in Russia – more than in any other country in the world. One
advantage is that all citizens are treated as if they have a direct stake in the
future success of the economy; if they opt to sell their vouchers for instant
gain, that is their 'choice'. In practice, however, many poorer citizens soon
feel compelled to sell just to survive, so that ownership becomes concen-
trated in ever fewer hands. Moreover, citizens do not have to use as much
initiative or take as much personal risk as they do in the bank credit system,
which could be seen as a disadvantage in economies trying to stimulate
entrepreneurship. Other countries that have either already introduced, or
else intend to introduce, this type of scheme include Moldova, Lithuania
and Ukraine.

   In the second type of citizen voucher system – which was adopted by
Czecho-Slovakia, and in a slightly different version was introduced in Bulgaria in January 1996 – citizens *purchase* investment vouchers from the
state. They can then exchange these for shares in joint stock companies. A
variation on this is the scheme approved by the Polish parliament in May
1993 and originally scheduled to be implemented from May 1994 (though it
still had not been by mid-1995). In this arrangement, most Polish citizens
would be able to purchase shares directly in national investment funds;
some citizens (such as pensioners) would be allocated shares free of charge.

   One advantage of the second method over the first is that it requires some commitment from citizens to the very concept of privatization, since they have to dig into their own pockets to become shareholders. Intuitively, a far lower proportion of citizens might be expected to obtain vouchers or shares in such a system than in one in which these are distributed free of charge. In practice, more than 8.5 million citizens – a substantial majority of the adult population – in former Czecho-Slovakia had bought such vouchers by late 1992. Since the price of an investment voucher was roughly equivalent to the average weekly wage in that country, the high level of public support for the scheme, encouraged by the 'get rich quick' atmosphere in which it was promoted, becomes clear. A 1992 survey suggested that a third of Polish citizens were intending to purchase shares under their government's mass privatization programme (Valencia and Frankl 1993, p. 60), though it remains to be seen whether or not this figure changes substantially by the time the scheme is actually introduced.

Although this second method is not without problems, it was sufficiently successful for a second round to be introduced in the Czech Republic itself in April 1994. Conversely, the Hungarian government had in 1993 been contemplating the introduction of such a scheme, but had by late 1994 indicated its preference for privatization through direct sell-offs (cash sales) rather than mass voucher schemes.

Employee share schemes   A more selective version of the above is one in which the employees of a particular enterprise are offered shares in it. In the July 1990 Polish privatization bill, for instance, it was envisaged that employees would be able to purchase shares in their own enterprises at half-price. As with the citizen voucher schemes, this encourages the sense of sharing in the economic future of one's country (or, more precisely, one's enterprise). But this system has the advantage over the more general one that employees not only have a vested interest in a particular enterprise but can also, assuming they continue to work for it, play a direct role in its success. They are thus encouraged to become more directly responsible than in the citizen voucher schemes.

The employee share scheme is one of the privatization methods adopted in Czechia. There the privatization ministry sought to ensure that no more than 10 per cent of the total stake in a given enterprise would be allocated via this system, a guideline the Poles also adopted in 1993. Slovenia has a higher cut-off level, having limited free employee shares to no more than 20 per cent of the total number of shares in a given enterprise (for further comparative analysis of this type of privatization see Bogetic 1993).

Foreign investment programmes

Although some post-communist governments (as in Azerbaijan, Hungary, Kazakhstan, Moldova) were in the early 1990s more enthusiastic about encouraging foreign investment than others (Poland, Czechia), all have now realized they cannot realistically hope to put their economies on a solid footing without external involvement. But the nature and scale of this can and does vary.

Joint ventures   In this arrangement, foreign investors either purchase a share in an existing enterprise (in the management of which they will henceforward have a direct say) or else invest jointly with the host country in a brand new project. This has a number of advantages for the post-communist country. First, additional funds (usually in hard currency) and/ or equipment flow into it. Second, the foreign partners often have expertise in the particular branch in which they are investing, so that the post-communist partners can gain knowledge and expertise vicariously. Third, the foreign partners will sometimes agree to purchase some of the output of the joint venture, which can be useful to a post-communist country seeking to increase its exports.

A drawback of this arrangement is that less of the profit stays in the country than in the case of a wholly domestically owned enterprise. Another potential problem is that the foreign investors can attempt to stipulate conditions the post-communist partners find difficult to accept. For instance, the former might insist on a reduction in the workforce in a region that already has high levels of unemployment. Moreover, many potential foreign investors have been wary of becoming involved in joint ventures when so many post-communist states have had ambiguous or constantly changing legislation on matters such as repatriation of profits, ownership of land and buildings, bankruptcy, etc. Thus, even where post-communist governments have been enthusiastic to pursue this method of (at least partial) privatization, they have not always been very successful.

Direct foreign investment   Here, foreign investors either buy out an existing firm or else wholly fund the establishment of a new one. The former approach usually occurs through one of three methods, depending on the way the price of a firm is determined. One way is for a government agency to specify a sale price. A practical problem with this approach, which soon became obvious in several east European states, is that it can be difficult to determine what a given factory etc. is worth when prices have for decades been set largely by planners rather than by the market. Partly for this reason, two other methods, tendering and auctions, have also been employed. Even though both have tended to be administered by state-run privatization agencies, these two methods are more genuinely market oriented than the first. In a tendering arrangement, the vendor invites written bids from potential purchasers and accepts what appears to be the best. Tenderers do not normally know what other tenderers are offering – at least until the final stages of the deal, when a given tenderer may be invited to increase its bid to counter a better offer from another tenderer. In an open auction, in contrast, potential purchasers work less in the dark in that they can instantly see what others are prepared to bid for a given unit.

Direct foreign investment has many of the same advantages and disadvantages as the joint venture arrangement, but often in more extreme form.

There are two variants on the normal conception of 'foreign' investment – one peculiar to the former GDR, the other more widespread. As in other areas, the GDR's approach to privatization was somewhat different from that of any of the other formerly communist systems, largely as a result of the country having been seen as part of a larger whole. Basically, the economy of the former GDR has been merged with a larger, well-established market economy (that of the former West Germany) to form a new economic unit. With the unification of Germany, east Germans could not legitimately complain about 'foreign' domination if west German entrepreneurs came in and purchased production units previously owned by the East German state. The sale of east German enterprises was handled by a privatization agency, the Treuhandanstalt, established in 1990 explicitly to sell off East German enterprises. Although the Treuhandanstalt sold many enterprises to non-Germans, most were sold to west Germans.

The other special version of 'foreign' investment, which is in some ways related to the first, is diaspora investment (that is, investment by natives of a given country who are now living abroad). Strictly speaking, this is not a distinct form of foreign investment. However, there has been a perception in many post-communist states that it is preferable to encourage investment by, say, Polish Americans in Polish industry than by non-Polish Americans. Certainly, it is understandable why many people in the post-communist world would believe that former citizens or their descendants – with their unique blend of wealth, expertise, family connections and often language skills – are considered more likely to settle in the post-communist country in the future than are investors with no ethnic or other ties to that country. It therefore makes sense to identify this particular form of privatization in its own right.

Three further approaches

In addition to the two major groups of privatization methods identified, of mass privatization and foreign investment, no overview would be complete without reference to the following three further approaches.

Extending bank credits   This method is associated primarily with small-scale privatization, although it can also be applied to large-scale. In the latter case, citizens with few resources wishing to buy shares either in a company being sold off by the state or – more likely – in an investment fund can borrow money from a bank to make their purchase. They then repay the bank over a set period of time, with interest. An advantage of this arrangement is that, since potential purchasers have to approach the bank themselves and commit to repaying a loan with interest, it encourages both risk-taking (entrepreneurship) and responsibility. In practice, one of the drawbacks has been that since the post-communist states had inherited such impoverished economies, many did not have sufficient funds to make much available to lending banks. Consequently, several governments have encouraged *foreign* banks to establish branches and to bring in their own funds from abroad. For some, this dependency on foreign banking capital renders their system subject to greater external influence than they would like. On the other hand, since the post-communist states have little experience with commercial, competitive banking, they can learn from the foreign banking methods being exercised on their own territory. Moreover, this is one way of attracting additional funds into a country without necessarily and directly transferring ownership of most privatized enterprises to foreigners.

Direct sell-offs to citizens   Since there were virtually no true capitalists in the communist era, it might appear strange that some post-communist governments (such as Hungary and Estonia) have placed great emphasis on selling off enterprises, mostly via tendering or auction,to anyone who can find the cash, including their own citizens. This is perfectly feasible, given the bank credit system. But one problem with the direct sell-off approach, at least in the very earliest stages of post-communism (before citizens have had much opportunity to build up capital reserves), is that many honest people suspected that some of their fellow citizens had been able to purchase factories etc. because of illegally acquired funds. Given the high levels of corruption and other forms of economic crime during the communist era (see L. Holmes 1993a), these suspicions were in some cases justified. But many post-communist politicians appear to have decided that the negative implications of this for regime and system legitimacy were outweighed by the positive implications for privatization – and hence, in the longer term, the economy and eudaemonic legitimation.

Restitution of property   The restoration of socialized property to its former (pre-communist) owners or their ancestors is yet another way of increasing the amount of private ownership in a system. Such restitution has in many cases occurred because of the post-communist authorities' sense of justice. Nevertheless, it does constitute a form of privatization – albeit mostly small in scale – with all the ramifications of this for the economy, society and politics.

Although no fewer than seven distinct approaches to privatization have been identified here, it should not be assumed that individual post-communist states choose only one of these methods, to the exclusion of others. In fact, all post-communist states have opted for *several* of these approaches. Moreover, one method is sometimes a precursor to another. For instance, citizens may borrow money from a bank (the method of 'extending bank credits') in order to purchase vouchers (the second variant of 'citizen voucher schemes') or buy directly (the method of 'direct sell-offs to citizens'). This all said, the particular blend of methods is unique to each country. Indeed, the relative salience of each approach in the overall privatization process varies over time, as governments change, as particular methods are rejected or completed, etc.

Perhaps surprisingly, given its reputation for adopting the 'shock therapy' approach, Poland has been one of the more cautious post-communist countries in the area of privatization. Whereas the GDR's Treuhandanstalt had by then listed approximately 11,000 enterprises for sale, Romania approximately 6,000 and Hungary 2,300, Poland had by the end of 1991 put up only 200 of approximately 7,500 enterprises and organizations (the reference here is to medium and large enterprises, as distinct from very small businesses – data from Kaser 1993, p. 386). This was despite the fact that the July 1990 Polish privatization bill had envisaged the eventual sale of state holdings amounting to 80 per cent of the economy. This point about Poland underscores the need to be cautious in classifying country A as having adopted a radical policy in economic transformation whereas country B has taken the more cautious route: closer analysis may reveal that country A adopted a radical policy in pricing and a cautious one in privatization, whereas country B did the opposite.

Although the analysis of privatization has focused on top-down approaches, that is, policies adopted by the state to encourage sales and investment, there has also been a limited amount of *local/'grass roots' privatization*. This has mostly been in the form of workers and managers joining forces and pooling resources to buy out the enterprise in which they all work. There were several cases of this in Poland in the early 1990s, for example (J. F. Brown 1994, p. 149, citing the *Economist*).

Problems of privatization

Many problems have emerged in the process of privatization. Although several Western analysts have pointed to the lack of an *entrepreneurial culture* as an explanation for the rather hesitant implementation of privatization, there are also many *structural reasons* for this. The major problem of a shortage of capital – as well as some of the ingenious methods devised to attempt to overcome this – has already been mentioned. Then there are *sociopolitical* reasons for slow implementation. A number of otherwise radically reformist governments have been cautious in their approach to privatization for fear that insufficiently sensitive policies might provide new owners with too much freedom to dismiss workers: the potential political implications for a government perceived to be indifferent to a growth in unemployment are obvious.

Another substantial problem is the inadequacy of the *legal framework* in so many post-communist states. As Michael Kaser (1993, p. 389) has pointed out, a properly functioning market economy requires four main types of legislative underpinning:

1 facilitating laws (laws that make it possible for a market economy to function properly, such as laws on contract);
2 prudential laws (laws that control the behaviour of financial institutions);

3 consumer protection laws, to set minimum standards for manufacturers
  and traders so as to protect purchasers against fraud, misrepresentation
  and poor quality goods;
4 economic regulation – control of prices etc. in public utilities such as
  water or electricity.

As Kaser goes on to argue, the post-communist states have so far tended to
concentrate on the first two of these.

But there is a fifth type of law that is particularly relevant in the post-
communist states, and which is not often to be found in other types of
transitional economy:

5 clarification laws – determining, in particular, who owns property.

This last area of legislation has been a minefield for post-communist governments. Many in eastern Europe have accepted the abstract notion of
restitution (returning property *or* compensating for loss of property). But
who is to be reimbursed and *how* have been highly contentious issues. For
instance, should the state recompense only those who themselves owned
property that was then forcibly seized by the communist authorities, or
should it take a broader approach and recompense their descendants? If
agricultural land was sequestered by the state decades ago and has since
been worked by farmers who have made it their home and their source of
income, is it fair to remove them and return the land to people who may
now live overseas or in cities far from the rural property (and who have
little or no knowledge of farming)? If it is considered appropriate to recompense a person or group of persons, could this be in the form of cash or
shares in companies rather than the actual land or buildings they used to
own? Should the post-communist states assume responsibility for redress-
ing the injustices perpetrated only by their immediate predecessors (that is,
the communists), or should they go further back, to the pre-communist
period? And assuming it is agreed that someone should be compensated in
kind, notably cash, how should the *sum* be determined? Should the claim-
ant receive a sum equal to the value of the property at the time the property
was seized, or at that price plus a supplement in line with officially registered inflation since the seizure, or at the current market price? How should
the latter be determined anyway, given the highly fluid and uncertain state
of the early post-communist economies? And should a potential purchaser
ever be the one responsible for compensating former owners?

All the above issues have arisen in the post-communist world since 1989,
and different countries – and different groups of politicians and economists
within one country – have reached different answers. It is well beyond the
scope of this chapter to provide even a cursory overview of these matters
(readers wanting details on individual countries could start their search with
Frydman et al. 1993). However, it should be noted that although many of
these problems may initially appear to be legal niceties, confusion over
various aspects of ownership has sometimes deterred would-be investors

and purchasers. This has only added to the problems of the already difficult privatization process, and hence of the general development and legitimation process of post-communist systems.

PRIORITIES

The very nature of post-communism is such that governments would not be expected to interfere in the economies to anything like the extent they did in the era of command economies. This said, post-communism is above all a *transitional* arrangement. Since the private sector is still fragile and emerging, governments are virtually *obliged* to play a relatively interventionist role in the economy and to specify certain priorities. After all, economic institutions cannot make their own decisions and play a relatively autonomous role until they have been established and their position vis-à-vis other institutions at least imperfectly defined within a framework of government policies and priorities. Indeed, in some post-communist states, the state has adopted what amounts to a mildly teleological approach in the economy; not *all* planning is considered anathema. President Niyazov's regime in Turkmenistan, for example, adopted an ambitious 'Ten Years of Stability' programme in 1993. This is designed to provide Turkmen citizens with a common goal to strive for, and to give his own government an image of knowing where it is heading.

One area where there appears to be proportionately less government spending in most post-communist states is defence. With the ending of the Cold War and the perceived need for much better satisfaction of the consumer, post-communist governments have less need and capacity to maintain the high levels of defence expenditure their predecessors did. This is in turn part of a move away from the privileging of the 'steel-eaters' that typified so many countries during the communist era. In fact, as post-communist countries move towards market economics, governments are in a much weaker position to privilege *any* sector or branch than they were when the communists were in power.

PERFORMANCE

Given all the problems and confusion identified earlier, plus the sheer scale of the task of totally transforming the economy of even the smaller ones, it is hardly surprising that the performance of the early post-communist states has by many criteria been unimpressive. It is also understandable why many potential investors have been cautious about making major investments in these countries until the governments have passed comprehensive and unambiguous legislation on ownership, repatriation of profits, taxation, etc. This uncertainty has been a major cause of poor performance in early post-communism.

The economic data on the early post-communist states are generally more reliable than those of the communist era (although extreme caution must still be exercised in the case of countries that remain highly disorganized, such as Russia). Performance is in most cases now being measured in a manner similar to that customary in Western states. The dramatic decline following the collapse of communism, and some of the difficulties experienced during the first years of post-communism, can be gleaned from tables 8.2 and 8.3.

In light of the problems in so many post-communist states of gathering accurate and complete information, the data should not be treated as sacrosanct. Nevertheless, it is clear that all post-communist economies experienced a *severe* contraction in the early 1990s. One of the most serious social problems this has led to is a marked increase in unemployment, to levels as high as 35 per cent in some relatively peaceful parts of the post-communist world (such as parts of Slovakia) – and an estimated 70 per cent in unstable areas such as Georgia. Since there had been little real unemployment in most communist states, most citizens were scarcely aware of the problems associated with it. Hence, such a sudden and dramatic rise in unemployment was even more traumatic for the populations of the post-communist states than it would be for Westerners (see chapter 9 for further details on unemployment).

At the same time, as many prices were allowed to find their own levels, virtually all post-communist states experienced severe inflation, as revealed in tables 8.4 and 8.5. At first glance, tables 8.2 to 8.5 tell a most depressing story. There has unquestionably been widespread and severe economic hardship in the early years of post-communism. Yet, as with all data, the reality behind the figures is more complex than the raw data can convey.

First, it must be remembered that many citizens of the post-communist

Table 8.2 Annual percentage growth of GDP in countries of eastern Europe

	1989	1990	1991	1992	1993	1994	1995[a]	1996[a]
Albania	9.8	−10.0	−27.1	−9.7	11.0	7.4	6.0	5.0
Bosnia-Hercegovina	1.6[b]							
Bulgaria	−0.6	−9.3	−11.7	−7.3	−2.4	1.4	2.0	3.0
Croatia	−1.9[b]	−8.5	−20.9	−9.7	−3.7	0.8	3.0	
Czechia	–	–	–	−6.4	−0.9	2.6	4.6	4.7
Czecho-Slovakia	1.4	−1.6	−14.7	−7.0	–	–	–	–
Hungary	0.7	−3.5	−11.9	−3.0	−0.8	2.9	2.0	3.0
Rep. of Macedonia[b]		−9.9	−10.7	−14.0	−14.1	−7.2	−3.0	3.0
Poland	0.2	−11.6	−7.0	2.6	3.8	5.1	5.9	5.0
Romania	−5.8	−5.6	−12.9	−8.8	1.5	3.9	6.9	4.0
Serbia-Montenegro[b]	–	–	–	−26.2	−27.7	6.5	6.5	6.0
Slovakia	–	–	−15.8	−6.0	−4.1	4.8	6.6	5.3
Slovenia	−2.7	−4.7	−8.1	−5.4	1.3	5.0	5.5	4.5
SFR Yugoslavia[b]	0.8	−6.0	−18.0[a]	–	–	–	–	–

[a] Estimates or forecasts.
[b] Gross Social Product.

Sources: EIU *Country Reports* and *Business Central Europe*, directly cited or calculated by the author.

Table 8.3 Annual percentage growth of GDP in countries of the FSU

	1990	1991	1992	1993	1994	1995[a]	1996[a]
Armenia	−7.2	−10.8	−52.4	−14.8	5.4		
Azerbaijan	−11.7	−0.7	−22.6	−23.1	−22.0		
Belarus	−3.2[b]	−1.2	−9.6	−11.6	−21.5	−10.0	−5.0
Estonia	−8.1	−11.9	−19.3	−2.1	4.7	3.8	3.5
Georgia[b]	−11.1	−13.8	−40.3	−39.1	−40.0		
Kazakhstan	−0.8	−11.8	−13.0	−12.9[a]	−25.4[a]	−10.0	−3.0
Kyrgyzstan	3.2	−5.0	−25.0	−16.0	−26.2[a]	−2.5	
Latvia	−3.4	−8.3	−32.9	−11.7	2.0	1.0	2.5
Lithuania	−6.9	−13.4	−35.0	−16.5	1.0	2.5	1.0
Moldova	−1.5	−18.0	−29.1	−8.7	−22.0	−1.0	6.0
Russia	−2.1	−12.9	−18.5	−12.0	−15.0	−2.5	3.0
Tajikistan[b]	−1.6	−12.5	−33.7	−28.0	−20.0[a]		
Turkmenistan[b]	2.0	−5.0	−5.3	−8.0	−10.0[a]	3.0	
Ukraine	−3.6[b]	−11.9	−17.0	−14.2	−24.3	−12.0	−3.0
Uzbekistan	1.6	−0.5	−9.6	−2.0	−2.6	−15.0	

[a] Estimates or forecasts.
[b] Net Material Product.

Sources: As for table 8.2.

Table 8.4 Annual inflation rate of consumer prices in countries of eastern Europe (per cent)

	1989	1990	1991	1992	1993	1994	1995[a]
Albania	0	0	37.0	226.0	86.0	20.0	10.0
Bosnia-Hercegovina	–	–	–				
Bulgaria	6.4	21.6	334.0	82.6	72.8	96.2	63.0
Croatia	–	–	–	665.0	1,517.0	−2.5	3.5
Czechia	–	–	–	–	20.8	10.0	8.9
Czecho-Slovakia	1.4	10.0	57.8	10.0	–	–	–
Hungary	17.0	28.9	34.8	23.0	22.5	18.8	27.0
Rep. of Macedonia	–	–	–	1,691.0	335.0	122.0	17.0
Poland	251.0	585.8	70.3	45.3	36.9	33.3	28.5
Romania	1.1	5.1	174.5	210.9	290.3	136.7	32.3
Serbia-Montenegro	–	–	–	9,237.0	116.5	0.0	80.0
Slovakia	–	–	–	–	23.2	13.4	9.9
Slovenia	–	–	117.7	201.3	32.3	19.8	13.0
SFR Yugoslavia	1,240.0	583.0	117.0[a]	–	–	–	–

[a] Estimates or forecasts.

Sources: As for table 8.2.

states *expected* pain. Many realized that the old-style command economies were failing, or had already failed, by many important criteria. In this sense, many post-communist governments enjoyed a honeymoon period; citizens were prepared to endure short-term suffering as long as there was light at the end of the tunnel.

Table 8.5 Annual inflation rate of consumer prices in countries of the FSU (per cent)

	1990	1991	1992	1993	1994	1995[a]
Armenia	10.3	100.0	825.0	3,732.0	5,273.0	
Azerbaijan	7.8	106.0	616.0	1,130.0	1,664.0	
Belarus	4.5	83.5	969.0	1,188.0	2,127.0	260.0
Estonia	17.2	210.6	1,069.3	89.0	47.7	29.0
Georgia	3.3	7.9	1,463.0	7,492.0	7,380.0	
Kazakhstan	4.2	90.9	1,513.0	1,571.0	2,000.0[a]	200.0
Kyrgyzstan	3.0	85.0	855.0	1,209.0	455.0[a]	30.0
Latvia	10.5	124.5	951.2	109.0	36.6	26.0
Lithuania	8.4	224.7	1,020.5	409.2	71.8	40.0
Moldova	4.2	98.0	944.0	688.0	108.0	25.0
Russia	5.0	92.6	1,354.0	883.3	320.0	197.0
Tajikistan	4.0	103.0	1,156.0	2,195.0	2,300.0[a]	
Turkmenistan	4.6	102.0	493.0	1,850.0	1,608.0[a]	800.0
Ukraine	4.2	91.2	1,310.0	4,735.0	891.0	380.0
Uzbekistan	3.1	82.0	528.0	1,312.0	820.0[a]	700.0

[a] Estimates or forecasts.

Sources: As for table 8.2.

Unfortunately, the suffering has been much deeper and more prolonged than almost anyone expected, and it is not surprising that many inhabitants of post-communist countries become angry when told by observers from affluent countries that four or five years of economic hardship is worthwhile if it places economies on a much stronger long-term footing. Yet the tables also reveal a marked slowdown in the decline of economic performance in most post-communist countries, and that some had already by 1993 – others by 1994 – either arrested the decline altogether or even entered a positive growth phase.

Moreover, the economic growth in most of these countries – parts of the FSU and former Yugoslavia being exceptions – is likely to improve further during the late 1990s if they more or less continue along their current paths (do not become populist dictatorships, for example), and as long as the West does not fall into a serious recession. A continuation of the current policies of marketization, privatization, legal clarification and formalization of so many aspects of ownership etc. will inspire greater confidence in investors, with positive knock-on effects. This said, high levels of inflation and unemployment are likely to continue to be serious problems for many countries for some time yet.

Second, there has been a marked improvement in both the *quality* and *availability* of goods in many post-communist countries. This is a function of several factors, including the general improvement in the consumer goods and service sectors, and a marked increase in trade with the West. At present many citizens feel frustrated when they can see the goods they want in their shops but cannot afford to buy them. However, this is another dimension of the 'light at the end of the tunnel' syndrome. During the communist era, many citizens had money to spend, but little to buy; over time, this meant that higher wages became increasingly ineffective as an incentive to greater productivity, with all the implications of this for economic growth. Under the new arrangements, in contrast, many people have already used up most of their savings. However, there is now a real incentive – for the more materialistically minded citizens at least – to work harder so that they can purchase goods which, though expensive, are at least available. This 'carrot' should act as a further stimulus to economic growth, with positive effects for most people.

Third, although the rate of privatization has been slower than some were hoping for, it has nevertheless been impressive in many countries, especially given the considerable problems identified earlier. Already by late 1992 the proportion of GDP emanating from the private sector (small, medium and large businesses) in most east European countries ranged from around 20 per cent in the Czech Lands, Slovakia and Bulgaria to over 40 per cent in Hungary and 45 per cent in Poland (Slay 1993, pp. 48–55). Figures 8.1 and 8.2 reveal that these proportions had already risen substantially by mid-1994. They also demonstrate that even many parts of the FSU, despite their slightly later transition to post-communism, had already made substantial progress in privatizing their economies.

The black market has not disappeared under post-communism, but the situation is likely to improve in the coming years. At present, in early post-

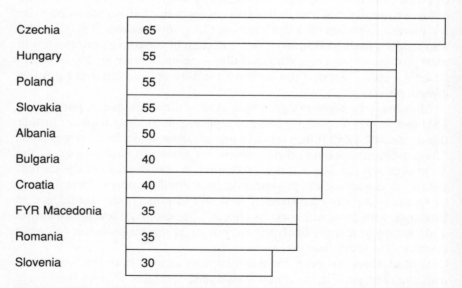

Figure 8.1 Approximate percentage share of the private sector in GDP in countries of eastern Europe, mid-1994, rank ordered (EBRD estimates, reproduced in *The European*, 21–7 Oct. 1994, p. 18; no data available for Bosnia-Hercegovina or Serbia-Montenegro)

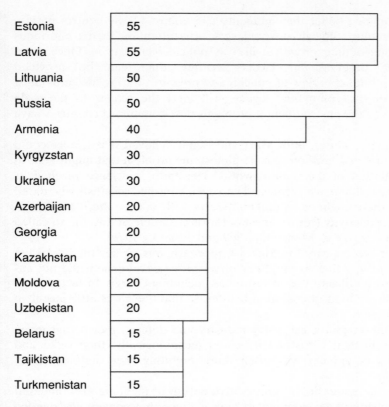

Figure 8.2 Approximate percentage share of the private sector in GDP in countries of the FSU, mid-1994, rank ordered (source as for figure 8.1)

communism, the lack of established authority in many countries (especially of the FSU) is one reason that mafia-style economic crime has increased in comparison with the communist period. But if growing numbers of citizens are able to afford more and more goods (as the balance between supply and demand evens out), and if the authority and legitimacy of post-communist regimes and systems increase, so the significance of many of the major reasons for black marketeering will begin to decline. Although their continued existence throughout the Western world is evidence that they will never disappear altogether, corruption and economic crime should become a less salient feature of everyday life than they currently are in so many post-communist states.

The Environment

One of the policy areas for which the communists can be most severely criticized is environmental management. Partly as a function of their

Marxist-Leninist belief that humanity can almost totally control nature, most communist officials devoted very little attention to the enormous damage some of their 'growth at all costs' policies were causing. Once again, this topic deserves far closer scrutiny than can be provided here. But a brief overview of policies and pressures during the communist era, and of the communist legacy, will alert the reader to the scale and nature of the environmental problems post-communist countries have inherited.

As intimated above, both Marx and Lenin believed that science could master nature and find solutions to almost any problem that might arise in the exploitation of the natural world. This faith in science reached its apogee under Stalin, who criticized and even punished scientists who dared to suggest there might be natural limits, especially in agriculture, to production and productivity (for the most notorious example of this, the so-called Lysenko affair, see Z. Medvedev 1969 and Joravsky 1970).

Another reason why the Stalinist approach was so destructive to the environment was that its emphasis on *extensive* development did not encourage more efficient use of resources, including energy. In fact, energy was very cheap in most communist states, so that there was little incentive to use it frugally.

Third, the emphasis on heavy industry and defence meant that many enterprises in light industry fell behind technologically; their older and more worn equipment was often more polluting than state-of-the-art technology.

Finally, the increasingly conservative nature of planning also hindered the emergence and development of radical, more environmentally friendly, new technologies.

The Stalinist model was modified, in some cases substantially, in most communist states during the 1950s and 1960s (the Soviet leadership eventually realized what a charlatan the pseudo-geneticist Lysenko was). Some of the changes were beneficial to the environment, and to thinking about humanity's relationship with nature more generally. Certainly, several communist states revealed greater sensitivity to the environment. Many established ministries or similar bodies to deal with ecological issues: Poland had a Ministry of Environmental Protection and Natural Resources, for example. Between 1957 and 1963, following Estonia's lead, all of the union republics of the USSR adopted laws on the conservation of nature (Komarov 1978, p. 63). And the GDR, in particular, had by the 1980s established relatively impressive recycling processes.

Despite such improvements, most communist states remained secretive about the environment until shortly before their collapse; as late as the mid-1980s, only Poland and Yugoslavia were fairly open about ecological issues (DeBardeleben 1991b, p. 17). While *glasnost* represented a significant move towards greater government openness and honesty in the USSR during the late 1980s, it should not be forgotten that the Soviet government was initially reluctant to release information about the worst environmental disaster ever in the communist bloc, the 1986 explosion at Chernobyl (see below). Only when the West raised the alarm did the Gorbachev government acknowledge that a major accident had occurred.

As will be demonstrated in chapter 10, unofficial environmental activists scored limited successes in some communist states during the 1970s and 1980s. Another source of pressure on communist governments was the West. Part of this influence was indirect: environmental activists were able to use Western reports in their endeavours to have their own communist governments adopt more environmentally friendly policies. But the West also attempted to exert pressure directly. One reason for this was a general issue of principle; as awareness of the global effects of many forms of pollution spread, so the developed states accepted some responsibility for setting an example and encouraging others to become more ecologically aware. Another reason, which applied particularly to countries such as West Germany, was more self-interested. Some West European states were being directly affected by the growing pollution emanating from Poland, Czechoslovakia and the GDR in particular. Although the Cold War meant that communist governments were loath to concede to Western pressure, they could not totally ignore it, since they had a vested interest in reducing tensions (and hence defence expenditure), increasing trade, gaining greater access to Western technology, and so on.

But there were also counterpressures. One was Comecon policies. One particularly relevant example that pertained from the mid-1970s (in the wake of the global 'oil crisis' of 1973) related to the fact that energy pricing within Comecon moved closer to world market prices. As the largest suppliers of fuels within the CMEA, the Soviets were no longer willing to subsidize, as they saw it, the costs of energy. In theory, one result of a large hike in energy prices could be more efficient use of energy; had this occurred in the communist world, this would almost certainly have had positive implications for the environment. But several East European states attempted to handle the problem of higher energy prices within Comecon by becoming more self-sufficient rather than more efficient. The GDR, notably, began to make much greater use of its own brown coal reserves; unfortunately, this coal is not only a much less effective source of energy than hard black coal or oil but also, when burning, pollutes the atmosphere far more. Unlike the GDR, communist Poland had good reserves of high-grade black coal. But, in their endeavours to improve the state of the economy, the Polish authorities sought to sell much of their best fossil fuel for hard currency and used the more polluting, lower-grade coal at home.

Overall, the impact of Marxist-Leninist ideology, Stalinist priorities, and economic imperatives greatly outweighed the newer counterweights of unofficial environmentalist movements and Western pressure in the communist world, and the post-communist countries have been left an appalling environmental legacy. This can be examined in terms of the soil, the water and the air.

The soil in many places was severely polluted by decades of communist environmental mismanagement. Excessive, inadequate or inappropriate use of fertilizer was a major cause of soil problems such as erosion of topsoil, salinization and chemical imbalance. By the mid-1980s, for example, acidification in Hungary was described by one specialist as 'very intense' in 30 per cent of the soil, while 70 per cent of soils were producing far too little nitrogen for good crop cultivation (cited in Kiraly 1991, p. 200).

Probably the best-known example of soil depletion was the disastrous exploitation of the so-called Virgin Lands in the USSR during the 1950s. Stalin's successor, Khrushchev, promised a substantial improvement in food supplies. In a manner typical of that era, the new Soviet leader sought to boost grain production through extensive methods. He brought over 30 million hectares of previously uncultivated (hence 'virgin') land in southern Russia and northern Kazakhstan into agricultural use, thereby dramatically increasing the total amount of arable land. Alec Nove (1992, p. 340) captures well the sheer scale of this project: 'Between 1953 and 1956 the amount of cultivated land was increased by 35.9 million hectares, an area equivalent to the total cultivated land of Canada. World history knows nothing like it.' Initially, the results were extremely impressive. But by the end of the decade inadequate replenishment of the soil had transformed much of the Virgin Lands into a giant dustbowl.

If a very parochial attitude is adopted, it could be argued that pollution of the soil affects only those living on or near it; although this is not strictly accurate, in that produce grown in that soil might be exported, for instance, it is true that soil pollution in one country is less likely to have major implications for other countries than does pollution of the water or air. These should therefore be considered.

A Soviet study published in 1984 argued that the GDR had the most severely polluted water in Eastern Europe, and that it was much more polluted than water in Poland and Czechoslovakia (in Ziegler 1991, p. 86). Nevertheless, according to some estimates, approximately half of Poland's lakes had by 1990 been contaminated by acid rain, while a staggering 95 per cent of the country's river water was deemed unfit for human consumption. By the same date, approximately half of Czecho-Slovakia's drinking water was contaminated.

A different problem is the overuse of water. During the 1970s the Soviets attempted dramatically to increase the cotton crop. As part of this programme, they made excessive use, for irrigation purposes, of the water in what was once the world's fourth largest inland sea, the Aral Sea in Kazakhstan and Uzbekistan. By the early 1990s there had been a decline in the volume of water in this sea, in comparison with the 1960s, of some 65 per cent. This led one commentator (Martin 1994, p. 43) to write, 'Most experts agree that the drying up of the Aral Sea is the greatest man-made catastrophe of modern times.'

One particularly disturbing aspect of communist disregard for water resources, the implications of which reach (and will continue to reach) far beyond the communist world, is Soviet dumping of radioactive waste into the sea. The Japanese, for example, have been very concerned in the 1990s about the effects on fish stocks of Soviet (and post-Soviet) dumping of nuclear waste into the Sea of Japan.

Turning now to air pollution: at the beginning of the 1990s the formerly communist countries of Eastern Europe accounted for approximately one-third of Europe's GDP but about two-thirds of its sulphur dioxide emissions. Expressed another way, the countries of Eastern Europe had been producing on average approximately four times more sulphur dioxide pollution – which is highly damaging both to the ozone layer and to human health – than the countries of Western Europe. Although such emissions declined by approximately 25 per cent in Western Europe during the 1980s, they increased (by approximately 4 per cent) in Eastern Europe. Perhaps the starkest contrast was between the two Germanies. By 1988 the level of East German emissions of sulphur dioxide per unit of GNP was more than 30 times higher than the West German level. One of the most visible signs of air pollution – in particular, of acid rain – was the considerable damage done to forests in the northern part of Eastern Europe. According to one estimate (cited in J. F. Brown 1994, p. 167), some 70 per cent of the forest trees in Czechoslovakia had by the early 1990s been damaged by pollution.

Without doubt, the best-known example of airborne pollution from one communist country affecting not only other communist states but also countries in Western Europe and even Africa and North America was the result of the accident at the Chernobyl (Ukraine) nuclear plant in April 1986. Although the type of reactor in which the accident occurred was different from those that predominated in Eastern Europe (or Western Europe), the Chernobyl disaster alerted citizens throughout the world to the dangers and ramifications of nuclear accidents, and to the fact that airborne pollution does not recognize either international borders or different types of politico-economic systems (on Chernobyl and its aftermath see Marples 1987, Z. Medvedev 1990, G. Medvedev 1991).

Summarizing the overall extent of pollution in the largest communist state, Russian economist M. Kozeltsev wrote:

> Under the communist system, the degradation of the environment reached an extreme ... Almost the entire map of the former USSR is covered by dark spots representing ecological crises or disasters. Altogether these represent about one hundred regions covering 3.7 million square kilometers, or 16 per cent of the whole territory of the former USSR. Given the size of the country and the scale of its industry (third in the world in terms of gross national product), it has had a significant impact on the global environment, depleting the world's natural resources and poisoning the environment with radioactive wastes. (1993, p. 59)

As for Eastern Europe, perhaps just as startling is the fact that an area covering most of the GDR and substantial parts of Poland and Czechoslovakia was by the end of the 1980s being identified by many environmental specialists as the most heavily polluted region on earth.

To conclude this discussion of the communist legacy, it is worth noting that in June 1990 the new (post-communist) federal environment minister of Czecho-Slovakia, Josef Vavrousek, stated publicly that life expectancy in

Northern Bohemia (a major manufacturing area, and one of the Czech Lands' major brown coal producing areas) was some ten years lower than the average in Western Europe, *due mainly to environmental pollution*. That the Czecho-Slovak population was well aware of environmental problems and seriously concerned about them is borne out by the results of an opinion survey of 1,500 Czech and Slovak citizens conducted in January 1990 and reported in the main Czecho-Slovak newspaper (*Rude Pravo*) in the following month. According to this, the state of the environment was considered one of the country's most urgent problems by a higher percentage (55 per cent) of respondents than was any other issue, including the 'state of public morale' (30 per cent) and 'health care and the cost of living' (24 per cent). When asked what problems the post-communist government should tackle first, 42 per cent of respondents identified 'solving environmental problems' – well ahead of 'social and health issues' (30 per cent) and 'supplying the domestic market' (26 per cent) (all details from Ramet 1995, p. 465). Surveys conducted in other countries at about the time of the collapse of the communist systems suggest similar concerns, and widespread support for environmental activist groups. For instance, more than three-quarters of those surveyed for a Bulgarian opinion poll in December 1989 approved of the unofficial ecological group Ecoglasnost – which was a far higher level of support than for any other official or unofficial organization (Ramet 1995, p. 462; on the USSR/Russia see Kozeltsev 1993, p. 71).

Given the survey data just cited, and the fact that governments in the post-communist era are supposed to be far more responsive to popular concerns than were their communist predecessors, it would be reasonable to assume that official policy in early post-communism has become far more environmentally friendly. Unfortunately, the available evidence does not clearly endorse this assumption.

There have certainly been *some* positive signs, as a brief comparison with the factors identified in the communism section as antithetical to the environment reveals. Thus, post-communist governments are not as ideologically insensitive to the environment as were Marxist-Leninists. Moreover, as positive economic growth begins to pick up, it is doing so more because of restructuring and intensive policies than extensive ones. Defence does not enjoy the privileged position it did, and many consumer goods industries are being modernized. The marked reduction of central planning, removal of subsidies, spread of competition and rapid moves towards market pricing (including in energy) are all counteracting the previous tendency for industries and sectors to resist change that might lead to greater efficiency and more environmentally friendly technologies. This trend is endorsed by the reorientation of the foreign trade of so many post-communist countries towards the West.

Several post-communist governments have taken concrete measures to protect and improve the environment. Many have replaced ministries or similar bodies from the communist period with revamped counterparts, and some have established additional bodies. Within Russia, for example, the Ministry of Ecology and Natural Resources has essentially replaced the Soviet All-Union Committee for Hydrometeorology and Environmental Control; but in addition, a new post of State Counsellor for Ecology and Public Health has been established, with the incumbent answerable directly to the president.

There has also been new legislation designed to improve the environment, although this is truer of some countries (such as the East Central European states) than of others (many of the states of the FSU). Post-communist governments in Poland, Hungary and Czecho-Slovakia quickly introduced laws based on the relatively high standards of official EC ecological guidelines, and Poland and Czecho-Slovakia offered government bonds for sale as a means of raising revenue for cleaning up the environment. In 1991, shortly before its collapse, the USSR introduced pollution charges whereby enterprises were to be taxed for each polluting element they released into the environment. In addition, some of the most polluting enterprises in several countries have been either temporarily or permanently shut down, and some of the potentially most dangerous nuclear reactors (such as the Kozloduy station in Bulgaria) subjected to more stringent safety codes.

Generally, post-communist governments have been far more open about the scale and nature of environmental pollution in their countries than were all but the most liberal of communist governments; in an October 1992 speech to the Russian parliament, President Yeltsin claimed: 'For the first time in 70 years, we are telling people openly and honestly about the scale of the ecological disaster we have inherited.'

Finally, since so many post-communist politicians are seeking to learn from and trade more with the West, market principles and Western emphasis in recent years on ecological matters are now very rarely treated as hostile capitalist propaganda.

Yet it would be quite wrong to infer from the above that the environment is now healthy, or even well on the way to recovery. Admittedly, the available evidence indicates a general decline in most forms of pollution in these countries during the 1990s. However, this is largely because of the marked decrease in manufacturing output, and does not *per se* provide any reason for continued optimism as these economies begin to pick up.

Some of the problems could be *relatively* easily solved. For instance, the current shortage of expertise in environmental management could be – in some cases already is being – solved by training personnel from the post-communist countries in Western countries more experienced in tackling such issues.

But there are also much bigger problems that cannot be overcome so readily. Thus there are often profound tensions between some of the policies and practices designed to improve the environment, on the one hand, and many of those designed, on the other hand, to foster economic growth and so enhance eudaemonic legitimation. Since all post-communist states currently have very limited resources available for investment, they frequently have to choose between the environment and modernization; unfortunately, if understandably, the latter usually takes priority. Some of the positive moves listed earlier are thus less impressive than they initially appear. The legislation in Poland and elsewhere passed in emulation of the EC, for instance, includes relatively distant deadlines for implementation – typically at the end of the 1990s or early next century. Even where legislation *is* intended to be immediately effective, it is often difficult to monitor adequately. Moreover, if proposals to shut polluting plants would increase unemployment, most post-communist governments will – again understandably – think twice about adopting them. This in turn renders it more difficult for the state to force private owners of enterprises to close plants on environmental grounds.

Another problem is that the West does not always exert the positive influence it might be expected to. There certainly has been pressure to meet minimum environmental standards, for instance from the World Bank, and from the European Commission, which in 1993 released an 'Environmental Action Programme for Central and Eastern Europe'. But the rhetoric and programmes of Western governments and supranational organizations are not always accompanied by action. Moreover, there is evidence that many private Western investors in the post-communist countries have not been insisting on environmentally friendly development. Indeed, some Western companies appear to have consciously sought to take advantage of early post-communism's slack or confused regulations on pollution control to turn a higher profit than they would have done in the more regulated West. Conversely, some more reputable Western firms have held back on investment precisely because of, *inter alia*, confusion over environment-related laws; many prefer to wait and see what the new legislation looks like before making final decisions on large-scale long-term investments (on all this see Baumgartl 1993). Some Western investors, it must be acknowledged, *have* been very responsible, introducing efficient scrubbers and other forms of pollution control in factories and processing plants. But there is a disincentive to continue doing this if competitors can produce similar items more cheaply (and hence increase market share) because they have not been required to install the most environmentally sensitive equipment.

Hence, while the effects of greater interaction with the West *should* eventually be beneficial to the post-communist countries, the current mixture of a need to attract investment at almost any cost and an inability to agree on and implement tough environmental legislation means that the implications of economic *rapprochement* with the West have been at best mixed, and in some cases downright detrimental to the environment.

Writing about eastern Europe – although her statement is equally true of the FSU – in 1992, Barbara Jancar-Webster (1993b, p. 4) concluded: 'Election rhetoric notwithstanding, no government has yet undertaken any serious remedial environmental program.' The situation has probably improved, but not markedly, since those words were written. Is there much likelihood of substantial improvement in the future?

Certainly, the *potential* for this exists. On the one hand, since many forms of pollution cross national boundaries, West Europeans should in future become more insistent on better care of the environment in post-communist countries. There is a reasonable chance that this will occur as Western economies pick up, enabling both governments and investors to look beyond the often narrow, short-term economic perspectives so many adopted in the early 1990s. The West needs to be sensitive in its endeavours, however, if it is not to appear to be a bully. On the other hand, perhaps enough politicians and citizens *within* the post-communist world will come to realize that unfettered economic development is in no one's long-term interests and that *sustainable* growth is needed, and will want to do something about it themselves. At that point, the environment will rapidly move up the agenda, to occupy the privileged position it briefly appeared to in a few countries just before and during the collapse of communist power. It is in everyone's interest that this occurs.

Conclusions

This chapter has highlighted some of the major problems and even contradictions of the post-communist economies; the wide range of often highly innovative methods proposed and introduced to deal with them; and the fact that several post-communist economies appeared by 1994 to have either turned the corner or to be about to do so – albeit following enormous declines in the earliest years of post-communism, and even though inflation, unemployment and the environment continued to be serious problems in most.

By the end of 1994 there were also just a few signs that some of the earliest stages of transition had already been completed in a few post-communist states. For example, the Treuhandanstalt was officially wound up at the end of that year, since it was considered to have achieved most of its objectives (a few remaining tasks were taken over by other organizations). And in a 1994 interview (in the *Weekend Australian*, 5–6 February 1994, p. 23), Czech Prime Minister Klaus argued that: 'We have crossed the Rubicon . . . When I talk about systemic change, which means changing the institutions, changing the rules, I would simply dare to argue that we are, to put it differently, on the other side of the Rubicon.'

But such signs of 'completion' are rare, and much still remains to be done even in the former GDR and Czechia. At this juncture, it is appropriate to make two important points about the prospects for the post-communist economies.

First, these cannot be isolated from the larger context in which they all operate. In particular, the extent and pace at which the countries of the EU pull out of the economic lethargy of the early to mid 1990s and sustain strong growth, and the degree to which the EU then opens up to other European countries (see chapter 11), will be of critical importance.

Second, many of the post-communist states *should* have good prospects in the medium to long term. Many of those currently experiencing particularly severe hardships – such as Russia, Azerbaijan and Georgia – are rich in natural resources. Many others that are less well endowed naturally have relatively well-trained workforces whose labour is still comparatively cheap by international standards. In addition, new investment in these countries could bring them up to the highest technological standards.

Unfortunately, it is not yet clear that or when such potential will be realized. The communist legacy was a very poor one and it was inevitable that there would be serious dislocations and suffering in the transition. Nevertheless, it is vital that the economic performance of the post-communist states shows even clearer signs of improvement soon, and that such improvement accelerates, since many governments are already well beyond the end of the honeymoon period. Since poor economic performance is so often linked with civil unrest and the emergence of extremist politics – topics considered in chapter 10 – the urgency of, for instance, establishing clear-cut economic laws and policies comes sharply into focus.

But before considering some of these particularly menacing aspects of post-communism, it is important to analyse one of the most significant double-binds for governments; it relates to the social implications of the economic difficulties elaborated in this chapter. Largely in order to modernize and restructure their economies and render them more efficient, most post-communist governments have had to permit some enterprises either to go bankrupt or to undergo substantial restructuring. In this restructuring process, production typically plummets, so that state revenue does too. Simultaneously, unemployment increases. Despite reduced income, the state must do what it can to alleviate suffering among the unemployed and low paid, for both humanitarian and legitimation purposes. This welfare dilemma is a substantial problem – and a major theme of the next chapter.

FURTHER READING

Two excellent introductions to the Soviet economy are Nove 1986 and 1992. On the East European economies see Lovenduski and Woodall 1987, chs 4 and 5, and Hohmann, Kaser and Thalheim 1975. An outstanding overview of communist economics generally is Kornai 1992, while Brus 1973 provides a most stimulating analysis of the interaction of politics and economics in the communist world.

There is a huge literature on post-communist transitional economies. However, much of it is highly specialized; beginners could usefully start with Aslund 1992, Keren and Ofer 1992, or J. F. Brown 1994, ch. 5. Lavigne 1995 is particularly useful, since it deals comparatively with both the communist and post-communist eras.

On environmental issues in the communist era see Volgyes 1974; Singleton 1987; Ziegler 1987; Pryde 1991; Feshbach and Friendly 1992.

Analyses of the environmental question in the late communist and early post-communist eras include DeBardeleben 1991a; Jancar-Webster 1993a; Carter and

Turnock 1993.

For up-to-date information, see the periodicals mentioned at the end of chapter 7, plus the quarterly EIU *Country Reports* and the monthly *Business Central Europe*. For more long-term, scholarly analyses see *Communist Economies and Economic Transformation* and *Economics of Transition*.

9

Social Policies and Problems

For many of their citizens, as well as for Westerners having sympathy for such systems, a major redeeming feature of communist states was their achievements in the field of social policy. While citizens often had only very limited freedoms of the kind most Westerners take for granted (of speech, travel, religious belief, etc.), they did in general enjoy free health care, free education, virtually guaranteed employment, inexpensive housing, state retirement pensions, cheap child-care facilities, etc. Indeed, so extensive were the provisions in most communist countries that the latter have been described as either 'cradle to grave' or 'womb to tomb' welfare states.

This chapter begins with a consideration of the achievements and problems of both communist and post-communist systems in five areas – health care, pensions, unemployment benefits, housing, and education; in short, the focus is on welfare in a broad sense. Following this, attention is directed towards explicitly gender-related aspects of social policy; this leads to a discussion of the position and particular problems of women in both communist and post-communist systems.

Welfare Policies under Communism

Although it was Wilhelmine Germany rather than any of the communist states that first introduced the welfare state (Rose 1991, p. 12), and while one or two East European countries had well-developed health care and pension schemes long before the communists took power (for instance, Hungary – see Pataki 1993a, p. 57), welfarism was an early and high priority of communist states. In all of them, one of the first priorities was to provide universal, free and state-supervised *medical services*. This aim was met by the 1920s in the case of the USSR, by the late 1940s in the case of all the East European states. Many of these countries used to boast of their achievements in these areas. For instance, the GDR authorities claimed in 1988 that they had 32.7 doctors for every 10,000 citizens, in comparison with 28.7 per 10,000 citizens in the FRG. In the same year, according to official CMEA statistics, Bulgaria had 37.5 doctors for every 10,000 people, Czechoslovakia had 36.6 and Hungary had 33.2. Whereas the USSR had only 1 doctor per 10,000 head of population in 1917, by 1987 this figure had climbed to 43.6 (Buckley 1990, p. 195). This compares with 13.6 and 25.2 doctors per 10,000 citizens in the USA in approximately the same years (1920, 1987).

For many years, the communists seemed genuinely to be improving the health of their citizens. Average life expectancy increased from approximately 32 years to almost 70 years between 1913 and the mid-1960s in the USSR (Powell 1991, p. 173); from 61.4 years to 71.5 years between 1952 and 1988 in Poland; and from 56.6 years in 1941 to 66.7 years in 1955 and 70.1 years in 1988 in Hungary. Disabled people were in most cases entitled to state-provided disability benefits and pensions.

But such data do not reveal the many problems there were with the medical services in many communist countries. Just four will be identified here.

First, although the authorities claimed that health-care services were free, in practice many citizens in the USSR, Hungary and other countries knew they could only obtain adequate and timely service if they paid doctors privately (usually illegally). That so many citizens opted to do this provides clear evidence of the inadequacy of the socially provided services.

Second, it should not be assumed that simply because country A has a higher number of doctors per 10,000 citizens than country B, this indicates better health-care services in the former. Sometimes, it reflects the fact that the medical technology in country A is inferior to that in country B. Certainly, the average level of medical technology in the communist world was well below that of the West.

Third, most people accept the unfortunate fact that the provision of medical services will never be ideal and that needs have to be prioritized. The essentially paternalistic and non-privatized nature of communist systems meant that most citizens had very little say in the prioritization of scarce resources and merely had to accept whatever choices were made by the politicians and bureaucrats on their behalf.

But perhaps the most damning criticism to be levelled against some communist states, notably the USSR, for much of the 1970s and 1980s was that they were caring so little for their citizens that average life expectancy was *declining*. Thus, having risen by 26 years between 1926 and 1972 (to 70), life expectancy fell again by 1985 to 69 (73 for women, 64 for men – Buckley 1990, p. 195). In this, the USSR diverged from the trend in most Western industrial countries. Although average life expectancy in the Soviet Union did marginally increase again in 1987 – largely, it seems, as a result of Gorbachev's anti-alcohol campaign (Manning 1992, p. 55) – the fact is that after seven decades of communist rule Soviet citizens could not rely on the state adequately to look after their most basic need and right, that to life. Essentially similar patterns could be found in Hungary (Heinrich 1986, p. 101), Poland and elsewhere.

It might be objected that citizens had only themselves to blame if, say, alcoholism was a major reason for the declining life expectancy. But this argument is hardly persuasive. First, it needs to be asked *why* alcoholism was increasing, *if* it was (for data on the USSR, and an analysis of the problems involved in obtaining a clear picture of the situation see Treml 1991). If one reason was a growing level of alienation in society as a result of the state's policies, then the state cannot be excused. Another reason was that the state-run health-care services were deteriorating, as a function of declining economic performance. Throughout the world, citizens' expectations of their health-care services, whether provided by the state or privately, are rising as developments in medical awareness and technology mean both that patients can expect better treatment across a wider range of ailments, and that such treatment – partly *because* of its development and increasing sophistication – becomes more expensive. Thus it is likely that if a state-funded health-care service is to keep pace with the advances of medical science, it will do so either in the context of a growing economy, or at the expense of other services such as defence or education, or through a higher tax burden on the citizens. In the case of the USSR from the late 1970s, the economy was growing only weakly, the defence burden was increasing and raising taxes was politically dangerous. Given the state's involvement in so many areas of citizens' lives, it is not surprising that medical services suffered.

As with health care, so in the field of *retirement pensions*, communist states in general achieved much. Such pensions were first introduced in the USSR in 1918, though at that time they were limited to the disabled elderly, and were in any case often not paid in practice. A more general scheme was introduced in 1928, though even then large numbers of Soviet citizens, including peasants (later collective farmers), were excluded until as relatively recently as 1965 (on all this see George and Manning 1980, pp. 37–43). Overall, however, retirement pension schemes in many communist countries improved the lot of ordinary citizens in comparison with the pre-communist era. By the 1980s the vast majority of citizens in the USSR and Eastern Europe were entitled to retirement pensions from the state, a situation which on one level compared favourably with the West. Moreover, the retirement age was lower in many communist states than in most Western states, at 60 for men and 55 for women in countries such as Bulgaria, Hungary and the USSR.

As in Western systems, so in the communist world the burden of retirement pension schemes increased over the years as people lived longer (mostly!), and enjoyed a longer average retirement period. Taking the USSR as an example, only 6.7 per cent of the population in 1939 were over 60 years of age, compared with 13.5 per cent by 1987 (Buckley 1990, p. 192). This placed an increasing burden on the state's resources.

In addition, citizens were subject to the paternalism of the state, and were not generally able to assume responsibility for their own old age in the sense of being permitted to subscribe to *private* retirement schemes. This problem was exacerbated by the fact that pensions in most countries were very low and not subject to automatic index-linking; the latter was only introduced in Poland as relatively late as 1986, for instance (Ksiezopolski 1990, p. 59). Moreover, some citizens complained that pension schemes took inadequate notice of the number of years worked and a person's qualifications; the *relatively* egalitarian system was thus criticized by some as unfair. Conversely, citizens with a below-average work record because they had gone out to work for fewer years than most people often received far less than others (see Deacon 1983, pp. 155–6; Deacon 1992a, p. 4); for them, the system was not egalitarian enough.

During the 1970s in particular, when many Westerners were criticizing the communist states for their lack of human rights, communist ideologues retorted by arguing that the *right to work* was a basic human right not acknowledged or respected in the West. Certainly, the record of most communist states in this field could by some criteria be interpreted as impressive. Unemployment hardly existed in most of these countries until very late in the communist era. As with all social phenomena, however, there were various ways of interpreting this, and the 'no unemployment' claims always had to be treated with caution.

Few, if any, of the communist states ever claimed to have no unemployment at all. Rather, the usual claim was that there was no systemic, long-term unemployment. Short-term unemployment, linked to structural changes in the economy, did exist. As technology changes, so some skills that were once needed become redundant, even in a socialist society. In this sense, some people in the communist world were made redundant in a technical sense. This said, most were retrained and found new positions. All this is a positive side of the equation.

But there were negative sides, too. In communist states, citizens had not only a *right* but also a *duty* to work. If people wanted to 'drop out' – for instance, to try their luck as artists or craftspersons – they usually had to hide this from the authorities. Normally, citizens could not claim unemployment benefits. Indeed, such benefits were rare in the communist world until well into the 1980s, as were unemployment exchanges.

This said, it should be noted that the USSR was the original trail-blazer among communist states, introducing an unemployment benefits scheme for some workers as early as December 1917 (George and Manning 1980, pp. 36–7). In practice, however, benefits were often not paid in the early years. Moreover, the scheme lasted only until 1930, when Stalin, as part of his all-out drive for industrialization, abolished it (Manning 1992, p. 38). Once this step had been taken, the USSR set a pattern that was more or less closely emulated by the other communist states. Not until the late 1980s did countries such as (still-communist) Poland and Hungary recognize the need to have a formalized benefits system for those for whom the state could not guarantee employment. In one sense, this represented recognition of failure by the state, given claims of no structural unemployment under communist rule. But at another level, it was better to acknowledge a problem ordinary citizens were aware of and to deal with it than to pretend it did not exist.

Another aspect of employment policy in communist states that would appear strange to many in the West – unacceptable to some – was the fact that the state sometimes played an important role in placing people in particular posts. For instance, most students in the USSR would expect to be informed by the authorities where they were to work following graduation from a university, at least for the first three years.

A third problem of employment policy was that many citizens were underemployed in one way or another. They would go to work but, once there, spend much of their time doing very little. It is a debatable point whether or not this is better than staying at home on unemployment benefits, especially if one's wage is similar to what, in another type of system, could be expected in benefits or social security payments.

Housing was yet another area in which the communists could from *some* perspectives be said to have scored significant successes. On an international comparative basis, a great deal of housing construction was undertaken in all of the communist states, and completely homeless people were far less visible than they are in so many Third World countries and, increasingly, the West. Housing was also generally very cheap, with average rents for state-provided accommodation amounting to only 3–5 per cent of household income in the USSR by the end of the 1970s (Kerblay 1983, p. 130; George and Manning 1980, p. 154), 10 per cent in the case of Hungary (Deacon 1983, p. 202). Starting with Poland in the late 1950s, some communist governments attempted to raise rents to levels closer to the actual costs of providing accommodation (Adam 1991b, p. 18); but fears of the potential social backlash meant that these attempts were typically half-hearted, and rents were still generally low by the late 1980s.

Once again, however, there were several negative dimensions to the communists' record on housing. One was that the *quality* of housing was often very poor. In many cases, several families would have to share a kitchen and bathroom. The actual *size* of apartments was generally small, and many families had to sleep in the same room they had used during the day as their sitting room. Anyone who has visited a large city in the FSU or Poland or Romania – or any other formerly communist state – will be aware, moreover, of the ugliness of the architecture in many parts of the cities. Functionality clearly dominated aesthetic appeal, and in some cases there would be literally kilometre after kilometre of essentially identical multistorey housing blocks. An advantage of the Western system is that the plurality of ownership of both land and construction firms means that the monotony of housing typical of so many cities in eastern Europe and the FSU is rarely seen.

Another problem was that the proportion of state expenditure devoted to housing construction and improvement tended to decline over time in many countries. As Buckley (1990, p. 192) points out, the proportion of capital investment allocated in the USSR to the housing stock amounted to 23.2 per cent in the period 1956–60, 13.6 per cent in 1976–80, and 12.0 per cent in 1986–90. In short, the share had virtually halved over a 30-year period.

To conclude this subsection, it is appropriate to point out that the CPSU's 1986 Party Programme set as one of the party's top priorities the provision of their own home or apartment for every family by the year 2000. This reflected the fact that housing shortages in the USSR often meant long waiting lists for an apartment. Hence, young married couples commonly had to spend their first years of marriage living with one set of parents in very cramped conditions. The potential negative effects of this on the various relationships in the household are obvious. This problem of long waiting lists was common throughout the communist world. For example, the waiting period for a state-owned apartment in Hungary as late as 1987 stood officially at 5.4 years. Yet this represented an improvement over the average waiting time during the 1981–5 quinquennium, when the figure was 6.9 years (Ferge 1991, p. 152).

Finally, turning to *education*: as with every other aspect of welfare considered here, the communists unquestionably achieved much in this area. This can be seen, for instance, in literacy rates. Thus the rate among Bulgarians over 15 years of age in 1946, shortly after the communists took power, was 75.8 per cent; within ten years, if the data are to be believed, this figure had risen to 85.3 per cent. At least equally impressive figures can be found in several other communist states, though it is difficult to obtain directly comparable data across countries. Thus the rates increased in Yugoslavia from 55.4 per cent in 1938, just a few years before the communists assumed power (Rusinow 1977, p. xviii), to 80.3 per cent in 1961 (the rates refer to those over ten years old); in Romania from 57 per cent (1930) to 88.6 per cent (1956); and in the USSR from 24.0 per cent (1897) to 51.1 per cent (1926)[1] (it should be noted that countries such as Czechoslovakia, Hungary and Poland already enjoyed high literacy rates *before* the communists came to power).

Universal, free education was a feature of most communist systems, and in some the legal minimum number of years of schooling increased substantially over the years. Thus the figure rose from seven to ten years in most of the USSR between 1957 and 1970. Not all communist states achieved as much, however. Thus the minimum number of years in Poland in 1950 was seven, a figure that increased to eight in 1961; but having announced during the 1970s plans to increase this to ten years, the Polish authorities dropped this proposal in 1982 (Kolankiewicz and Lewis 1988, pp. 54–5). Many new schools and universities were established in the communist world, and, at a formal level at least, the arts and sciences were treated with respect.

But there were also several drawbacks with the communist approach to education. Here, the focus will be on three closely connected ones. First, creative and critical thinking was generally discouraged. Children and young adults (even at university level) were for the most part encouraged to learn by rote. While this meant that many people educated in communist systems often had an impressive level of factual knowledge by international standards, their critical faculties were underdeveloped.

Second, their knowledge was often one-sided – presented, as it was, through the prism of Marxism-Leninism – without them necessarily being very aware of this. This lack of critical faculties, coupled with a limited awareness of alternative ways of perceiving the world, is one of the many factors hindering the successful development of post-communism, in that initiative and entrepreneurship – whether in more economic or more political spheres – were for so long discouraged.

Third, there was the problem of targeting, that is, privileging some groups while depriviliging others. In the early stages of communist rule, some countries (such as the GDR and the USSR) consciously privileged the offspring of working-class parents in terms of university admissions, whereas the sons and daughters of 'bourgeois' parents found it very difficult to gain admission. Although this policy tended to be replaced over time by more meritocratic principles, such 'affirmative action' could lead to long-term resentment.

Before concluding this section on the communist era, one important point about welfare still needs to be made, since it is another factor helping to explain why communists in power typically experienced declining levels of legitimacy among the masses. This is that there was a serious and growing discrepancy between the values they purported to espouse and their actual behaviour. In marked contrast to their professed commitment to equitable access to medical facilities, senior communist officials lived in a world detached from that of the masses, giving them access to far superior medical care. This was in the form of so-called 'closed facilities' for the elite. According to Field (1993, p. 3, citing Christopher Davis's 1979 doctoral thesis), as of 1979 only 0.1 per cent of the Soviet population had access to these elite facilities, while almost 5 per cent has access to superior facilities that did not quite match the standards of the 'closed' facilities. Not only did a mere 5 per cent enjoy much better facilities than the other 95 per cent, but – again according to Field (ibid., citing a 1987 Soviet source) – by the late 1980s approximately 50 per cent of all doctors in Moscow worked in these superior or elite hospitals and clinics. The elite also had access to special schools, better housing and various other privileges.

It could be retorted that all this was very similar to the West. In most countries, there is a fairly readily identifiable elite that enjoys access to private clinics, private schools, vastly superior housing, etc. But there was an important difference between this and the communist system, in that communists claimed to be committed to an eradication of the more blatant dimensions of stratification. In fact, some forms of elitism and inequality in most communist countries (the GDR was something of an exception) *increased* over time (see, for instance, Lane 1982, pp. 61–2), even though these allegedly socialist societies were supposed to be moving closer to communism (on the tensions between elitism and egalitarianism in communist states see Connor 1979, Lane 1982). It was less the elitism *per se* than the hypocrisy of the elite that annoyed so many citizens.

Welfare Policies under Post-Communism

In the early to mid 1990s, the top priority of all the post-communist governments has been to place their economic systems onto a sound footing. This focus on the economy has meant that public welfare issues have not generally enjoyed the level of attention they might have done in a more settled and prosperous period. Yet the sheer scale and nature of the economic problems of early post-communism mean that governments *must* devote attention to welfare issues: so many ordinary citizens are suffering in the transition period that a protective cushion has to be created if the new post-communist governments are to retain power and build up legitimacy. This need for extensive welfare programmes at a time when governments can ill afford them constitutes the *welfare dilemma* of post-communist states.

Although this is a universal problem, the different political orientations of various governments mean that the amount of attention devoted to welfare issues varies quite considerably from country to country. In some of those countries where the government has been dominated by advocates of a more radical economic transformation policy, such as Poland until late 1993, there has in general been less concern with welfare than in those countries where there is a stronger residue of communist values, such as Romania, Bulgaria, Lithuania or Ukraine. One notable exception to this generalization was Czecho-Slovakia, which introduced *relatively* generous and comprehensive social welfare policies soon after the communists were removed from power (Deacon 1993, p. 230), despite its fairly radical approach to economic transformation. The five areas of welfare analysed for the communist period can now be considered.

Health care

An important change in the area of health care policy was the enthusiasm of several early post-communist governments (including Bulgaria, Czechia, Hungary – less so Slovakia) for a private sector. But while some have encouraged across-the-board privatization, none has yet proceeded very far in this direction. Admittedly, a substantial proportion of the pharmacies in many countries have been privatized, and doctors have been permitted to establish private practices in addition to their work in public hospitals and clinics. But there has been relatively little true privatization of health insurance schemes. Rather, many countries have opted for a system in which the state establishes or encourages what might be called semi-autonomous and semi-private health insurance schemes. Typically, the state has sought to divest itself of direct responsibility for administering health care, but still feels responsible for regulating the new schemes (for instance, in determining how they should be funded). It also typically feels responsible for ensuring that the weakest and poorest in society are still provided for, and hence reimburses the new insurance schemes for medical services rendered to the unemployed, the elderly, etc. Understandably, though regrettably, there have been many teething problems with these new semi-autonomous health insurance schemes. The relationship between them and the state is still crystallizing and is often strained.

At the same time, several post-communist countries (including Czechia and Poland) have passed legislation to put state-run hospitals and other medical institutions on to a proper cost-accounting basis.

There has been encouragement in some countries (such as Czecho-Slovakia, Poland) of charity-based welfare schemes, often run by the church. These are not a total innovation of the post-communist era; they were reasonably well developed in the communist GDR, for instance, where both the Evangelical and Catholic churches offered care to citizens (Diakonie and Caritas respectively – see L. Holmes 1986b, pp. 97–8; on the rise of charity in the USSR during the 1980s, see Matthews 1991). Nevertheless, their role appears to have increased in the 1990s.

In sum, the funding and management basis of post-communist health care has in many countries become more pluralistic, more autonomous of the state and in *some* ways more responsible and better regulated, for instance in bringing previously *de facto* but 'under-the-counter' private practices into the open. This legalization of genuinely private medical practice *should* in the future result in a decrease in the level of 'corruption' (here meaning the technically illegal payment of medical personnel by private citizens for services)[2] in the health-care industry. At present, however, there is still widespread use of bribes, which are often solicited. Poland, for example, has so far permitted only a very limited private sector; given problems in the state-run facilities, many hospitals and clinics have encouraged patients to make 'voluntary' contributions (Vinton 1993c, p. 57). Furthermore, it is clear from the 1995 clampdown on 'corruption' in the impoverished Bulgarian health-care system that there may continue to be problems of pecuniary impropriety for some time to come even in those post-communist states that have in recent years provided a greater stimulus to the private sector (on the Bulgarian clampdown see Gomez 1995, p. 40).

Unfortunately, the encouragement of private or semi-private and more responsible health-care funds in so many countries at present comes nowhere near matching the marked reduction in real state expenditure on health care. For instance, Poland devoted approximately 5.1 per cent of GDP to this in 1990, but at a time when the size of the economy had shrunk significantly; the 1993 Polish budget envisaged a decline in health-care spending of some 10 per cent in real terms in comparison with 1992 (Vinton 1993c, p. 57), even though such spending still represented a significant proportion (14 per cent) of the state budget. The figures for early post-communist Russia are even more depressing. In 1992, only 6.2 per cent of the state budget and 2.3 per cent of GDP was allocated to health care; this not only represented a real cut in comparison with 1991, but also constituted only about 50 per cent of what many analysts believed was necessary to ensure minimally adequate facilities (Davis 1993b, p. 39). Even allowing for the emergence of a small private sector and a nascent semi-private sector, the overall situation had deteriorated markedly. The situation was no better in 1993: the state-managed sector was to have received approximately 60 million roubles, but in fact received only about one-third of this. The gravity of the situation becomes even clearer when the rapid inflation of the period is taken into account.

The poor economic situation in the early 1990s has resulted in a situation in which many hospitals and other medical institutions have fallen increasingly into debt. One result has been shortages of medications, especially high-quality imported ones. Moreover, many health-care workers, including doctors and nurses, have become increasingly despondent as their real incomes have failed not only to keep up with inflation, but also with the incomes of other groups. This helps to explain the 'corruption' referred to above, why some doctors have emigrated, and why there have been strikes by many health-care workers in several post-communist states. While some governments have been addressing the problem of underpaid and over-worked health-care personnel recently, none has fully overcome it. A final ramification of the poor economic situation is that an increasing number of citizens have been expected to pay a higher proportion of the cost of their prescription medicines, which has predictably been unpopular.

Given all this, it is not surprising that there has been an overall *decline* in both health-care facilities and the average state of citizens' health in most countries during the first years of post-communism. One indication of this is the data on infant mortality rates. According to official data, these rose in Russia from 17.4 per 1,000 live births in 1990 to 18.8 in the first half of 1993 (Davis 1993b, p. 38), and in Lithuania from 10.3 in 1990 to 16.4 in 1992 (Girnius 1993b, p. 53). In the early 1990s, Albania and Romania had the highest infant mortality rates in Europe (Ionescu 1993, p. 60), a situation which had not changed by mid-decade.

Mortality rates generally are also far from impressive. For instance, the 1992 Hungarian rate of 13.9 per 1,000 head of population was worse than the 1960s average of 10 per 1,000 (Pataki 1993b, p. 50). Average life expect-ancy figures continued to fall, sometimes at an accelerating rate, in a number of early post-communist states. In Russia, for instance, the figure declined from 69.2 years in 1990 to 67.2 in the first half of 1993 (Davis 1993b, p. 38; for a particularly detailed and scholarly analysis of mortality and morbidity rates in the FSU, especially Russia, in the 1980s and 1990s see Ellman 1994). As of 1992, the Hungarian figure was 69.6 – slightly lower than in 1988, and five years lower than in Western Europe (Pataki 1993b, p. 50). The 1992 figure in Lithuania was 70.5 years, some two years less than it had been in 1987 (Girnius 1993b, p. 53). And Bulgarian life expectancy in 1995, according to a UN Human Development Report, is 71.2 years – almost *four years* less than it was in 1991.

Admittedly, caution must be exercised in comparing communist and post-communist data, not only for the reasons cited in chapter 8, but also because the methods for calculating mortality rates etc. in the two eras differ in some countries (Girnius 1993b, p. 53).[3] Moreover, lower birth-rates in many countries mean that the proportion of elderly people in the overall population is growing, which also tends to push up mortality rates. But even allowing for these factors, there is little doubt that the general health of citizens has deteriorated in early post-communism. Davis (1993a, p. 34) has summarized the overall situation as follows:

On the whole . . . the picture is a negative one . . . Nutritional, infectious, social, and degenerative diseases have become more widespread. Medical facilities are underfunded and afflicted by shortages of all categories of supplies ... The diminished effectiveness of health institutions in the face of increasingly widespread illness has resulted in rising invalidity and mortality rates and falling life expectancy throughout Eastern Europe and the former Soviet Union.

The British periodical *The Economist* (7 January 1995, p. 43) described the current position more dramatically: 'Communism could seriously damage your health; but post-communism is proving even worse.' Even if it is borne in mind that *some* of the deterioration in health is more a function of citizen 'choice', such as increased smoking and drinking, than of the direct effects of spending cuts by the state, the question arises of the extent to which such increases in bad habits are a function of the greater stress and general insecurity in these countries during the 1990s.

Given sharply reduced population growth rates, the population of some post-communist countries is declining at present; as Eberstadt points out:

In the first half of 1993, there were four deaths for every three births in Bulgaria; three deaths for every two births in Estonia. Throughout 1992 and 1993, Eastern Germany was burying two people for every baby born. In the first nine months of 1993, according to official figures, Moscow saw two-and-a-half times as many deaths as births; for St Petersburg, the ratio of deaths to births was nearly three to one. Such disparities were last seen in Russia during Operation Barbarossa and the seige of Leningrad. (1994, p. 55)

In examining the causes for rising mortality rates, Eberstadt concludes that 'adjustment to life after communism is proving not just difficult but positively traumatic throughout the entire former Soviet bloc' (p. 56).

Clearly, the health-care situation of early post-communism has been bleak. But it would be misleading not to point to one or two blades of grass that were beginning to emerge on this landscape by the mid-1990s. According to data from UNICEF, two post-communist states – Czechia and Slovakia – experienced a decline in mortality rates in 1993 in comparison with 1989. The earlier cited article in the *Economist* (7 January 1995, pp. 43–4) related this to increased public health expenditure, including on medical salaries, and to low unemployment levels (in that the unemployed in most societies tend to eat less well than the employed, and to have more habits and illnesses related to stress and low self-esteem, which in turn means they die younger on average). Given the economic growth figures cited in chapter 8, and the positive knock-on effects these are likely to have in the future both on the funding of health-care facilities and on employment prospects, there is room for cautious optimism that the average standard of health of citizens in several post-communist states will improve in the coming years. It certainly needs to.

Retirement pensions

The situation regarding retirement pensions in early post-communism is also strongly affected by the generally poor state of the economies. Thus pensions are in several countries (such as Czechia) supposed to remain at the same ratio to average earned incomes as they were, which might at first glance look like a form of index-linking. But true index-linking is related to inflation rates – the increasing cost of goods and services – rather than the income of others. Thus, when it is borne in mind that in real terms (purchasing power, rather than the mere number of roubles, leva, crowns, etc., received) average earned incomes in virtually *all* post-communist countries[4] were falling in the early 1990s, it becomes obvious why the guarantee of fixed ratios is not as attractive a promise as it might initially appear.

Another aspect of post-communist approaches to pensions that is subject to differing interpretations is policies on retirement age. In Bulgaria it seems that the effect of 1991 legislation is in practice to *reduce* the retirement age, as long as an individual has been working for at least 25 years, from the previous 60 for men to 57 years of age, and from the previous 55 for women to 52 years. Although a minimum pension level was set at the time this legislation was introduced, this was stated in terms of leva, not proportion of average income; in an inflationary era, it is not clear that this is any better than the Czecho-Slovak ratio system. Moreover, approximately a quarter of the population is now of pensionable age (Gotovska-Popova 1993, p. 46), partly as a result of such relatively young retirement ages; this is a comparatively high figure, and it is unlikely that Bulgaria will be able to afford to maintain pensions at similar real levels in the future. It should be noted that some countries have *raised* or are contemplating raising the retirement age. This is true of both Hungary and Slovakia, for instance.

One potential effect of changing the retirement age in any country is that it can have an impact on unemployment levels. Thus, *reducing* the retirement age should – other things being equal – reduce unemployment levels, as the retirees free up posts they previously occupied. However, not all retirees are replaced, and another potential effect of lower retirement ages is to increase the proportion of non-productive population, thus placing a greater burden on those who are in work.

From the above, it should be clear why it is not possible to state categorically which of the various approaches to pensions being adopted by post-communist states is 'best'. The answer to this depends partly on the criteria applied, and partly on the actual outcome of the policy. On the latter dimension, at least, it will be some time before the relative merits of the differing approaches being adopted by the post-communist states can be properly evaluated.

Employment and unemployment

The issue of unemployment soon emerged as a serious and difficult one for the majority of post-communist states. Although Russia *officially* had an enviably low rate of only 2.1 per cent[5] and the Czech Republic only 3.1 per cent by late 1994, the rate was in double figures in several countries (13.5 per cent in Bulgaria, 14.3 per cent in Slovakia, 14.4 per cent in Slovenia and

16.5 per cent in Poland – all data from *BCE*, December 1994/January 1995, p. 73). High unemployment levels are a serious problem in *any* country, since they tend to be accompanied by, for instance, rising crime rates and declining production. The former problem is reflective of an even deeper problem with unemployment, that is the negative psychological effects on those who have either lost their jobs or who have never even been able to enter the workforce (notably school-leavers).

Following the lead of Poland and Hungary, other countries have set up unemployment benefits schemes. As with other aspects of the transition to post-communism, in many cases the change began in the late communist era. Thus the first unemployment exchanges opened in the USSR in July 1991, *before* the banning of the CPSU and the subsequent break-up of the Union.

Although many of the problems of unemployment are common to the numerous post-communist countries, the solutions adopted vary. For instance, post-communist governments have reached different conclusions as to who should fund unemployment schemes, how long recipients should be eligible for support, how much benefit a person should receive relative to the minimum wage, and what scale of differentials there should be.

In terms of funding, countries can opt for one or more of three main sources: employer contributions, employee contributions and general state revenue. In practice, many states are opting for a mixed arrangement. Bulgaria did so in 1991: the fund for unemployment benefits is financed jointly from the state budget and by employers. Similarly, Poland and Russia have systems under which employers pay a 2 per cent payroll tax as their contribution to the unemployment benefits fund, which is then topped up by the state; in Russia, this payroll tax may soon be increased to 2.5 per cent (Morvant 1995a, p. 47). Czecho-Slovakia and Hungary went further, opting for a mixed system that would be funded from the state budget, by employers, and by employees themselves (Castle-Kanerova 1992, p. 109; Okolicsanyi 1993, p. 12). The employers' payroll tax in Hungary was raised in January 1993 to 7 per cent, which is comparatively very high, while the employee contribution was set at 2 per cent of gross wage or salary.

Following a June 1991 decision by the Ministry of Labour and Social Care, the level of unemployment benefit in Bulgaria was set at 80 per cent of the salary/wages a person was paid during his or her last 12 months of employment, subject to the rider that the sum received should not fall below the minimum wage level, or be more than four times this amount (Deacon and Vidinova 1992, pp. 83–4). In the earliest phase of post-communism, Bulgaria appears to have had the most generous unemployment benefits scheme (Deacon 1992b, p. 171). The benefits were not as generous in Czecho-Slovakia, for instance, where they were normally set at 60 per cent of the person's most recent earnings for people living in the Czech Lands, and 65 per cent for those in Slovakia; but by 1993, the enormous drain of unemployment benefits on the Bulgarian system had resulted in a reduction of benefits to the Czech level of 60 per cent, while Slovak benefits had also gone down to this proportion (Scarpetta and Reutersward 1994, pp. 257, 282). As in the original Bulgarian arrangement, there was a proviso in the earliest Czecho-Slovak legislation to ensure that benefits at least matched minimum income levels; by 1993, neither Czechia nor Slovakia had such provisions, while the minimum level in Bulgaria had declined to 90 per cent of minimum wages (ibid.). One way in which individuals could increase their benefits in Czecho-Slovakia was by register-ing for a retraining programme: the authorities saw this as evidence of flexibility and a willingness to make an effort to help the country's moderniz-ation, and so were prepared to reward people for their attitudes. Bulgaria, among others, subsequently adopted a policy rather similar to that adopted in the early 1990s by the Czecho-Slovaks; in March 1993, a scheme was introduced whereby unemployed people who had completed a retraining course were to receive an additional 15 per cent, while the young (up to 30 years of age) long-term unemployed would receive a bonus merely for enrolling and participating in a retraining programme (see Gotovska-Popova 1993, p. 45).

Poland and Russia are two of the many post-communist states that have a sliding-scale approach to unemployment benefits. In order to provide meaningful support to people temporarily unemployed, probably through no fault of their own, the Polish authorities originally set benefit levels at 70 per cent of past earnings for the first three months. After this, however, the levels fell quite dramatically to 50 per cent for the next six months, and to only 40 per cent after that (the percentages were much lower by 1993, though there was still a sliding scale – see Scarpetta and Reutersward 1994, p. 282). Russia's system is slightly more generous – at least in terms of percentages of earnings, though not necessarily in terms of purchasing power. Thus, following a three-month period in which retrenched workers may receive severance pay from their previous employer, the unemployed receive from the State Employment Fund 75 per cent of their previous average monthly wage for the first three months, 60 per cent for the next four months, and 45 per cent for the next five months (Marnie 1993, pp. 18, 20–1; Morvant 1995a, p. 46). Such periodic reduction schemes are designed to assist the unemployed, while simultaneously providing them with an incentive to find a new job as soon as possible. Indeed in Poland, unem-ployed persons who refuse either two jobs offered by a job centre or a retraining or public works programme forfeit their entitlement to unem-ployment benefits (Deacon 1992b, p. 172). One final point to note is that once a person reaches the end of their unemployment benefits entitlement period, many states provide no further assistance. This is true of Russia, for instance.

Some early post-communist states opted to help the unemployed more in terms of compensation (notably for price rises) than in extremely generous benefits of the sort seen in Bulgaria. Poland is one country which soon developed a sophisticated mechanism for such compensation. In contrast, Russia had made little headway on this front by 1994.

Housing

The situation regarding housing is in many ways similar to that in other areas. Thus states are in general attempting to divest themselves increasingly of this responsibility, while market forces are to set the prices of rents and properties. In the longer term, this supply-and-demand orientation towards housing should result in a drastic reduction in waiting lists, and more young couples should be able to live on their own from the time they decide they want to live together. But in the early stages of post-communism, there have emerged a number of problems with the housing situation.

First, rents have in many cases risen far more steeply than incomes. In several countries – including Czecho-Slovakia, Poland, Hungary – early post-communist governments opted to reduce rent subsidies in stages (usually planned to occur over a three-year period), so that citizens were not suddenly hit by huge increases. Nevertheless, rent increases have still generally been above wage rises, and citizens know they will be increasing further. In countries such as the FSU, where rents accounted for only 3 per cent of household costs on average in 1991, the notion that rents might reach similar levels, relative to household income, to those typical in many Western countries – that is, 20–40 per cent – is causing considerable anxiety and distress; the post-communist Hungarian authorities soon accepted 20 per cent as a reasonable figure for the proportion of income spent on accommodation (Deacon 1992b, p. 171). One ramification of all this is that in some housing estates in the post-communist world, *none* of the tenants has been paying rent (Deacon 1993, p. 237); clearly, it is not merely many of those renting who have suffered in early post-communism, but also some of the property owners (including the state). The rent issue must be seen as one of the many factors accounting for the relatively low levels of real support for so many post-communist governments, and hence as a potential contributory factor to a legitimation crisis of one kind or another.

Second, problems have arisen concerning the ownership of some rental property, which has implications for the availability of accommodation and hence rent levels, as well as for the security of sitting tenants. Several post-communist governments have been committed to restitution of property seized by the communists; but in most cases, it takes time to investigate claims and reach a decision about ownership. This can lead to a feeling of insecurity among tenants in disputed property. Not only are they unsure about the new levels of (private) rent, but they often cannot be certain that the 'new' (that is, reinstated) owners will continue to rent out the large house that is currently let as a number of apartments. Perhaps the new owners would rather renovate the house and live in it themselves, or else rent the entire house as one unit to a 'new bourgeois' family (on this problem in Czecho-Slovakia see Castle-Kanerova 1992, p. 112).

Third, there has been dissatisfaction over what is perceived to be unjust treatment of people who want to purchase the apartment they are currently renting. Some local authorities have been more willing than others to sell off formerly state-owned apartments, for instance. And some individuals and couples find it easier than others both to obtain and to afford a mortgage.

Fourth, one of the problems of the economic uncertainty and inflation in so many countries in their early post-communist stage has been that building projects planned in the late communist era were either abandoned or not even started. In Poland, for instance, 'Rocketing building costs left half a million uncompleted housing units by mid-1990, and 1990 saw fewer completions (132,500) than 1989 (150,200). Banks refused credit to the co-operatives because repayment could not be guaranteed, while few private borrowers could afford the astronomical interest rates' (Millard 1992, p. 136). This problem has been further exacerbated by the fact that many of the mass-produced, prefabricated residential towers that were constructed during the communist era had a life expectancy of only 20 to 25 years; many are thus either rapidly approaching their 'use-by' date or have already passed this in recent years. While the housing supply situation should improve over time, it is clear that in some cases it actually deteriorated in early post-communism.

Finally, some resentment has been caused by the explicit rejection by many post-communist politicians of the notion that citizens have a *right* to housing. Thus the first post-communist minister of housing in Poland, Aleksander Paszynski, argued that housing is a commodity like any other, and that people should pay a market price for what many of them, after years of living under communism, consider basic needs and rights (Millard 1992, p. 135).

Education

Official attitudes towards education have changed significantly in most post-communist states. This is one area in which, by many criteria and depending on one's own ideological perspective, there could be seen to have already been substantial improvements in several countries. Thus the compulsory study of Marxism-Leninism that was still a feature of several (though not all) communist countries in the late 1980s has, as would be expected, been abandoned. Conversely, religious schools were rapidly legalized in several countries, including Czecho-Slovakia and Hungary. In some ways surprisingly, given the country's strong Catholic traditions, the right of priests to offer optional religious education in schools was debated for some time in Poland; not until mid-1993 was it formally accepted by the government that religion could be taught in state schools, as long as such teaching was in line with programmes devised by the Catholic Church.

While free, state-sponsored education was still to be the norm in post-communist countries, the right to establish privately funded schools was introduced early on in several of these states. For example, Poland's first private schools of the post-communist era began operating in 1990.

Given the poor economic situation in most countries, it is hardly surprising that the educational sector has borne its share of suffering in the early post-communist era. For instance, pure research institutions, such as the Academies of Sciences, have been in a parlous situation in several countries. Since basic schooling has been seen by most post-communist governments as more important than retraining, many vocational schools, adult education centres and correspondence schools have been subject to (often substantial) funding cuts – to such an extent that many have had to close down altogether. In contrast to what appears to be the general trend, Russia was in the early 1990s tending to place more emphasis on vocational training at the expense of academic training (Deacon 1992b, p. 173).

One area in which there has been at least commitment to an improvement in the educational system is in the approach to creativity and critical analysis. As mentioned earlier, a salient feature of education in most communist countries was an emphasis on rote learning, with little stress on – and often active discouragement of – individual initiative, criticism and creativity. Although it would be too crude, and going too far, to suggest that school-children were indoctrinated to 'toe the line', empirical studies have shown that obedience and uncritical learning of textbooks inspired by the communist party were the norm. In the post-communist era, such overt and monistic indoctrination is in most countries being replaced by a far more pluralistic approach.[6] There is also greater freedom of choice of subjects.

The Gender Issue

In many books and university courses, well-intentioned moves to include gender issues that were for so long overlooked unfortunately refer to 'the problem of women' or, somewhat less problematically, 'women's issues'. These phrases are themselves in many ways male-oriented, in that they can suggest either that women constitute a problem (and, implicitly, that men do not) or that there are many major problems women experience in isolation. In fact, many of the problems women face relate to male dominance in so many areas of life. Not only are men as much a part of the problem as are women, but all but the most radical, separatist (and sexist!) feminists or masculinists will accept that problems that have traditionally been seen as primarily female – whether it be lower average wages, sexual harassment at work, domestic violence, the double or triple burden, or even many aspects of parenting – can only be solved by women and men working together to overcome what are in many ways two sides of the same coin. As Charlotte Masaryk, writing early in the twentieth century, expressed it, 'solving the female question means solving the male question as well. Both concern sheer humanity' (cited in Havelkova 1993, p. 62).

This said, it must also be acknowledged that men and women do not always suffer equally or in the same way from society's problems. It is not sexist to argue, merely empirically the case, that policies relating to childcare and domestic chores often impact more directly and immediately on women than on men, for instance.

Like most themes in this book, the gender issue deserves much fuller analysis. Given the limitations here, there is a focus on a selective range of topics – including gendering in the workforce; gendering in the political system; and aspects of childbearing and childrearing.

THE COMMUNIST ERA

For their times, the classic theorists of communism – Marx, Engels and Lenin – had progressive attitudes towards gender. All of them recognized that women were often less free than men, for instance in that so many were economically dependent on men (notably as wives). They recognized that there was a relatively clearly defined gender division of labour in capitalist societies of the nineteenth and, in Lenin's case, early twentieth centuries; broadly speaking, men went out to work and were paid for it, women stayed at home, performed domestic tasks (including childrearing), and were not directly paid for it. They argued that many bourgeois men married women for their appearance and for their own ego (that is, their wives were essentially status symbols), rather than for true love; Marx appears rather naively to have believed that proletarian marriages were generally based on more egalitarian bases and love.

The solution to many of these inequalities, for the founding fathers of communism, was to 'liberate' women by granting them proper access to the workforce. This would render women less economically dependent on men. In addition, they advocated the granting of equal rights to women in education, politics and before the law. Finally, Engels in particular argued that many domestic chores that were in practice performed mostly by women and for no pay, such as cooking and cleaning, should be socialized and paid for from public funds.

Ultimately, however, the classical Marxist theorists considered class domination more significant than patriarchy, and maintained that if the working class as a whole were to be liberated, working-class women would be *ipso facto*. This position, and their belief that there was a natural division of labour in the sex act and in childrearing, have been criticized by many feminists (on this and the gender-related views of Marx, Engels and Lenin more generally see Vogel 1983).

The privileging of class analysis over theories of patriarchy resulted in conflicts on occasion between Lenin and some of the leading female Bolsheviks, notably Kollontai and Armand. Although he was prepared to see special organizations established to look after women's issues – the so-called *zhenotdely* ('women's departments') – Lenin remained convinced that female emancipation was not to be treated separately from what he saw as the most significant struggle, that between classes.

The notion that women could be liberated by incorporating them into the *paid workforce* resulted in communist governments actively encouraging women to go out to work. As a result of such policies, communist states had among the highest rates of female participation in work in the world, marginally higher even than many of the most advanced capitalist states. In 1988 the female participant rate (women as a percentage of the total workforce) was in the USSR 50.8 per cent, in Hungary 46.0 per cent, in Romania 40.0 per cent and in the GDR 49.9 per cent (Corrin 1992c, p. 241);

by way of comparison, according to International Labour Office statistics the 1988 rates were 42.3 per cent in the UK, 44.4 per cent in the USA, 39.7 per cent in the FRG and 41.3 per cent in Australia. Considering labour participation from another perspective, more than 70 per cent of women of working age in Eastern Europe were by the end of the 1980s either employed or else in work-related training; the figure reached 91 per cent in the GDR, compared with 55 per cent in West Germany (Einhorn 1993, p. 116), and almost 96 per cent in Czechoslovakia in 1986 (Siklova 1990, p. 193). Such were the achievements in this area that this variable was one of the most frequently cited by communist governments when claiming that women had been liberated and were treated equally with men.

Many Western critics, including several feminist writers, have argued that these data should be contextualized. One charge is that women were actually being used by a male-dominated political elite to assist with the economic development of the state. Although there is some truth in this, it should not be overlooked that many men were also subjected to harsh working conditions for relatively little reward during most of the communist 'revolutions from above'. Nor should it be forgotten that both men and women usually benefited to some extent as economies developed. The issue is thus less straightforward than it might initially appear.

A more convincing criticism is that the workforces in many communist states were gendered along traditional lines. Thus women were heavily over-represented in some countries in the so-called 'caring' professions, such as health and education. In 1985, 69 per cent of doctors in the USSR were women (the ratios of male to female doctors were more evenly balanced in the GDR and Hungary, however). In the GDR during the 1980s, all creche and kindergarten teachers were women, as were 77 per cent of school-teachers (Einhorn 1992, p. 143). Although women did perform some tasks in communist states that they are even now rarely seen performing in the West, such as repairing roads, these were marginal exceptions to the general point that many jobs in the communist world were predominantly performed by women (including being a secretary – as in the West), others overwhelmingly by men.

Even in those occupations where women predominated, there was often a discernible, gender-based hierarchy. Thus the further up the health and education professions one looked, the more likely it became that a given post would be occupied by a man rather than a woman.

Partly as a function of the last point, average female wages were only 66–75 per cent of average male wages in Eastern Europe by the late 1980s (for details see Einhorn 1993, esp. pp. 122–3, 268).

The *political system*, too, was basically male dominated in communist systems, and many of the patterns already noted in the case of the workforce were repeated in the political representative bodies. In general, the higher up the political ladder one looked, the lower the proportion of women. This meant that there were far fewer female voices in the organizations that really mattered (in terms of policy formulation), and correspondingly less likelihood not only of having policies introduced that were designed to improve the lot of women, but even of getting issues related primarily or exclusively to women on to political agendas.

An analysis of Soviet, East German, Hungarian and Polish central state organs will quickly and clearly demonstrate this point. In the USSR, 31.1 per cent of seats in the lower house of the legislature (Soviet of the Union) were occupied by women in 1988; in December of the same year, only one of the 107 members (that is, 0.9 per cent) of the Council of Ministers was a woman. The comparable data for the GDR are 32.2 per cent and 2.3 per cent (December 1988); for Hungary 20.9 per cent and 5.3 per cent (May 1989); and for Poland 20.2 per cent and 4.3 per cent (October 1988; most of these data have been calculated by the author – for fuller details on female representation in legislatures see table 9.1 on p. 258). Only one communist state, Yugoslavia, ever had a female prime minister (Milka Planinc, from 1982 to 1986).

Since the party tended to dominate the state in communist systems, data on female representation in the highest party organs are even more instructive. Thus, women occupied 27 per cent of seats at the 1986 (Twenty-Seventh) CPSU Congress, and constituted 29 per cent of the party's total membership (and 53 per cent of the Soviet population). But the Congress was a relatively weak body in comparison with the Central Committee and the most powerful body of all in most communist systems, the Politburo. It is therefore far more significant that only 4.4 per cent of CPSU Central Committee members in 1986 were women – and that there was not a single woman in the Politburo. In fact, there were only ever four women in the Soviet Politburo (E. Stasova for two months in 1919, E. Furtseva 1956 to 1961, A. Biryukova 1988 to 1990, and G. Semenova 1990 to 1991; of these, Biryukova was only a candidate – that is, non-voting – member anyway, as was Furtseva from 1956 to 1957). One final point to note is that female representation even in the CPSU Congress declined markedly at the Twenty-Eighth Congress (1990), falling to 7.3 per cent at a time when their share of total party membership had increased slightly to 30.2 per cent (Lentini 1994, pp. 2–3).

Moving to Eastern Europe: the figures on female representation within the communist party as a whole, the Central Committee and the Politburo during the mid to late 1980s[7] were respectively, 35.5%, 10.5% and 7.7% in the GDR; 32.1%, 17% and 18.2% in Hungary; 27.6%, 11% and 8.7% in Poland. These data largely speak for themselves.

At present, though perhaps not for long, *childbearing* is still an exclusively female activity. But communist states did not invariably accept that it was for individual women or couples to decide whether or not to have children, how many to have, etc. On the issue of the optimal number of children, there was no consensus in the communist world. At one end of the spectrum was the People's Republic of China, which in the late 1970s introduced a 'one-child policy'. Under this, couples were encouraged – later permitted – to have just one child; if they had more than one, they were penalized. The reason for this policy was to slow down or even reverse the population explosion; China has easily the largest population in the world (currently approximately 1.2 billion), and in the 1980s – even with a one-child policy – it was increasing (net) at an annual average of 14 million people.

Whereas the Chinese government was attempting to reduce the rate of population growth, the Romanian authorities were actively encouraging women to bear as many children as possible. The main reason for this appears to have been that Ceausescu wanted to ensure an adequate workforce in the future to build socialism, although on occasion he also suggested it was to align Romania with the Third World (in which birth-rates were, on average, high).

This aggressively pro-natalist policy was first introduced in 1966, shortly after Ceausescu came to power (1965). The first clear indication of the changed approach was the new abortion law of 1966, which made it much more difficult for a woman to have an abortion; until then, following a 1957 law, abortions had been easy to obtain. The Romanian birth-rate had been falling in the first half of the 1960s and Ceausescu was determined to reverse this trend. His new policy initially had the desired effect. The birth-rate in 1966 was 14.3 per 1,000 population, and in 1967 27.4 per 1,000, so that the figure almost doubled in one year.

Unfortunately for the government, the policy's success was relatively short-lived, and by the 1980s the Romanian authorities were taking further measures to encourage women to bear children. This included financial incentives, increased propaganda on the joys of motherhood, official en-couragement of popular tolerance of single motherhood (this was taboo in traditional Romanian culture) – and even state recommendations on how frequently couples should engage in sexual intercourse (3–4 times per week)! The authorities are also alleged to have attempted to coerce rural women into signing contracts requiring them to bear at least four children.

But these policies were far from totally successful either. A major reason was the appalling living conditions in Romania, which dissuaded many would-be parents. Another was that many Romanians associated high birth-rates with Romanies (gypsies), from whom they wanted to distance themselves. One of the most unambiguous signs of a tightening of policy – a more coercive approach – came in December 1985, when abortions be-came even more difficult to obtain. At the same time, childless couples and single women aged 25 or above were penalized (through monthly deduc-tions from their wages/salaries) even more than they had been since 1977, unless they could provide good medical reasons for having no offspring. The penalties for doctors who helped women terminate a pregnancy were also increased, with imprisonment of between one and six years being quite likely for any doctor found guilty of performing an abortion (all informa-tion on Romania from Kligman 1992).

Other countries were generally less draconian. Abortions were *relatively* easy to obtain in many communist states by the 1970s and 1980s – Albania and Hungary being two exceptions – and contraceptive methods, albeit often primitive, were reasonably accessible. However, high rates of abortion in countries like the USSR were partly a function of the underdeveloped situation regarding contraception (for many women, abortion *was* their form of contraception). This helps to explain why some Soviet women had up to 12 abortions, which can hardly be seen as progressive or indicative of a state that is anxious both to liberate and to care properly for its female citizens. In some countries, access to an abortion depended very much on who you were and who you knew. During the later communist era, for instance, abortions were often unavailable to married women in Bulgaria or Hungary if they had fewer than two children (Petrova 1993, p. 23, and Morgan 1985b, pp. 290–1); as with Romania, this was in line with the pro-natalist line of the respective governments.

On the surface, the conditions for childrearing were comparatively good in some communist states. Child-care facilities were, by international standards, well developed in some countries, such as the GDR, and often either free or else inexpensive. This said, in most cases it was not until well into the 1960s that creches and kindergartens were constructed (Corrin 1992b, p. 8). Moreover, facilities were not widely available in countries such as Hungary and Poland. Even by 1989 only 8.6 per cent of children of the appropriate age in Hungary, and 4.4 per cent in Poland, had a place in a creche (Einhorn 1993, p. 262 – it should be noted that the percentage had decreased in both countries since 1985, when the figures stood at 12.3 per cent and 5.1 per cent respectively). In practice it was often older relatives, especially grandmothers, who were expected to look after young children while their parents were out at work.

Many communist states had relatively liberal divorce laws, and divorce rates were comparatively high in countries such as the GDR (at 38.5 per cent of the marriage rate in 1986) and the USSR (at 34.7 per cent in 1986). But others had much lower rates of divorce. In some, notably Poland (at 20.3 per cent of the marriage rate in 1986), this was probably due to social attitudes – the strong Catholic tradition – as much as to communist policy. In others, such as Bulgaria and Romania (at 15.1 per cent and 20.5 per cent respectively in 1986), the government's strongly pro-natalist policies were the principal reason, since these resulted in laws that strongly discouraged divorce (all data in this paragraph have been calculated by the author on the basis of figures in SEV Sekretariat 1990, p. 66).

Several of the points made in the preceding paragraphs are essentially quantitative. But there are many more qualitative aspects of the gender divide and gender politics that need to be considered if the inequalities between men and women during the communist period are to be appreciated.

As noted above, one of the founding fathers of communism (Engels) had argued that the liberation of women involved not only granting them access to the paid workforce, but also socializing domestic work. He favoured the spread of cheap public canteens, for instance, so that people (empirically, in most cases women) would not have to spend so much time devising meals, shopping for food and cooking. There were some experiments along these lines in the communist world, one of the most significant being in China during the Great Leap Forward (1958–60). But such experiments were very limited in their success, partly because many women disliked the impersonality of this communal dining and having to give up what they saw as one of their 'natural' tasks.

Another qualitative point – although it can to some extent be quantified – is that the emphasis most communist states placed on heavy industry, at the expense of the manufacture of durable consumer goods, meant that domestic chores were more onerous than they needed to be, given the level of technological development in the world. Theoretically, this should affect everybody equally; in practice, surveys and experience indicate that women mostly performed domestic chores like cleaning, so that a shortage of high-quality domestic appliances (vacuum cleaners, high technology cooking equipment, washing and drying machines, etc.) made life harder for women than it would have been had the state not prioritized defence and heavy industries.

THE POST-COMMUNIST ERA

As writers such as Molyneux (1990) have pointed out, the politically more liberal – less centralized, hierarchical and closed – systems of most post-communist countries should in theory lead to an improvement in the lot of women (as well as men). In practice, it is not clear that this is beginning to occur yet, for reasons suggested towards the end of this section and in the next chapter. First, however, it is worth comparing the situation of the post-communist world with that of the communist in terms of the factors singled out for analysis.

The workforce

Regarding traditional genderings of the workforce, the evidence from early post-communism does not suggest any dramatic change in most areas. The caring professions, for instance, are still dominated by women, and it looks as though female penetration of traditionally male occupations such as mining will be as long and difficult a task as it has proved to be in the West.

This said, there is at least one area in which the situation *may* have markedly deteriorated – unemployment. There is evidence that some professions traditionally dominated by women have been shedding staff in early post-communism. Thus many child-care facilities have either contracted or shut down altogether as the 'user pays' principle has spread. More significantly, women often took part-time or less skilled work in the communist era – precisely, in many cases, because they had the other burdens of running a home and rearing children (hence the double or triple burden of going out to work, doing domestic work, child-caring), and it is often these sorts of jobs that disappear first in a deteriorating economic situation. It appears that in early 1992 just over half of the officially unemployed in Bulgaria, Czecho-Slovakia and Poland were women, while over 60 per cent of those unemployed in Romania and east Germany were; a staggering 75 per cent of the jobless in the FSU and Latvia were female. In contrast, women accounted for only 42 per cent of the officially unemployed in Hungary by the same date (all data from Corrin 1993, p. 200).

However, it must be acknowledged that the situation is unclear, and that there is evidence and reason to infer that women might over time fare *better* than men as a result of the economic restructuring of early post-communism. Thus Kligman (1992, p. 400) makes the point that heavy industries are among those being phased out, often to be replaced by consumer goods industries. This can often be to the employment advantage of women (see also Acsady 1995, p. 22; Stastna 1995, p. 26). Moreover, Kligman goes on to argue that precisely the fact that women have tended to be in lower-paid jobs is good reason for inferring that they might fare better in a tight economic situation. Then there is the point that since women have higher average qualifications than men in several post-communist states, the move to more sophisticated industries and general economic moderni-zation might well favour women (for this argument and evidence to this effect from Poland, Hungary and the GDR, see Funk 1993, p. 7). In short, the picture is hazy.

Nevertheless, there are areas relating to employment in which women *definitely* appear to be faring worse in the early stages of post-communism. Thus, because of their childbearing and child-rearing responsibilities, many women have had prolonged spells either out of the workforce altogether or else working only part-time (which is part of the reason why they have not generally reached as high a level in a given hierarchy as males of a similar age). Under post-communism, it appears that some women are virtually being punished, financially at least, for taking time out of the paid workforce. This emerges clearly from the following quotation from Deacon concerning unemployment benefits in Poland and Hungary:

> in Poland when women registered for the new unemployment benefit the law was rapidly changed to disqualify from receipt of benefit those who had not worked for at least six weeks in the previous twelve months. The likely outcome is the continuation of grants and allowances for the early years of motherhood but the removal of the right to work without loss of status and salary. In Hungary this right was abolished in July 1991. (1992b, p. 174)

(For a brief update on the Hungarian situation, revealing a further deterio-ration, see Acsady 1995, p. 23.)

Finally, women might be worse off as a result of *others'* unemployment. The limited evidence from Western countries – and common sense – sug-gest the strong probability that women in the post-communist world are being subjected to more domestic violence as a result of higher unemploy-ment among males; at the time of writing, however, the author was unaware of any data to substantiate this assumption (though see Morvant 1995b, p. 7; Acsady 1995, p. 23).

Political representation

The situation regarding female representation within the institutionalized political system has also markedly deteriorated from many perspectives. As Corrin (1992c, p. 248) has observed: 'During 1989 women were highly visible on the streets in demonstrations, organising meetings, electioneering and voting. When the new governments were being formed, however, and people were taking their places in the new power structures, women seemed to disappear from view.' While this is a slight exaggeration, there is no doubt that far fewer women are represented in parliaments etc. than was the case in the late communist era. In Albania, for instance, following the 1991 election only 3.6 per cent of parliamentarians were women, even though the state had originally assigned 30 per cent of seats to female occupants (Emadi 1993, p. 93). Moreover, there was almost 29 per cent female representation in the late communist period. By June 1994 the average percentage of female representation in national legislatures in the transition states was only 8 per cent, 1 per cent lower than the world average, and fully 10 per cent lower than the Western average (Morvant 1995b, p. 8). Data on representation in individual countries during the

Table 9.1 Percentage of women in national legislatures

	1945	1950	1988	June 1991	May 1996
Albania	3.6	14.0	28.8	3.6	5.7
Bulgaria	5.7	15.0	21.0	8.5	13.3
Czecho-Slovakia	n.a.	n.a.	29.5	8.7	10.0[a]
GDR	–	27.5	32.2	(20.4)[b]	–
Hungary	3.1	17.2	20.9	7.0	11.1
Poland	n.a.	0.0	20.2	13.5	13.0
Romania	n.a.	7.2	34.4	3.6	4.1
USSR	n.a.	19.6	31.1	15.6	10.2[c]
Yugoslavia	n.a.	n.a.	17.7	17.7	2.9[d]
Australia	1.3	0.8	6.1	6.7	15.5
Finland	9.0	9.0	31.5	38.5	33.5
France	5.6	6.8	5.7	5.7	6.4
FRG	–		15.4	(20.4)[b]	26.2
Japan	n.a.	2.6	1.4	2.3	2.7
UK	3.7	3.3	6.3	6.3	9.5
USA	n.a.	2.1	6.7	6.4	11.0

In bicameral legislatures, the figure is for the lower house.
[a] Czechia; figure for Slovakia is 14.7%.
[b] By June 1991, the two Germanys had unified and hence had a unified legislature.
[c] This figure is for Russia.
[d] Rump Yugoslavia.

Sources: Compiled by the author on the basis of data in Inter-Parliamentary Union. *Distribution of Seats Between Men and Women in National Parliaments: Statistical Data from 1945 to 30th June 1991* (Geneva: Inter-Parliamentary Union, 1991); Inter-Parliamentary Union, in a private communication to the author.

communist and post-communist eras, and on some Western legislatures, can be found in table 9.1.

The data may be even more disappointing than they initially appear, in that the percentages might have been still lower in some countries had it not been for the electoral system. This point emerges from Kiss's observation (1991, p. 53) that a substantial majority of female members of the 1990 Hungarian parliament were there as a result of having been included on their parties' lists, not because they had been elected as individuals in the single-member constituencies. One small ray of hope in all this is that the proportion of women in *some* legislatures, including the Czech and the Bulgarian, had begun to creep up by the mid-1990s (to 10 per cent and 13.3 per cent respectively). But with the figure below 3 per cent in Ukraine, for example (Bohachevsky-Chomiak 1995, p. 12), there is a long way to go.

In those countries where the communists were still in power as of early 1993, female representation in the legislature remained high by international standards (though still low in terms of population proportionality) – at 20.1 per cent in North Korea, 21.3 per cent in the PRC and 33.9 per cent in Cuba. On one level, it could be argued that it is better to have even 3–4 per cent representation in a body that really debates issues – where delegates really have a voice – than 33.9 per cent or 20.1 per cent representation in a body that always follows a party-dictated line and votes unanimously (for the record, debating was *reasonably* open in the Cuban legislature during the 1980s according to Azicri 1988, pp. 103–4, but highly controlled in the Korean). But this is a contentious point; if *men* also have to toe the line in a communist legislature, the all-important question is how well represented women are in the very top bodies, where the really significant decisions are made. As already indicated, women were *very* poorly represented in communist politburos and Councils of Ministers, so that the real impact of relatively high levels of representation in the legislature should not be exaggerated. This said, and as table 9.2 demonstrates, female representation in post-communist *cabinets* (often the top decision-making bodies)[8] is essentially as poor as it was in the communist era.

As in the West, there is also a fairly obvious division of labour at the ministerial level. Thus women tend to occupy portfolios relating to health care, welfare, education, youth matters and women's affairs, but are rarely seen in defence, foreign affairs, police affairs (the so-called power ministries) or transport. As one small ray of light in this rather depressing picture, it is worth noting that post-communist Lithuania, Poland and Bulgaria have all had female prime ministers, albeit for brief periods (respectively, Kazimiera Prunskiene from 1990 to 1991, Hanna Suchocka from 1992 to 1993 and Renate Indzhova in late 1994; for a factual overview of women in governments, unfortunately only analysing the situation as of October 1991, see Inter-Parliamentary Union 1992, pp. 157–66).

Overall, it is far from clear that the lot of women has improved at all in terms of representation and 'voice', even if the data on communist and post-communist political institutions are unpacked. Indeed, and as mentioned above, it has in some ways deteriorated.

Table 9.2 Number and percentage of women in selected cabinets

	July 1991		December 1993		December 1994	
	Actual number (Females/Total)	%	Actual number (Females/Total)	%	Actual number (Females/Total)	%
Albania	2/15	13.3			0/16	0.0
Bulgaria	1/19	5.2			2/17	11.8
Czechia	–	–	0/19	0.0	0/19	0.0
Czechoslovakia	1/16	6.3	–	–	–	–
Hungary	1/17	5.9	0/18	0.0	1/14	7.1
Poland	0/20	0.0	1/20	5.0	1/21	4.8
Romania	0/25	0.0			0/26	0.0
Slovakia	–	–	3/18	16.7	3/18	16.7
USSR[a]	1/64	1.6			1/30	3.3
Yugoslavia[b]	0/19	0.0			2/17	11.8
Australia	1/17	5.9	1/18	5.6	1/17	5.9
Finland	7/17	41.2	6/17	35.3	4/16	25.0
France	4/33	12.1	3/30	10.0	2/22	9.1
Germany	4/22	18.2	4/20	20.0	3/18	16.7
Japan	0/13	0.0	3/21	14.3	2/14	14.3
UK	0/22	0.0	2/22	9.1	2/23	8.7
USA	2/18	11.1	3/18	16.7	3/15	20.0

[a] Russia in 1993 and 1994.
[b] Serbia-Montenegro in 1994.

Sources: Dolling 1991, p. 277 (1991 data); Koole and Mair 1994 (1993 data), p. 224; calculated by the author on the basis of *KRWE* (1994 data).

The reasons for the decline in female representation in legislatures and lack of improvement in executives are several. One is that many communist governments used to have representation quotas for bodies such as legislatures and party congresses. In other words, it was precisely *because* the communist party exercised so much control over politics that women were, if still not equally and adequately, at least better represented in formal terms than women in most Western countries. The removal of central control, with the citizenry permitted to choose their representatives freely, has resulted in the disappointing representation levels revealed in table 9.1.

Probing one level deeper, as to *why* women fare so relatively poorly in freely contested elections, at least two closely related factors need to be highlighted. One is that many women themselves apparently believe that public politics – in parliament, for instance, as distinct from personal politics in the home and at work – is 'men's business'. This inference is compatible with the findings of an April 1995 survey conducted in 11 post-communist states (including five in the FSU), which indicated that in most, men were approximately twice as likely as women to have a serious interest in politics and to have ever joined a political party (Gigli 1995, esp. pp. 18, 20). This is presumably one of the reasons why the percentage of female candidates in post-communist parliamentary elections has generally been low (15 per cent for the 1990 Bulgarian election, 9 per cent for the 1990 Hungarian election, 8.9 per cent for the 1990 Romanian election and 14 per cent of the single-member constituency candidates in the 1995 Russian election – data from Inter-Parliamentary Union 1992, pp. 132–6 and OMRI *Special Report* 14, 15 December 1995), which is the second factor. If only a small number of women stand for election, it is not surprising that so few get elected. All this said, there is conflicting evidence on whether or not women turn out to vote proportionately less than men under post-communism. Funk (1993, p. 12) seems to suggest that they do. However, this point is not entirely clear, since the gendering of voting patterns in many recent elections has yet to be analysed. What is clear is that the April 1995 survey referred to above suggests there is almost no difference between male and female participation in elections. Although it is possible that the different pictures painted by Funk and Gigli reflect changes from the early to the mid 1990s, this would not apply in all cases, since not all had had fresh elections since Funk was writing. Nevertheless, *if* it is the case that women are now voting in greater numbers than they were in the earliest days of post-communism, this would be one small reason for being optimistic that increasing political participation will eventually result in more female candidates, and ultimately in better political representation.

Childbearing

The situation regarding childbearing appears to be mixed. In most countries, marketization and an opening up to trade with the West have made contraceptives more readily available. For many, this represents an improvement. Similarly, as post-communist states generally believe in far less interference in the private lives of their citizens, the actively pro-natalist policies that were typical of the USSR, Romania and Bulgaria have been replaced by policies that leave it to women to decide whether or not to have children and how many. Indeed, as has been shown, there are now financial disincentives in some countries for women who drop out of the paid workforce to bear and rear children. While some radical environmentalists and feminists would applaud the effects of (though not the motivation for) such policies, most people would probably consider this unfair.

The other side of the coin, however, is that abortions have become more difficult to obtain in many countries, including Poland, Hungary and the former GDR. Notable exceptions to this generally conservative trend are Romania, where abortions became fully legal the day after the execution of the Ceausescus, and Albania, where abortion was legalized in 1992.

In the case of the GDR, during the early post-unification phase east German women were permitted as easy access to abortions as they had enjoyed when the GDR existed; East Germany had had far more liberal laws than the FRG. Indeed, together with property matters, the law on abortion was one of only two areas of legislation in which the former GDR and the former FRG initially continued to have separate laws after the October 1990 unification. But this was always intended to be short-term and in mid-1992 the German parliament passed pan-German legislation that, though not as liberal as the former East German law, was far more liberal than the FRG's own law until then. But that was not the end of the story. Conservatives in Germany soon challenged the new legislation through the Federal Constitutional Court, which in May 1993 ruled it unconstitutional. Eventually, in mid-1995, a new abortion law was passed; though considered relatively liberal by the standards of the former FRG, the new legislation still makes abortions more difficult to obtain than they were in the GDR.

In Poland, with its strong Catholic tradition, public debates about abortion started in the 1920s and resulted in a 1932 law that forbade abortion in all but exceptional cases. In 1956 the communists replaced the 1932 law with a new one that made it much easier for women to have an abortion. This law was supplemented by a set of guidelines from the Ministry of Health in 1959 that made it easier still. But, following a proposal from Catholic deputies in October 1988, a draft new law was submitted to the Polish parliament in the late spring of 1989 (that is, still during the communist phase). This led to heated debate both within and beyond parliament, especially once communist power had fully collapsed. Within the legislature, formal debates were held from the (northern) summer of 1990. Many Catholics sought to have the 1956 Act annulled, as they had on various occasions since its promulgation (during the communist era, the Polish legislature was often more like a real debating chamber than its equivalents in most other East European countries). Despite a petition signed by approximately 1.3 million citizens demanding a referendum on this issue, the parliament and president eventually agreed to enact legislation without reference to the masses. In March 1993 a new law became effective that rendered it far more difficult for women to have abortions (on the history of the abortion issue in Poland see Heinen 1992 and Jankowska 1993). Although the new law was not quite as restrictive as some Catholics had hoped for, it certainly represented a *significant* change from the communist era.[9] The impact of the 1993 legislation is reflected in the number of legal abortions being performed: in 1994 there were only 786 according to official statistics, compared with approximately 130,000 to 140,000 a year during the 1980s (*Economist*, 27 May 1995, p. 56; Fuszara 1993, p. 242).

Turning now to childrearing, the fact that child-care facilities have been either contracting or shutting down has led to serious resentment in some countries, including the former GDR. The situation has not been as serious in other countries. In Bulgaria, for instance, almost all children aged between three and six years old could be found a kindergarten place in 1990, although some have criticized the quality of these (see Petrova 1993, p. 27).

The point made earlier about the availability of contraceptives also applies to domestic appliances; high quality electrical goods designed to make housework easier are now readily available in most post-communist states, although their affordability at a time when the living standards of many people have been dropping is a different matter.

New issues

Some areas in which there was little concern for women under communism have *become* issues in the politically freer atmosphere of post-communism.

Thus pornography was not a major issue in most communist states, whereas newsstands in many parts of the post-communist world now freely display magazines, calendars, etc., that many would consider pornographic and offensive. A combination of a deteriorating financial situation for many women and the less draconian approach of post-communist governments has resulted in a marked growth in prostitution and the sex industry generally; for many observers, Budapest has now replaced Amsterdam as *the* red light district of Europe, while it is claimed that many young Russian women consider prostitution to be the most prestigious and desirable profession (see Lissyutkina 1993, p. 275).

The situation regarding feminism and feminist movements is considered in chapter 10. For now, and as a partial counterweight to the mostly depressing picture just painted, the point should be made that many women in the post-communist states are enjoying what many Western feminists see as the dubious joy of greater freedom to be 'feminine'. Many women are defending and participating in beauty contests, for instance, arguing that these were not permitted in the communist era because of the prudishness of most communist authorities. In a similar vein, many women in eastern Europe and the FSU are enjoying the wider availability of cosmetics, and of magazines that cater specifically to women's interests but which do not contain the political moralizing and cant of so many women's magazines of the communist era.

Finally, and considering a quite different form of 'liberation', many lesbians (as well as male homosexuals) are beginning to find life a *little* easier under post-communism than it was in the communist era. Although the GDR had a small lesbian movement by the late 1980s (Schenk 1993, p. 163), this was an exception: in the vast majority of communist systems, female homosexuality was an all but invisible phenomenon both to most of society and to the state. In the 1990s this is beginning to change; what appears to have been the first organized meeting of lesbians in Russia took place in Moscow in 1991, for instance (Funk 1993, p. 11; Waters 1993, p. 293). However, it should be noted that while many governments have more openly recognized and accepted lesbianism, social attitudes in many countries are still very conservative and disapproving, sometimes more so than of male homosexuality (see Hauser et al. 1993, p. 268; Panova et al. 1993, p. 20).

For reasons analysed in the next chapter, feminist movements are not yet a major force in post-communist politics. But at least the scene has been set for them to develop autonomously once the citizens of the post-communist societies really turn the corner economically and can start thinking about the quality of life and their role in politics, rather than merely day-to-day subsistence.

Summary and Conclusions

Whether one compares welfare policies or gender issues during the communist and post-communist eras, the pictures are mixed. In important ways, the situation is *worse* under early post-communism than it was under late communism. There is less security, and to some extent greater invisibility for women.

Part of the explanation for this is a purely economic one. With declining GNP and production in the first years of post-communism, many citizens – and certainly the new governments – were more concerned with basic survival than with improving welfare provisions or addressing gender-related issues. Concerning the former, governments have been attempting to transfer much of the financial responsibility for the welfare system on to employers, for instance. But the load has been almost unbearable. Total on-costs (for social security, health care and unemployment schemes) for employers in Russia, Poland and Hungary, for instance, amount to 39 per cent, 48 per cent and a staggering 51 per cent respectively (Marnie 1993, esp. p. 18; Vinton 1993d, esp. p. 4; Okolicsanyi 1993, esp. p. 13). This has led some more conscientious employers (those who attempt to pay in full and on time) to declare bankruptcy, while others have simply refused to pay. Either way, the state faces a serious problem, especially since the first option only adds to the unemployment levels and hence increases demand on an even more underfunded welfare system.

But there is more to the problem of welfare than just this economic explanation. Some post-communist politicians have been *ideologically* committed to an ending of the 'cradle-to-grave' state, and concerned about the demotivating effect of too much welfare at a time when economies need to be put on a secure footing. They believe they must encourage the development of individual responsibility, initiative and risk-taking, a process they perceive as being hindered where there is an overly protective welfare state.

To regard the current situation only, or even primarily, from the perspective of governments and new elites is too narrow. Citizens, too, have to learn to articulate and aggregate demands. For decades they have been actively discouraged from voicing their dissatisfactions and making demands; although the situation improved in the late 1980s, it was still within a communist system that many believed might at any moment clamp down again, as did the Chinese communist authorities in June 1989. It is hardly surprising, then, that citizens need time to learn to form themselves into effective groups making demands of governments, and to accept this as fully legitimate. They need to learn that the state does not make all the decisions about the allocation of resources on its own, and that a modern liberal-democratic state is far more subjected to citizen demand than is the 'vanguard'-style communist state.

Having made this point, it is clear from the situation of many of the most advanced and wealthy Western states that citizens in the post-communist world are never going to be able to enjoy the levels of welfare and subsidy they once did. States all over the world are currently attempting to reduce their involvement in both the economy and social welfare. It is a sad irony that, where greater intervention in the economy and the boosting of the welfare state were once intended to save capitalist states, the costs of both have in recent decades become so high that more and more states feel compelled to reduce their involvement if they are to avoid total fiscal crisis and ultimately perhaps collapse (on this dilemma see O'Connor 1973 and Offe 1984).

Turning specifically to the position of women, there is much truth in Sabrina Ramet's depressing statement that 'Communism was a seriously flawed system but is being replaced in Eastern Europe not by emanations of goodness and light but by seriously flawed systems with different flaws. Of these flaws, the most grievous is surely the insensitive refusal to accord women equal dignity and status' (1993, p. 527). Yet it would be defeatist and unrealistic, even demeaning to women, to suppose that just because this is largely the situation in the early to mid 1990s, it has to stay this way. In time, and with improving economies, women in the post-communist countries will learn to empower themselves; *if* they are already turning out to vote more than they were at the beginning of the 1990s, this is a step in the right direction. But there is a need for a major cultural shift, and this can never occur overnight, whatever the culture. As the memory of the all-embracing state fades for women – and indeed for all citizens – so they will learn to make demands of the new kind of state, as is appropriate in a pluralistic democracy. This brings us to an appropriate point from which to move to the next chapter, in which the role and nature of social movements and civil society more generally in both late communism and early post-communism are considered.

Notes

1 As Lane points out (1978, pp. 488–9), some of the marked improvement between the 1897 and 1926 censuses was due to pre-revolutionary (i.e. non-communist) policies. He goes on to show, however, that the Soviet government could certainly claim *some* of the credit and that literacy rates had shot up to 81.2% by 1939.
2 The word corruption is in inverted commas here because it usually refers to the abuse of *public office* for private gain; since many doctors, for instance, are simultaneously state employees and self-employed, and since they are not office-holders in any meaningful sense, the questionable activities of some of them would not be classified as corruption by most serious analysts.
3 The implication here is that formerly communist states that move to the methodology used by the World Health Organization (WHO) for measuring infant mortality will, because of the stricter criteria, show an increased rate. It should therefore be noted that some of the figures cited in this section, notably those on infant mortality in Russia, are based on a constant (non-WHO) methodology and thus reveal an unambiguous increase in mortality rates. According to one Russian source (cited in Marnie 1993, p. 22), the infant mortality rate in Russia in 1991 using the WHO method of calculation was 21 per 1,000 births, rather than the 17.8 cited in official Russian statistics. This compares with a rate of 8.9 per 1,000 births in the USA in the same year.
4 The former GDR might be an exception.
5 But note that the head of Russia's Federal Employment Service, Fedor Prokopov, stated in a January 1995 article (cited in Morvant 1995a, p. 46) that he believed that 7.1% of the workforce was unemployed, while another 6.4% was working substantially reduced hours.
6 This is less true of parts of the FSU, however. It was a cause for concern when the Belarusian president, Lukashenka, announced in August 1995 his intention to

replace all post-communist textbooks in the schools with books from the Soviet era.
7 The data here all relate to the years 1985–8, but unfortunately individual figures refer to slightly different points in time; however, they convey a reasonably accurate overall picture of the situation.
8 Where there is a strong presidency, this can be seen either as the top decision-making body or else to share this status with the cabinet (depending on the actual country and period). Since there is no female president in the post-communist world, this caveat only strengthens the general point being made here.
9 When the so-called former communists came to power following the September 1993 elections, they attempted to liberalize the law, but President Walesa refused to approve any changes.

FURTHER READING

On welfare policies generally during the communist era see George and Manning 1980 (on the USSR) and Deacon 1983 (comparative). On health care and its problems see Kaser 1976 and Davis 1989; on housing see Sillince 1990 and Turner, Hegedus and Tosics 1992.

On welfare generally in the final stages of communist power and the early stages of post-communism see Adam 1991a and Deacon et al. 1992.

On health care in the post-communist era see the various articles in *RFE/RL Research Report*, vol. 2, no. 40 (8 October 1993), pp. 31–62.

On social security in the post-communist era see the various articles in *RFE/RL Research Report*, vol. 2, no. 17 (23 April 1993), pp. 1–23; Boeri 1994 (specifically on unemployment).

On education under post-communism see A. Jones 1994; Karsten and Majoor 1994.

On women under communism and post-communism see Jancar 1978; Wolchik and Meyer 1985; Corrin 1992a; Einhorn 1993; Funk and Mueller 1993; Rueschemeyer 1994; and the numerous articles in *Women's Studies International Forum*, vol. 17, nos 2–3 (1994), pp. 267–314, and in *Transition*, vol. 1, no. 16 (1995), pp. 2–28.

10

Civil or Uncivil Societies?

The focus in chapter 7 was on the more formally organized aspects of politics, notably the state and political parties. But politics is about power relationships of any kind; a valuable contribution of much feminist analysis has been to emphasize that politics starts in small-scale human relationships – between partners, parents and children, etc. Unfortunately, these more personal aspects of politics lie beyond the scope of this study. But the reader would form a quite incomplete picture of politics beyond the level of individual relationships if there were no consideration here of politics other than those of the state and parties. This chapter focuses on such extra-institutional politics. In the first section, there is an examination of both the concept of civil society and the emergence and role of social movements (excluding nationalism). Following this is an analysis of what many consider to be the most salient and dangerous feature of post-communist politics, nationalism and ethnic politics. As with previous chapters, this one is structured so as to highlight similarities and differences between the late communist and post-communist eras; yet again, it has to be highly selective.

On Civil Society

Starting in Poland in the 1970s (Pelczynski 1988, Arato 1991, p. 161), but accelerating dramatically from the late 1980s, was a scholarly interest in analysing developments in the late communist and then in the early post-communist eras in terms of civil society (see, for instance, Kukathas et al. 1991, Rau 1991a, Lewis 1992, R. Miller 1992a). Very crudely, the argument was that society was reasserting itself, in particular vis-à-vis the state; one clear sign of this was the emergence of autonomous or semi-autonomous groupings. This development encouraged a questioning of some of the most influential interpretations of communist politics, particularly totalitarianism. A salient feature of a totalitarian system, according to theorists such as Hannah Arendt (1951), was that it *atomized* society. In other words, individuals no longer formed into the subgroupings typical of most complex societies but, largely because of widespread fear of the state, kept very much to themselves. Even the other members of one's family were not necessarily to be trusted. During the 1930s the Soviet authorities made a 14-

year-old boy, Pavlik Morozov, a hero of the USSR for denouncing his own father,[1] so that it becomes clear why such fears developed in society. By the 1970s and 1980s, in contrast, people were beginning in some communist countries to form bonds and groupings again to pursue all kinds of activity.

But should such activity be interpreted as indicating the emergence of *civil society*? The answer to this depends largely on what is understood by the term. Historically, it can be traced back to Cicero in Rome in the first century BC, and has surfaced on various occasions since. It enjoyed a positive connotation in much of the writing up to the eighteenth century, as in Adam Ferguson's *An Essay on the History of Civil Society* (1767). But Marx treated the concept in a largely pejorative way, seeing it as a term that encapsulated the salient features of a selfish and self-satisfied bourgeois society. The term was relegated to the back burner for much of the twentieth century, until there was a resurgence of interest in it in both Eastern and Western Europe during the 1970s (on the history of the concept of civil society see Black 1984, esp. pp. 32–43).

Even though it is once again in vogue, the term civil society is highly contentious. For some (see Kukathas and Lovell 1991, esp. p. 21), it is more or less coterminous with the market, in that market economies operate primarily on the basis of interaction between independent groups of individuals – companies, craft guilds, family businesses, etc. – rather than via the state's plan and ministries. For others (see Rigby 1991, 1992), this essentially economic interpretation is too narrow, being but one part of civil society. For these analysts, civil society refers to the establishment and functioning of social activities and groupings independent of the state, although they can and should interact with the latter. Such activities include economic ones, but also religious ones, and any non-governmental organizations (political, social, professional, sports, private educational or medical institutions, etc.). Thus Robert Miller (1992b, p. 1), apparently paraphrasing East European dissident intellectuals, defines civil society as 'a sphere of social activity free of the interference of the communist party-state', while Hosking (1992a, p. 1) defines it as 'institutions and associations independent of the state and the ruling party'.

Clearly, both of the definitions just cited are focusing on civil society in the communist era. But, as already described, the term developed long before any communist system had been established, and can refer to activities in the post-communist era. In this context, it is interesting to note that when the Russian Constitutional Commission's draft constitution was published in May 1993 (in *Rossiiskaya Gazeta*, 8 May 1993, pp. 9–13), the whole of section three was headed 'Civil Society' (*Grazhdanskoe Obshchestvo*). In line with the broader interpretation of civil society, the chapter headings of this section were 'Property, Labour, Entrepreneurship', 'Social Associations' (*Obshchestvennye Ob"edineniya*), 'Training, Education, Science, Culture', 'The Family' and 'Mass Information'; these headings reveal that some senior Russian officials had opted for the broader definition of civil society.

Another contested aspect of civil society relates to the *legitimacy* of its various components. For many observers, it is not necessary for there to be a formal recognition by the state that the groupings that make up civil society have a right to exist; for them, the fact that social movements such as autonomous trade unions have come into existence is sufficient to start referring to the emergence of civil society. For others, such as Graeme Gill (1991 and 1993, p. 226), there can be no serious talk of civil society until and unless this has been recognized by the state (that is, has been fully legitimized, not merely *self*-legitimized). This is an important theoretical point, but requires further consideration. In particular, does the point still pertain if a given state *itself* enjoys a low level of legitimacy? If a state has lost most of its authority, or else never acquired much to start with, why should civil society require its approval before analysts will recognize its existence? It should be clear that this issue is highly germane to a study of the late communist and early post-communist eras.

In addressing this question, it is useful to consider Michael McFaul's (1993, p. 3) proposal that the term 'a-civil' society be applied to a situation in which 'a great many activities take place outside the state, but with no direct connection, indirect leverage, or even desire for connection with or influence over the state.' Such a situation would not constitute a proper civil society for either Gill or Rigby (1991, esp. p. 110), since it meets neither the former's concern about legitimacy nor the latter's requirement that there be a symbiotic relationship between civil society and the political order for the former to flourish. On the other hand, McFaul's suggestion represents an attempt to categorize a phenomenon that was observable in parts of the communist world in the late 1980s (for McFaul, most clearly in Hungary), and which does appear to be closely related to many conceptions of civil society. Of course, since McFaul himself specifically labels this phenomenon 'a-civil society', he cannot be criticized for identifying as civil society something others would not.

Some of the conceptual difficulties identified in the previous few paragraphs cannot be fully resolved, to no small extent because analysts employ different criteria and initial premises. However, a partial resolution can be found by adopting a *dynamic* interpretation of the concept of civil society. This can be done by focusing on the term *emergence*, which implies a process and perhaps stages. Thus it is quite possible to argue that there are signs of a *nascent* civil society (the establishment of various autonomous social/economic/political/religious etc. organizations), but that it has not yet fully *emerged* (has not been legitimized by the formal political system). For some commentators (see Rau 1991b, esp. pp. 12–17, and 1991c), emerging civil society was a major reason for the collapse of communist power.[2]

Certainly, the increasing encouragement of some forms of private initiative and entrepreneurship in so many late communist states means that Gill's notion of *legitimate* autonomous behaviour pertained to some extent (it was usually limited to small-scale activity) in the economic sphere. In addition, the fact that the Polish government recognized Solidarity for approximately 15 months in 1980–1, to such an extent that it was prepared to negotiate with it and even invited its leaders to participate in economic decision-making, meant that this was a legitimated autonomous organization that clearly straddled the economic and political spheres. If the economic activity could be argued to relate merely to a narrow definition of civil society, the political activity constituted clear evidence of emerging civil society in the broader sense.

Other pieces of evidence of emerging civil society include the independent peace movements in the GDR and Hungary, and environmental movements in the USSR and Bulgaria. Some observers, such as Di Palma (1991b), also see the intellectual dissidents and their impact on the broader society in which they operated as evidence of a nascent civil society. For Di Palma, it is precisely because a civil society was beginning to emerge in many late communist systems that there is a real chance for democracy to establish itself under post-communism.

For many, Di Palma included, mass demonstrations by citizens against the state do not *per se* reflect an emerging civil society. The latter term implies something more profound and enduring than ephemeral outbursts of discontent or euphoria.

So far in this discussion, there has been no explicit consideration of the term *civil*. Edward Shils argues in a 1991 article that civil society has three main components. The first two are necessary but insufficient conditions: autonomous institutions distinguishable from the family, clan, locality and state; and the separation of such institutions from the state, at the same time as they interact with it. But the third is also crucial. This is what Shils, building on a line of thought that can be traced back centuries, calls 'a widespread pattern of refined or civil manners' (1991, p. 4). There might, for instance, be a situation in which autonomous institutions are in conflict with each other and the state, and in which such conflicts are not being properly arbitrated; according to Shils, such a conflictual and unregulated situation does not constitute civil society. For him, all the main players must accept the rules of the game, including faith in the referee, for there to be genuine civil society. This emphasis on respect for rules of the game by both the state and social organizations is compatible with the conception of legal-rationality that informs this book; together with mutual legitimation by both agencies (the state and the social organizations), it is taken here as a necessary component of *true* civil society (as distinct from merely *emerging* civil society).

Civil society and social movements

For many analysts, especially of late communism and early post-communism, one of the clearest indications of emerging civil society is the development of *social movements*. While these can constitute only *part* of civil society – other vital components include political parties and private businesses – their existence and status usually serve as a good indicator of the extent to which civil society has established itself.

Unfortunately, there is no universally agreed definition of social movements. Pakulski has provided a valuable if somewhat abstract definition: 'recurrent patterns of collective activities which are partially institutionalised, value oriented and anti-systemic in their form and symbolism' (1991, p. xiv). The reference to recurrent patterns and partial institutionalization means that Pakulski's definition is compatible with Di Palma's point that spontaneous, short-lived mass demonstrations do not *per se* constitute a form of social movement activity or evidence of civil society. However, the use of the term anti-systemic, which could be seen as taking one step further J. Cohen's (1983) argument that social movements represent an attempt to challenge the state to deepen democracy, fits poorly with conceptions of civil society that emphasize the state's recognition of social organizations, the interaction of the latter with the state, and perhaps even with Shils's notion of all agencies working to the same basic rules of the game. It is therefore not surprising that Pakulski himself (1991, p. 86) maintains that the usefulness of seeing social movements as part of civil society depends very much on the definition of the latter being employed.

A distinction is often drawn in the literature between 'old' and 'new' social movements (see Touraine 1985, Jennett and Stewart 1989a). The former include trade unions, business groups and arguably nationalists, whereas examples of the latter are feminists, environmentalists, gay and lesbian activists and animal rights activists. Unfortunately, problems arise in using the same label to describe diverse types of groups, even if a distinction is drawn between old and new. This is only partly because one group is largely based on class or ethnicity while the other (the new) typically cuts across more traditional identities. Perhaps even more important are the different operational styles and natures of the two types. The so-called old social movements are typically highly organized, relatively exclusive, and seek to exert direct influence on the state's decision-makers. They are, in essence, potential or actual pressure groups. In contrast, new social movements are usually loosely structured, have more open membership, and are more concerned with changing society's dominant values, attitudes and behavioural patterns than with direct interaction with the state. While they *do* sometimes act as pressure groups, to change the law on affirmative action or prevent a forest being logged for instance, their broader objective is to 'transform existing cultural patterns' (Jennett and Stewart 1989b, p. 1).

Given the differences just identified, it might appear advisable to reserve the use of the term social movements exclusively for what many call *new* social movements, and to call the old movements pressure groups. Unfortunately, such an apparently sensible solution is not without problems either, as becomes particularly obvious when examining the late communist and early post-communist world. Solidarity, for instance, was on one level a trade union and attempted to pressure the government; but on another, it sought to change dominant attitudes and behaviour, and was in many ways anti-systemic.

It should by now be very obvious that and why the concepts of civil society and social movements are *both* problematic, and that these problems are compounded by attempts to link them too closely. In a sense, it would be justifiable to abandon the two terms. On the other hand, both occur frequently in recent analyses, and both are valuable heuristically. While neither concept can be defined to everyone's satisfaction, it has to be recognized that the debates on them have opened up important new avenues to explore, particularly in terms of state–society relationships and legitimacy. It would therefore be irresponsible to omit them from an analysis of late communism and post-communism. But it would be equally irresponsible to move straight to a discussion of sub-elite politics, and the interaction between movements and the state, without explaining how the terms are understood in the present analysis.

For our purposes, for an organization (here very loosely interpreted, to include even relatively unstructured social movements) to be considered relevant in the context of the emergence of civil society, it must be autonomous (self-initiated, self-motivated and self-legitimated), and must more or less adhere to a set of rules. However, although it has already been argued that Shils is correct to emphasize respect for the rules of the game, it must also be acknowledged that *particularly* in a period of transition, rules may be vague or disputed. Indeed, unless the concept of civil society is to imply a static and conservative situation – the sort of cosy division of labour between the state and certain social groupings Marx saw as typifying bourgeois society, and that in recent decades has often been visible in countries adopting a corporatist model (on corporatism see Williamson 1985, Cawson 1986) – there must always be room for rules to be challenged and changed, and for a creative tension between the state and society. Respect for the rules of the game in an unstable and transitional period such as late communism and early post-communism is seen here as no more than a commitment to seek to promote or defend one's interests through *peaceful* channels. This is a broader conception of the rules of the game than one that focuses on a state-imposed legal framework.

Further, and in line with the argument above concerning the dynamics of civil society, it is maintained here that in the earliest stages of the emergence of civil society it is *not* necessary that autonomous organizations interact with or are legitimated by the state. From this perspective, it would be difficult to argue that there was not even a primitive *basis* of civil society in some communist countries by the 1970s. But it is also maintained here that if the next stage in the emergence of civil society is to be reached, there needs to be some recognition by the state of the right of such organizations to exist, and some form of interaction between the two. It is not necessary for *all* autonomous organizations to interact with the state in any meaningful political sense, merely that there is some mutually legitimated interaction between those that external observers would consider political in a reasonably broad sense and the authorities.

Various kinds of social grouping are considered in the following analysis. Some are clearly new social movements, by almost all definitions. Others would be considered social movements by some analysts and not by others, for reasons that will by now be obvious. The concern here is not to consider only groups that would generally be accepted as social movements, but rather any social grouping that meets our criteria for being relevant to the emergence of that vague but not meaningless concept, civil society.[3] For want of a better term, and while being fully cognisant of the potential problems with this, such groupings are here called social movements. This is justified on the grounds that the primary interest here is in the reassertion (or, more accurately in the case of several countries, the assertion) of society vis-à-vis the state, rather than in winning or even competing in semantic competitions.

SOCIAL MOVEMENTS DURING THE LATE COMMUNIST ERA

Claims that all communist states were always totalitarian are not very enlightening. They typically lack sufficient nuancing about the significant differences that existed between Stalin's USSR and either Tito's Yugoslavia or Kadar's Hungary, or even between Stalin's USSR and Gorbachev's USSR. Certainly, as terror became ever less salient a feature of most communist states – from the 1950s on – so there were signs, albeit at first very small ones, of autonomous social activity.

Brief reference has already been made to the dissidents; they are considered below. In some ways even more significant in terms of civil society were the private peasants in Poland and Yugoslavia from the 1950s, since they constituted a semi-autonomous and more or less legitimate private economic group. Moving to the 1970s and 1980s, the emergence and development of small-scale private businesses in many countries of Eastern Europe and the USSR can be seen as further evidence of nascent civil society (see Aslund 1985). Although it was still premature to identify an emerging bourgeoisie proper, there can be little question that, even by Marxist criteria, a petty bourgeoisie was beginning to develop in most of these countries (Albania was a notable exception).

By the late 1980s, the seeds were being sown for the development of an increasingly autonomous economic sector and class. One important symbol of this was the development of the cooperatives in the USSR. These had existed in pre-revolutionary and early communist Russia, but had been phased out in the 1930s. Following the promulgation of a law on them in July 1988, cooperatives were rapidly established in most sectors, including manufacturing, services, trade, agriculture and construction. Already by June 1989 there were more than 200,000 cooperatives, employing almost 3 million Soviet citizens. This development was not clearly self-initiated, since many members of the Soviet political elite themselves believed in the need to encourage such economic activity, as part of their attempts to improve economic performance for eudaemonic legitimation. Hence, as with several of the developments identified in the previous paragraph, some analysts would not recognize this as part of emerging civil society. However, the movement soon developed its own identity and momentum. Over time, therefore, it *did* become part of emerging civil society.

If doubts about the applicability of the concept of civil society to the economic sphere are less about legitimacy than about self-initiation and motivation, the problem is more or less reversed when considering autonomous political and *religious* activity. Considering the latter first, Albania was the only communist state ever to ban religion formally. However, Marxism-Leninism was an avowedly humanist ideology; its adherents regarded religion as largely metaphysical mumbo-jumbo which had emerged in a more superstitious age and was now largely outdated. Hence, communists were never comfortable with religion. In particular, they never fully recognized or legitimized the organized church. In some communist countries, there were understandable, if not defensible, reasons for this. Notably in Poland, when a Pole was elected to the position of Pope in 1978, the communist authorities realized that the status of the Roman Catholic Church in their country would be raised to an even more elevated position than it already enjoyed, thus threatening their own position. Since John Paul II has proven to be a more overtly political pope than some of his predecessors, there was some justification for the concerns of the Polish authorities about the potentially inspirational and destabilizing effect he and the church might have on the Polish masses. Indeed, Solidarity always made clear its support for the Catholic Church. The church in Poland was not the only one to become increasingly assertive in the communist world. Another good example was the Evangelical Church (and, to a much lesser extent, the Roman Catholic Church) in the GDR. In the early 1980s, in particular, this played a significant role in the unofficial peace movement in East Germany; the same was true, to a lesser degree, of the church in Hungary (on the churches under communism see Miller and Rigby 1986, Ramet 1989).

From this cursory overview, it should already be clear that the boundary between the reactivation and development of religion and the reinvigoration of politics sometimes overlapped in the communist world. The spotlight turns now to more explicitly *political* self-motivated activity in late communism.

For many observers, the starting point for such an analysis should be with the *dissidents*. These became a discernible phenomenon in the 1960s and 1970s. In the USSR, they emerged mainly in the late 1960s, largely because members of the creative intelligentsia – in particular – considered that the Brezhnev–Kosygin leadership team that had come to power in late 1964 was reneging on the modest liberalization introduced by Khrushchev from the mid-1950s to the early 1960s. They began to write and disseminate analyses of the system, details of harsh treatment by the authorities, examples of the state breaking its own agreements, etc. Most of these articles and pamphlets were handwritten or typed on thin paper, and recipients were often requested to make an additional copy before passing on the documents. This was necessary because the state controlled virtually all photocopying facilities and it would have been dangerous to have attempted to use these for this kind of material. In this way, many copies of the same document were eventually in circulation. This process was known as *samizdat* – literally self-publishing – and the very inclusion of the word 'self' to describe this kind of activity indicates its independence of the state (for a useful overview of Soviet dissent see Reddaway 1983). Very soon, albeit with different local flavours, dissidence was increasing in many of the more northerly countries of Eastern Europe (see Tokes 1979); it never became a salient feature of politics in Albania, Bulgaria or Romania, though there was an active Yugoslav dissident movement (see Sher 1977).

Many dissidents were treated harshly by the authorities, but most revealed impressive resilience, and often found some new stimulus to activity. In the mid-1970s, for instance, the fact that several communist states signed the 1975 CSCE Accords (the so-called Helsinki Agreement) led various dissident intellectuals in several countries to establish Helsinki monitoring groups. Unfortunately, such groups were typically harassed by the communist authorities.

Dissidents worked mostly either individually or else in small groups, so that many have questioned the validity of referring to dissident *movements*. Such reservations are largely valid. On the other hand, despite the small numbers of dissidents, some of their *ideas* were gradually filtering into mass society in some countries, and in this sense their role should not be underestimated (see Taras 1992a).

In any case, in at least one country – Poland – the role of the dissidents in the emergence of significant autonomous political activity was *clearly* significant. Following mass unrest in 1976, a number of dissident intellectuals linked up with working-class activists to form an organization (eventually known by the acronym KSS-KOR) that would attempt to defend workers against state harassment. It was to no small extent as a result of this collaboration that Solidarity emerged and played the significant role it did in Polish politics in 1980–1 (see Bernhard 1993, Karabel 1993).

The fact that some leading dissidents became popular heroes, and that citizens wanted them to play a major role in the politics of late communism and early post-communism, testifies to the widespread perception that several of them had played an important role in the delegitimation and then collapse of communism. Vaclav Havel in Czecho-Slovakia and then Czechia is the most obvious example; others include Andrei Sakharov (USSR), Zviad Gamsakhurdia (Georgia), Adam Michnik and Jacek Kuron (Poland).

But the existence of these small groups of intellectuals was not the only evidence of emerging independent political activity in late communism. While it has already been explained why short-lived mass demonstrations etc. did not *per se* qualify for inclusion in an analysis of the emergence of civil society, there are more than sufficient examples of ongoing, self-initiated political activity in the late communist era to permit references to emerging civil society in the political sphere.

First and foremost, mention must be made of Solidarity in Poland. While there were attempts elsewhere to establish autonomous *trade unions* (such as Klebanov's Free Trade Union Association in the USSR – see Haynes and Semyonova 1979), independent labour movements were not a salient feature of politics in most communist states until very late in the communist era, if at all.

Another type of group was mentioned earlier, and can now be briefly considered. This is the *independent peace movements* in Eastern Europe. A major impetus for the emergence of these groups was the 1979 NATO offer to the USSR not to expand and modernize US medium-range nuclear missile forces in Europe if the USSR would remove new SS-20 missiles it had installed in Eastern Europe in 1977; conversely, deployment of new American missiles would start at the end of 1983 if the Soviets did not respond positively (this was NATO's so-called twin-track or double-track decision – see Holloway 1983, esp. pp. 70–8; Nogee and Donaldson 1988, esp. pp. 326–30). Unfortunately, the USSR did not respond sufficiently to this offer. But in the four-year period of grace NATO granted the USSR (1979–83) before it began to install Cruise and Pershing missiles, many East European citizens revealed they were prepared to stand up and criticize the USSR's policy. The best example was the GDR, where the peace movement not only became a significant independent organization in its own right, but also spawned environmentalist and feminist groups (on the GDR see Mushaben 1984, L. Holmes 1992; on peace movements more generally in late communist Eastern Europe see Tismaneanu 1990).

Certainly, *environmentalist movements* became a growing force in the sub-elite politics of many late communist societies, although, with the notable exceptions of Bulgaria (see chapter 3), Czechoslovakia and Hungary (see Fisher 1993, esp. pp. 99–102), it would be going too far to suggest they became a major force in politics. Nevertheless, nascent independent ecological groups received a major boost from April 1986, when citizens of the USSR and Eastern Europe were directly exposed to the effects of the Chernobyl nuclear explosion. As citizens in so many communist countries were informed of the precautions they had to take (what they should and should not eat and drink, for instance), so their consciousness about the potential and actual dangers of nuclear power was necessarily raised. Although awareness of environmental problems became much more acute after 1986, it would be wrong to infer that there were no unofficial environmentalist organizations prior to this. Among those formed long before Chernobyl were the Polish Ecological Club (established September 1980) and the Danube Circle in Hungary (established 1983).

Feminism was not a major force in any of the communist states, even in late communism. One of the many reasons was that several states were particularly heavy-handed with groups of women who attempted to form feminist movements. Typical of the ideological attacks on them were the 'six points' made by various official spokespersons in Yugoslavia in the early 1980s. According to them, there were six mortal sins of feminism: it was an imported ideology; it represented a love of power; it was elitist; it constituted uninstitutional activity; it encouraged 'apoliticization'; and it did not sufficiently relate class analysis to the women's question (Drakulic-Ilic 1985). Most readers will immediately appreciate the hypocrisy and contradictoriness of many of these charges against feminism. The Yugoslav authorities were on one level reacting to an attempt by Yugoslav women to establish an autonomous feminist movement, which had resulted in the holding of a 'neo-feminist' conference in Belgrade in 1978. This movement had not progressed very far, however. Similarly, women in Leningrad (now St Petersburg) produced a document known as 'The Almanac: Women and Russia' in 1979; they were interrogated and in some cases arrested and exiled for their efforts (see Holt 1985).

It is worth noting that one of the most frequent criticisms of feminism from the communist authorities was that it was a bourgeois ideology and hence, *ipso facto*, to be rejected. But there was far more to the rejection than this, and it was not simply that communists were suspicious of *any* self-initiated political activity. The communist states, like all others (the Nordic countries being the least guilty of this – see Kelder 1994), were male dominated. Whereas male communist officials could at least appreciate why some citizens would protest about Chernobyl, since even the officials had children who could be affected by the fall-out, there was no inherent reason why they should identify with feminist groups, especially very critical ones.

Before concluding this brief overview of social movements in the communist world, one important point still needs to be made. Most independent groups, especially those that could in any meaningful sense be described as political, had something in common with each other: state oppression. Many of them temporarily overlooked their substantial differences in terms of attitudes and interests because of their common goal of fighting the state for the right to exist and disseminate views. The church, peace groups and feminists therefore often collaborated with each other during the communist era. The loss of this commonality, determined by time and place – and based, ironically, on state oppression – is just one of many factors helping to explain the relatively sorry state of these groups in early post-communism.

SOCIAL MOVEMENTS DURING THE POST-COMMUNIST ERA

Many observers have been very disappointed with the development – or lack of it – of social movements and various other aspects of emerging civil society in early post-communism. There are several reasons for this situation.

Starting with the issue of autonomous economic activity, it is by now clear that there have been significant problems with the way this has developed. The economic and legal dimensions of this transformation having been considered in earlier chapters, the focus here is on political and social aspects.

There is no question that new entrepreneurial classes are emerging in all post-communist states, albeit slowly in countries such as Albania and several states of the FSU. Some of these are already relatively significant numerically; others are still so small that the shortage of risk-takers is hampering economic development. But at least two additional major problems are already crystallizing. One is that societies are stratifying far more than they already were, and not all citizens appreciate that this is probably necessary if the economies are to modernize and grow. The second is that criminal elements are becoming so dominant among the new entrepreneurial class in some post-communist countries (notably Russia – but the problem can also be found in Poland, Czechia, etc.) that the very notion of private economic activity is evoking increasingly negative reactions.

Returning to the discussion of civil society outlined above, it is clear that much private economic activity is being consciously *sponsored* by the state (voucher systems, enabling legislation, etc.). In this sense, what is normally accepted as a key feature of civil society – independent, *self-initiated* activity – is not emerging in as clear-cut a form in post-communism as might have been expected. Nor is it clear that such activity is legitimate. In that the *state* is encouraging private activity, clearly this has been *officially* legitimized. But does *popular* legitimacy matter? If it is accepted that this *is* significant, then it is of concern that some opinion surveys conducted in several countries in the 1990s indicated that the increasingly privatized system, and by extension the people running or engaged in it, did not enjoy widespread popular legitimacy (see McIntosh et al. 1994, esp. pp. 498–500). This inference is to some extent endorsed by the so-called pink revolution (see chapter 12).

It would be largely inappropriate in the much freer atmosphere of post-communism to refer to dissident movements as such.[4] Conversely, a boosting of the role of autonomous *trade unions* would be anticipated. While workers have gone on strike on numerous occasions in the post-communist era, research to date suggests that the trade unions are often much less organized and effective, and have less worker support, than might be expected (see Cook 1995). There are various explanations for this. One is the lack of experience of autonomous organization. Another is a feeling among some workers that the unions are too remote and/or untrustworthy (for evidence of this among Russian workers see Rose 1995, p. 37). A third relates to the economic restructuring of early post-communism. This has led to a significant rise in unemployment, at the same time as the welfare state is in most cases finding it difficult to keep the unemployed from falling below the poverty line. This encourages competition for jobs, which in turn favours employers and weakens the bargaining role of unions.

The role of *the church* has in some important ways been enhanced. Citizens throughout the post-communist world are now legally free to practise religion. As indicated in chapter 9, legislation has been enacted in several countries that permits religious education in schools. In this sense, the post-communist states are becoming more like Western states. Unfortunately, greater tolerance by the state has in some cases been accompanied by greater intolerance by citizens, who use religious differences as a pretext for open conflict with their neighbours. Much of this issue is considered in the next section, under ethnic politics. At this juncture, it is worth noting that the church has in some cases not merely been revitalized as a *religious* organization, but has also become even more active *politically*. Perhaps the most visible example of this is on the issue of abortion; this too is considered briefly below, in the discussion of post-communist feminism.

The evidence so far suggests that the three types of new social movement considered earlier (peace movements, environmentalists and feminists) have in general become *less* active in early post-communism than they were in late communism. In the case of the *peace activists*, this is hardly surprising. The Cold War is over and the nuclear threat *appears* to be less than it was (although it would be unwise to be overconfident on the latter point, given the continuing instability in Russian and Ukrainian politics and the growing number of countries worldwide that either already have, or appear likely soon to have, nuclear weapons). The Soviet army has disbanded, and its remnants have either left or are soon to leave most of the countries of the former Soviet empire. The process of converting parts of the defence industry into civilian-oriented industries in countries such as Russia, Ukraine, Slovakia, Czechia, Bulgaria, etc., is proceeding, even if not invariably smoothly (on the problems faced by the armaments industries, including conversion, see Clarke 1994a and 1994b; Bush 1994a and 1994b). In short, while the world is still a dangerous place and in many ways more unstable than it was until the late 1980s, there is less *raison d'être* for the peace movement. Moreover, it should not be overlooked that some of the 'peaceniks' of the late communist era took their stand as much to protest against the communist authorities as because of their commitment to the cause of international peace. Indeed, some East German 'peaceniks' of the mid-1980s apparently became so in the belief that this might lead to their deportation to the West; since it did for some, it is understandable that many citizens saw protesting against communist militarism as a possible (and highly desirable) one-way ticket to the FRG.

Most of the above arguments do not apply to *environmentalists* or feminists. Certainly, the concerns they had in the 1980s have not diminished in the 1990s. Each group can be examined separately.

Many new 'green' parties were formed in the late 1980s and early 1990s. East European examples include the Romanian Ecological Movement (established late 1989); the Polish Green Party (originally the Polish Ecological Party – established September 1988); the Albanian Ecology Party (December 1990); and a German green party that was formed in late 1989 and which linked up with the West German Greens and other East German citizens' movements to contest the December 1990 pan-German elections under the umbrella organization 'Alliance 90' (all from DeBardeleben 1991b, p. 9; D. Hall 1993, p. 16). In the FSU, parties and other organizations emerging in late communism which then continued into early post-communism include the Estonian Green Movement (1988), the Georgian Green Movement (1988), the Belorussian Ecological Union (1989), and Green World (Ukraine – 1989). The dates of the establishment of the above reveal that many of these organizations were formed while the communists were still in power, demonstrating once again that it is often inappropriate to draw overly sharp distinctions between the late communist and early post-communist periods. In other cases, mainstream parties had a strong green orientation or faction (as with Democratic Russia, established in 1990 – see Duncan 1992, p. 98; Alliance of Free Democrats in Hungary, established in 1988 – Korosenyi 1991, p. 70).

While none of the green organizations has fared well in the various post-communist elections held since 1990, some of the mainstream parties with a strong green interest have performed creditably, notably the AFD in Hungary and the UDF in Bulgaria. Moreover, some of those who were environmental activists during the communist period now occupy positions in post-communist state administrations (Szacki et al. 1993, pp. 19–20). While it must be acknowledged that many of these appear to have lost their interest in the environment at present, this might be rekindled in the future; if this happens, their official standing should ensure they will be influential in future policy-making and implementation. But at present, and although there continue to be environmental activists, many politicians and citizens are more concerned with keeping their jobs and surviving than they were, and this is depleting the ranks of the environmental movements that emerged in late communism.

In some ways, the state of *feminism* in the post-communist world is the most depressing of all the social movements considered here. In the words of Gail Kligman, commenting on recent developments in Eastern Europe, 'the relationship between national liberation and "women's liberation" is seemingly an inverse one' (1992, p. 401); while two Slovak feminists lament, with regard to the former Czecho-Slovakia, 'For some time we have asked ourselves why the words "emancipation of women" have become such objects of derision and irony even among women,' (Kiczkova and Farkasova 1993, p. 84); and Elizabeth Waters, writing on the FSU, states that 'women are tired of politics and exhausted' (1993, p. 300).

As many commentators have observed, there has tended to be a 'retraditionalization' in post-communist societies, with returns to a conception of women as home-makers, to the family, to femininity, and – to a lesser extent – to religion. This is on one level part of the backlash against communism. It also relates to the belief, whether justifiable and realistic or not, that life was better in the pre-communist era. Admittedly, this interest in traditional values had surfaced among some politically aware women during the communist era (see Waters 1993, p. 287); but it appears to have intensified greatly in the 1990s. It could be that this will prove to be a relatively short-lived retraditionalization; as people travel more and are better integrated into the rest of the non-communist world, so some of the sentimentality about the past may be replaced by more forward-looking attitudes.

But what is the current position of feminism in the post-communist world? In attempting to answer this, it is useful to begin by considering the state of women's groups; unfortunately, this must be based on the rather sketchy, changing and often contradictory information available. Following this, some of the major issues such groups are addressing and that they might address in the future will be considered.

One kind of women's group has largely disappeared under post-communism, namely state-sponsored ones. Since these were in general meant to reflect the interests of the communist state, not only were they not very progressive by the standards of most Western feminists, but they were in some ways even anti-feminist and encouraged conformity. Their disappearance should thus be no cause for concern, although as of 1992 some were still in existence (as in Hungary – Adamik 1993, p. 208).

Conversely, for those who believe in a woman's right to choose whether or not to have a child once she has conceived, some of the new groups that have emerged in post-communism will be anathema. In 1991, for example, a new 'right-to-life' group in Hungary requested the Constitutional Court to declare the country's pro-abortion laws unconstitutional. Although the court ruled that it was not in a position to make such a declaration, it did require parliament to pass a new law by the end of 1992 (Adamik 1993, p. 208); the legislature complied, as a result of which abortions have in recent years become harder to obtain in Hungary than they were during the communist period. Apparently, as of early 1992 only one tiny group, the Feminist Network (established 1990), had sought to counter the right-to-lifers. Yet the Hungarian debate on abortion was often heated; in the words of Eva Fodor: 'In the course of the debate . . . the discourse surrounding the abortion issue underwent a metamorphosis from liberal humanitarianism to religious dogmatism of the kind that has become familiar in the United States' (1994, pp. 183–4).

Similar developments, that is the emergence of both more conservative and more progressive groups concerned with essentially female issues, are occurring elsewhere in the early post-communist world. In addition, as with the environmental issue, there are just a few indications that some political parties are beginning to include feminist concerns and ideas in their programmes, or at least to realize that there is an issue here. As of 1992, the Labor Party and the Social Democrats in Russia exemplified this (Waters 1993, p. 300), while the establishment of Women of Russia in 1993 (see chapter 7) and similar bodies in Belarus and elsewhere means there are political parties that on one level explicitly represent women. Moreover, the limited evidence garnered by Funk (1993, p. 9) suggests there are small green shoots of progressive feminist movements emerging and growing in Poland, Slovakia, what was the GDR, and what was Yugoslavia; there is remarkably little evidence of any such developments in Romania and Bulgaria.

The range of issues that might well be more fully addressed by feminist groups in the future is extensive, and can largely be inferred from the numerous problems identified in the last chapter. One relates to women's control over their own bodies. In the current climate in many post-communist states, the fact that the communists approved of abortion, whereas the church often disapproved, has led many politicians and citizens (female as well as male) to seek to limit or forbid access to abortions. This sometimes results in major confrontations between the church, particularly the Roman Catholic Church, and feminists. Many women (and men) will also need to demand better contraceptive facilities and education. The situation in terms of employment/unemployment is not clear at present (see chapter 9), with women having proportionally higher unemployment rates than men in some countries (including Romania, Czechia, Poland and the former GDR) and lower ones in others (Hungary). But gross and obvious inequities in this area will sooner or later result in the emergence of raised women's consciousness and, presumably, action to counter such inequities. Similarly, although child-care should be the equal responsibility of both mothers and fathers, it is likely that more women than men in post-communist states will see it as their task to improve child-care facilities.

As Hana Havelkova (1993) points out, it is important not to over-generalize about 'the' situation of women in post-communism (a point that applies to virtually any aspect of post-communism). Thus some issues are more salient in some post-communist countries than in others. For instance, the issue of divorce appears to have been a more contentious one in Hungary than it has been in most other post-communist states (Funk 1993, p. 9). But at the same time, commonalities should not be overlooked. While the salience of individual aspects of gender politics varies from country to country – indeed region to region, towns versus villages, ethnic group to ethnic group, age group to age group, etc. – most of the basic issues are common.

One of these is violence against women. As indicated in chapter 9, there are very few statistics on this for the post-communist world. Even if there were more, many would have to be treated cautiously, as *minimum* figures, since so much violence in the home never gets reported (the situation is similar in the West). But one very visible and pressing issue in the 1990s has been the widespread, *state-legitimated* rape and killing of women in the former Yugoslavia, especially Bosnia-Hercegovina. As well-known radical American feminist Catherine MacKinnon and many others have been arguing since the early 1990s, there is an urgent need for women (and men) both in post-communist societies and elsewhere to organize to have the international community not merely condemn war-related rape but treat it as a true war crime, with all the potential sanctions this connotes. Such demands have at last met with some success; in June 1996, for the first time, the Hague-based International Criminal Tribunal for the Former Yugoslavia began treating rape as a war crime.

On Nationalism and Ethnic Politics

For many, nationalist movements are simply another form of social movement. In this sense, it would have been appropriate to have considered them in the previous section. However, nationalism and ethnic politics constitute a much larger topic than merely nationalist movements. Moreover, ethnic tensions have become so significant a feature of politics in parts of the post-communist world that some commentators believe they are both *the* distinguishing feature of post-communism, and that they constitute a major threat to the development of *civil* society.[5] They are therefore treated in their own right in this chapter.

Nationalism is a highly complex phenomenon that assumes many forms. If sense is to be made of some of the conflicts and developments in the post-communist world, it is necessary to isolate these forms. In order to understand nationalism itself as a concept, it is important to consider the root or core of the word, that is, nation.

In the past, many writers have tried to define nations in terms of the commonalities of a group of people. Such commonalities might include language, religion, territory and that elusive concept, culture. In recent years, most analysts have come to accept that while several or all of these common attributes might indeed be found in a group describing itself as a nation, it is ultimately self-perception that defines the latter. Paraphrasing Seton-Watson (1965, p. 5), a nation exists if an active and substantial section of its members believes it exists. Inasmuch as a nation is something that exists primarily in the mind – in the collective consciousness – it is understandable why Benedict Anderson (1991, p. 6) has described it as 'an imagined political community'. There may well be important *symbols*, such as a shared language, a focus on certain events and heroes of the past, etc., but ultimately, the nation is a social construct. It is important to bear this in mind when considering examples of ethnic conflict in the post-communist world.

Nationalism can, *with important reservations explained below*, be described as the ideology of a nation. For the purposes of the discussion here, ideology is simply, if not unproblematically, understood as a complex set of mostly normative ideas used to define, guide and/or justify a particular group (in this case a nation) and its activities. The ideas might be formally and overtly disseminated – in schools, in the media, in activists' speeches, etc. Alternatively, or in addition, they might filter through to the individual's consciousness subtly and covertly. This might be through members of the family, friends, etc., who themselves may be largely unaware that they are passing on the (nationalist) code or value system. The true nationalist's primary identification is with the nation, rather than with class or gender for instance.

Caution must be used in describing nationalism as an ideology because, unlike most ideologies, it does not *per se* provide guidelines on several key aspects of social organization, notably on how to structure and manage a political or an economic system. Rather, it is little more than a general 'principle, which holds that the political and the national unit should be congruent' (Gellner 1983, p. 1). In this sense, it is an *incomplete* ideology, and needs to be linked in a particular case to a true ideology (such as liberalism, conservatism, socialism or communism) if it is to play an ongoing role in a system.

As mentioned above, nationalism assumes many forms. One division is between *official* and *unofficial* nationalism.[6] The former refers to the efforts of a state to inculcate and strengthen a state-oriented *national identity* (on this see Smith 1991), as well as to its work in structuring a state system in line with the perceived needs of the nation; this process is often referred to as nation-building. In contrast, unofficial nationalism is often, though not invariably, directed against an existing state, and emerges primarily from within society rather than the state. Of course, the world is a dynamic place, and today's unofficial nationalism can be so successful, in the sense of achieving its aim of creating a new state or fundamental change in an existing state, that it becomes tomorrow's official nationalism.

Unofficial nationalism can be subdivided into at least four types – unitarism, autonomism, separatism (or secessionism) and irredentism. *Unitarist* nationalism refers to attempts by one ethnic group, usually the numerically dominant one within a given state, to create or encourage the development of a common identity with and among most or all of the other ethnic groups in the state. This is intended to be an integrative rather than a disintegrative form of nationalism. Although unofficial nationalists who have espoused this form of nationalism often have much in common with the state's official ideologists, they can also embarrass or be at odds with the latter. This is sometimes because of their own insensitivity to the cultures and aspirations of other ethnic groups. Alternatively, or in addition, it can be because the central authorities do not wish to appear to be favouring the dominant ethnic group over ethnic minorities.

Unlike unitarist nationalism, both *autonomist* and *separatist* (secessionist) nationalisms are basically disintegrative. Both may well be counter-hegemonic, resisting the dominance of the largest ethnic group and/or the existing state (which itself may be dominated by the largest ethnic group). The main difference between these two forms of nationalism is that autonomists seek greater freedom to manage their own affairs *within* an existing political unit, whereas separatists (secessionists) want full independence, in the sense of breaking away from the existing unit (state) to form their own.

The fourth type of nationalism can in fact be either official or unofficial. It can also be both integrative and disintegrative simultaneously. This is *irredentism*. Here a group (of unofficial nationalists) in country A wants to break away from it and link up with country B, typically because they feel themselves to be closer ethnically to the major group inhabiting country B than to that of country A. It is also possible that the government of country B (official nationalists) will encourage the ethnically related or homogeneous group in country A to break away from it and join their country. It should thus be clear why this is simultaneously official and unofficial, integrative and disintegrative, depending on whether the focus is on country A or B.

In the real world, and as alluded to in the references to occasional overlap and interaction between official and unofficial versions, some examples of nationalism straddle, blend or blur the ideal types identified in the above taxonomy.[7] This will become clear below, when examples of nationalism in the post-communist world are considered.

On one level, nationalist politics is ethnic politics. Indeed, *ethnos* (the root of the word ethnic) was the classical Greek word for nation, which is derived from the Latin word *natio*. Certainly, many people use these terms interchangeably. But there are some phenomena that have yet to be discussed and for which, for the sake of clarity, the term ethnic politics can be reserved. Moreover, most analysts maintain that nationalism is a modern phenomenon, dating from no earlier than the eighteenth century. Given this, it becomes clear that, since both the ancient Greeks and the Romans had terms for the nation, but apparently no conception of nationalism, there must be more to ethnic politics than merely nationalism.

In this book, the phrase *ethnic politics* is used to refer to conflict either between two (or more) ethnic groups in society, or between an ethnic group and the state, but in which there is no suggestion of substantially changing political structures or raising national consciousness as such. In one form of this, the ethnic group is demanding greater justice – equal rights with other citizens in the state – and sees its perceived (and possibly actual) unjust treatment as being a function of its ethnic difference.

A related form of ethnic politics is *racism*. For analytical purposes, this can be held to assume three forms, although in the real world these often overlap. The first and mildest form holds that particular traits are determined by race.[8] At the other end of the spectrum is what should properly be called *racialism*,[9] when superiority is claimed by one group (or more than one) over other groups on the basis of actual or alleged biological differences considered by the first group(s) to be significant. In between these two is a form of racism that maintains that there are distinctive races and that these should be largely or completely kept apart. Although this form of racism does not *necessarily* involve the concept of hierarchy that is a key feature of racialism, in practice there is often an unspoken assumption by such racists that their race – and its culture – is better than those of others.

Having identified the major forms of nationalism and ethnic politics, communist policy on them can be briefly analysed, following which is a much longer subsection on the situation under post-communism.

THE COMMUNIST ERA

According to many Marxists, nationalism is a temporary phenomenon linked closely to a particular phase of capitalist state-building, especially in nineteenth-century Europe. For Marx himself and many of his followers, nationalism was an ideology created by bourgeoisies to encourage the proletariat in a given territory to believe it had more in common with 'its own' capitalist class than it did with workers in other parts of the world. According to this argument, it was in the interests of national bourgeoisies to make German or French workers believe in Germany or France rather than in the common interest of the proletariat worldwide. If the latter consciousness were to develop, the national bourgeoisies would be threatened. Marx argued that the working classes really have no nation, and advocated socialist or proletarian internationalism. Indeed, the slogan at the end of Marx's best-known and most widely read tract, *The Communist Manifesto*, is 'Workers of all countries, unite!'

Although communist systems were all, in theory, committed to this argument, perceived practical needs often shifted actual policy away from such internationalism. The process became very pronounced under Stalin, with his 'socialism in one country'. Once the USSR had adopted this policy, the precedent had been set for subsequent communist leaderships to incorporate official nationalism into state ideology (see Zwick 1983). This they often did in their endeavours to gain legitimacy: in that communists mostly took power in existing nation-states (the GDR was an exception), there was often a belief that an appeal to *some* pre-communist traditions, notably love of the nation (*patriotism*), would enhance communist legitimacy. As mentioned in chapter 2, communist leaderships often also attempted to enhance their legitimacy by emphasizing *contemporary* achievements, such as sports; this was another dimension of official nationalism.

In those communist states that were radically multi-ethnic, notably the USSR and Yugoslavia, the authorities sought to promote loyalty to a state rather than to a particular ethnic group. Thus citizens of the USSR were encouraged to think of themselves more as Soviets than as Georgians or Ukrainians or even Russians. Similarly, citizens of Yugoslavia were to some extent discouraged from perceiving themselves above all as Croats or Slovenes or Serbs, etc.

If their pronouncements are to be accepted at face value – and we shall never know how genuine a Tito or a Brezhnev was when they made them – many communist leaders appear to have believed that 'the' problem of nationalism had been basically solved within their own societies. By this they meant that unofficial nationalisms and traditional ethnic rivalries had been overcome, and that the 'new socialist persons' who putatively constituted the citizenry were committed both to the state in which they lived and to genuine socialist internationalism. Late communism and early post-communism has amply demonstrated the erroneousness of such assumptions.

But before examining the evidence on this, it is important to note that there were numerous examples during the communist period of all the kinds of nationalism that have been identified here (see L. Holmes 1986a, pp. 326–41). Until towards the very end of the communist era, however, excesses of unofficial nationalism were usually suppressed quite forcibly by the coercive organs of the communist state (examples include in Croatia, Lithuania and Ukraine in the early 1970s, Kosovo in the early 1980s, and nowadays in Tibet).

THE POST-COMMUNIST ERA

The events of 1989–91 in the communist world have been described in this book, with reservations, as the double-rejective revolution. One of these rejections, of external domination, can be seen as a good example of nationalism, although in some cases it was of a particular kind that does not fit neatly into the usual taxonomies. Here, members of a given country believe that their state has not *in practice* been treated as a fully sovereign and independent entity, despite its formal status in international law. They therefore wish to assert, and have universally recognized, their full sovereignty and independence.[10] While most nationalists within the USSR or Yugoslavia were clearly irredentists, autonomists or secessionists, many of those in Eastern Europe were not advocating structural change as such. Rather, in countries like Poland or Hungary, the states *were* formally sovereign and independent, but many citizens and some politicians considered they were still too much under Soviet influence. This is therefore best understood as a specific type of nationalism that blends elements of autonomism and secessionism and nation-building.

Ethnic politics also played a role in the 1989–91 revolutions. Perhaps the clearest example was in Romania. It will be recalled from chapter 3 that it was the state's treatment of someone defending the rights of Hungarians in Transylvania, Father Tokes, that is seen by many commentators as the trigger for the anti-Ceausescu revolution of December 1989.

Unfortunately, the nationalism that was one part of the double-rejective revolution has in many countries gained a momentum of its own and become a negative phenomenon in post-communism. While the external observer can often understand and accept that nationalism directed against domination is basically justified (in that sense it is 'good' nationalism), the situation changes if it starts to become chauvinistic or racist. Arguably the least acceptable form of such nationalism is where members of the dominant nations do not accept the new situation, and attempt to retain control of nations that have declared their independence of a larger state of the communist era.

Czecho-Slovakia

Consideration of the three states that were federal during the communist era reveals quite different processes of disintegration. The smoothest break-up was of Czecho-Slovakia. It will be recalled that this originally came into existence in 1918, and that it was federalized in 1969 as a result of the so-called Prague Spring. By 1992 a small number of the leading politicians in both the Czech Lands and Slovakia had reached agreement that it would be better for all concerned if Czecho-Slovakia were to work not as a more genuinely equal federation, but as two separate states. Surveys taken of the citizens in the Czech Lands and Slovakia just months before the division of the country at the end of 1992 revealed that majorities in both wanted to remain part of one larger whole. Admittedly, Czechs tended to favour a somewhat more integrated arrangement than did Slovaks. But two politicians in particular – Klaus in the Czech Lands, Meciar in Slovakia – were committed to a dissolution, and in their respective posts of recently mandated (by the June 1992 elections) Czech and Slovak prime ministers, they were in a strong position to realize this.

A major reason for the agreement to divide Czecho-Slovakia was that Klaus and Meciar had very different views on the best way forward.

Klaus had long been one of the most consistently pro-market and pro-privatization leaders in the post-communist world, whereas Meciar believed the state should play a significant role in the running of the economy. These positions could not be reconciled, Klaus dismissing as unworkable Meciar's notion of a confederal state comprising two sovereign units. The two men agreed to disagree, and Czecho-Slovakia split into two independent states from 1 January 1993 (on all this see Pehe 1993). As predicted by many, this had an almost immediate positive economic effect on the already stronger Czech Lands. In contrast, Slovakia, which was less developed and more dependent on traditional and often outdated industries, initially fell further behind its neighbour; this said, it began to recover much sooner than predicted by many economic analysts.

Czecho-Slovakia's population had long had a reputation for being acquiescent and peace-loving when faced with adversity (they are sometimes contrasted with the Poles in this context). Certainly the disintegration of the country, based partly on Czech and Slovak nationalism, was extraordinarily peaceful; it has been described as the 'velvet divorce'. However, whether the whole process was as democratic, smooth and legally proper as it might have been can be questioned. For instance, the Slovak National Council unilaterally declared Slovak sovereignty in mid-July 1992, thereby so upsetting the Czecho-Slovak president (Havel) that he resigned within one hour of hearing the news. Moreover, according to the legislation still in force in mid-1992, a dissolution of the state could occur only if a majority in at least one of the two republics had expressed its desire to secede in a referendum. But the two prime ministers argued that a referendum would be an expensive formality, and therefore submitted new proposals for a dissolution. Although these did not proceed smoothly through the Federal Assembly, by late 1992 many parliamentarians appear to have accepted that the country was going to divide anyway, so that it was better for this to occur in an orderly manner than in a chaotic (and possibly violent) one. Despite some reluctance earlier in the year, the Federal Assembly finally agreed to a dissolution bill on 25 November 1992, just weeks before the country split. Privately conducted surveys continued to suggest, however, that neither Czech nor Slovak majorities wanted total separation (for a collection of views on why Czecho-Slovakia split up see Musil 1995).

It is not clear that 1 January 1993 represented the end of this story. One of the most contentious issues within the Czech Lands during 1992 was the issue of Moravia and Silesia. It will be recalled from chapter 3 that what are normally called the Czech Lands consist of Bohemia, Moravia and parts of Silesia (the rest of the last of these is in Poland). In the early 1990s, a number of Moravians and Silesians were arguing that the Czech Lands were being dominated by the Bohemians: for example, the capital of Czechia, Prague, is also the Bohemian capital. This debate filtered right up to the level of the Czech parliament, when it was debating a new Czech constitution. Some opposition politicians advocated the federalization of the Czech Lands themselves, as a way of ensuring that Moravia and Silesia did not lose their identity within the Czech Republic. Although the majority of parliamentarians voted against this proposal, on the grounds that it could encourage further disintegrative nationalism and possibly even separatism, it is not clear that Moravian and Silesian nationalists will simply accept this. There could yet be further structural changes in the Czech Republic as a result of nationalist politics. Much will depend on the new republic's economic performance.

USSR

In the case of Czecho-Slovakia, the leaderships of what were essentially only two parts (the last point notwithstanding) had to negotiate the dismemberment of the country. But the USSR was far bigger and more complex, and negotiations on its restructuring were far more difficult. In the event, the Soviet negotiations failed. Whereas the Czecho-Slovak dissolution was planned in advance and implemented in an orderly manner, the USSR just fell apart! The process had already been under way before mid-1991, with most pressure coming from the Baltic republics and Georgia. But following the dismal coup attempt of August 1991, the efforts Gorbachev and others had made to reach agreement on a new, much looser arrangement essentially came to naught. Many republican elites now understandably believed that there was a risk of another coup attempt, and that this time the plotters might learn from the bungling of the August 1991 group. Given that the principal motivation for the August coup was the plotters' resentment about the imminent *de facto* near break-up of the Soviet Union and their desire to re-establish a strong multi-ethnic USSR, it becomes clear why so many political elites outside Russia declared their republic's independence in the days and weeks following the failed attempt. Expressed simply, they sought to detach their countries from the USSR before powers in Moscow had an opportunity to tighten control once again.

Given the sheer scale of the Soviet Union, with 15 republics and well over 100 hundred ethnic groups officially recognized, the dissolution was *relatively* peaceful. Certainly there was, and in some cases continues to be, armed resistance to the actual or proposed political restructuring (or the absence of this) in parts of the FSU. Among the main examples are the bloody conflicts between Armenia and Azerbaijan over Nagorno-Karabakh (13,000 deaths are estimated to have resulted from this by 1993 – Gitelman 1994, p. 245); fighting between the Georgian 'unitarist' authorities and both South Ossetian autonomists (who want the reinstatement of the South Ossetian autonomous region that was abolished in 1990) and irredentists (who would prefer to leave Georgia and join the North Ossetians within the Russian federation) and Abkhazian autonomists and separatists (see S. Jones 1992, 1993); and tensions between Russians (including Russian troops) and the Moldovan authorities over the left bank of the River Dnestr (see Kolsto et al. 1993 and the various articles in *Transition*, vol. 1, no. 19, pp. 2–20).

If the many verbal and legal conflicts are added to these armed conflicts – many of which are on one level territorial disputes – the situation looks even worse. Not only did the USSR contract and convert into the much looser and possibly ephemeral CIS at the end of 1991, but even *within* the biggest partner, Russia, the demands for autonomy grew at an alarming rate in the early 1990s. In some cases, such as the demand of St Petersburg (the renamed Leningrad) for equal status with the new republics within the Russian federation, the claims cannot be described as nationalist or ethnically based. They are, rather, a reflection of a loss of faith in the central authorities, and a belief among local elites that their administrative unit would function better if they had greater control. In this sense, this is primarily an example of *regionalism*. But *some* of the demands for more autonomy or actual independence have unquestionably been examples of nationalist politics within the Russian federation. One example is Chechnya, which *de facto* separated from Ingushetia in November 1991 and claimed independence of Russia; the dissolution of what had been Checheno-Ingushetia was soon recognized by Moscow, whereas Chechen independence was not. It was primarily this that eventually resulted in the outbreak of fighting between Chechens and Russian troops in late 1994. Other Russian republics that have sought either greater autonomy or total independence include Tatarstan (see Teague 1994) and Bashkortostan (see Todres 1995).

By late 1992, the nationalist conflicts in parts of the CIS were so intense that some countries had indicated their intention to leave the Commonwealth. In October 1992, for example, the Azerbaijani legislature voted unanimously *not* to endorse the CIS treaty; Azerbaijan subsequently withdrew from the CIS. Then, in December, Moldovan President Snegur announced that his republic would not sign the treaty either; although the official reason given was that there was a centralizing tendency within the CIS to which Moldova objected, it seemed clear that the principal reason was that several leading Russian politicians had been supporting the Russian forces on the left bank of the River Dnestr. Yet both countries subsequently came back into the fold, despite continuing reservations: Azerbaijan decided to rejoin the CIS in September 1993, and Moldova finally agreed to join its economic alliance in April 1994, while remaining outside its military alliance.

Many more cases of nationalism of various sorts could be cited from the contemporary CIS. But this would not alter the basic picture, which is one of an enormous number of nationalist claims and counterclaims. All of this is giving cartographers either nightmares or a bonanza.

One further aspect of the situation in the FSU during the 1990s warrants comment. This is that many of the political elites in the successor states of the FSU have had to engage in a new form of state-building and creation of a national identity. It has come as a surprise to many in the West to discover that many Russians are finding it difficult to identify with Russia or to feel anything they can recognize as distinctly 'Russian'. They have for centuries been part of a Russian empire, and evidently many identify far more readily with this larger entity than with 'just' Russia (which remains territorially the largest country in the world – on the issue of Russian identity see Shearman 1994). This is part of the explanation for the St Petersburg demands noted earlier. It also helps to explain the success of Zhirinovskii and his expansionist Liberal Democrats in the December 1993 elections. Yet two quite different reactions to this problem of Russian identity can be observed here. Many of the St Petersburg demonstrators preferred to relate to a local unit than to the Russian federation; in short, they were focusing on a much *smaller* unit. For many Zhirinovskii supporters, the promise of a reconstituted Russian empire (that is, a *larger* unit) was an attractive one.

Evidently, many Central Asians are also finding it difficult to relate to their new states. As Bess Brown observes:

> For the five Central Asian republics – Kazakhstan, Uzbekistan, Kyrgyzstan, Turkmenistan and Tajikistan – the collapse of the USSR and their de facto independence at the end of 1991 was an unexpected event for which no-one in the new states was prepared, psychologically, politically or economically ... The first year of independence of the Central Asian states was dominated, therefore, by the new countries' efforts to come to terms with a statehood that for all of them, except Uzbekistan, had little precedent. (1993, p. 25)

The fact is that there was *relatively* little national awareness in most of this part of the world before the establishment of Soviet republics there in the 1920s. For instance, much of the population of Kazakhstan had been nomadic before the incorporation of the area into the Russian empire in the nineteenth century, while Tajikistan hardly existed as an entity in its own right prior to 1929. Despite the predictions of some (see Carrere d'Encausse 1981), this area was not a major source of separatist nationalism in the 1980s, and in the early 1990s the countries largely accepted rather than passionately agitated for independence. Official nationalism is now very much part of government agendas in most of these states. It might even be that part of the reason for the increasingly authoritarian leadership in most of these countries is the leaders' perceived need to develop a strong and unified identity among the populations.

Yugoslavia

In many ways, the most tragic transition to post-communism and a restructured political system has been Yugoslavia's. Since much of the break-up was elaborated in chapter 3, the whole story will not be recounted here. However, since the situation in Bosnia-Hercegovina has so dominated the world's media in recent years, and since it will not cease to be a historically significant event in the future, an overview of that particular problem is appropriate.

As already indicated, Bosnia-Hercegovina has a long and complex history. Many of those who agreed to become Muslim in the fifteenth and sixteenth centuries were ethnically Serbs; indeed, Serbs had first settled in Bosnia no later than the seventh century, and Bosnia was a part of Serbia until the tenth. Over the centuries, Serbs and Croats settled in the area, so that by the 1990s Bosnia-Hercegovina was a complex mixture of Muslims, Serbs, Croats and others (for details see L. Cohen 1995, p. 241). The

declarations of independence by Slovenia and Croatia in June 1991 (following declarations of sovereignty in July 1990 and December 1990 respectively) led many essentially unitarist nationalists in Serbia, including some
in the government, to go on the offensive, wondering where the disintegration of the country would end. This antagonized the non-Serbs in the
former Yugoslavia, who in many cases believed that the Serbs were bent on
defending a Serbian-dominated and still quasi-communist system.

In one sense, the Bosnians were unfortunate in their timing. In declaring
their country's sovereignty and then independence *after* the Slovenes and
Croats, in October 1991 and March 1992 respectively, the Bosnian government was adding salt to an already sore Serbian wound. However, there was
far more to the Bosnian situation than this. Its ethnic diversity rendered it
very different from the far more homogeneous Slovenia and Croatia. First
Serbia, then Croatia, became increasingly concerned that 'their own' people
within Bosnia-Hercegovina might be treated as second-rate citizens by
the ethnically largest group, the Muslims, in an independent Bosnia-
Hercegovina. At the same time, and perhaps as an even more significant
factor, both Serbian and Croatian leaders believed that if Yugoslavia was
doomed anyway, then they should attempt to maximize their territories
before the post-Yugoslav arrangements became too consolidated and recognized in international law. This is the background to the horrendous fighting
that started in Bosnia-Hercegovina in the (Northern) spring of 1992.

During 1992 and 1993, both Western governments and international
organizations such as the UN sought not to take sides too clearly, on the
grounds that to do so might inflame the situation and turn it into a full-scale
war. They therefore imposed a trade and arms embargo on Serbia, in the
hope that the Serbs would be forced through economic and military necessity to cease their hostilities and atrocities in Bosnia-Hercegovina. They
also refused to supply arms to the Muslims of Bosnia-Hercegovina, and
would not fight to defend them. Rather, they proposed a division of Bosnia-
Hercegovina that would have given Serbs, Croats and Muslims different
parts of the former republic, depending on which group was numerically
dominant in a given area. One problem with this proposal – the so-called
Vance–Owen plan (after its American and British authors) of January
1993[11] – was that it would have created islands of Serbs and Croats, whereas
Serbian and Croatian authorities sought an arrangement that would give
them areas contiguous with Serbia and Croatia respectively, so as to create
new and larger unified states of Serbia and Croatia. Moreover, many parts
of Bosnia-Hercegovina, including the capital Sarajevo, were so ethnically
mixed that the notion of a neat division of the republic was flawed.[12] It was
not surprising that the plan eventually came to naught.

By mid-1995 the Bosnian issue looked no closer to resolution than it had
in 1992–3. Moreover, by the time of its fiftieth anniversary in 1995, the UN
had proven itself a most ineffectual organization, above all because of its
record of weakness and indecision in Bosnia. Not until the end of August
1995, and the start of Operation Deliberate Force, did the UN – via NATO
– start using real force against the Bosnian Serbs. This show of strength had

the desired effect on the warring parties. Following a US initiative and prolonged negotiations, the so-called Dayton Peace Accord was eventually signed by the Bosnian, Croatian and Serbian presidents in Paris in December 1995. This envisaged a single Bosnian state comprising a Croat-Muslim Federation and a Serbian Republic. It remains to be seen whether or not this agreement really does bring about a long-term resolution of the Bosnian issue. Problematic as the Bosnian conflict has been, it might prove even more difficult to improve the UN's public image.

One of the most appalling aspects of the break-up of Yugoslavia during the 1990s, about which the UN has done remarkably little, has been the so-called *ethnic cleansing*. Although recently applied mostly to Bosnia-Hercegovina, there are many examples and varieties of it in the post-communist world (as there were in the communist), and it is worth focusing on the phenomenon.

Ethnic cleansing is nothing new. It can be traced back almost three thousand years to the Abyssinians (see Bell-Fialkoff 1993). In the context of Bosnia-Hercegovina, it refers above all to the forced transfer of people who had been living in one area to another, because of their ethnicity. As already indicated, Bosnia-Hercegovina was a patchwork quilt in terms of the distribution of ethnic groups over its territory; indeed, while some centres were overwhelmingly Serb, Croat or Muslim, many were genuinely multicultural. One of the aims of the Serbs, in particular, was to remove non-Serbs from such multi-ethnic areas if they were geographically adjacent to Serbia or else predominantly Serbian settlements further inside Bosnia-Hercegovina, so as to create a single greater Serbia. Thus hundreds of thousands of people were forced out of their homes and made to move to areas in which the Serbs had less interest. Moreover, many thousands of women were raped by soldiers, in some cases apparently receiving official encouragement.[13] This is seen, *inter alia*, as a way of terrorizing women into vacating an invaded area. It is also designed to sully the putative purity of an ethnic group's next generation, and to render women less attractive in the future to 'their own' men in the hope that this will result in a decline in that group's population growth rate. Not only is the use of these various forms of coercive violence repugnant and morally reprehensible, but it is in practice often arbitrary anyway. In Bosnia-Hercegovina, as in so many parts of the world (especially multi-ethnic areas), widespread intermarriage means that it is frequently unclear who is a member of a given ethnic group and who is not; if it is borne in mind that many Bosnian Muslims have their ethnic origins in Serbia, the absurdity of the situation becomes as clear as its horror. Related to this is the bitter irony that many rape victims subsequently give birth as a result of the rape, producing what is in effect the opposite of what those who consider themselves the victors are seeking; far from maintaining 'ethnic purity', the newborn children of mixed ethnicity can be argued to be 'diluting' the blood of the rapists.

The forced and often violent resettlement of people in the former Yugoslavia was in the early to mid 1990s the most overt and well-publicized example of ethnic cleansing in the post-communist world. But it was not the only case. There were several allegations of it in Tajikistan and Georgia, for instance.

Further examples

A more subtle form of cleansing is being practised by some post-communist governments. Here, the authorities marginalize or harass particular ethnic minorities, with the (usually unstated) aim of encouraging them to move. A wide range of techniques is employed. One is for police physically to harass groups. Romanies (gypsies), whom some are blaming for substantial increases in crime rates in countries such as Czechia, Hungary and Romania, have been subject to this (on Romanies and their situation under post-communism see Barany 1994 and 1995, Crowe 1995, Lemon 1995). Another is where governments pass new citizenship laws that deprive some long-term residents (and former citizens) of full rights. These are generally targeted at ethnic minorities, seemingly in the hope that these will eventually feel sufficiently marginalized to 'return' whence they came. Many Russians in Estonia, for instance, have been affected by such legislation.[14] This is a quite different situation from that in Bosnia-Hercegovina, and it would be totally inappropriate to lump the actions of the Estonian and some other FSU governments in the same basket as those of the Bosnian Serbs. Outsiders can probably sympathize to a *limited* extent with the Estonian position, since many Estonians feel they were subjected to Russian domination for decades and now wish to ensure they do not once again become, as they see it, second-rate citizens in their own country. Their position could be seen as fragile anyway, since they constituted only just over 60 per cent of the population of Estonia at about the time the country declared independence (1991; the population figures are actually for 1989). However, it also needs to be borne in mind that many Russians have been living in Estonia for two or more generations and in a real sense have no home other than Estonia. This is why the word return is in inverted commas above. (For two quite different views of the Estonian citizenship issue see Kionka 1992, Park 1994. Latvia has also considered such exclusionary policies – see Girnius 1995a, p. 16. More generally on citizenship policies and laws in several parts of the FSU see Barrington 1995.)

The problem of citizenship is a difficult one. In a democratic system, governments often reflect popular moods; they need to if they wish to be re-elected. Thus if the dominant ethnic group opts to keep its distance from 'others', governments will often feel compelled to pursue policies that reflect these wishes. This said, many governments could make much greater efforts to change dominant attitudes: state–society relations are interactive.

There is considerable evidence of overt racism among both government officials and the population in many post-communist states. In addition to the prejudice against Romanies already mentioned, one of the best documented cases is of *anti-semitism*. There is a long history of anti-Jewish feeling in both Poland and Russia, in particular, dating back to the communist and pre-communist periods. In Poland, for example, a major purge of intellectuals in 1968 was directed above all against Jews. In the post-communist period, there was a slur campaign against Tadeusz Mazowiecki when he ran for the Polish presidency in late 1990; despite being a Catholic, there were rumours he had Jewish ancestry, which allegedly had a negative impact on his results in the elections (Roskin 1993, p. 55). Ironically, there have also been suggestions that the anti-semitic leader of the Russian Liberal Democrats, Zhirinovskii, has Jewish ancestry, and that he applied in the early 1980s to emigrate to Israel (see Morrison 1994, pp. 25–8).

According to Brym and Degtyarev (1993, p. 2), Russia has the world's largest combined population of Jews and anti-semites. It also has a long tradition of anti-semitism, as revealed graphically yet subtly in the short stories of Isaac Babel. In October 1992 a telephone survey was conducted of just over 1,000 Muscovites, most of whom were prepared to reveal their views on a wide range of issues. One of these was their attitude towards Jews. In contrast to the findings of some opinion surveys (see Gudkov and Levinson, cited in Brym and Degtyarev 1993, p. 3), the October 1992 survey suggested that a depressingly high percentage of those interviewed either believed that Jews were partly responsible for Russia's contemporary woeful situation, or else did not know (that is, were not prepared to say Jews were *not* responsible).[15] Apparently, many were prepared to blame 'the West' for Russia's problems, and believed 'Zionism' played a major role within the West (many Slovaks apparently have similar attitudes – see Brym and Degtyarev 1993, p. 11 n18). Such scapegoating attitudes are and have been all too familiar around the world, and are hardly conducive to improved understanding and better relations between peoples.

Despite the strength of the anti-semitic mood in many parts of eastern Europe and the FSU, there are, except in Russia and Hungary, very few Jews still living in these countries (Hockenos 1993, p. 271), partly as a function of anti-semitism in the past. In short, much of the current anti-semitism is directed against an almost non-existent 'other'. This merely endorses the argument that much of the racism and ethnic hostility in the post-communist world – generally, not just against Jews – reflects the extreme frustration of citizens, many of whom seek to cope with their feelings of helplessness by blaming others for their situation, even when it should be patently obvious that these 'others' play a very minor role in the given society. The violence and xenophobia of many skinheads in these countries can be understood partly from this perspective.

The reader could be forgiven for concluding by this stage that nationalism and ethnic hostilities have become one of the salient features of post-communism. To some extent, this is true. However, the notion that ethnic identity is all-important to citizens throughout the post-communist world cannot go unchallenged, and there is some counter-evidence to much of the above.

Not all ethnically homogeneous groups (to the extent that any truly are) living in currently divided or separate political units are anxious to link up with their ethnic kindred. Two of the best examples are the Moldovans vis-à-vis Romania, and the Hungarians vis-à-vis Transylvania (Romania) and Vojvodina (within Serbia). In the case of the former, opinion polls, a March 1994 referendum, and the amount of support for the man who placed Moldovan independence above all else (including unification with Romania), President Mircea Snegur, indicate clearly that irridentism is not a major force in today's Moldova. This is despite the fact that many would argue that Moldovans and Romanians are ethnically the same.[16] Similarly, it appears that most Hungarians feel they have enough problems of their own, without wanting to add to these by incorporating the troubled and economically less developed Transylvania and Vojvodina (interview with E. Hankiss, Oxford, May 1993).

A ten-point analysis

This last point raises an important issue. Since evidence of *some* nationalism and ethnic conflict can be found in most parts of the contemporary world, the question arises as to why it becomes so much more significant at some points in time and in some places than in others. In short, what leads to the rise and demise of nationalism and ethnic politics?

A ten-point analysis of the reasons for unofficial nationalism and ethnic conflict was provided by the author in an earlier book (L. Holmes 1986a, pp. 341–5); this model can be readopted here, with only minor modifications in light of recent developments and the fact that the model is now being applied to post-communist rather than to communist states. The ten points are as follows.

Historical tradition   There may be a tradition of hostility between two or more ethnic groups, in many cases dating back centuries. The antagonisms may relate to territory, religious differences, former domination, past wars and atrocities, etc.

Official and unitarist nationalism   Nationalism by the state and/or of the dominant ethnic group can stimulate and encourage greater national self-awareness among minority groups. This is even more likely to occur where official nationalism and unofficial unitarist nationalism coalesce.

Rapid modernization and/or revolutionary change   If regimes attempt rapid, extensive and significant change in society, there can be a backlash. This can also occur if there is a sudden radical change of politico-socio-economic system as a result of a revolution. Traditional value systems come under pressure in both processes, which can have a destabilizing effect on many citizens. The atavism inherent in many forms of nationalism can act as a magnet and source of assumed stability for people who have been disoriented by the rapid and extensive changes, and who feel they are losing or have lost their *identity*. This is even more the case if a post-revolutionary situation is characterized by an ideological void and/or a rapidly changing class structure and/or a fragile state structure. All three of these factors can be found to varying degrees in the post-communist countries. Since many citizens cannot find in ideology or class or a strong state a sufficient focus for self-identification, the nation can be an effective alternative.

Political structures   A political structure that is perceived as having been imposed from above, such as a federal system, can become the focus of nationalist agitation once the whole political system is challenged.

Political climate   A liberal phase of a government's rule can sometimes encourage (unofficial) nationalist activists to become more outspoken, which may lead to a general increase in unofficial nationalism. This can in turn result in a more repressive policy, with a regime introducing legislation to suppress what are perceived to be the excesses of unofficial nationalism, xenophobia, right-wing extremism, etc.

Poor regime performance   One of the main reasons for changes in the intensity of nationalist feelings is regime performance, particularly in the economic sphere. In the most common scenario, deteriorating economic performance, especially when reflected in growing unemployment, encourages unofficial nationalism and/or ethnic politics. But poor regime performance in the economic sphere can also lead a government itself to seek scapegoats. In such circumstances, it too becomes more nationalist, even racist, in its endeavours to enhance its own legitimacy. By late 1993, for instance, poor economic performance in Slovakia was encouraging what many saw as increasing racism by the Meciar government, which sought to blame the Hungarian minority for some of Slovakia's problems.

A rider to this argument is that poor regime performance in a neighbouring state or political unit that is ethnically very close to a given state might actually result in a *reduction*, or at least no increase, in irredentist nationalism. Moldovan and Hungarian attitudes cited earlier can be interpreted in part from this perspective.

Perceptions of unequal or unjust treatment   If an ethnic group believes it is being underprivileged by the authorities relative to other groups, this can exacerbate tensions both between that group and the state and between it and other groups.

Conversely, some hitherto privileged groups believe they *should* continue to receive better treatment than others, and resent policies designed to assist those the state perceives as underprivileged. Such a situation can also result in nationalist and ethnic politics of various kinds.

Regime sycophancy towards a foreign power   If citizens believe their own leaders are being too sycophantic towards a dominant foreign power, one result can be growing unofficial nationalism. While post-communist leaders are not *generally* obsequious towards the FSU/Russia in the way most of their predecessors were,[17] there is a danger that some will become increasingly fawning towards Western institutions (the EU, NATO, etc.). Since many *West* Europeans have become more nationalistic partly because of integrative moves within the EC/EU, there is a distinct possibility that a similar phenomenon will occur in coming years in some post-communist countries, especially those admitted to the EU.

Direct and indirect external stimulation   Nationalism among the members of one group can intensify either as a result of direct interaction with other nationalist groups or because they are inspired by the perceived success of other nationalist groups with whom they are not in meaningful contact. It should be obvious that the media can and do play a major role in this stimulation. This is even more true nowadays, since the publishing atmosphere in most countries is markedly more liberal than it was during the communist period – though still not as liberal as in most Western countries (see conclusions to this chapter) – and access to the Internet has increased dramatically (for details see Woodard 1995).

Alternative organizations and leadership   Increases in nationalist and ethnic politics can sometimes be related to changes in organizations around which nationalists can rally. And for a movement to be successful, it must have effective leadership; indeed, the role of leaders is often critical.

The *balance* of the above factors varies according to time and place and group. However, it seems likely that the 'escape to ethnicity' that appeared to be so much a part of the early post-communist scene will become less salient if political structures and practices crystallize, and if economic situations improve. It is not strictly accurate to argue that ethnic politics is never a serious problem when an economy is performing well: if a society is basically wealthy but distribution is perceived by some groups as inequitable, if dominant groups are insensitive, or if there is temporary large-scale unemployment, then nationalist and ethnic politics may still play a major role (Canada and Belgium exemplify this). But such tensions rarely become as violent as the nationalist and ethnic politics in very unstable, insecure and basically impoverished societies. There is little need for scapegoats where there are no major problems.

On the other hand, a legacy of extreme nationalist and ethnic violence *can* take generations to overcome. A sudden cessation of hostilities in the former Yugoslavia would not end all tensions, since so many people have been negatively affected by the fighting that there will be hatred and a desire for revenge for years to come. But one should not necessarily be unduly pessimistic about the medium- and long-term future of the Yugoslav successor states – or others – either. The French and the Germans, for instance, soon learnt to live together in peace again after the Second World War, as did the Americans and Australians with the Japanese.[18] Common economic interests often override ethnic tensions in the longer run. Once again, the future of post-communism depends very much on economic performance and, more broadly, the legitimacy of the new systems.

Conclusions

At the beginning of this chapter, the term civil society was considered primarily from social science perspectives. According to such definitions, there have been unmistakable signs of an emerging civil society since late communism. But if, in line with Shils (1991), the term civil is considered in its everyday sense, it is clear from the contents of this and earlier chapters that there is much about early post-communism that is *un*civil. The rules of the game remain contested, and there are still high levels of prejudice and violence in many places. The environment is not as high a priority for many citizens as it was in late communism. The situation for women and feminism is from some important perspectives deteriorating in many countries. Thousands of lives have been ruined and even lost as a result of the related phenomena of nationalism, ethnic conflict and territorial disputes. Ethnic cleansing has been a salient feature of politics in parts of the former Yugoslavia and USSR, and might be spreading. Some well-regarded analysts (see, for instance, Touraine 1994) are claiming that Western Europe is moving towards, or is already in, a post-national phase. This conclusion is at least premature, perhaps even erroneous. Nevertheless, it is a reflection of the differences between most of Western Europe and most of the post-communist world that such a claim applied to the latter would seem absurd (though see Hobsbawm 1992, pp. 163–92).

One reason for the problems of emerging civil society in the post-communist world relates precisely to the point made by so many analysts concerning the symbiotic relationship between the state and society. Thus Fish (1995) argues persuasively that many of the problems currently being experienced by Russian civil society (or, in his preferred terms, 'movement society') can be explained partly in terms of the near-chaotic situation of the state. Were the latter to consolidate more, the chances of a more coherent and effective civil society developing would be increased.

Another – related – reason is that the uncertainty and instability of early post-communism is leading many citizens to search harder for their own ethnic identities – in language, territory, history, etc. Generally, seeking to strengthen one's own identity involves becoming more exclusionary towards others – to seek clearer demarcation from 'them'. This is hardly conducive to the development of Shils's notion of 'civil' society.

But it would be irresponsible and misleading to leave the reader with only negative impressions about civil society and its prospects. What must never be overlooked is that so many citizens have been in a learning mode in the early stages of post-communism. Women, for instance, had very little experience of organizing themselves autonomously under communism, and will need time to develop both a consciousness of their own situation and of how to organize to do something about it. In this context, the fact that what is basically a women's party performed respectably in the 1993 and 1995 Russian elections must be seen as encouraging, even if the party does not consider itself feminist in the way most Westerners would understand this.

It will take time for citizens to appreciate fully that civil society and liberal democracy is not merely liberating, but also places far more responsibilities on individuals. Citizens have for so long been used to the paternalistic state that essentially determines what they can and cannot do and have, that it will take some years yet for them to appreciate that if they want change, they must assume much of the responsibility for this themselves. They must, in short, empower themselves. This does not necessarily mean they should act as individuals; they may well have to form into groups in the era of modern, mass society. They may also have to enlist outside support.

As individuals and groups assume increasing responsibility in the economic sphere, so economies *should* improve, which in turn should lead to a reduction in the ethnic tensions and will permit people to think beyond the narrow issue of economic survival. At that point, they will have the 'luxury' of being able to examine other problems in their lives, such as pollution and sexism and ethnic intolerance.[19] Fortunately, now that communism has been overthrown, when they *do* have the time and opportunity to focus on these other matters, many will be able to do something about them without repression by the state. Although emerging civil society in early post-communism appears in many countries to be decidedly uncivil from some perspectives, the longer term prognosis should not necessarily be seen in pessimistic terms, and certainly not exclusively by reference to current difficulties. Everything is still new and uncertain, and could go either way; this theme is explored further in chapter 12.

Before concluding this chapter, however, it is worth considering two aspects of civil society that have not yet been mentioned; the mass media, and lustration (sometimes called decommunization). Although neither relates directly to either social movements or nationalist/ethnic politics, no discussion of moves towards civil society and democracy in the post-communist world would be complete without reference to them.

Genuinely autonomous mass media should be a feature of developed civil society. There is no question that both the printed and broadcast media in most parts of the post-communist world are immeasurably more autonomous than they were for most if not all (depending on the country) of the communist era. The range of views expressed is also much broader. Yet there are still signs of excessive government interference in many countries. While there are limitations on the media in the West too, these mostly relate to security matters, with overt and partisan interference being rare. In contrast, several post-communist governments have censored or even shut down newspapers, or removed editors and television chiefs, because they have been considered too critical or partisan. This might not be particularly surprising in post-communist countries that have made relatively little progress towards democracy, such as Belarus, where newspapers appeared in December 1994 with blank spaces because of government censorship. But it is of concern that in countries that appear to be taking big strides towards democracy in other ways, post-communist governments continue to hound the media. A prime example is Hungary, where renewed government interference in 1995 led to much criticism (see *Transition*, vol. 1, no.

10, pp. 17–18). Two of the ways in which the kind of interference seen in Belarus, Hungary and elsewhere might be reduced is to increase the privatization of the media and to introduce and enforce media protection laws. Both of these measures should bring about greater media autonomy, while the second should also clarify what the state considers unacceptable. Once again, a problem of early post-communism relates to ambiguity about the rules of the game (for introduction to media issues in the post-communist world see *EECR*, vol. 2, no. 3, pp. 41–53, and the entire issue of *Transition*, vol. 1, no. 18).

In the context of post-communism, lustration is the process whereby the state investigates the activities of individuals during the communist era, with a view to punishing them in some way for behaviour considered unacceptable.[20] Many observers were initially apprehensive that new post-communist regimes would use lustration as a way of wreaking revenge on officials from the communist era or, in a period of privation, of finding scapegoats by claiming that current problems were the result of such officials' past actions. In fact, while many governments passed legislation on lustration, hardly any used this to any meaningful extent in the early 1990s. The one major exception was Germany, where many either lost their posts or else were not promoted because of past activities (on all this see S. Holmes 1994). By the mid-1990s it seemed clear that most governments intending to try former communists were likely to target only the most senior officials, usually for their alleged role in acts of violence or treason against the citizenry or large-scale corruption during the communist era. Examples of senior officials charged in this way include Honecker, Zhivkov, Alia, Jaruzelski and Jakes. In all of these cases, however, either the case was eventually dropped or the prison sentence was cut short.

The lustration issue is highly contentious. It can be argued that individuals should not now be tried for obeying orders under a different system, or according to 'bourgeois' codes they themselves once (or still) consider(ed) illegitimate. While there is some weight to this argument, some values and rights are universal. Corruption was illegitimate anyway during the communist era; the use of extreme violence against citizens in the name of an ideology would nowadays be seen by many around the world as impermissible. Given all this, the way in which most post-communist regimes have so far actually applied their lustration laws – particularly in targeting those ultimately responsible for ordering the use of extreme force against citizens, rather than everyone who in any way collaborated with the secret police, for instance – must on balance be seen as very civil (for an interesting approach to the whole issue of dealing with the communist past see Rosenberg 1995). As Wiktor Osiatynski (1994, p. 41) observes: 'It may . . . turn out that the failure of decommunization and resistance to the retributive phase of the revolution – with its predictable violence, injustice and destructiveness – will be praised, in the future, as one of the most important successes of the postcommunist transformation.' It can only be hoped that post-communist governments continue to adopt a sensible and sensitive approach to lustration.

Notes

1 This was for involvement in what the authorities claimed were anti-Stalin activities. The father was subsequently executed, while the son was murdered in September 1932 by a group of peasants that included his uncle.

2 Conversely, some analysts all but dismiss the role of civil society in the collapse of communist power – see e.g. Szakolczai and Horvath 1992.

3 Despite this, neither political parties nor private economic activity are considered in this chapter, even though their role and status constitute key indicators of the level of development of civil society. The reason for this exclusion is simply that they were analysed in chapters 7 and 8 respectively.

4 This is not to deny the existence of political prisoners in some post-communist states, such as Uzbekistan.

5 It is in this context that Vladimir Tismaneanu (1992, esp. pp. 279–88) has highlighted the tension between democracy and what he calls ethnocracy in the post-communist world.

6 These terms overlap considerably with what others call respectively 'civic' and 'ethnic' nationalism.

7 For instance, *local* officials belonging to an ethnic minority may make autonomist demands of the *central* authorities in a federal system; while such activity is treated here as unofficial nationalism (since it represents a challenge to the official integrative policy of the state), the fact that it emanates from local *officials* testifies to the limitations of the official/unofficial distinction.

8 Race has traditionally been seen as an essentially biological concept. But its validity is increasingly being questioned by sections of the scientific community, who suggest that it is more of a socially constructed subjective concept than an objective phenomenon.

9 However, this term has been going out of favour in everyday usage in recent years. For this reason, and also given the argument here that different forms of racism sometimes overlap and blur, the term racialism will not be used here beyond this semantic discussion.

10 When referring to political units, the terms 'sovereign' and 'independent' are often used interchangeably in everyday parlance. In the case of states that are not part of a federal unit, this common blurring does not pose any major problem for the discussion here. In formally federal states, however, the distinction matters. In such arrangements, sovereignty is by convention – and here – taken to mean that the laws of a given unit (a republic in the Soviet, Yugoslav or Czechoslovak cases) take precedence over federal laws if these conflict, at the same time as the unit remains part of the federation. Hence sovereignty in such a situation represents something less than full independence. In the context of the terminology used in this book, those calling for sovereignty alone would be autonomists, whereas those advocating full independence would be secessionists.

11 For a map of Vance and Owen's proposed division of Bosnia-Hercegovina into ten provinces see L. Cohen 1995, p. 254.

12 The Vance–Owen plan did envisage one ethnically mixed province, which would have included Sarajevo; but there was ethnic mixing throughout Bosnia-Hercegovina.

13 According to EC and some other estimates, up to 20,000 women may have been raped during the first few months of the Bosnian conflict, mostly by Serbs. Some have claimed such figures are exaggerated (see L. Cohen 1995, p. 270), while others consider them conservative and believe up to 50,000 women may have been raped in the same period (see e.g. *The Independent* [London], 6 January 1993, p. 7). The most important point is not the actual number, but that even one rape is one too many.

14 Indeed, many of the approximately 25 million Russians living beyond Russia's borders but still within the FSU (in what the Russians often call 'the near abroad') have in the 1990s been feeling marginalized, as ethnic majorities in these other former Soviet republics seek to strengthen their own national identities by excluding others.

15 Several other analysts argue that Brym and Degtyarev are exaggerating the level and danger of anti-semitism in Russia, although they do accept there is a problem – see Gibson 1994a and 1994b; Hesli et al. 1994.

16 Reflecting the instability of the region, however, many Moldovan students and teachers protested in March and April 1995 in favour of calling their language Romanian rather than Moldovan. But the evidence does not suggest this reflected any widespread desire to link up with Romania. President Snegur made it clear towards the end of April that he agreed the national language of Moldova should be called Romanian. Unfortunately, this increased tensions between the president and the Moldovan parliament.

17 *Some* citizens have seen presidents Kuchma in Ukraine and Lukashenka in Belarus, and former Latvian prime minister Valdis Birkavs – to cite just three examples – as too accommodating of the Russians. There is abundant evidence that others have supported their leaders' attempts to improve relations with Moscow, however.

18 There is *some* weight to the argument that this analogy is inappropriate, since the USA and Australia are not immediate neighbours of Japan; this is why the Franco-German relationship is cited first here. In terms of feuding neighbours, there are also enough instances of what appeared until recently to be completely intractable ethnic and nationalistic conflicts now moving (albeit falteringly) towards reconciliation and resolution to suggest that a totally pessimistic outlook on former Yugoslavia is unjustified. A prime example is South Africa; *perhaps* even the two Irelands will prove to be, too.

19 Even political activism requires funds, especially if it is to be ongoing; a shortage of these is yet another factor explaining the rather sorry state of social movements in early post-communism.

20 Similar activities are not entirely unknown in the West; two of the best examples are McCarthyism in the USA during the 1950s and the *Berufsverbot* in West Germany during the 1970s.

FURTHER READING

On civil society in late communism and early post-communism see Kukathas, Lovell and Maley 1991; Rau 1991a; Lewis 1992; R. Miller 1992a. Two standard recent works on civil society more generally are Keane 1988 and Cohen and Arato 1992.

For useful general analyses of social movements see Touraine 1981, 1985; Pakulski 1991; Tarrow 1994.

On workers and trade unions under post-communism see the various articles in *CAPCS*, vol. 28, no. 1 (1995), pp. 3–118; Thirkell, Scase and Vickerstaff 1995.

For analyses of late communist and early post-communist environmentalism see Jancar-Webster 1993a (esp. part 2), while the sources listed at the end of chapter 9 provide much useful material on feminism.

On nationalism in late communism and early post-communism see Gitelman 1992; Bremmer and Taras 1993; Bugajski 1995; Kupchan 1995; Pavkovic, Koscharsky and Czarnota 1995. Two of the standard works on political (particularly right-wing) extremism in the post-communist world, much of it relating to nationalist and ethnic politics, are Hockenos 1993 and Held 1993; see too the entire issue of *RFE/RL Research Report*, vol. 3, no. 16 (22 April 1994).

For more general introductions to nationalism see Anderson 1991; Kellas 1991; Hobsbawm 1992.

11

Changing Allegiances

This book's primary focus is on domestic developments in the post-communist states. But in an era of increasing interaction between states and of globalization, it is impossible to make sense of domestic politics without some consideration of the international context within which they operate. For instance, the economic policies of the post-communist states cannot be properly understood without an awareness of the kinds of conditions international organizations such as the EC/EU, the IMF, the World Bank and the EBRD have required these countries to fulfil before they will release funds. Similarly, in 1995 both NATO and the EU produced guidelines on the criteria these countries must meet before their requests for membership can be seriously considered.

When US President Reagan referred in the 1980s to the USSR as an 'evil *empire*', he was only reiterating a term that had been in use since at least the 1950s. With so much of Eastern Europe falling under increasing Soviet influence during the 1940s, analysts of Soviet foreign policy such as David Dallin (1951) characterized the USSR as a new empire (see also Grove Haines 1954, Seton-Watson 1961, Ionescu 1965). Admittedly, it was a peculiar sort of empire, since it often cost the Soviets dearly to maintain control over what were referred to by some as the USSR's satellites (for a brief but insightful analysis of the complexities of this issue see Dawisha 1990, pp. 109–21). Nevertheless, for more than four decades, and in various ways, the USSR exerted influence and control over most of the communist states of Eastern Europe; the only real exceptions to this were Yugoslavia from 1948 and Albania from about 1960. In the first part of this chapter, the focus will be on the ways this influence was exercised in the areas of politics and ideology; military-strategic affairs; and economic and trade matters. In the second part, these three areas will be considered in the context of post-communism. How and why the old allegiances broke down will be analysed, as will their replacements.

Before this, however, two themes and two contexts need to be identi-fied.[1] The first theme, which acts as a backdrop to much of the chapter, is that the numerous bi- and multilateral *international* relationships that will be analysed in one sense reflect the *domestic* politics and relationships of communist and post-communist systems. Thus, during most of the commu-nist era both the domestic systems and international relations (within the

Soviet bloc) were relatively authoritarian, hierarchical, simple and stable. Conversely, the post-communist systems are more pluralistic, egalitarian (in *some* ways), complex and unstable. Both the domestic and international scenes are currently typified by a plethora of new organizations and relationships that are still crystallizing.

The second, closely related theme is that both the domestic scene and international relations are not merely in a state of flux but also of contradiction. For instance, most of the east European states seek closer relationships with powerful countries and blocs, such as Germany, the EU and NATO, yet at the same time are determined to maintain their only recently gained independence of more powerful states. There is also a tension between theory and reality at both the international and the domestic levels. In the case of the latter, this is reflected in the abstract commitment to marketization and democratization on the one hand, and, on the other, the fears many post-communist politicians have of the destabilizing effects the implementation of these policies is having and is bound to have. In the area of international relations, many on both sides of the old divide are now appreciating that, for all the ideological rancour and sabre-rattling, the Cold War era (approximately 1947 to 1990) had a certain stability that, as memories of its worst features fade, can appear increasingly attractive to some. On both the domestic and international scenes, centrifugal and centripetal forces currently coexist.

The two contexts in which much of what follows must be located and analysed can now be considered. The first is the double-rejective revolution: the two rejections have had major implications for the kinds of decisions makers of foreign policy in the various countries have taken and feel able to take. Just as Marxism-Leninism imposed certain constraints on policy-makers, so the rejection of that ideology, and of dominance by the country in which it originated, has limited the options available.

The second context is that of instability and global recession. The reasons for the relative instability of the transitional countries of post-communism are obvious, given that they are attempting such comprehensive and rapid change. Less obvious is the instability of the West, especially Western Europe. Yet the problems resulting from the unification of Germany; tensions within the EC/EU; the growing unpredictability of the electorate in so many countries; and the increase in racial tensions and neo-fascist activities (often exacerbated by migration to the West from the post-communist world) – all this testifies to the fact that the West has in the 1990s been in a period of greater uncertainty than for many years. The recession in the West in the early 1990s – initially in the USA and the UK, subsequently in Japan and continental Western Europe – was intimately connected to and helps to explain these manifestations of instability. The West was becoming more introspective and self-protective, which necessarily impacted in various ways on the post-communist world, including on its attempts to move closer to the West.

The Communist Era

Considering first *political and ideological relations* – until the late 1980s, the structures and even policies of the communist states of Europe were remarkably similar. Admittedly, the two states that were not part of the Soviet bloc (Yugoslavia and Albania) diverged more from the norm than the other countries of communist Eastern Europe; but even *their* political and ideological systems and policies were closer to the Soviet model and practices than to Western or even most Third World systems.

From 1947 to 1956, Moscow's attempts to impose ideological conformity were made primarily through Cominform, although this organization's precise role was never clearly defined. With its abolition in April 1956, Soviet efforts to limit diversity were directed through other channels, including diplomacy, economic leverage and threatened or actual military might.

One other method used by Moscow to keep the East European states in check was interference in their leadership politics. The aim was to ensure that politicians sufficiently sympathetic to the USSR were brought to power and maintained there. But a leader who had once been very loyal to the USSR would sometimes clash with Moscow, usually because of a belief that the Soviets were pursuing their own interests too much at the expense of the leader's own country. A good example was Walter Ulbricht, leader of the GDR from 1950 to 1971. Having once been a very loyal ally of the Soviets, Ulbricht came into conflict with them at the end of the 1960s. As part of the East-West detente, the Soviets sought to improve relations with the FRG; Ulbricht believed this would be at his country's expense and attempted to hinder various moves towards rapprochement. But the Soviets were unwilling to permit even a loyal ally to block what they saw as, *inter alia*, an easy path to more advanced technology. They therefore played a significant role in removing Ulbricht and replacing him in May 1971 with someone (Erich Honecker) who would be more compliant. This was a significant example of the way in which the Soviets used to interfere in the domestic politics of the East European states.

The principal mechanism through which the USSR used to exercise *military* influence over the countries of Eastern Europe was the WTO (Warsaw Treaty Organization, or Warsaw Pact). Although many believe the WTO was created as a direct response to the West's formation of NATO (the North Atlantic Treaty Organization), this is not the case: NATO was established in 1949, whereas the WTO came into being in 1955. Among specialists, there are two main explanations for the formation of the Warsaw Pact.

The first is one provided by the USSR and other communist states themselves. According to this argument, the WTO was established as a direct response to the remilitarization of West Germany and its integration into the Western military alliance (that is, NATO). These developments were perceived by the Soviet bloc as a serious threat. Germany had invaded

Czechoslovakia in 1938, Poland in 1939, and had reneged on a 1939 non-aggression treaty with the USSR and invaded it in 1941; it is therefore understandable that the countries of the region, excluding Yugoslavia, banded together to form their own military alliance.

The second explanation, which is not incompatible with the first, is that the Soviets were concerned that Austria had just set a precedent some of the East European states might wish to emulate. Until 1955, Austria had been occupied by both Western forces and the Soviets as part of the post-Second World War agreements on securing peace in Europe. But these troops were withdrawn in 1955 on the understanding that Austria would remain a neutral in international affairs. This meant the Austrians could not join any military alliance. The Soviets were concerned that some of its allies/satellites would seek a similar neutrality, which would have substantially reduced Soviet influence in those countries. Moscow's suspicion was not entirely unfounded, as events in Hungary in late 1956 demonstrated (see chapter 3).

This second explanation developed into what has been called the Remington thesis on the role of the WTO. According to this, the WTO existed more as a 'channel for communication or even conflict resolution' (Remington 1971, p. 8) between the USSR and its East European neighbours than as a military bloc to counter NATO. In a sense, the WTO can be seen to have existed as an instrument of coercive control over its allies. Certainly, the only time WTO troops were deployed for real military action was in 1968, when they were used to suppress the Czechoslovak experiment in 'socialism with a human face'; the order to invade emanated ultimately from the Kremlin. This led the West to start referring to the Brezhnev Doctrine, named after the then General Secretary of the CPSU. According to this, the Soviets claimed the right to intervene, even militarily, in the affairs of countries they considered part of their sphere of influence if, as they perceived it, domestic developments in those states threatened the international socialist order.

There were many tensions within the WTO between 1955 and 1991. For instance, the Romanians protested about the invasion of Czechoslovakia and refused to participate in it. During the 1980s there were disputes over the question of nuclear weapons and advanced military technology. Several East European leaderships, notably the East German and Czechoslovak, objected that the USSR was not treating them as equals within the WTO on matters regarding the deployment of nuclear warheads in Europe. Several also complained that the Soviets sometimes supplied more sophisticated equipment to Third World countries, especially in the Middle East, than to its own allies. It therefore came as no surprise that the new post-communist leaderships soon indicated their unwillingness to be dominated any longer by the USSR/Russia within a military alliance.

The principal organizational structure through which the Soviet-oriented communist countries *traded* and agreed on *economic policies* was the

CMEA (Council for Mutual Economic Assistance, or Comecon). This was founded in January 1949, principally as a reaction to the Marshall Plan (or Marshall Aid Program) of 1947. Under this, the USA had offered to help finance the economic recovery of individual European states, subject to such countries meeting certain criteria. The Soviets soon decided this was an attempt to spread American liberal-democratic ideas in Europe. Partly in order to counter this, as well as to maximize their own influence in countries where the communists had only recently come to power and were not yet clearly secure, the Soviets urged the formation of Comecon.

CMEA played a relatively insignificant role during the 1950s, but from the end of that decade the Soviets sought to upgrade it and to have it play a far greater role in the domestic economies of the member states. This led to a fairly open dispute with Romania, which during the early 1960s complained that the Soviets were attempting to impose their own views on the other member states without adequate consultation or sensitivity. Although the Soviets essentially lost that debate, they now sought to intensify the processes of integration and standardization within CMEA.

This process of integration continued into the 1970s, when Comecon also expanded by admitting two additional non-European members: Cuba and Vietnam joined in 1972 and 1978 respectively (Mongolia had joined in 1962). The CMEA was thus deepening and widening simultaneously.

It was also during the 1970s that CMEA began to change its pricing policies, which caused tensions between the USSR and some of its main trading partners. By the end of the decade, many resources were being charged at prices related to world market levels. This revealed that Comecon was not immune to the vagaries of the international economic system. It can also be seen as the start of a process whereby the non-Soviet members of CMEA became increasingly aware that the system in which they had been operating was becoming less secure. No longer could they rely on the USSR for a ready supply of raw materials (including fuels) at well below market prices. Indeed, the somewhat complicated system now used within the CMEA for determining prices meant that the East Europeans sometimes paid more for items such as fossil fuels, notably oil, than they would have done had they been able to purchase on spot markets such as Rotterdam's. From an East European perspective, it could appear that the Soviets were wanting to have their cake and eat it. Objectively, however, the Soviets could often have made better profits by selling the produce they exported to their CMEA partners on the international market. They would also have been paid in hard currency.

By the 1980s many East Europeans had concluded that they would fare better were their country to be part of the EC rather than the CMEA. The impressive growth rates of earlier years had by now been replaced by modest ones in most communist countries, while the economies of Western Europe were growing impressively again after their downturn of the mid-1970s.

The Post-Communist Era

POLITICAL AND IDEOLOGICAL RELATIONS

The *relative* homogeneity of the communist era has been replaced in the 1990s by a far more diverse situation. In previous chapters, it has been demonstrated that there is a wide variety of political and economic patterns in the post-communist world. No longer do the countries of eastern Europe emulate the Soviet or Russian model; if anything, it is the reverse (since the Russian anti-communist revolution occurred approximately two years after most of those in Eastern Europe, the Russians sometimes learn vicariously from the east Europeans). It is true that, in framing new constitutions for example, many east Europeans studied in particular the German model. But this is a fundamentally different situation from that during the communist era, since the east Europeans are not being pressured to copy a 'big brother'; they now choose for themselves whom to emulate, if anyone.

Despite this diversity, the commonalities of the double-rejective revolutions have resulted in discernible post-communist patterns. On the ideological front, for instance, there was in the early years of post-communism the widespread rejection of grand theories mentioned in the first chapter. The other similarities have already been elaborated in earlier chapters and need not be repeated here.

MILITARY/STRATEGIC RELATIONS

As argued in chapter 2, Gorbachev's unambiguous abandonment of the Brezhnev Doctrine and adoption of the so-called Sinatra Doctrine at the end of the 1980s is justifiably seen by many as a major factor explaining the collapse of East European (and in the longer term Soviet) communist power.

This change was part of Gorbachev's overall approach in foreign policy, which was described by the Soviets themselves as *new political thinking* (see A. Brown 1992c, p. 1). The Soviet leader believed, almost certainly correctly, that the USSR's interference in the affairs of other communist states was hindering its own development. This was not simply because of the financial costs, but also because Western disapproval of Soviet behaviour rendered it more difficult for the USSR to obtain Western assistance in its endeavours to accelerate economic development. Thus, by relinquishing control over the external empire, Gorbachev hoped to secure several advantages.

Yet it would be wrong to infer that Gorbachev was willing to permit the complete dissolution of the Soviet bloc. That he was not can be seen quite clearly in his approach to the WTO. By the beginning of the 1990s the Soviet leader appeared to have accepted that its days as an instrument of *military* coercion were over. But he still believed it could continue to exist as an agency of *political* cooperation.

It became clear by 1990 that the dominant view in the newly emerging post-communist states of eastern Europe was quite different from Gorbachev's, however. At the June 1990 WTO summit meeting, major changes were agreed in principle that were soon interpreted as heralding the possible dissolution of the WTO. Another clear indication that the putative *raison d'être* of the WTO was now in doubt was the announcement by both NATO and WTO spokespersons at the Paris CSCE[2] summit of November 1990 that the two military alliances no longer regarded each other as enemies.

Early in 1991, Czecho-Slovakia, Poland and Hungary publicly announced their intention to cease cooperating with the WTO from July 1991. As if this were not serious enough from the Soviet perspective, the Hungarian legislature went even further and voted to accept what it understood to be a NATO offer of associate (non-voting) membership. Hence one member of the WTO was not merely rejecting the organization but even dared to declare it would join what had for decades been regarded as the ultimate threat from the enemy camp.

At about the same time as their north-western neighbours were making these statements, Bulgarian and Romanian leaders declared the WTO to be an anachronism. The Warsaw Pact was collapsing before the Soviets' eyes.

But Gorbachev was not prepared to concede defeat so readily. He wrote to the leaders of all the member states in mid-February recommending the liquidation of just the military structures by April 1991. Gorbachev hoped to be able to retain a rump WTO in the form of a purely political integrative structure. It looked for a brief period as if the east Europeans might be prepared to agree to such a dramatically diluted version of the WTO. For instance, each member state of the WTO signed a protocol in late February 1991 that cancelled the validity of all military agreements and structures of the WTO with effect from the end of March, but that also, and despite obvious reluctance on the part of some countries, constituted an agreement to a temporary transformation of the political structures into a voluntary consultative organization.

Even this fragile shell of what had once been the most serious military threat to the West was too much for many east Europeans, however; they sought the total dissolution of the WTO. This occurred in July 1991 with the signing of a protocol in Prague. This document advocated a gradual shift towards pan-European security structures, on the basis of agreements reached at the November 1990 CSCE summit. Although the Prague protocol did not officially come into force until the parliaments of the member states had ratified it, the WTO had now *de facto* ceased to exist. The Soviets were by this stage so engrossed in their own domestic squabbles, especially those between Gorbachev and Yeltsin, that they had little energy or inclination to resist the will of the east Europeans.

Yet there remained a number of issues to resolve between the USSR/ Russia and its former allies. One was the matter of Soviet troops still

stationed in eastern Europe. This problem did not arise in the cases of
Bulgaria and Romania, neither of which had had any permanently stationed Soviet troops since the 1950s. In the cases of Hungary and Czecho-
Slovakia, the issue was resolved at about the same time as the WTO was
finally dissolved; the last Soviet troops were withdrawn from the two countries in late June 1991. But the Polish case was problematical. As of mid-
1991 there were still approximately 50,000 troops stationed in Poland, and
Warsaw wanted them removed before the end of the year. The USSR, on
the other hand, did not plan to withdraw the last of its troops until the end
of 1993. Following numerous rounds of negotiations, the last Russian troops
finally left Poland at the beginning of October 1993; this was three months
early by Soviet/Russian reckoning, but almost two years later than the
Polish government had wanted.

A second issue was that of compensation for damage caused by the
Soviet military presence. For example, Hungary lodged a claim with the
USSR or its successors for approximately 1,700 million US dollars to cover
the costs of, *inter alia*, repairing the environmental damage it alleged the
Soviets had caused since 1956 (that is, since the Soviets had invaded and
then 'occupied' Hungary). Much of this issue was resolved during 1993. In
June, Hungarian President Goncz visited Russia and agreed to cancel over
half his country's claim in return for 28 Russian-built fighter aircraft. And in
September, Poland agreed to drop its claims for compensation after the
Russian state agreed to transfer ownership of all its property in Poland to
the Polish state.

The military links between Russia and its former WTO allies were thus
almost completely severed by 1993 and most aspects of this relationship had
been tidied up to mutual satisfaction. However, tensions arose between
Moscow and various east European capitals in late 1993, as Russia began to
criticize the attempts by several of its former allies to join NATO.

As already indicated, the WTO and NATO had formally 'buried the
hatchet' by late 1990. Then in November 1991, NATO and the former
members of the WTO, including all the former Soviet republics except
Georgia, conjoined to form the North Atlantic Cooperation Council
(NACC). At this stage, the Russians appeared to have no problem with the
notion that its former allies would move closer to NATO. Even as late as
August and early September 1993, President Yeltsin was still stating publicly that Russia had no objections to Polish, Czech and Hungarian attempts
to join NATO.

But Yeltsin had changed his position dramatically by the end of September 1993. Following the forced closure of parliament, the Russian president
became much more hawkish in his foreign policy statements. This was to no
small extent because of pressure from the Russian military and other coercive organs of the state on which Yeltsin had now become more dependent
for keeping order in an increasingly chaotic polity. At the end of September
1993, Yeltsin wrote to various Western leaders warning them against any
expansion of NATO eastwards. Following this, various spokespersons of
the so-called 'power ministries' (those connected with the state's coercive

activities, including those for defence and internal security) became increasingly outspoken in their criticisms of the attempts by the Visegrad Four to join NATO. For instance, in late November 1993, the head of Russia's foreign intelligence services (Primakov) made it clear at a press conference that Russia would feel seriously threatened by an expanded NATO that extended as far as its borders, and would have to alter its defence policies dramatically were this to eventuate. He also referred to the danger of increasing restlessness among the Russian military were NATO to expand in this way.

With statements such as Primakov's, Yeltsin's apparent volte-face, and the impressive performance of Zhirinovskii's ultranationalist and expansionist Liberal Democrats in the December elections, it is not surprising that so many post-communist leaderships beyond Russia became increasingly alarmed by Moscow's mood of late 1993. Far from being intimidated into withdrawing their applications to NATO, the Polish, Czech and other leaderships stepped up the pressure on the West to admit them. Meanwhile, other post-communist countries were joining the ranks of applicants. In January 1994, Lithuania became the first former Soviet republic to make a formal application to join NATO. This reflected widespread fear among Balts and others that Zhirinovskii was serious in his commitment to reconstitute the former Russian empire, and that he was likely to become more and more influential within the Russian polity.

By this stage, however, the West was becoming increasingly uneasy about many of the developments in the post-communist world, and appeared to be unwilling to take sides too clearly in the disputes between Russia and its former WTO allies. Early signs that the West was less enthusiastic than it appeared to have been in 1989 or 1990 to admit the post-communist states to its ranks were clearly visible by March 1992 at the latest. At that time, the then Secretary-General of NATO, Manfred Woerner, indicated during visits to Poland and the Baltic states that although NATO was committed to ensuring that no security vacuums would emerge in eastern Europe, it would be unable to offer either formal security guarantees or full membership to countries in the region in the foreseeable future.

The West's reluctance to become over-involved, and its commitment to seek a middle path between the east European and Russian positions, resulted in the adoption by NATO in January 1994 of US President Clinton's proposal for a 'Partnership for Peace' policy. Under this, any former WTO country was to be permitted to participate in certain NATO exercises and formally to express security concerns to NATO, but little else. While states such as Romania welcomed this move as a step in the right direction, others such as Poland made clear their disappointment that the West had not gone further. There was also disappointment in some quarters that, apparently, some countries were not to be granted full NATO membership in the foreseeable future.

Nevertheless, the Partnership for Peace compromise did achieve tangible results. Within one year, not only had all the east European states (except for some in former Yugoslavia) applied to join the programme, but so had all the FSU states apart from Tajikistan (details of joining dates are in Mihalka 1995a, p. 85). Moreover, three joint field exercises had been conducted by the end of 1994. The first of these was held in Poland in September and involved troops from Bulgaria, Czechia, Lithuania, Poland, Romania, Slovakia and Ukraine, as well as from six Western states.

For many post-communist states, these joint exercises represented a symbolically important move towards the consolidation of new allegiances. But they also highlighted the many practical problems involved in attempts to integrate NATO and post-communist states. In addition to the not insignificant cost factor, the exercises revealed serious problems of communication (the NATO command language is English, of which few east European officers have adequate knowledge and experience), incompatibilities of equipment and techniques, different conceptions of appropriate command structures, etc.

Such problems of interoperability are substantial. On the other hand, their exposure during the joint exercises served two useful purposes. First, they revealed that Western concerns about premature military integration had a real basis. Second, they helped to frame the future agenda by clarifying the areas that required most effort if incompatibilities were to be overcome. Hence they made it that much more likely that the day would come when the post-communist states were sufficiently close to NATO norms to be eligible for full membership.

Unfortunately, it is not clear that costs and interoperability problems are the most significant ones facing the east Europeans in their bids to join NATO. Just as important are the serious rifts within NATO itself, about which the post-communist states can do little. Until mid-1995 these differences manifested themselves above all in relation to the Bosnian issue (see chapter 10) and, partly connected with this, to policy on Russia. Each of these deserves consideration.

Whereas the West Europeans had tended to prefer a cautious approach to Bosnia and had sought peace at almost any cost,[3] the Americans became increasingly irritated at the blatant Serb disregard for the international community and humanitarian pleas. The US position hardened after the shift to the right of the US Congress following the November 1994 elections, resulting in the July 1995 statement that the US would lift its embargo on arms sales to the Bosnian Muslims. This also helps to explain the start of the NATO bombing campaign against the Bosnian Serbs (Operation Deliberate Force) at the end of August 1995 – which revealed that the West Europeans had now adopted a tougher stance too – and US pressure on the Serbs, Croats and Muslims to agree to a peace plan.

One reason why the West (until the fairly open rifts of early to mid 1995, this means here both the USA and Western Europe) was for long so indecisive about the Bosnian issue was that it preferred not to antagonize the Russians, who often claim to be traditionally close to the Serbs.[4] Several Western experts advised policy-makers that isolating the Russians by actively countering the Serbs in Bosnia would only play into the hands of

Russian extremists; given that Russia was to have parliamentary elections in December 1995 and presidential ones in June 1996, such an approach was seen by some policy advisers as counterproductive, perhaps even dangerous. Certainly, Operation Deliberate Force was strongly criticized by Moscow, although Russian reactions also highlighted differences within the leadership.

This leads to the reasons that relate *directly* to Russia. Moscow has long wanted a special relationship with NATO, and many Russian politicians believe that their country's size, recent history as a superpower, and nuclear arsenal all mean that it should be treated differently from the east European states. Western leaders cannot agree on how far to meet this Russian demand. Russia did (as of 1995) officially have a special relationship (an Individual Partnership Programme), but the nature of this remained vague.

Despite the differences among Western leaders, agreement on the issue of closer military involvement with the east European states appeared to have been reached by late 1994. Following an American initiative in October, NATO foreign ministers agreed in early December to produce within one year a clear set of criteria for full membership of NATO. This was less than many east European leaders wanted, in that they sought not only a clear set of criteria but also a timetable for the process of admission. On the other hand, it was enough to annoy the Russians. Almost as soon as NATO announced its plans, Russian Foreign Minister Kozyrev, who was in Brussels for the NATO meeting, announced he would not after all sign an implementation plan as part of the Partnership for Peace agreement he had signed back in June. He claimed there was a significant difference between cooperation (that is, the Partnership for Peace programme) with NATO and the enlargement of NATO through the admission of new (east European) members, on the grounds that the former improved relations whereas the latter constituted a threat to Russia. But Kozyrev's actions in December were essentially posturing. To start with, he had been informed in advance that NATO was to introduce the one-year feasibility (admission criteria) study. Moreover, the NATO proposal of December 1994 envisaged seeking the approval of Russia before any major changes in NATO membership were to be made (Clarke 1995, p. 27). Hence, and although the precise details of the nature of Russian participation were still not clear, Russia *was* being treated as a special case in comparison with the other post-communist states. Despite its December posturing, Russia formally accepted a NATO proposal for NATO–Russian dialogue in May 1995.

Nevertheless, there was still confusion within the Western alliance by the end of 1995 about its relationships with both eastern Europe and Russia. The publication of its 'Study on Enlargement' – the promised set of admission criteria – in September only highlighted this. On the one hand, the first chapter stated that 'Decisions on enlargement will be for NATO itself,' while a section specifically on relations with Russia in chapter 2 also declared that 'NATO decisions . . . cannot be subject to any veto . . . by a non-member state.' Yet in the very same section on relations with Russia, the study claimed there would be 'no "surprise" decisions . . . that could affect

the interests' of Russia and that 'the enlargement process . . . will threaten
no one' (the NATO document is extracted in *Transition*, vol. 1, no. 23, pp.
19–26). A generous interpretation of the above is that NATO would keep
Russia informed of all its major decisions, perhaps even discuss these before
they are finalized, but would ultimately make up its own mind. But the
possibilities for conflicting interpretations of these statements are manifest.
The study was also ambiguous about future members. It simultaneously
listed criteria to be met by new members (chapter 5) and stated (chapter 1)
that 'There is no fixed or rigid list of criteria for inviting new member states
to join.' Since it also provided no timetable for admission, many east Europeans were as baffled and irritated by the document as the Russians. Con-
firmation that the West was taking a slow and cautious path came in
December 1995, when a meeting of NATO foreign ministers declared there
would be no discussion of new membership before 1997 at the earliest.

It is not clear that the West *should* seek to placate the Russians too much
– certainly if its main reason is concern that if it does not it might help to
bring an extremist government to power in Moscow. First, Russian internal
problems appear to some observers to be so serious that extremists might
come to power *anyway*, whatever the West does or does not do or say.
Second, a larger, more powerful NATO should be a better shield against a
Russia led by extremists. It is reasonable to assume that if expansionists
within Russia were to come to power, they would be more apprehensive
about invading former WTO members that had become NATO members
than if these countries were not part of a military bloc. Moreover, it should
not too readily be assumed that some of the more aggressive rhetoric of the
Russian extremists would be translated into actual policy even if they did
come to power. This said, it *is* understandable why many post-communist
governments have been so anxious to join NATO since the 1993 (and 1995)
Russian elections. Since all of the east European states are much smaller
than Russia (let alone the CIS), and since none of them has a nuclear
arsenal (unlike Russia or Ukraine), it was perfectly reasonable that they
should look to NATO to become their new protector.

Although it is appropriate in this subsection to concentrate on the relationship between the post-communist states and NATO, other alliances
need also to be mentioned. Particularly in light of the tensions that have on
occasion arisen between the USA and Western Europe, it is not surprising
that the West Europeans have been considering beefing up an organization
that has so far been the EU's defence arm essentially in theory only, the
West European Union (WEU).[5] Although established in the mid-1950s and
reactivated in 1984, this organization has not so far played a significant role
in West European defence. But it could become a powerful military organization in the future. Those post-communist states that eventually secure full
membership of the EU will be eligible for admission to the WEU.[6] Bowker
(1995, p. 83) is probably correct in observing that the Russians would feel
less threatened by the admission of east European states to the WEU than
they would by such states enjoying full membership of NATO – assuming
the Russians themselves are not members – even if the WEU is substan-

tially upgraded, simply because the USA cannot be part of the WEU (for a different view on Russian responses see Wohlfeld 1995, esp. p. 36). However, whereas NATO has sought to involve Russia in its activities, the WEU has no plans to offer associate partner status to Moscow. Although this can be justified on the grounds that, geographically speaking, far more of Russia is located in Asia than in Europe, such a position could be interpreted as offensive to the Russians.

Finally, brief mention must be made of the Collective Security Pact signed by several CIS members in May 1992. At the CIS summit held in Tashkent that month, Armenia, Kazakhstan, Kyrgyzstan, Russia, Tajikistan and Uzbekistan all agreed to cooperate closely on defence matters. It is interesting to note that it was mainly Central Asian states that signed this with Russia, and agreed in April 1994 that Russia should be responsible for defending their southern borders; many of the other CIS states have preferred to retain full control of their defence, and have in some cases opted for bilateral treaties with other CIS members. A good example is the military cooperation pact signed by Ukraine and Moldova early in 1993.

ECONOMIC AND TRADE RELATIONS

As with military relations, so in the area of international economics and trade there has in the 1990s been a clear attempt by the east European post-communist states to reorient themselves away from the USSR/Russia and towards the West. Indeed, Russia itself has also sought to interact economically far more with the West, at the expense of its former primary trading partners. But, once again, the post-communist states have discovered that the initial enthusiasm with which they were greeted by the West has been fairly rapidly replaced by a more hesitant approach, so that by 1994 many were feeling rejected, even bitter.

The emergence of post-communism soon led to a fundamental questioning of the CMEA. A clear indication of this came at the January 1991 Moscow meeting of the CMEA Executive Committee, at which the executive announced its approval of 'proposals for the radical overhaul of the system of economic cooperation by member states, including a draft charter for a new organization'. This proposal revealed that the Soviets, in particular Gorbachev, were still unwilling to renounce altogether the notion of an integrating economic body for the USSR and eastern Europe. In essence, the January 1991 meeting agreed to disband the CMEA and replace it with a new body, the Organization for International Economic Cooperation (OIEC). Although Yugoslavia had never been a member of the CMEA and Albania had not been one since the 1960s, both countries were to be invited to join the OIEC. The new organization was to be based in Budapest.

But the decision to establish the OIEC was taken within days of the introduction of compulsory hard-currency trading within the CMEA. This replaced the system of conducting transactions in transferable roubles, which were now abolished. The transfer to the new system meant that the

CMEA countries were required to generate far more hard currency than previously, a change that encouraged the formerly communist states to look westwards rather than to what had until then been their principal trading partners. An understandable reaction was that of the Hungarian parliament, which voted within days of the establishment of the OIEC to seek closer ties with both the Council of Europe and the EC.

Given the westward imperative just described, plus the attitudes reflected in the double-rejective revolution, it is hardly surprising that the OIEC was stillborn. In its (and the CMEA's) place, most of the post-communist states have tended to opt for one or both of two main paths.

First, many have been forming regional economic groupings, although the intended and actual level of integration within these has varied markedly. Some of them are made up exclusively of formerly communist states. Others link such states with Western – or, in the case of some of the Central Asian and Transcaucasian states of the CIS, Islamic – countries. So many of these have been formed since the end of the 1980s that only some of the more significant are listed here.

Foremost is the CIS itself. Although this is often seen as a successor to the USSR (minus the Baltic states), it does not seem inappropriate to argue that a primary function of the CIS so far has been to act as an economic integrator and common market for most of the former Soviet republics, even if its track record on this has been less than impressive. There have for instance been a number of economic squabbles within the CIS, many concerning the use of a common currency. Nevertheless, most of the former Soviet republics had realized within a year or two of the dissolution of the USSR that they were mutually dependent. Much as some of them might prefer to be quite independent of Russia, the wariness of the West about becoming too closely involved with most of them, plus the reality that Russia has enormous reserves of natural resources (including energy-related ones) that are likely for the foreseeable future to be more readily accessible to most of them than sources elsewhere, has led these countries to a reluctant pragmatism. It therefore came as little surprise when plans to establish a formal economic union were announced at the May 1993 CIS summit in Moscow, or when six CIS states (Armenia, Belarus, Kazakhstan, Russia, Tajikistan and Uzbekistan) agreed to create a new rouble zone in September 1993.

However, as with so many aspects of the CIS, the economic grouping situation has yet to stabilize. Despite claims by Russian Deputy Prime Minister Shokhin in September 1994 that an interstate economic committee just established was comparable to the European Commission, economic cooperation and integration within the CIS still rests on very shaky foundations (the Azerbaijani and Turkmeni prime ministers refused to sign the September 1994 agreement anyway). Individual member states continue to propose and form new subgroupings with other FSU states,[7] while at the same time joining economic blocs straddling or outside the CIS. An example of the latter is the Economic Cooperation Organization (ECO), originally formed in 1985, and which since 1992 has linked the Central Asian states and Azerbaijan with Afghanistan, Iran, Pakistan and Turkey; ECO has as its ultimate objective the creation of a (non-Arab) Islamic common market. On one level, such developments are not necessarily abnormal, in that many countries in the world are members of several organizations simultaneously. Against this is the fact that many of the groupings proposed or actually established by CIS states are either stillborn, ephemeral or have hazily defined objectives and structures.

To a much lesser extent, this point about fluidity also applies to many of the non-CIS post-communist states. Among the many groupings these have formed or joined are the Central European Initiative (originally comprising Austria, Croatia, Czecho-Slovakia, Hungary, Italy, Poland and Slovenia, and established in January 1992 on the basis of what had started life in 1989 as the Danube-Adria Group, it subsequently admitted Bosnia-Hercegovina and the Republic of Macedonia, and in 1996 is to admit Albania, Belarus, Bulgaria, Romania and Ukraine); the Council of Baltic States (incorporating ten states in the Baltic region, including Poland, the three Baltic states and Russia, it was formed in March 1992 following a German-Danish initiative); and CEFTA (the Central European Free Trade Agreement, established in December 1992 on the basis of the Visegrad Four, augmented in January 1996 by Slovene membership, while other countries such as Ukraine have expressed an interest in joining) (for listings and analysis of these and other organizations see Bakos 1993, Clarke 1993, Reisch 1993b, Vachudova 1993).

Several of these new groupings have as one of their primary aims closer links with the EU, with full membership being an ultimate goal. This leads to the second path adopted in the early 1990s: both individual and groups of post-communist states have made concerted efforts to move closer to the major West European economic groupings. Thus EFTA (the European Free Trade Association, until the end of 1994 comprising seven countries – Austria, Finland, Iceland, Liechtenstein, Norway, Sweden, and Switzerland) signed Free Trade Agreements with Bulgaria and Hungary in March 1993, following similar agreements with Czecho-Slovakia in March 1992 and with Poland and Romania in December 1992. Although the Free Trade Agreements invariably exclude some items, they symbolize a commitment on both sides to much freer trade in the future. There have, in addition, been much looser Declarations on Cooperation between EFTA and some of the other post-communist countries (Slovenia, May 1992; Albania, December 1992).

For the post-communist states, the formation of the EEA (European Economic Area, comprising EFTA – minus Liechtenstein and Switzerland – and the EU) in March 1993[8] meant that closer cooperation with EFTA could be another method of moving closer over time to the EU. After all, EFTA is not nearly as important to these countries in the long term as the EU. This is especially so since January 1995, when Austria, Finland and Sweden became full members of the EU and hence were no longer part of EFTA. Concrete moves to develop closer links with the EC/EU have been taken by several post-communist states. Thus Association (or Europe)

Agreements with the EC were signed by Czecho-Slovakia, Hungary and Poland in December 1991, by Romania in February 1993 and by Bulgaria in March 1993. However, it is worth noting that the first of these to become operational, the Polish and Hungarian, did so only in February 1994. Shortly thereafter, in April 1994, the Hungarians and Poles again attempted to force the pace by submitting formal applications for full membership of the EU; by January 1996, they had been joined by Bulgaria, Czechia, Estonia, Latvia, Lithuania, Slovakia and Romania. Meanwhile, looser Trade and Economic Cooperation Agreements, under which the EC agreed to reduce a number of import quotas and to render development assistance, were signed with a number of other post-communist states, including Albania and Slovenia.[9]

As indicated above, it is not only the east Europeans who have been attempting to reorient their trading focus. Russia has also sought to move closer to the West economically, at the expense of its traditional principal trading partners in eastern Europe. This can be inferred from the following trade statistics. In 1980, 49.0 per cent of Soviet exports went to CMEA partners, while 48.2 per cent came from them. The respective figures for 1989 were 55.2 per cent and 56.3 per cent. But in the first half of 1992, only 21.2 per cent of Russia's exports went to former CMEA partners, while a mere 15.4 per cent of imports were from these countries. By the first half of 1993, the figures had dropped even further, to 18.6 per cent and 12.9 per cent respectively. Although it is difficult to compare data directly because they refer to money value (and are thus affected by exchange rates, the conversion to hard-currency transactions within CMEA at the beginning of 1991, etc.), the above statistics reflect an unambiguous reorientation in Russian foreign trading practices. Russia also signed a loose Partnership and Cooperation Agreement (PCA)[10] with the EU in June 1994 – as did Ukraine and Moldova in June and November 1994 respectively – and a Trade and Economic Cooperation Agreement in July 1995. In 1994, several other CIS states (Armenia, Georgia, Kazakhstan and Kyrgyzstan) signalled their interest in signing PCAs with the EU, although the latter made clear that political stability and a genuine commitment to economic reform were prerequisites to negotiations.

Western Europe's cautiousness, sometimes even coolness, towards eastern Europe and the FSU has manifested itself in a number of incidents that, while each being relatively minor in itself, cumulatively reflect the underlying strains in current East–West relations. One of the main sources of friction has been what many post-communist states perceive to be a double standard on the part of many West European governments and the EC/EU. The latter strongly advocate free market economics, yet are sometimes protectionist in their own practices. This has led critics, from both the West and the East, to refer to a 'fortress Europe' mentality within the EU during the 1990s.

The latter phenomenon has manifested itself in a number of tensions between the EC/EU and the east European states. A prime example was the meat dispute of 1993. In April the EC banned the import of meat, live

animals and dairy produce from all the countries of Central and Eastern
Europe. This step was taken after cases of foot-and-mouth disease were
discovered among live animals exported from Croatia to Italy without the
appropriate documentation. On the day following the announcement of the
EC ban, Hungary and Poland retaliated by imposing their own bans on a
number of EC products. Over the next few days, Bulgaria, Czechia and
Slovakia followed suit. Towards the end of the month, the EC lifted the
bans on most countries, following their acceptance of a number of conditions. But the ban on imports from Poland – by far the largest of the
affected states in terms of population – was not lifted until mid-July, following protracted and sometimes heated negotiations. Even then the EC imposed a minimum price for Polish cherries in West European markets,
which the Poles claimed was above the average market price. As had
happened with dairy produce in the early 1990s, the Poles believed the EC
was discriminating against their products and breaking the rules of free
market competition.

These examples are but the tip of the iceberg. They testify to the underlying tensions in the 1990s between a Western Europe that has been experiencing more economic (and related social) problems than usual, and a
post-communist world that would very much like to join the Western clubs,
but which has sometimes been treated like a poor and unreliable neighbour
that does not yet have the necessary credentials. This is all the more galling
for many east Europeans when they examine the trade statistics between
the EC/EU and themselves. These reveal that the trade balance in the early
1990s was very much in the EC's favour, so that Western Europe, for all its
coolness towards them,[11] was actually profiting from its poor neighbours.
Although such a trade imbalance is not unusual when less developed economies seek rapid modernization and technological upgrading, it is obvious
why this would be vexing. As the final straw, while east Europeans were
running a trade deficit with the EC, Russia was enjoying a healthy surplus,
of approximately 4 billion US dollars in 1993.

Under pressure, the EU agreed in 1994 to produce a set of criteria to be
met by intending members before their applications would be seriously
considered. This led to the adoption by the EU in May 1995 of a 300-page
White Paper that spelt out certain prerequisites for membership, though
still no target dates. Eventually, in December 1995, the EU indicated that
negotiations on the east European and Baltic applications would probably
commence in the latter half of 1997. While this was still not a clear indication of when applicants might hope to become members, at least the train
was still moving. It remains to be seen if any concrete deadlines can be
agreed in 1997.

The EC/EU is not the only major Western institution to have irritated
some of the post-communist states in the early 1990s because the latter
perceived either unfair treatment or excessive interference in their internal
affairs. Both the IMF and the World Bank have also had altercations with
several of these countries. In January–February 1993, an IMF delegation
spent two weeks in Hungary, at the end of which it refused to lift a tempo-

rary ban on a previously agreed credit arrangement. The reason given was that the Hungarian government was planning to permit what the IMF considered to be too large a budget deficit for the years 1994 through 1996. And in July 1993 an IMF delegation to Romania censured the government for inadequate progress in restructuring state enterprises and lowering inflation.

Conclusions

It is by now evident that many post-communist states have in the 1990s been attempting to move away from many of their former allegiances towards what they perceive to be potentially far more rewarding ones. But it has also been demonstrated that the West has been less enthusiastic about much closer relations with many of these states than appeared likely at the time of the anti-communist revolutions; this can be seen in both the military and the economic contexts.

In the military sphere, the Warsaw Pact is no more, but Russia continues to exert an influence on its former allies, albeit usually indirectly. This is partly because the West has permitted Russia to do so. While there are perfectly sound reasons for the Western position, it is important not to alienate and weaken the fledgling democracies in so many post-communist countries simply for the sake of one former quasi-imperialist power that is finding it difficult to accept its new reduced role. The West should have learnt certain lessons in the twentieth century about the dangers of appeasing extremists, whether fascist or communist or ultranationalist. If it is not to lose even more credibility than it already has over its botched handling of Bosnia to mid-1995, the West should make it quite clear to Russia in regard to these post-communist states – now internationally recognized as sovereign and independent – that any attempt either to incorporate or interfere with them against their will will be resisted by force.

In the economic sphere, it is not simply a matter of the post-communist states meeting certain criteria. The EU has many problems of its own. Western Europe has taken decades to reach its current stage of integration, and still has far to go before it reaches the level aspired to by the more ardent advocates of a unified Europe. It has constantly to seek compromise positions between those of its members that would prefer a widening (expanded membership) of the organization, and those that would at this stage prefer to deepen the integration process between the 15 existing members. The difficulties encountered in admitting Austria, Finland and Sweden, and in the adoption of the Maastricht Treaty in the early 1990s, amply demonstrated that both the wideners and the deepeners will have an uphill struggle to achieve their objectives. Given this, West European fears that their achievements could be jeopardized by admitting countries that are still unstable and only slowly developing truly democratic and market-oriented cultures become easier to understand. If one adds to this the fears the poorer members of the EU (such as Greece and Portugal) have about competition from any post-communist states admitted as full members, it becomes clear why the east Europeans and Balts will have to work long and hard to secure admission.

The West's hesitancy can also be partly explained by its wish to be on good terms with as many post-communist states as possible. Many Westerners appreciate the reasons for so much antipathy towards and fear of the Russians from both east Europeans and citizens of some of the former Soviet republics. Yet they cannot directly empathize. Moreover, it is often and justifiably argued in the West that it is dysfunctional to keep focusing on the past and to feed past hatreds. Russia is *also* post-communist – even following the 1995 elections (see next chapter) – and the sooner politicians in other post-communist countries fully acknowledge this, the more the position of reformers within Russia will be strengthened vis-à-vis their extremist opponents (which is not to say that this situation should not be reassessed *if* extremists both come to power in Russia *and* then pursue expansionist policies).

Thus the West's apparent reluctance to embrace the post-communist states of eastern Europe as warmly as the latter might prefer can be interpreted from radically different though not mutually exclusive perspectives. At least the post-communist states can complain more openly now than they could when they were members of the WTO and the CMEA, which is a healthy improvement. All of these states are still in a learning situation, and few had to come to grips with all the complex realities of the world when they were part of a bloc dominated by a superpower. They are currently learning aspects of realpolitik, including that it would be in nobody's interest for the rest of the world to ostracize or marginalize the world's largest country.

Despite the current tensions in East–West relations and the internal problems of the EU, the West must do everything possible to overcome its reservations. If one of the major arguments of this book – that post-communist governments need to acquire a degree of eudaemonism-based legitimacy if post-communism is to develop into stable democracy based on legal-rationality – is correct, then the West has to make even more strenuous efforts to help foster economic development in these transitional states. This argument can be framed in terms of vested self-interest (rational choice). First, the West can benefit itself economically by encouraging the development of consumerism (preferably bearing ecological concerns in mind!) in the post-communist states, thus creating the potential for major new markets for Western products. In this sense, the poorer EU states that fear competition should stop looking at future expansion as a zero-sum threat in which the gains for the east Europeans would be at their expense, but rather as an enormous opportunity.[12] Second, it might find that a refusal to interact sufficiently with the transitional and fragile systems of eastern Europe and the FSU will play into the hands of extremist politicians in the post-communist world who have simple but dangerous slogans. If such people come to power, they could threaten the West and the world order generally, especially if they succeed in potentially very powerful – and at the time of writing still nuclear – countries such as Russia or Ukraine.

While advocating that the West should do all it can to help the fledgling and fragile post-communist systems, it is ackowledged that much has already been done. According to EU statistics, the EC and its member states provided assistance worth approximately 70 billion US dollars – or 60 per cent of the total – to the CIS states alone between September 1990 and July 1994. The European Bank for Reconstruction and Development (EBRD) was established primarily by Western states in April 1991 explicitly to help most of the post-communist countries with their economic transitions; after a rocky start, the bank was by the mid-1990s playing a useful role in the privatization and economic development programmes of these states.

It is further acknowledged that there are practical limits to the scale of assistance from the West; as the Western economies pick up, so the possibilities for such assistance should also increase. But economic assistance is not all, or necessarily the most important thing, the post-communist states need. Just as important is the matter of attitude, and that the West practises rather better than it has been doing its alleged commitment to free competition and open markets. The freeing of the international market envisaged as a result of the successful conclusion of the Uruguay Round of the GATT (General Agreement on Tariffs and Trade) in December 1993 and the establishment of the WTO (nowadays meaning the World Trade Organization) from January 1995 should be beneficial to many of the post-communist states, with their relatively well-developed industrial bases and low labour costs.

Ultimately, the FSU, eastern Europe and the West all need to coexist. But securing the optimal balance is extraordinarily difficult, which helps to explain some of the ambiguities in Western policy identified in this chapter. It is in no one's interest, perhaps least of all that of the east Europeans, for the West to appear to be marginalizing Russia for the sake of the latter's former allies and partners. Rather, the West must work incrementally to improve relations with *all* the post-communist states, sometimes appearing to favour one group, at other times another. If the east Europeans do not recognize this, there is a danger they will finish up being as marginalized as many believe they were during the communist era. The forging of new allegiances is a complex and sensitive issue.

Most of this section has focused on eastern Europe and Russia. But some of the other post-communist states do not fit easily into the general patterns described. Thus, while several of the Central Asian and Transcaucasian states have sought to improve their relations with the West, they have also fostered closer ties to states in which Islam plays a dominant cultural role.

Of the latter, those that appeared most interested in developing better relations in the early 1990s were Turkey and Iran. The West could not raise serious objections to closer relations between countries such as Azerbaijan or Kazakhstan and Turkey: after all, the latter is a member of NATO. But the very strained relations between Iran and the West since the late 1970s meant that approaches by the Iranian government to new governments in

Central Asia were a cause of concern to the USA and various other Western powers. At the time of writing, however, this issue was less sensitive than it had been in 1991 or 1992. Not only is Islam a relatively heterogeneous religion and ideology, but many of the politicians in the former Central Asian republics are aware that economic links with successful and developed economies in both the West and East/South-East Asia are likely to be more beneficial to their own economies, and therefore to their own legitimacy, than are connections with troubled economies and governments such as Iran's. Only if such politicians are ousted by fundamentalist rebels is there much likelihood of markedly closer relations between some of the post-communist states and some of the Middle Eastern countries.

Notes

1 Parts of the present chapter are very similar to L. Holmes 1995. This is because both pieces were written at about the same time and deal with many of the same issues.

2 The Conference on Security and Cooperation in Europe, established in 1972. It became the Organization for Security and Cooperation in Europe (OSCE) in December 1994.

3 Some West European leaders were more hawkish on this issue than others. Soon after coming to power in 1995, President Chirac of France publicly declared his frustration at what he saw as the excessively conciliatory approach of many of his West European allies and drew comparisons with the appeasement policies towards Nazi Germany during the late 1930s. He must be seen as having played a role in the hardening of European attitudes that led to Operation Deliberate Force and, eventually, European acceptance of the US-sponsored peace agreement on Bosnia.

4 Russians who claim this have a selective memory, however; the relationship was decidedly cool in the 1940s and the 1950s, for instance.

5 Although the WEU is often described as the EU's defence arm, it does not include Denmark or Ireland or the three countries that joined the EU in January 1995 (see next subsection).

6 Nine post-communist states (Bulgaria, Czechia, Estonia, Hungary, Latvia, Lithuania, Poland, Romania and Slovakia) were admitted as *associate* partners of the WEU in May 1994.

7 Kazakhstan, Kyrgyzstan and Uzbekistan did so in January 1994, apparently because of frustration at the lack of progress towards real economic integration within the CIS.

8 It only became operational in January 1994, however.

9 These are often precursors to more substantial agreements; for instance, Slovenia initialled a Europe Agreement in May 1995.

10 These involve even less than Trade and Economic Cooperation Agreements, but are important symbols of a longer-term commitment to closer cooperation.

11 It should in fairness be pointed out that some West European states have been much warmer towards their post-communist neighbors than have others. The Germans have consistently been the most welcoming, while the southern members of the EU have tended to be the least.

12 Some of the southern European states, notably Greece, Portugal and Spain, would also do well to remember that they were themselves transitional and rather unstable societies in the 1970s and early 1980s, and that the EU helped them to stabilize by admitting them as full members.

FURTHER READING

On Soviet relations with Eastern Europe see Dawisha and Hanson 1981; Dawisha 1990; Pravda 1992. On the Warsaw Pact see Clawson and Kaplan 1982, while Brabant 1980 provides a detailed analysis of the CMEA.

A comprehensive overview of Russia's relations with the rest of the CIS is Dawisha and Parrott 1994, while Shearman 1995 provides details on Russian foreign policy in the 1990s. On post-communist relations with NATO see the various articles in *Transition*, vol. 1, no. 23 (1995), pp. 5–43, 64, while relations with the EU are considered in Mihalka 1995b.

Part IV

Conclusions

12

Some Concluding Remarks

Since there are concluding sections to each of the chapters on post-communism, it is unnecessary to summarize the various findings again here. However, an overall assessment is appropriate.

The post-communist countries have manifestly experienced severe difficulties in their first half-decade. Welfare and health-care systems are overloaded and in most cases grossly inadequate. Life expectancy has declined in many countries. Workers are still not defending themselves through unions as well as they might. Citizens are not forming themselves into autonomous groups to promote the environment or gender equality to anything like the extent this occurs in many Western countries. Racism, ethnic conflict and other forms of intolerance are widespread. The media in most countries are still being subjected to excessive government interference. Inflation and unemployment remain too high in many countries (though dropping in several). Then there are the tensions between the various agencies of the state; these are resulting in some countries in near stalemate, in others in an accumulation of presidential powers that increase the possibilities of eventual dictatorships. All this might lead to the conclusion that post-communist states have little chance of developing into stable consensual democracies that look after their citizens adequately, have healthy economies and are based on the rule of law.

Yet for all its major problems, post-communism has also already achieved much in its short life. It has been emphasized that the transitions currently being made by these countries are unprecedented in their range and ambitions. Given the legacy of communism, the score-card to date is even more impressive, especially outside the CIS. Political institutions are crystallizing: most presidential and parliamentary processes are beginning to settle down; elections are being held and are becoming more regularized; political parties are consolidating; constitutional courts are functioning and often display high levels of independence and fairness; and so on. Economic achievements are also considerable. Growth figures indicate a modest but real turnaround by the mid-1990s in all countries outside the CIS and former Yugoslavia; the prognoses for future growth are encouraging, even for many CIS and former Yugoslav states. Industries are being modernized. Given the enormous difficulties facing the post-communist economies, the levels of privatization achieved by 1994 can only be described as extraordinary. Although social movement activity is generally disappointing, at least the framework now exists for boosting this in the future. And while so many east European states wanting to join the West – primarily through member-ship of NATO and the EU – are finding the path rockier than expected, they *are* progressing.

Clearly, the achievements are greater and the prospects brighter in some countries than in others. The Visegrad countries are in general doing quite well (though several political developments in Slovakia during 1995 and 1996 were a cause for concern). On the other hand, many of the CIS states are still either highly unstable or increasingly dictatorial, or both. Many of the Balkan states fall somewhere in between these two extremes. But the overall equation is, marginally and on balance, positive.

Having assessed the early stages of post-communism, the layout of the rest of this chapter can be considered. It starts with a brief but important point about the *stages* – or dynamism – of post-communism. This is followed by four general questions about its current and future situation. The first is whether or not recent electoral results in various countries constitute evi-dence of a 'pink revolution'. Second, the interesting if problematic issue of 'normalcy' in the post-communist countries will be explored. Third, the legitimation crisis argument used to explain the collapse of communist power will be applied to the post-communist world, as one way of interpret-ing recent developments from a deeper theoretical perspective. Finally, a very brief overview of possible future scenarios is provided.

On Early Post-Communism

One feature of early post-communism is that most countries have already experienced at least two distinct stages. The first can be called the euphoric or elated stage. This lasted at most a year or so in most cases, and in some only months. During this phase, expectations within individual countries about the future were not merely optimistic but often unrealistic. This first period was soon followed by a longer, pessimistic phase.

It is tempting to call the first phase the dream period and the second the rude awakening. But this could be misleading. It is not a matter of being unrealistic in the early stages and realistic now. A better analogy would be to see the first stage as a drunken one, in which people were light-headed after having overthrown or in other ways disposed of communist power, and the second as a sobering-up period. This metaphor does not draw as sharp a qualitative distinction as the dreaming/waking one. Moreover, its images of abnormality – drunkenness and hangovers are not the norm for most people – and slight distortion of 'reality' enhance its utility.

There are a few indications that a new third phase – a more realistic and balanced one – may now be emerging in *some* of the post-communist states, especially the Visegrad ones. Ironically, perhaps the best sign of this is a widespread change of attitude towards what some observers describe as 'the former communists'; they constitute the focus of the following section.

A Pink Revolution?

At the time of the 1992 Lithuanian elections, several Western journalists raised the alarm that the communists were on the march back to power (on these elections see Girnius 1992). This view was endorsed in September 1993, when the results of the Polish elections led to headlines such as 'Socialist swing shocks West' (*The Australian*, 22 September 1993). While some commentators were sober in their interpretations of these results (see Meth-Cohn 1993), even specialist analysts such as Louise Vinton (1993b, p. 21) referred to them as 'a major political earthquake' (for further analyses of the 1993 Polish elections and the move to the left see Zubek 1994, Chan 1995). By December 1994 the trend had spread to Hungary, where the successor to the communist party performed better than any other in the parliamentary elections (see Fitzmaurice 1995), and to Bulgaria; it reached Russia by the end of 1995. (Some have suggested the Estonian elections of March 1995 were also part of this trend. Most specialists agree there was a marked move towards more left-wing – in the conventional Western sense –parties in these elections, but that this did not represent a return of the communists. For an analysis of the Estonian elections and their aftermath see Girnius 1995b.)

The election results in most of these countries (Bulgaria perhaps being an exception) were seen by some as particularly significant for two main reasons. First, the 'former communists' had earlier been decisively removed in these states, and were now being *returned*. In this sense, the results were perceived as cause for greater concern than those in Ukraine (1994 elections) or Romania (1992 elections), since it could be argued that in these cases 'former communists' had immediately succeeded the communists anyway.

Second, the 'former communists' were in the cases of Lithuania, Poland and Hungary being returned in countries often seen in the past (see Heller 1984, esp. pp. 137–8) as among the most hostile to communist power. In fact, this assessment was not true of Hungary by the 1980s; Kadar became increasingly popular over the decades, and his successors – reform communists – were largely credited with the extremely smooth transition from communism to post-communism (for May 1989 survey data on popular attitudes towards Kadar's communist successors see Ramet 1995, p. 467). But there is no denying that Poland appeared by many criteria to be the *least* likely candidate in the post-communist world to return 'former communists' to power. After all, there had been more displays of public hostility to the communist governments in Poland between the late 1940s and 1989 than in any other communist state. Moreover, Poland was the first country to 'turn the corner' economically; while this must be contextualized, in that positive growth was from a very low base following two years of serious decline, its symbolic significance should not be underestimated.

Given all this, some electronic media commentators began to refer to a 'pink revolution' in the post-communist world, and predicted that other countries would also 'return' to communist rule. Whether or not this is happening or is likely to happen is of importance, so that the claims of such commentators need to be addressed.

Post-communism cannot jettison all of its communist baggage overnight. In chapter 1, some of the more abstract dimensions of this point were elaborated. A more practical aspect is that a complex and long-standing system cannot be totally and instantly replaced in terms of its *personnel*. Even Lenin and the Bolsheviks acknowledged the need to use the expertise and experience of what they called bourgeois specialists. As the problems of early post-communism have become increasingly obvious, and as the Soviet domination factor has receded, so many citizens have begun either to forget or else to reassess various aspects of communist rule. Many have begun to realize that some of the experience of the former communist elites might be useful, even necessary, to the better functioning of the new system. Consequently, the fact that political sociologists are discovering increasing evidence of elements of continuity between communist and post-communist administrative elites should not *per se* be a cause for major alarm (on elite continuity see Baylis 1994).

There is undoubtedly considerable resentment in many countries at the so-called '*nomenklatura* privatization', in which many who enjoyed power and prestige under communism now constitute a significant component of the new capitalist elites. But at the same time, many citizens also accept that there are positive aspects to this, for instance in terms of experienced managers taking the reins of the rapidly changing economies. To some extent, a basically similar argument can be made about politicians. Most of these, in any system, have to learn the art of government and politics over time. This is even more true of post-communist countries, since there was no general culture of competitive politics on which budding politicians could draw and in which they had grown up. Politics operated within a limited framework in which the communists dominated and set the rules. Many of the leading figures of the genuinely new parties of late communism and early post-communism were simply much less experienced at government than were their communist counterparts (including those who joined successor parties to the communist party).

This point about political experience should not be exaggerated: relatively few communist politicians had learnt the art of parliamentary debate, for instance, for fairly obvious reasons (though this was changing in some countries in the last years of communist power, giving the communist politicians another headstart on the others in the 1990s). Nevertheless, as time has passed, and as non-communists in power have made mistakes and adopted unpopular policies, some citizens have decided it is worth capitalizing on the organizational and other experience of some of the 'former communists'. As one (unnamed) correspondent in the *Economist* wrote: 'When communism collapsed and free elections followed, democrats could offer what voters most wanted at the time: untarnished pasts. Since then, purity has come to look like mere inexperience. Voters have reacted against government by musicologists (Lithuania) and historians (Hungary). The ex-communists are, after all, political professionals' (16 April 1994, p. 54).

Second, even quite sensationalist journalists have mostly used the term *pink* revolution rather than *red*. This suggests it is only a moderate version of 'communism' that is being chosen. There is no call (yet!) by the elected 'former communists' – even when they continue to call themselves communists, as in Russia – for a return to the one-party state, democratic centralism, the dominance of Marxist-Leninist ideology, or even the centrally planned and socially owned economy. Therefore, the significance of the fact that people who were once members of the communist party are now running for office should not be exaggerated. Moreover, many who were until the recent revolutions members of the communist party were so primarily because of opportunistic, career-related reasons rather than genuine commitment to communist ideas and ideals. Hence it should not automatically be assumed that anyone who was once formally a communist is at heart still a true Marxist-Leninist. It is because of all this that the term 'former communists' is invariably written with inverted commas in this part of the argument.

Third, scrutiny of the election results in Lithuania, Poland, Hungary, Bulgaria and Russia reveal that many voters did *not* opt for communist party successor organizations (compare parties italicized and not italicized in tables 7.1 and 7.2 on pp. 157–65). This makes the notion of a widespread demand for a return to communism even less convincing.

Fourth, and perhaps most important, the so-called pink revolution should be interpreted primarily as *protest* voting. Given the high inflation and unemployment rates, plus the general sense of insecurity, in early postcommunism, it is understandable that so many voters have wanted to change their parliaments and governments in the hope of improvement. At the risk of sounding patronizing, this can be seen as a clear indication of the rapid political maturing of the 'infantilized' electorates (see chapter 1), who now feel genuinely free to vote left or right depending on the performance and political persuasion of those in power prior to the elections. In the particular case of Poland, the fact that it experienced what was in many ways the most radical and rapid transformation (the 'shock therapy' approach) of all was a major reason for the backlash: people were suffering and, since the signs of improvement were only just beginning to show in 1993, could not be confident that the positive turnaround would be sustained and to their advantage. Endorsing the argument that much of the support in the various elections was essentially backlash voting rather than indicative of a deep-seated and long-term commitment to the communists or their successors, the March 1995 Lithuanian local elections revealed a strong shift away from the governing party. Thus the first country to return 'former communists' was showing its displeasure at their performance. This phenomenon is likely to be repeated in the other countries in the future, including at general elections.

Finally, the notion of the pink revolution can only be fully evaluated by including some consideration of what the 'former communists' have done once in office. In fact, the new governments have pursued policies remarkably similar to those of their predecessors. Thus, writing a little over a year after the Lithuanian Democratic Labour Party replaced Sajudis, Girnius argued that 'Lithuania's domestic and foreign policy did not undergo major changes in 1993' (1994, p. 99). The budget adopted in March 1994 by the Polish parliament revealed that economic policy under Prime Minister Waldemar Pawlak looked similar to that of his 'radical marketeer' predecessor, Hanna Suchocka; this was even more true of Pawlak's successor, Jozef Oleksy. Similarly, the new Hungarian government of 'former communists' did not act *markedly* differently either from its own predecessors or its Lithuanian and Polish counterparts. Although the new Bulgarian government was in the first half of 1995 seeking to distance itself from its predecessor in several policy areas, it also remained commited to continued marketization and privatization, as revealed by the implementation of the citizen voucher scheme from January 1996. For it does seem that no one has been able to find a better general approach to economic policy than the basically market-oriented one adopted in one form or another in almost all post-communist states in the early 1990s. The more 'former communists' adopt policies that are fundamentally similar to those of other major parties, the less distinctive they become. This in turn may well mean that an increasing number of voters come to accept the near inevitability of the general policy direction being taken – albeit in various permutations and at different paces in individual countries – in the post-communist world, and that there is no realistic alternative to pain in the short term.

The one case in which a 'return' to communist power might be of real concern is Russia. Not only did the communists perform better there than any other party in the 1995 parliamentary elections, but communist leader Zyuganov was front runner in the opinion polls for much of the time in the lead-up to the 1996 presidential election. Yet even if Zyuganov were to become president – and it appeared increasingly possible by May 1996 that President Yeltsin would succeed in fending off his main challenger – it is not clear he would seek or be able to change Russia's direction as *fundamentally*, in either the political or the economic sphere, as many Western observers and Russians themselves believe. Rather, the real danger would be if a communist president and parliament were to make a serious attempt at reinstating the USSR (probably excluding the Baltic states) or even the former Soviet external empire. If they *were* to do this – and pre-election rhetoric in a country with as many problems as Russia has is likely to be far more extreme than actual policies would be once former oppositionists assume power – it would not be their communist orientation as much as their Russian nationalism and expansionism that would threaten both their neighbours and world peace.

In sum, the so-called pink revolution is understandable; its significance should not be exaggerated (it is certainly more pink than a revolution); and it might even reflect an underlying rapid development of a genuinely democratic culture. This is *not* to argue against the possibility of a return to authoritarian left-wing systems or of Russian expansionism in the future; rather, it is to point out that recent developments need to be kept in perspective.

The reference to the rapid development of a more democratic culture has led some to suggest that post-communism is, albeit via a very bumpy path, leading many formerly communist states towards 'normality'. This is a highly loaded and problematic term, and warrants examination.

On 'Normal' Politics

What would be considered 'normal' in a country that has long been a dictatorship might seem quite abnormal to someone from a First World democracy, and vice versa. This obvious point highlights the fact that there is no universal conception of normal politics. In fact, a comparative analysis just of First World politics soon reveals some relatively significant differences between countries. Thus an American is likely to have a quite different conception of the role of political parties and the head of state (president) from that of a German. Each country has its own unique political culture.

Nevertheless, there are sufficient *fundamental* similarities between most First World states to warrant reference to normal Western politics (for an analysis of what this might mean see L. Holmes 1994), just as there were enough commonalities between communist states to justify references to the normal communist way of doing things, notwithstanding the significant differences between, for instance, Yugoslavia and Albania.

With these introductory points in mind, no fewer than three approaches to normal politics will be elaborated here, while a fourth will be introduced towards the end of the discussion.

The first approach is to consider normalcy from the perspective of *the West*, particularly Western Europe. This might initially appear to be ethnocentric, and perhaps even smack of 'cultural imperialism'. But the fact is that many east Europeans and European citizens of the FSU – less so citizens of the former Central Asian republics of the USSR – describe themselves as Europeans *culturally*, not merely geographically, and are consciously and overtly attempting to move closer to West European culture, including its general model of politics and economics. This was clear in the Russian case even under Gorbachev, when he referred (first in 1985) to a 'common European home'; two further indications came in June 1994, when the Russian government finally agreed to join NATO's 'Partnership for Peace' programme, and when Yeltsin himself signed the PCA at the Corfu summit of the EU committing his country to closer economic integration with the EU and greater political convergence between Russia and

Europe. Thus this first approach to normalcy is justified less in terms of Western ethnocentrism than of the professed self-perceptions and objectives of so many post-communist leaders and intellectuals.

The second approach derives in part from a definition of post-communism given by Vaclav Havel in 1991. According to the then Czecho-Slovak president, post-communism is 'a long forgotten history coming back to haunt us, a history full of thousands of economic, social, ethical, territorial, cultural and political problems that remained latent and under the surface of totalitarian boredom' (cited in the *Sunday Age*, Melbourne, 17 May 1992, p. 10). This second approach refers to the *pre-communist traditions* of the post-communist countries, and the principal focus is on perceptions of a *return* to normal.

The third approach also implies a return to the past, but in this case to the much more recent past, that is, the *communist era*. Most citizens in the post-communist world have spent the majority of their lives under such a system, so that this can with justification be seen as the most convincing interpretation of normal.

It should be fairly obvious that these three conceptions of normalcy are to a large extent mutually exclusive. For instance, with the exception of Czechoslovakia, none of the communist states had had much pre-communist experience with liberal democracy, and very few had had an advanced, industrialized market economy. In this sense, the first and second conceptions are incompatible. Yet far from these incompatibilities causing a problem, they are useful, since they highlight the fact that there cannot be a straightforward answer to the question 'are post-communist politics becoming normal?' The answer depends not only on how current and future likely developments in the post-communist states are interpreted, but also on which definition of normalcy is being used.

In addition to these problems, there is the point that there might be different answers to the question of normalcy, depending on the particular state or states under consideration. One country might currently look as though its leaders and/or citizens are attempting to return to the pre-communist past, a second might appear to be sliding back towards (or else hardly to have left) the communist era, while a third seems determined to move in the direction of a Western model.

Finally, there is the further complication that a particular country might appear to have been attempting to recreate aspects of the pre-communist past (the second conception of normalcy identified earlier) in the earliest years of post-communism, but subsequently to have decided to move towards the first conception.

Given these numerous and largely insurmountable difficulties, it should be clear why the very question 'Is post-communist politics becoming normal?' is too vague to be answered. If it is to be of any value to discussion, the questioner must specify the preferred meaning of 'normal', the country or countries at issue and the specific period to be considered. Moreover, it is empirically difficult to answer the question at this stage, precisely because of the continuing uncertainties in even the most apparently settled of the post-communist states; the pink revolution is but one sign of this.

At the beginning of this section, reference was made to a *fourth* possible meaning of normal. This one largely transcends cultural and temporal specificities, and in this sense could be seen to be more useful than the other definitions. For many ordinary people in societies with quite different traditions and at very different levels of economic development, normality is essentially coterminous with high levels of stability and predictability – with well-established and defined patterns of behaviour. After all, this is what norms are.

This everyday sense of normal can be applied to the post-communist world with fewer problems than the first three meanings, although the point about needing to specify the country and period *still* pertains. According to this approach, the post-communist world is necessarily abnormal, since it has recently undergone revolution, is still transitional, and its end destination(s) remain(s) unclear. Only when reasonably clear patterns of political behaviour have been established in a given post-communist country, so that prediction *within relatively limited parameters* is possible, can there be meaningful references to normal politics. At that point, the particular post-communist state will no longer be transitional, and hence no longer post-communist. From the perspective of this fourth conception then, post-communism and normality are mutually exclusive, and the latter will take *time* to develop; all that might be said is that a given state appears to be moving towards normalcy, and hence away from post-communism.

Legitimation, Legitimation Crises and Post-Communism

In chapter 2, ten modes of legitimation were identified and implicated in four kinds of legitimation crisis (see pp. 44–5, 52–4); in this section, these will be applied to the post-communist world, both in an endeavour to make more sense of it theoretically, and as a basis for further discussion once this book has been set aside.

Evidence of the first kind of legitimation crisis – legitimation shifts – is not difficult to find in most post-communist countries. In the first, euphoric stage of post-communism, there was understandably a mixture of legitimation modes. Countries such as the Baltic states harked back to pre-communist traditions (seen in the partial or total reinstatement of the pre-communist constitution), which might at first glance be taken as evidence of a return to old traditional legitimation. However, there were many aspects of the pre-communist period that were *not* emphasized at this stage. For example, there were few calls for a return to authoritarianism, which, in various forms, had typified so many of these countries before the communists took power. Many countries had also had monarchies, and there was little pressure for a return of these. A closer analysis of the situation suggests that what initially might have looked like old traditionalism was much more like official nationalism. The resurrection of old constitutions was primarily part of the first rejection (that is, of external domination): Balts were no longer prepared to work to constitutions they perceived as having been imposed by the Russian-dominated Soviet system.

Another dominant mode in this earliest stage was charismatic legitimation. Many citizens revered new 'national hero' leaders who had defied the authorities during the communist era, and who had in many cases paid the price through prison sentences or other forms of punishment. This applies, for instance, to Gamsakhurdia in Georgia, Walesa in Poland, Havel in Czecho-Slovakia and Tudjman in Croatia. Even former senior communist politicians who were seen to have stood up to less liberal communist leaderships were in some cases now treated with great admiration, even as charismatic leaders; examples include Yeltsin in Russia and Dubcek in Slovakia.

In these earliest days, there was also a form of teleological legitimation, as post-communist leaders promised major transformations of the economic and political systems. However, this was incomplete teleologism, since both the end goal and the means for achieving it were ultimately vague. This was partly a function precisely of the greater political freedom of the period, and the relatively underdeveloped skills of compromise and constructive debate between people of different views. Given the widespread rejection of grand theories, teleological legitimation was from the start unlikely to prove as effective for post-communist regimes as it had for some early communist regimes.

Since the approach to new traditionalism used in this book cannot, by definition, be used by a new system, it need not be considered. In terms of domestic modes, this leaves only eudaemonism and legal-rationality.

Ideally, most post-communist governments would probably prefer to be legitimized in the medium term above all on the basis of eudaemonism. Most citizens of communist states had been deprived of much that Westerners take for granted, especially in terms of the choice and availability of consumer goods, and most post-communist politicians have been aware that they would gain even greater support and kudos through improving living standards than through increasing political and human rights. But the communist economic legacy was a very poor one. Moreover, the post-communist governments' attempts at major economic reconstruction were bound to cause severe dislocation: the road could not merely be patched up or resurfaced, but had to be completely remade. This helps to explain many of the tensions of the second phase of post-communism. Until the new road is open and the traffic flowing freely, there will be frustrations, resentments, intolerance and other negative phenomena. In short, it is still too early for eudaemonic legitimation to be the salient mode of legitimation; if even Poland, with its positive growth rates since 1992, cannot satisfy citizens sufficiently to avoid a return of 'former communists', there is little hope in the immediate future for other post-communist governments.

According to writers such as Poggi (1978, pp. 101, 132), the only mode of legitimation appropriate to a stable modern state – which is surely what most post-communist states ultimately hope to become – is the legal-rational. There is no inherent reason why post-communist states cannot move increasingly towards legal-rational legitimation, since there is no ultimate contradiction between this mode and the current ideology (such as it is) as there was under communism. There are numerous signs that legal-rationality is in principle being increasingly adopted. But it is ironic that the very instability and problematic nature of early post-communism renders it difficult for politicians and others to place too much emphasis on legal-rationality, since it is clear to all that the essential orderliness and predict-ability associated with the concept have yet to be firmly established.

The three external modes of legitimation have played a perceptible role in the legitimation process of post-communist regimes. Most post-communist governments were soon recognized by both international or-ganizations and other governments. In the case of several of the former republics of Yugoslavia, it could even be argued that external recognition was a major factor encouraging them to continue challenging Belgrade at a time when it was becoming ever clearer that the Yugoslav army would be used against republics attempting to secede. This was particularly true of Slovenia and Croatia, for whom German – and then more general Western – support was an important factor encouraging the post-communist leaders to follow through with their commitment to sovereignty and independence.

Informal external support has also been important to several post-communist governments. This is sometimes of a largely verbal nature, in the form of general statements of support from leading Western politicians, or as foreign government backing of a given post-communist government in its struggle either with another state (as with Turkish and Iranian support for Azerbaijan in its fight with Armenia) or with sections of its own population or political opposition (as with Western endorsement of Yeltsin in his struggle with the Russian parliament in September–October 1993, or of Kazakhstan's President Nazarbayev when he shut down his parliament in March 1995 – see Pannier 1995, esp. p. 66).

At other times, the informal support is more tangible. This can be in the form of fighting-related military assistance – troops and/or weapons (as with Russian support for Georgia in its struggle with the Abkhazians) – or of aid and strictly defensive (humanitarian) military support (such as UN involve-ment in Bosnia-Hercegovina). In all such cases, the regime receiving sup-port can use this in its attempt to gain greater legitimacy with its own population (by arguing that 'others can see the justness of our cause – we're doing the right thing'). Another form of concrete support is financial. Thus the IMF or the World Bank might guarantee a new loan on the grounds that it has faith in a given post-communist government's economic policies. This loan might alleviate economic suffering and thus increase support for a government. Sometimes, conversely, the post-communist government will blame international financial organizations for austerity measures it is adopting. This can be a useful form of scapegoatism in a difficult situation; it is a common scenario in early post-communism, given the severity of the economic problems. By deflecting some of the popular criticism on to an external agent, the government might improve its own image and perhaps its legitimacy.

There are numerous ways in which the existence of an external role model might help a post-communist regime's self-legitimation even when it knows it enjoys limited legitimacy among the mass citizenry. The most obvious case is where a government persists with an unpopular policy because it genuinely believes this to be in the long-term interests of the country. It does so because it considers there is only one kind of system (typically, 'Western') that can work in the long run, even if citizen patience for such a complex and prolonged operation is rapidly running out, or has already done so. Moreover, it can be encouraged by the fact that other countries are attempting similar restructuring and are experiencing similar problems; in terms of self-legitimation by reference to an external role model, however, such peer comparisons are most effective if at least one of the other countries actually seems to be succeeding in moving towards its objectives. For this reason, the legitimacy of post-communism generally is closely linked to those countries that currently look as if they might be stabilizing politically and, in many ways even more important, improving economically. As of 1995 the fates of Poland and the Czech Republic were therefore of far wider importance than merely for their own populations.

In sum, the very instability of post-communism has led, and will continue to lead, to changing emphases on the various modes of legitimation.

By 1994, it was already clear that the second minor type of legitimation crisis – abnormal regime change – could also affect post-communist countries. Several countries had had a number of short-lived governments. Often, the change of government was reflective of tensions between presidents and parliaments. In other cases, it reflected the inability of parties and coalitions to compromise sufficently. In both situations, the problem derived primarily from the very newness, fragility and uncertain legitimacy of post-communist political institutions.

Instances of the third type of legitimation crisis – reversion to coercion – can also already be found in the post-communist world. Perhaps the most widely reported example was Yeltsin's use of force against the Russian parliament in October 1993. Other examples include Shevardnadze's imposition of martial law on the Georgian government in December 1992; Iliescu's use of force (including by thuggish miners transported into Bucharest, since the Romanian president was unable to rely on the police and the army to carry out his orders) against demonstrators in June 1990; and various measures adopted by the parliament and President Rakhmonov in Tajikistan in late 1992 and early 1993.

However, the Russian example, as well as various cases that could be cited under the second type of crisis, reflect an aspect of legitimation crises that both distinguishes post-communist ones from those in the communist era, and makes the determination of the existence or not of the fourth kind particularly difficult. By and large, communist power systems were relatively homogeneous; Rigby has described them as 'mono-organizational' (for his most comprehensive analysis and application of this concept see Rigby 1990, where a 'distilled' six-point version can be found on p. 6), while Waller (1993) refers to the 'communist power monopoly'. Most analysts were with considerable justification prepared to see a relatively simple dichotomy between the regime and the people, or the political system and the citizenry, or the state (broadly understood, to include the party) and society. But what happens when there is an overt, major conflict *within* the state, *between* different institutions? On one level, this is still a regime crisis and is not qualitatively different from the situation in which one regime replaces another under abnormal circumstances. Ultimately, it still represents a conflict essentially *within* the political institutional framework, and it matters little whether this is vertical (one leadership team replaces another) or horizontal (one institution comes to dominate another); it is not yet *systemic*.

What of the possibility of identity crisis and extreme legitimation crisis, and, as a corollary, system collapse? In a very real sense, it is inappropriate to refer to system collapse, or even its possibility, when a system has not yet properly crystallized. If post-communism is essentially about *transition*, then, it can be argued, it is necessarily going to be replaced by something more defined, and probably more enduring, that can be called a system. But is this argument overly rational and formal – precious, even?

The application to post-communism of the notion of identity crisis and collapse becomes highly problematical if it is assumed that *only* a crystallized system can experience such difficulties. But if it is accepted that a regime and *emerging* system can also collapse, partly or largely because of an identity crisis, and can be replaced by something that has fundamentally different values, then a *modified* version of the fourth type of legitimation crisis *is* possible under post-communism. This differs from the second type of legitimation crisis in that this one brings about a basic change of direction, whereas the second type brings much less significant change. But what sort of identity crisis could occur in a post-communist country?

Leaders such as Yeltsin or Klaus argue publicly that there is a necessary connection between market-oriented economic reform and political reform in a pluralist direction. Given this, it would be difficult for such leaders to introduce an essentially dictatorial regime at the same time as they claim to be continuing in the same basic direction in economic policy. To do so would be evidence of an identity crisis that might well be overcome only by a reversion to coercion.

But what is to be made of the fact that so many citizens were already showing a lack of faith in the basic direction of post-communism within a year or so of the collapse of communist power? Does this suggest that there was a legitimation crisis of post-communism, and, if so, of what sort was it?

Before answering this question, it is necessary to provide some evidence of the popular mistrust of post-communism.

In November 1992 a survey of some 8,000 citizens in eight former Soviet republics (approximately 1,000 citizens in each of the three Slavic states/ regions of Belarus, Ukraine and the European part of Russia, in the three Baltic states, and in two of the Trancaucasian states) was conducted on behalf of the European Commission. In all but one of the former Soviet republics (the exception being Lithuania), a higher proportion of respondents thought that their situation had been better under late communism ('the previous political system') than it was under post-communism. In the Slavic states, those believing life was better under the old system than under the new outnumbered those having the opposite opinion by approximately 3:1. Even in Estonia – where it might have been expected that many citizens would be pleased about their newly independent and non-communist status – more than twice as many respondents felt life was better under the old system (details in Rhodes 1993). Opinion surveys conducted in Romania between late 1991 and mid-1995 suggested that the confidence in the future revealed there by more than half of the respondents in 1991 had declined by 1993. By then, only 43 per cent of respondents considered that Romania was heading in the right direction – precisely the same percentage as believed it was heading in the wrong direction (for details see Shafir 1993). By June 1995, the latter figure had increased to 51 per cent, while only 30 per cent of respondents still believed their country was going down the right path (David 1995, p. 2). Numerous other polls could be cited to endorse the suggestion that there was considerable faith in the future in many post-communist states in the immediate aftermath of the collapse of communist power, but that this declined dramatically in many countries relatively shortly afterwards (for some fascinating survey data from several Eastern European countries during and since the late 1980s see Ramet 1995, pp. 461–82; for readily accessible comparative east European data on attitudes towards regime change see Rose and Mishler 1994, Rose and Haerpfer 1994a; for some of the most detailed sets of data, on both eastern Europe and Russia, see the numerous New Democracies and New Russia Barometer reports produced jointly by the Centre for the Study of Public Policy at the University of Strathclyde and the Paul Lazarsfeld Society in Vienna). What should be made of such data?

The first point is that all survey data should be treated with caution. There are numerous methodological assumptions involved in both gathering and interpreting such data, and survey findings should never be fetishized. Nevertheless, it is also true that we have no better method for gauging attitudes and values, and it cannot usually be proven that the data are false.

So let us assume such data *are* more or less correct; after all, they largely accord with yet more subjective methodologies (small-scale interviews, perceptions by scholars and journalists, common-sense interpretations of human reactions to major economic and social problems, etc.), and recur in so many countries that there is no convincing reason to be overly sceptical about them. Even if they do accurately reflect opinions at the time they were conducted, it is not clear such opinions matter very much – in the sense of endangering the political order – in the relatively short term. This is much more the case for post-communist states than for their predecessors, since citizens now have reasonably open channels for expressing their discontent. The most obvious escape valve is the ballot box. Moreover, there is now far less of an obvious alternative to the general policy directions being adopted by post-communist governments than there appeared to be in late communism. These last two points are borne out by the pink revolution. In a very real sense, the more voters engage in protest voting, only to discover that the previous opposition group now in power is no better able to overcome fundamental difficulties than was the group it replaced, the more post-communism will be transformed into a true *system*, in which citizens accept that there is little realistic alternative. This might not appear to be a very solid basis for legitimacy; but it is worth asking whether or not this might be true of some Western systems (increasingly so by the 1990s). At least it suggests the need to be wary of reading too much into survey findings when discussing legitimacy and legitimation crisis in the post-communist world. Attitudes are still changing rapidly and do not necessarily endanger post-communism in the short term; it is certainly not clear they reflect a current profound (extreme) legitimation crisis, *especially if leadership groups retain faith in what they are doing.*

But what of the longer term? Can post-communist regimes evolve into legal-rational systems? The point has been reached at which it is worth briefly considering future possible scenarios.

The Future

Some more adventurous analysts (see Agh 1993, Brzezinski 1993b, Lewis 1993) have produced various scenarios of the future of post-communism. Although many of these are complex and sophisticated, most can be reduced basically to four possible scenarios.

The first is what can be called 'becoming like the West'. In this picture, a post-communist country is gradually transformed into a stable pluralist democracy. Stable is not to be equated with static: change occurs, but is mostly piecemeal and can be accommodated without fundamental threat to the system. The economy functions primarily according to market and private-ownership principles, although it is ultimately mixed; certainly the state plays a role in the economy, although the level of this varies from country to country. Above all, this system is typified by a general commitment to 'rules of the game'; there is a well-established democratic culture and a solid commitment to legal-rationality. None of the post-communist states either is, or could be expected to be, close to this yet – though countries like Poland, the Czech Republic, Hungary and Slovenia were by 1995 closer to it than most of the other post-communist states.

The second scenario is of an authoritarian system. Some writers produce fine gradations of this, and it can be argued that a distinction should be drawn between populist, nationalist, military and perhaps even communist (assuming the possibility of a return to an old-style communist system, even though there are no convincing signs of the possibility of this at present) versions of this. However, there is a real danger of devising highly complex schemas that draw unhelpful distinctions between essentially similar arrangements. For instance, post-communism has already demonstrated that there is usually a very close connection between populism and nationalism.

In fact, the only significant potential differences between these forms of authoritarianism are how they arise and what approach is adopted towards the economy. Thus, in terms of legitimacy and levels of coercion, a distinction should be drawn between authoritarian systems that emerge as a result of the will of a majority of citizens, and those that are imposed by a small minority. To illustrate this by way of example, it would surely be important to distinguish a Russian regime led by Zhirinovskii or Zyuganov (or someone like them), but which has been properly elected, from one in which a group of military officers seized power. If the former were more popularly legitimate, it is also likely it would function better; for one thing, the international community would be less able to criticize a regime that has been popularly mandated than a self-installed one, and hence less able to impose economic sanctions and take other steps designed to 'punish' a new government economically (unless, of course, such a regime were to threaten other countries as a result of expansionist policies, which changes the whole situation). Equally, one should distinguish between regimes that opt for a basically capitalist system, albeit with a relatively high level of state involvement in the economy, and those that seek a return to many elements of the command economy. Thus authoritarian regimes that might seek to emulate the economic model (and success!) of the Asian Tigers are likely to be more successful in the longer term than those that seek a return to basic elements of the communist economic system.

The third scenario is of essentially directionless long-term transition, in which governments change with abnormal frequency, and keep attempting to change direction. This picture reveals no discernible long-term pattern; since the so-called pink revolutions have witnessed little *fundamental* change of direction in Lithuania, Poland, Hungary, or even Bulgaria, they do *not* constitute an example of this scenario. The continuing confusion in Russia, on the other hand, could as of early 1996 be seen as exemplifying it.

The final scenario cannot and should not be described; it cannot be predicted, since it does not fit neatly into any pre-existing categories. If the collapse of communist power has not taught us that, for all our models and social science sophistication, we cannot always predict future possibilities, then there is little hope that we can learn from our mistakes.

Although different scenarios have been described here, it should not be assumed they are mutually exclusive. A given country might elect an authoritarian leader and later decide this was a worse choice than the alternatives. At that point, the electorate might bring in a team more committed to 'the Western model', vague though that may be. In other words, a particular country might move between categories over time.

While it is interesting to speculate on how particular countries will fare over the next few years, it is beyond the scope of this book to do this for nearly 30 post-communist countries. Certainly, groups of countries could be clustered into the different scenarios, according to the author's calculations and intuitions; as indicated earlier, most Central Asian states were by 1995 tending towards the authoritarian scenario, while the Visegrad countries (with the possible exception of Slovakia) were closest to the Western. But unless there were an explanation as to why any given state had been classified in a particular way, such an exercise would be almost worthless; after all, the factors taken into consideration and the relative weighting attributed to them would be different in each case, even for countries within the same category. For this reason, it is more valuable to consider the factors that will be of relevance in explaining why a given country moves into one scenario at a given point in time rather than into another. As with every other topic addressed in this book, this question cannot be dealt with as thoroughly as it deserves to be; but it is still better to place it on the agenda – probably for further debate in tutorials – than to ignore it altogether. Thus the following factors will be involved in determining which path (scenario) will be taken by a given post-communist state in the future.

Political culture   There is an enormous number of subvariables in this category, including experiences under pre-communism, communism and post-communism; religious traditions; traditional attitudes towards both authority and democracy; level and type of external influences; ethnic diversity; proximity to the West or other models. Many more variables could be identified. Unfortunately, the sheer range means that it is impossible to predict precisely *which* components of the political culture will become salient under certain conditions. Many commentators have in the past focused on Poland's Roman Catholic tradition, for instance – yet the 1993 Polish election results have been interpreted as reflecting a widespread disillusionment with the role of the Catholic Church in politics (see Sabbat-Swidlicka 1993). Here then, a largely unexpected result occurred because most commentators had misjudged Polish attitudes towards both the church and the communist past, while they had also underestimated the potential influence of West European views on Poles with respect to a woman's right to choose to have an abortion or not.

In short, while the concept of political culture is useful, its primary value is in helping to understand developments *ex post facto* rather than for prediction.

Quality of leaderships   One of the great ironies of early post-communism is that the economic and social instability of the early years virtually necessitated strong leadership, despite the putative commitment of many politicians to Western-style democracy and the depersonalization of politics. The future of post-communism in all countries will depend partly on the quality of leaders, both those in power and those who seek to replace them. Moreover, the correlation between leaders' qualities and the values they espouse will be important: other things being equal, strong leaders who can acquire widespread support will be able to gain greater legitimacy for their values and policies. There is one major exception to the validity of this general statement: strong leaders who adopt foreign policies that threaten others will lose international legitimacy, which will eventually result in a decline of their popular legitimacy.

The international economic climate Ultimately, only post-communist countries themselves can improve their lot. Nevertheless, they need external assistance and support. Wealthier, more established systems have a moral duty towards the post-communist states and a vested interest in helping them to stabilize and, eventually, to 'come into the fold' (to be permitted to join organizations such as the EU and NATO); it is in almost no one's interest to see extremist regimes come to power in these countries, particularly if they are expansionist.

This said, there are limited funds available for bailing out weak regimes worldwide; the post-communist countries are in a long queue of states seeking Western aid, Most Favoured Nation status, etc. Attitudes in the post-communist countries towards the West and liberal democracy will continue to be affected by Western behaviour towards those states – although it must be emphasized that this is a two-way street, and Western attitudes, including willingness to invest, are affected by what post-communist governments themselves do.

Economic performance Probably the most important factor determining the future of post-communist systems will be their economic performance. Poland's success in recent years might suggest that other states should have adopted a more radical approach to economic transformation than they did. But the honeymoon period in the post-communist world is over and the window of opportunity to adopt such an approach has now *probably* shut (though Ukraine might be argued to have shown in 1994–5 that it is never too late). While the main indicator of economic performance will be overall growth and development, the level of suffering and decline in living standards for most citizens in early post-communism means there will have to be reasonably equitable distribution of new wealth if systems are to stabilize and increase their legitimacy. While citizens will almost certainly have to accept on an ongoing basis higher levels of insecurity than they were used to under communism, governments will also have to reduce the current high levels of social tension by developing proper safety nets (welfare states) akin to those typical in several West European countries. Most – probably all – post-communist states are too fragile and have a citizenry that remembers too well the better aspects of communism to sustain the gross inequalities and underdeveloped welfare system of some Western countries.

As stated at the beginning of this book and by now proven, post-communism is a complex dynamic phenomenon. Parts of this book will be redundant, or at least history, even by the time it is published. This matters not; if readers have gained a deeper knowledge of and greater interest in this subject, the primary objective will have been met.

Bibliography

Acsady, J. (1995) 'Shifting Attitudes and Expectations in Hungary', *Transition*, vol. 1, no. 16, pp. 22–3.

Adam, J. (ed.) (1991a) *Economic Reforms and Welfare Systems in the USSR, Poland and Hungary* (London: Macmillan).

Adam, J. (1991b) 'Social Contract', in Adam 1991a, pp. 1–25.

Adamik, M. (1993) 'Feminism and Hungary', in Funk and Mueller 1993, pp. 207–12.

Agh, A. (1993) 'The "Comparative Revolution" and the Transition in Central and Southern Europe', *Journal of Theoretical Politics*, vol. 5, no. 2, pp. 231–52.

Agh, A. (1995) 'The Experiences of the First Democratic Parliaments in East Central Europe', *Communist and Post-Communist Studies*, vol. 28, no. 2, pp. 203–14.

Agh, A. (ed.) (1994) *The Emergence of East Central European Parliaments* (Budapest: Hungarian Centre for Democracy Studies Foundation).

Agh, A. and Ilonsaki, G. (eds) (1996) *Parliaments and organised Interests* (Budapest: Hungarian Centre for Democracy Studies Foundation).

Almond, G. (1970) *Political Development* (Boston: Little Brown).

Amin, S. (1974) *Accumulation on a World Scale* (New York: Monthly Review Press).

Anderson, B. (1991) *Imagined Communities* (London: Verso).

Apter, D. (1965) *The Politics of Modernization* (Chicago: University of Chicago Press).

Arato, A. (1982) 'Critical Sociology and Authoritarian State Socialism', in J. Thompson and D. Held (eds), *Habermas: Critical Debates* (London: Macmillan), pp. 196–218.

Arato, A. (1991) 'Revolution, Civil Society, and Democracy', in Rau 1991a, pp. 161–81.

Arel, D. and Wilson, A. (1994) 'The Ukrainian Parliamentary Elections', *RFE/RL Research Report*, vol. 3, no. 26, pp. 6–17.

Arendt, H. (1951) *The Origins of Totalitarianism* (London: Allen and Unwin).

Arendt, H. (1965) *On Revolution* (New York: Viking).

Aslund, A. (1985) *Private Enterprise in Eastern Europe* (New York: St Martin's).

Aslund, A. (1992) *Post-Communist Economic Revolutions* (Washington D.C.: Center for Strategic and International Studies).

Aslund, A. (1993) 'The Gradual Nature of Economic Change in Russia', in Aslund and Layard 1993, pp. 19–38.

Aslund, A. and Layard, R. (eds) (1993) *Changing the Economic System in Russia* (London: Pinter).

Avineri, S. (1968) *The Social and Political Thought of Karl Marx* (Cambridge: Cambridge University Press).

Avtorkhanov, A. (1967) *The Communist Party Apparatus* (Cleveland: World Publishing).

Azicri, M. (1988) *Cuba* (London: Pinter).

Bakos, G. (1993) 'After COMECON: A Free Trade Area in Central Europe?', *Europe-Asia Studies*, vol. 45, no. 6, pp. 1025–44.

Barany, Z. (1994) 'Living on the Edge: The East European Roma in Postcommunist Politics and Societies', *Slavic Review*, vol. 53, no. 2, pp. 321–44.

Barany, Z. (1995) 'Grim Realities in Eastern Europe', *Transition*, vol. 1, no. 4, pp. 3–8.

Barker, R. (1990) *Political Legitimacy and the State* (Oxford: Oxford University Press).

Barrington, L (1995) 'The Domestic and International Consequences of Citizenship in the Soviet Successor States', *Europe-Asia Studies*, vol. 47, no. 5, pp. 731–63.

Batt, J. (1991) *East Central Europe from Reform to Transformation* (London: Pinter).

Bauman, Z. (1993) 'A Post-modern Revolution?' in Frentzel-Zagorska 1993, pp. 3–19.

Bauman, Z. (1994) 'A Revolution in the Theory of Revolutions?', *International Political Science Review*, vol. 15, no. 1, pp. 15–24.

Baumgartl, B. (1993) 'West Provides No New Aid to Clean Up Eastern Europe', *RFE/RL Research Report*, vol. 2, no. 29, pp. 41–7.

Baylis, T. (1994) 'Plus ça change? Transformation and Continuity among East European Elites', *Communist and Post-Communist Studies*, vol. 27, no. 3, pp. 315–28.

Baylis, T. (1996) 'Presidents versus Prime Ministers: Shaping Executive Authority in Eastern Europe', *World Politics*, vol. 48, no. 3, pp. 297–323.

Beetham, D. (1991) *The Legitimation of Power* (London: Macmillan).

Bell-Fialkoff, A. (1993) 'A Brief History of Ethnic Cleansing', *Foreign Affairs*, vol. 72, no. 3, pp. 110–21.

Bernhard, M. (1993) *The Origins of Democratization in Poland* (New York: Columbia University Press).

Bianco, L. (1971) *Origins of the Chinese Revolution 1915–1949* (Stanford: Stanford University Press).

Bicanic, I. and Dominis, I. (1993) 'The Multiparty Elections in Croatia: Round Two', *RFE/RL Research Report*, vol. 2, no. 19, pp. 17–21.

Black, A. (1984) *Guilds and Civil Society in European Political Thought from the Twelfth Century to the Present* (London: Methuen).

Blondel, J. (1990) *Comparative Government* (New York: Philip Allan).

Boeri, T. (ed.) (1994) *Unemployment in Transition Countries* (Paris: OECD).

Bogetic, Z. (1993) 'The Role of Employee Ownership in Privatisation of State Enterprises in Eastern and Central Europe', *Europe-Asia Studies*, vol. 45, no. 3, pp. 463–81.

Bohachevsky-Chomiak, M. (1995) 'Practical Concerns and Political Protest in Post-Soviet Ukraine', *Transition*, vol. 1, no. 16, pp. 12–17.

Bollobas, E. (1993) '"Totalitarian Lib": The Legacy of Communism for Hungarian Women', in Funk and Mueller 1993, pp. 201–6.

Bowker, M. (1995) 'Russian Policy Toward Central and Eastern Europe', in Shearman 1995, pp. 71–91.

Boycko, M. and Shleifer, A. (1993) 'The Voucher Program for Russia', in Aslund and Layard 1993, pp. 100–11.

Bozoki, A., Korosenyi, A. and Schopflin, G. (eds) (1992) *Post-Communist Transition* (London: Pinter).

Brabant, J. van (1980) *Socialist Economic Integration* (Cambridge: Cambridge University Press).

Braybrooke, D. and Lindblom, C. (1970) *A Strategy of Decision* (New York: Free Press).

Bremmer, I. and Taras, R. (eds) (1993) *Nations and Politics in the Soviet Successor States* (Cambridge: Cambridge University Press).

Brinton, C. (1965) *The Anatomy of Revolution* (Englewood Cliffs: Prentice Hall).

Brown, A. (ed.) (1992a) *New Thinking in Soviet Politics* (London: Macmillan).

Brown, A. (1992b) 'New Thinking on the Soviet Political System', in Brown 1992a, pp. 12–28.

Brown, A. (1992c) 'Introduction', in Brown 1992a, pp. 1–11.

Brown, A. (1996) *The Gorbachev Factor* (Oxford: Oxford University Press).

Brown, A. Kaser, M. and Smith, G. (eds) (1994) *The Cambridge Encyclopedia of Russia and the Former Soviet Union* (Cambridge: Cambridge University Press).

Brown, B. (1993) 'Central Asia: The First Year of Unexpected Statehood', *RFE/RL Research Report*, vol. 2, no. 1, pp. 25–36.

Brown, J. F. (1991) *Surge to Freedom* (Durham, N.C.: Duke University Press).

Brown, J. F. (1994) *Hopes and Shadows* (Durham, N.C.: Duke University Press).

Brugger, B. and Reglar, S. (1994) *Politics, Economics and Society in Contemporary China* (London: Macmillan).

Brus, W. (1973) *The Economics and Politics of Socialism* (London: Routledge and Kegan Paul).

Bruszt, L. (1992) '1989: The Negotiated Revolution in Hungary', in Bozoki, Korosenyi and Schopflin 1992, pp. 45–59.

Bryant, C. and Mokrzycki, E. (eds) (1994a) *The New Great Transformation?* (London: Routledge).

Bryant, C. and Mokrzycki, E. (1994b) 'Introduction: Theorizing the Changes in East-Central Europe', in Bryant and Mokrzycki 1994a, pp. 1–13.

Brym, R. J. and Degtyarev, A. (1993) 'Anti-Semitism in Moscow: Results of an October 1992 Survey', *Slavic Review*, vol. 52, no. 1 (Spring), pp. 1–12.

Brzezinski, Z. (1989) *The Grand Failure* (New York: Scribners).

Brzezinski, Z. (1993a) *Out of Control* (New York: Scribners).

Brzezinski, Z. (1993b) 'The Great Transformation', *National Interest*, no. 33, pp. 3–13.

Buckley, M. (1990) 'Social Policies and New Social Issues', in White, Pravda and Gitelman 1990, pp. 185–206.

Bugajski, J. (1995) *Nations in Turmoil* (Boulder: Westview).

Bungs, D. (1993) 'Twenty-Three Groups Vie for Seats in the Latvian Parliament', *RFE/RL Research Report*, vol. 2, no. 23, pp. 44–9.

Bush, K. (1994a) 'Aspects of Military Conversion in Russia', *RFE/RL Research Report*, vol. 3, no. 14, pp. 31–4.

Bush, K. (1994b) 'Conversion and Privatization of Defense Enterprises in Russia', *RFE/RL Research Report*, vol. 3, no. 17, pp. 19–22.

Callinicos, A. (1991) *The Revenge of History* (Cambridge: Polity)

Cardoso, F. (1973) 'Associated-Dependent Development: Theoretical and Practical Implications', in A. Stepan (ed.), *Authoritarian Brazil* (New Haven: Yale University Press), pp. 142–76.

Carew Hunt, R. (1963) *The Theory and Practice of Communism* (Harmondsworth: Penguin).

Carnahan, R. and Corley, J. (1992) 'Czechoslovakia – June 8 and 9, 1990', in Garber and Bjornlund 1992, pp. 112–34.

Carothers, T. (1992) 'Romania – May 20, 1990', in Garber and Bjornlund 1992, pp. 75–94.

Carr, E. H. (1966) *The Bolshevik Revolution*, vol. 2 (Harmondsworth: Penguin).

Carrere d'Encausse, H. (1981) *Decline of an Empire* (New York: Harper and Row).

Carter, F. and Turnock, D. (eds) (1993) *Environmental Problems in Eastern Europe* (London: Routledge).

Castle-Kanerova, M. (1992) 'Social Policy in Czechoslovakia', in Deacon et al. 1992, pp. 91–117.

Cawson, A. (1986) *Corporatism and Political Theory* (Oxford: Blackwell).

Chan, K. (1995) 'Poland at the Crossroads: The 1993 General Election', *Europe-Asia Studies*, vol. 47, no. 1, pp. 123–45.

Chesnaux, J. (1979), *China: The People's Republic 1949–1976* (Hassocks: Harvester).

Chesnaux, J., Bastid, M. and Bergere, M.-C. (1976) *China: From the Opium Wars to the 1911 Revolution* (New York: Pantheon).

Chesnaux, J., Le Barbier, F. and Bergere, M.-C. (1977) *China: From the 1911 Revolution to Liberation* (Hassocks: Harvester).

Chin, J. (1993) 'Political Attitudes in Bulgaria', *RFE/RL Research Report*, vol. 2, no. 18, pp. 39–41.

Chirot, D. (ed.) (1991) *The Crisis of Leninism and the Decline of the Left* (Seattle: University of Washington Press).

Chossudovsky, M. (1986) *Towards Capitalist Restoration?* (London: Macmillan).

Clark, W. (1993) *Crime and Punishment in Soviet Officialdom* (New York: Sharpe).

Clarke, D. (1993) 'Europe's Changing Constellations', *RFE/RL Research Report*, vol. 2, no. 37, pp. 13–15.

Clarke, D. (1994a) 'Eastern Europe's Troubled Arms Industries: Part 1', *RFE/RL Research Report*, vol. 3, no. 14, pp. 35–43.

Clarke, D. (1994b) 'Eastern Europe's Troubled Arms Industries: Part 2', *RFE/RL Research Report*, vol. 3, no. 21, pp. 28–39.

Clarke, D. (1995) 'Uncomfortable Partners', *Transition*, vol. 1, no. 2, pp. 27–31.

Clawson, R. and Kaplan L. (eds) (1982) *The Warsaw Pact* (Wilmington: Scholarly Resources).

Cliff, T. (1974) *State Capitalism in Russia* (London: Pluto).

Cohan, A. S. (1975) *Theories of Revolution* (London: Nelson).

Cohen, J. (1983) 'Rethinking Social Movements', *Berkeley Journal of Sociology*, vol. 28, pp. 97–113.

Cohen, J. and Arato, A. (1992) *Civil Society and Political Theory* (Cambridge, Mass.: MIT Press).

Cohen, L. (1995) Broken Bonds (Boulder: Westview).

Colton, T. and Tucker, R. (eds) (1995) *Patterns in Post-Soviet Leadership* (Boulder, Colo.: Westview).

Connor, W. (1979) *Socialism, Politics, and Equality* (New York: Columbia University Press).

Cook, L. (1995) 'Workers in Post-communist Poland, Russia and Ukraine', *Communist and Post-Communist Studies*, vol. 28, no. 1, pp. 115–18.

Corning, A. (1993) 'The Russian Referendum: An Analysis of Exit Poll Results', *RFE/RL Research Report*, vol. 2, no. 19, pp. 6–9.

Corrin, C. (ed.) (1992a) *Superwomen and the Double Burden* (London: Scarlet Press).

Corrin, C. (1992b) 'Introduction', in Corrin 1992a, pp. 1–26.

Corrin, C. (1992c) 'Conclusion', in Corrin 1992a, pp. 236–55.

Corrin, C. (1993) 'People and Politics', in White, Batt and Lewis 1993, pp. 186–204.

Cotta, M. (1994) 'Building Party Systems after the Dictatorship: The East European Cases in a Comparative Perspective', in Pridham and Vanhanen 1994, pp. 99–127.

Coulson, A. (ed.) (1995) *Local Government in Eastern Europe* (Aldershot: Elgar).

Crampton, R. (1987) *A Short History of Modern Bulgaria* (Cambridge: Cambridge University Press).

Crampton, R. (1990) 'The Intelligentsia, the Ecology and the Opposition in Bulgaria', *World Today*, vol. 46, no. 2, pp. 23–6.

Crampton, R. (1994) *Eastern Europe in the Twentieth Century* (London: Routledge).

Crawford, B. (ed.) (1995a) *Markets, States and Democracy* (Boulder: Westview).

Crawford, B. (1995b) 'Post-Communist Political Economy: A Framework for the Analysis of Reform', in Crawford 1995a, pp. 3–42.

Crowe, D. (1995) *A History of the Gypsies of Eastern Europe and Russia* (New York: St Martin's).

Cutwright, P. (1963) 'National Political Development: Measurement and Analysis', *American Sociological Review*, vol. 28, no. 2, pp. 253–64.

Cviic, C. (1991) *Remaking the Balkans* (London: Pinter).

Dahrendorf, R. (1990) *Reflections on the Revolution in Europe* (London: Chatto and Windus).

Dallin, D. (1951) *The New Soviet Empire* (London: Hollis and Carter).

Dallin, A. and Breslauer, G. (1970) *Political Terror in Communist Systems* (Stanford: Stanford University Press).

David, I. (1995) *Public Opinion Barometer* (Bucharest: Center for Urban and Regional Sociology).

Davis, C. (1989) 'Priority and the Shortage Model: The Medical System in the Socialist Economy', in C. Davis and W. Charemza (eds) *Models of Disequilibrium and Shortage in Centrally Planned Economies* (London: Chapman and Hall), pp. 427–59.

Davis, C. (1993a) '*Eastern Europe and the Former USSR: An Overview*', *RFE/RL Research Report*, vol. 2, no. 40, pp. 31–4.

Davis, C. (1993b) 'The Former Soviet Union', *RFE/RL Research Report*, vol. 2, no. 40, pp. 35–43.

Dawisha, K. (1990) *Eastern Europe, Gorbachev, and Reform* (Cambridge: Cambridge University Press).

Dawisha, K. and Hanson, P. (eds) (1981) *Soviet-East European Dilemmas* (London: Heinemann).

Dawisha, K. and Parrot, B. (1994) *Russia and the New States of Eurasia* (Cambridge: Cambridge University Press).

Deacon, B. (1983) *Social Policy and Socialism* (London: Pluto).

Deacon, B. (1992a) 'East European Welfare: Past, Present and Future in Comparative Context', in Deacon et al. 1992, pp. 1–30.

Deacon, B. (1992b) 'The Future of Social Policy in Eastern Europe', in Deacon et al. 1992, pp. 167–91.

Deacon B. (1993) 'Social Change, Social Problems and Social Policy', in White, Batt and Lewis 1993, pp. 225–39.

Deacon, B. and Szalai, J. (eds) (1990) *Social Policy in the New Eastern Europe* (Aldershot: Avebury).

Deacon, B. and Vidinova, A. (1992) 'Social Policy in Bulgaria', in Deacon et al. 1992, pp. 67–90.

Deacon, B. et al. (1992) *The New Eastern Europe* (London: Sage).

DeBardeleben, J. (ed.) (1991a) *To Breathe Free* (Washington D.C.: Woodrow Wilson Center Press).

DeBardeleben, J. (1991b) 'Introduction', in DeBardeleben 1991a, pp. 1–21.

Dempsey, J. (1993) 'East European Voices', in White, Batt and Lewis 1993, pp. 280–8.

Dennis, M. (1988), *German Democratic Republic* (London: Pinter).

Deutsch, K. and Smith, D. B. (1987) 'The Federal Republic of Germany – West Germany', in R. Macridis (ed.), *Modern Political Systems* (Englewood Cliffs: Prentice Hall), pp. 160–250.

Diamond, L., Linz, J. and Lipset, S. M. (eds) (1988–9), *Democracy in Developing Countries* (4 vols, Boulder: Rienner).

Di Palma, G. (1991a) 'Legitimation from the Top to Civil Society: Politico-Cultural Change in Eastern Europe', *World Politics*, vol. 44, no. 1, pp. 49–80.

Di Palma, G. (1991b) 'Why Democracy Can Work in Eastern Europe', *Journal of Democracy*, vol. 2, no. 1, pp. 21–31.

Dittrich, K. (1983) 'Testing the Catch-All Thesis: Some Difficulties and Possibili-

Bibliography

ties', in H. Daalder and P. Mair (eds), *Western European Party Systems* (London: Sage), pp. 257–66.

Djelic, B. and Tsukanova, N. (1993) 'Voucher Auctions: A Crucial Step toward Privatization', *RFE/RL Research Report*, vol. 2, no. 30, pp. 10–18.

Dolling, Y. (ed.) (1991) *Who's Who of Women in World Politics* (London: Bowker-Saur).

Dominguez, J. (ed.) (1982) *Cuba: Internal and International Affairs* (Beverly Hills: Sage).

Dos Santos, T. (1970) 'The Structure of Dependence', *American Economic Review*, vol. 60, no. 2, pp. 231–6.

Drakulic-Ilic, S. (1985) "Six Mortal Sins" of Yugoslav Feminism', in Morgan 1985a, pp. 739–41.

Dreyer, J. T. (1993) *China's Political System* (New York: Paragon House).

Dukes, P. (1990), *A History of Russia* (London: Macmillan).

Duncan, P. (1992) 'The Rebirth of Politics in Russia', in Hosking, Aves and Duncan 1992, pp. 67–120.

Dunlop, J. (1993) 'Russia: Confronting a Loss of Empire', in Bremmer and Taras 1993, pp. 43–72.

Dunn, J. (1989) *Modern Revolutions*, 2nd edn (Cambridge: Cambridge University Press).

Duverger, M. (1954) *Political Parties* (London: Methuen).

Duverger, M. (1980) 'A New Political System Model: Semi-Presidential Government', *European Journal of Political Research*, vol. 8, pp. 165–87.

East, R. (1992) *Revolutions in Eastern Europe* (London: Pinter).

Eberstadt, N. (1994) 'Demographic Disaster: The Soviet Legacy', *National Interest*, no. 36, pp. 53–7.

Einhorn, B. (1992) 'German Democratic Republic – Emancipated Women or Hardworking Mothers?' in Corrin 1992a, pp. 125–54.

Einhorn, B. (1993) *Cinderella Goes to Market* (London: Verso).

Eisenstadt, S. (1992) 'The Breakdown of Communist Regimes', *Daedalus*, vol. 21, pp. 21–42.

Ellman, M. (1969) *Economic Reform in the Soviet Union* (London: PEP Publishing).

Ellman, M. (1993) 'Multiple Causes of the Collapse', *RFE/RL Research Report*, vol. 2, no. 23, pp. 55–8.

Ellman, M. (1994) 'The Increase in Death and Disease under "Katastroika"', *Cambridge Journal of Economics*, vol. 18, pp. 329–55.

Emadi, H. (1993) 'Development Strategies and Women in Albania', *East European Quarterly*, vol. 27, no. 1, pp. 79–96.

Engelbrekt, K. (1993) 'Reinventing the Bulgarian Secret Services', *RFE/RL Research Report*, vol. 2, no. 47, pp. 41–9.

Evans, G. and Whitefield, S. (1993) 'Identifying the Bases of Party Competition in Eastern Europe', *British Journal of Political Science*, vol. 23, pt 4, pp. 521–48.

Fane, D. (1993) 'Moldova: Breaking Loose from Moscow', in Bremmer and Taras 1993, pp. 121–53.

Ferge, Z. (1991) 'Recent Trends in Social Policy in Hungary', in Adam 1991a, pp. 132–55.

Feshbach, M. and Friendly, A. (1992) *Ecocide in the USSR* (New York: Basic Books).

Field, M. (1993) 'Post-Communist Medicine: Morbidity, Mortality and the Deteriorating Health Situation', May 1993 revised version of an unpublished paper presented at the Conference on the Social Legacy of Communism, Washington D.C., Feb. 1992.

Fish, M. S. (1995) *Democracy from Scratch* (Princeton: Princeton University Press).

Fisher, D. (1993) 'The Emergence of the Environmmental Movement in Eastern

Europe and its Role in the Revolutions of 1989', in Jancar-Webster 1993a, pp. 89–113.

Fitzmaurice, J. (1995) 'The Hungarian Election of May 1994', *Electoral Studies*, vol. 14, no. 1, pp. 77–80.

Florinsky, M. (1969) *Russia: A Short History* (Toronto: Collier-Macmillan).

Fodor, E. (1994) 'The Political Woman? Women and Politics in Hungary', in Rueschemeyer 1994, pp. 171–99.

Frank, A. (1969) *Development and Underdevelopment in Latin America* (New York: Monthly Review Press).

Frazer, G. and Lancelle, G. (1994) *Zhirinovsky (London: Penguin)*.

Frentzel-Zagorska, J. (1989) 'Semi-free Elections in Poland', unpublished paper presented at the Australasian Political Studies Association annual conference, Sydney.

Frentzel-Zagorska, J. (ed.) (1993) *From a One-Party State to Democracy* (Amsterdam: Rodopi).

Friedrich, C. and Brzezinski, Z. (1965) *Totalitarian Dictatorship and Autocracy* (Cambridge: Harvard University Press).

Frydman, R., Rapaczynski, A. and Earle, J. et al. (1993) *The Privatization Process in Central Europe* (London: Central European University Press).

Fukuyama, F. (1989) 'The End of History?' *National Interest*, no. 16, pp. 3–18.

Fukuyama, F. (1992) *The End of History and the Last Man* (New York: Free Press).

Fukuyama, F. (1993) 'The Modernizing Imperative', *National Interest*, no. 31, pp. 10–18.

Funk, N. (1993) 'Introduction: Women and Post-Communism', in Funk and Mueller 1993, pp. 1–14.

Funk, N. and Mueller, M. (eds) (1993) *Gender Politics and Post-Communism* (New York: Routledge).

Fuszara, M (1993) 'Abortion and the Formation of the Public Sphere in Poland' in Funk and Mueller 1993, pp. 241–52.

Garber, L. (1992) 'Bulgaria – June 10, 1990', in Garber and Bjornlund 1992, pp. 135–60.

Garber, L. and Bjornlund, E. (eds) (1992) *The New Democratic Frontier* (Washington D.C.: National Democratic Institute for International Affairs).

Garton Ash, T. (1989) *The Uses of Adversity* (London: Granta).

Garton Ash, T. (1991) *The Polish Revolution* (London: Granta).

Gellner, E. (1983) *Nations and Nationalism* (Ithaca: Cornell University Press).

George, V. and Manning, N. (1980) *Socialism, Social Welfare and the Soviet Union* (London: Routledge and Kegan Paul).

Gerth, H. and Wright Mills, C. (1970) *From Max Weber* (London: Routledge and Kegan Paul).

Gibson, J. (1994a) 'Understandings of Anti-Semitism in Russia: An Analysis of the Politics of Anti-Jewish Attitudes', *Slavic Review*, vol. 53, no. 3, pp. 796–806.

Gibson, J. (1994b) 'Misunderstandings of Anti-Semitism in Russia: An Analysis of the Politics of Anti-Jewish Attitudes', *Slavic Review*, vol. 53, no. 3, pp. 829–35.

Gigli, S. (1995) 'Toward Increased Participation in the Political Process', *Transition*, vol. 1, no. 16, pp. 18–21.

Gill, G. (1991) (Book review), *Australian Journal of Political Science*, vol. 26, no. 3, p. 594.

Gill G. (1993) 'The Soviet Transition and "Democracy from Above"', in White, Gill and Slider 1993, pp. 212–29.

Gill, G. (1994) *The Collapse of a Single-Party System* (Cambridge: Cambridge University Press).

Girnius, S. (1992) 'The Parliamentary Elections in Lithuania', *RFE/RL Research Report*, vol. 1, no. 48, pp. 6–12.

Girnius, S. (1993a) 'Problems in the Lithuanian Military', *RFE/RL Research Report*, vol. 2, no. 42, pp. 44–7.

Girnius, S. (1993b) 'Lithuania', *RFE/RL Research Report*, vol. 2, no. 40, pp. 53–5.

Girnius, S. (1994) 'Lithuania: Former Communists Fail to Solve Problems', *RFE/RL Research Report*, vol. 3, no. 1, pp. 99–102.

Girnius, S. (1995a) 'Reaching West while Eyeing Russia', *Transition*, vol. 1, no. 1, pp. 14–18.

Girnius, S. (1995b) 'A Tilt to the Left', *Transition*, vol. 1, no. 9, pp. 28–31.

Gitelman, Z. (1991) 'Glasnost, Perestroika and Antisemitism', *Foreign Affairs*, vol. 70, no. 2, pp. 141–59.

Gitelman, Z. (ed.) (1992), *The Politics of Nationality and the Erosion of the USSR* (New York: St Martin's Press).

Gitelman, Z. (1994) 'Nationality and Ethnicity in Russia and the Post-Soviet Republics', in White, Pravda and Gitelman 1994, pp. 237–265.

Glenny, M. (1990) *The Rebirth of History* (London: Penguin).

Glenny, M. (1993) *The Fall of Yugoslavia* (London: Penguin).

Goldman, M. (1991) *What Went Wrong with Perestroika* (New York: Norton).

Goldstein, J. (1995) 'The Coming Chinese Collapse', *Foreign Policy*, no. 99, pp. 35–52.

Gomez, V. (1995) 'News of Note Across the Region', *Transition*, vol. 1, no. 4, pp. 40–3.

Gonzalez, E. (1974) *Cuba under Castro* (Boston: Houghton Mifflin).

Gorbachev, M. (1987) *Perestroika* (London: Collins).

Gotovska-Popova, T. (1993) 'Bulgaria's Troubled Social Security System', *RFE/RL Research Report*, vol. 2, no. 26, pp. 43–7.

Gray, J. (1977) 'China: Communism and Confucianism', in A. Brown and J. Gray (eds), *Political Culture and Political Change in Communist States* (London: Macmillan).

Grofman, B. and Lijphart, A. (eds) (1986) *Electoral Laws and their Political Consequences* (New York: Agathon).

Grove Haines, C. (ed.) (1954) *The Threat of Soviet Imperialism* (Baltimore: Johns Hopkins University Press).

Gurr, T. R. (1970) *Why Men Rebel* (Princeton: Princeton University Press).

Habermas, J. (1973) 'What Does a Legitimation Crisis Mean Today? Legitimation Problems in Late Capitalism', included in W. Connolly (ed.), *Legitimacy and the State* (Oxford: Blackwell, 1984), pp. 134–79.

Habermas, J. (1976) *Legitimation Crisis* (London: Heinemann).

Hall, D. (1993) 'Albania', in Carter and Turnock 1993, pp. 7–37.

Hall, J. (1995) 'After the Vacuum: Post-Communism in the Light of Tocqueville', in Crawford 1995a, pp. 82–100.

Halligan, L. and Mozdoukhov, B. (1995) *A Guide to Russia's Parliamentary Elections* (London: Social Market Foundation).

Hancock, D. and Welsh, H. (eds) (1994) *German Unification* (Boulder: Westview).

Harasymiw, B. (1969) 'Nomenklatura: The Soviet Communist Party's Leadership Recruitment System', *Canadian Journal of Political Science*, vol. 2, no. 3, pp. 493–512.

Harding, N. (1983) *Lenin's Political Thought* (London: Macmillan).

Hardt, J. (1977) 'Summary', in Joint Economic Committee, East European Economies Post-Helsinki (Washington D.C.: US Government Printing Office), pp. ix–xxiv.

Harman, C. (1983) *Class Struggles in Eastern Europe 1945–83* (London: Pluto).

Hauser, E., Heyns, B. and Mansbridge, J. (1993) 'Feminism in the Interstices of Politics and Culture: Poland in Transition', in Funk and Mueller 1993, pp. 257–73.

Havelkova, H. (1993) 'A Few Prefeminist Thoughts', in Funk and Mueller 1993, pp. 62–73.

Haynes, V. and Semyonova, O. (eds) (1979) *Workers Against the Gulag* (London: Pluto).

Heinen, J. (1992) 'Polish Democracy is a Masculine Democracy', *Women's Studies International Forum*, vol. 15, no. 1, pp. 129–38.

Heinrich, H-G, (1986) *Hungary* (London: Frances Pinter).

Held, J. (ed.) (1992) *The Columbia History of Eastern Europe in the Twentieth Century* (New York: Columbia University Press).

Held, J. (ed.) (1993) *Democracy and Right-Wing Politics in Eastern Europe in the 1990s* (New York: Columbia University Press).

Heller, A. (1984) 'Legitimation', in F. Feher, A. Heller and G. Markus, *Dictatorship Over Needs* (Oxford: Blackwell), pp. 137–55.

Herspring, D. (1995) 'The Russian Military: Three Years On', *Communist and Post-Communist Studies*, vol. 28, no. 2, pp. 163–82.

Hesli, V., Miller, A. and Reisinger, W. (1994) 'Comment on Brym and Degtyarev's Discussion of Anti-Semitism in Moscow', *Slavic Review*, vol. 53, no. 3, pp. 836–41.

Hill, R. (1994) 'Parties and the Party System', in White, Pravda and Gitelman 1994, pp. 88–108.

Hinton, H. (1978) *An Introduction to Chinese Politics* (New York: Holt, Rinehart and Winston/Praeger).

Hobsbawm, E. (1992) *Nations and Nationalism since 1780* (Cambridge: Cambridge University Press).

Hockenos, P. (1993) *Free to Hate* (New York: Routledge).

Hohmann, H.-H., Kaser, M. and Thalheim, K. C. (eds) (1975) *The New Economic Systems of Eastern Europe* (London: Hurst).

Holloway, D. (1983) *The Soviet Union and the Arms Race* (New Haven: Yale University Press).

Holmes, L. (1981) *The Policy Process in Communist States* (Beverly Hills: Sage).

Holmes, L. (1986a) *Politics in the Communist World* (Oxford: Oxford University Press).

Holmes, L. (1986b) 'The State and the Churches in the GDR', in Miller and Rigby 1986, pp. 93–114.

Holmes, L. (1992) 'The GDR: The Search for Autonomous Patterns of Development', in Miller 1992a, pp. 65–83.

Holmes, L. (1993a) *The End of Communist Power* (Cambridge: Polity Press).

Holmes, L. (1993b) 'On Communism, Post-Communism, Modernity and Post-Modernity', in Frentzel-Zagorska 1993, pp. 21–43.

Holmes, L. (1994) 'Normalisation and Legitimation in Postcommunist Russia', in White, Pravda and Gitelman 1994, pp. 309–30.

Holmes, L. (1995) 'Russia's Relations with the Former External Empire', in A. Saikal and W. Maley (eds) *Russia in Search of its Future* (Cambridge: Cambridge University Press), pp. 123–41.

Holmes, S. (1994) 'The End of Decommunization', *East European Constitutional Review*, vol. 3, nos. 3–4, pp. 33–6.

Holmes, S. (1995) 'Conceptions of Democracy in the Draft Constitutions of Post-Communist Countries', in Crawford 1995a, pp. 71–81.

Holt, A. (1985) 'The First Soviet Feminists', in B. Holland (ed.), *Soviet Sisterhood* (London: Fourth Estate), pp. 237–65.

Hosking, G. (1992a) 'The Beginnings of Independent Political Activity', in Hosking, Aves and Duncan 1992, pp. 1–28.

Hosking, G. (1992b) *A History of the Soviet Union* (London: Fontana).

Hosking, G., Aves J. and Duncan, P. (1992) *The Road to Post-Communism* (London: Pinter).

Howard, D. (ed.) (1993) *Constitution Making in Eastern Europe* (Washington D.C.: Woodrow Wilson Center Press).

Huang, Y.-S. (1995) 'Why China Will Not Collapse', *Foreign Policy*, no. 99, pp. 54–68.

Hunter, S. (1993) 'Azerbaijan: Search for Identity and New Partners', in Bremmer and Taras 1993, pp. 225–60.

Huntington, S. (1987) 'The Goals of Development', in Weiner and Huntington 1987, pp. 3–32.

Huntington, S. (1991) *The Third Wave* (Norman: University of Oklahoma Press).

Huskey, G. (1993) 'Kyrgyzstan: The Politics of Demographic and Economic Frustration', in Bremmer and Taras 1993, pp. 398–418.

Inter-Parliamentary Union (1992) *Women and Political Power* (Geneva: Inter-Parliamentary Union).

Inter-Parliamentary Union (1995) *Parliaments: World Directory 1995* (Geneva: Inter-Parliamentary Union).

Ionescu, D. (1993) 'Romania', *RFE/RL Research Report*, vol. 2, no. 40, pp. 60–2.

Ionescu, G. (1965) *The Break-up of the Soviet Empire in Eastern Europe* (Baltimore: Penguin).

Jancar, B. (1978) *Women under Communism* (Baltimore: Johns Hopkins University Press).

Jancar-Webster, B. (ed.) (1993a) *Environmental Action in Eastern Europe* (Armonk, N.Y.: Sharpe).

Jancar-Webster, B. (1993b) 'Introduction', in Jancar-Webster 1993a, pp. 1–8.

Jankowska, H. (1993) 'The Reproductive Rights Campaign in Poland', *Women's Studies International Forum*, vol. 16, no. 3, pp. 291–6.

Jasiewicz, K. (1993) 'Structures of Representation', in White, Batt and Lewis 1993, pp. 124–46.

Jennett, C. and Stewart, R. (eds) (1989a) *Politics of the Future* (Melbourne: Macmillan).

Jennett, C. and Stewart, R. (1989b) 'Introduction', in Jennett and Stewart 1989a, pp. 1–28.

Joeste, M. et al. (eds) (1991) *The Baltic States* (Tallinn, Riga and Vilnius: Estonian, Latvian and Lithuanian Encyclopedia Publishers).

Jones, A. (ed.) (1994) *Education and Society in the New Russia* (Armonk, N.Y.: Sharpe).

Jones, A., Connor, W. and Powell, D. (eds) (1991) *Soviet Social Problems* (Boulder: Westview).

Jones, S. (1992) 'Revolutions in Revolutions within Revolution: Minorities in the Georgian Republic', in Gitelman 1992, pp. 77–101.

Jones, S. (1993) 'Georgia: A Failed Democratic Transition', in Bremmer and Taras 1993, pp. 288–310.

Joravsky, D. (1970) *The Lysenko Affair* (Cambridge: Harvard University Press).

Jowitt, K. (1992) *New World Disorder* (Berkeley: University of California Press).

Kaminski, B. (1991) *The Collapse of State Socialism* (Princeton: Princeton University Press).

Karabel, J. (1993) 'Polish Intellectuals and the Origins of Solidarity: The Making of an Oppositional Alliance', *Communist and Post-Communist Studies,* vol. 26, no. 1, pp. 25–46.

Karsten, S. and Majoor, D. (eds) (1994) *Education in East Central Europe* (New York: Waxmann Munster).

Kaser, M. (1976) *Health Care in the Soviet Union and Eastern Europe* (London: Croom Helm).

Kaser, M. (1993) 'The Marketization of Eastern Europe', in J. Story (ed.), *The New Europe* (Oxford: Blackwell), pp. 378–96.

Keane, J. (ed.) (1988) *Civil Society and the State* (London: Verso).

Kelder, M. (ed.) (1994) *Women and Government* (Westport: Praeger).

Kellas, J. (1991) *The Politics of Nationalism and Ethnicity* (London: Macmillan).

Kennedy, P. (1987) *The Rise and Fall of the Great Powers* (New York: Random House).

Kennedy, P. (1993)   *Preparing for the Twenty-First Century* (New York: Random House).

Kerblay, B. (1983)   *Modern Soviet Society* (London: Methuen).

Keren, M. and Ofer, G. (eds) (1992)   *Trials of Transition* (Boulder: Westview).

Kettle, S. (1995)   'Of Money and Morality', *Transition*, vol. 1, no. 3, pp. 36–9.

Kiczkova, Z. and Farkasova, E. (1993)   'The Emancipation of Women: A Concept that Failed', in Funk and Mueller 1993, pp. 84–94.

Kionka, R. (1992)   'Estonian Political Struggle Centres on Voting Rights', *RFE/ RL Research Report*, vol. 1, no. 24, pp. 15–17.

Kiraly, Z. (1991)   'Recent Hungarian Approaches to Agricultural Pollution', in DeBardeleben 1991a, pp. 197–209.

Kirchheimer, O. (1966)   'The Transformation of the Western European Party System', in J. LaPalombara and M. Weiner (eds) (1966), *Political Parties and Political Development* (Princeton: Princeton University Press), pp. 177–200.

Kirschbaum, S. (1995)   *A History of Slovakia* (New York: St Martin's).

Kiss, Y. (1991)   'The Second "No": Women in Hungary', *Feminist Review*, no. 39, pp. 49–57.

Kitschelt, H. (1992)   'The Formation of Party Systems in East Central Europe', *Politics and Society*, vol. 20, no. 1, pp. 7–50.

Kligman, G. (1992)   'The Politics of Reproduction in Ceausescu's Romania: A Case Study in Political Culture', *East European Politics and Societies*, vol. 6. no. 3, pp. 364–418.

Kolakowski, L. (1981)   *Main Currents of Marxism* (3 vols, Oxford: Oxford University Press).

Kolankiewicz, G. and Lewis, P. (1988)   *Poland* (London: Pinter).

Kolsto, P., Edemsky, A. and Kalashnikova, N. (1993)   'The Dniester Conflict: Between Irredentism and Separatism', *Europe-Asia Studies*, vol. 45, no. 6, pp. 973–1000.

Komarov, B. (1978)   *The Destruction of Nature in the Soviet Union* (London: Pluto).

Kontorovich, V. (1993)   'The Economic Fallacy', *National Interest*, no. 31, pp. 35–45.

Koole, R. and Mair, P. (1994)   'Political Data in 1993', *European Journal of Political Research*, vol. 26, nos 3–4, pp. 221–9.

Kornai, J. (1992)   *The Socialist System* (Princeton: Princeton University Press).

Korosenyi, A. (1991)   'Revival of the Past or New Beginning? The Nature of Post-Communist Politics', *Political Quarterly*, vol. 62, no. 1, pp. 52–74.

Kozeltsev, M. (1993)   'Old and New in the Environmental Policy of the Former Soviet Union', in Jancar-Webster 1993a, pp. 58–72.

Kramer, M. (1993)   'From Dominance to Hegemony to Collapse: Soviet Policy in East-Central Europe 1945–1991', unpublished paper.

Ksiezopolski, M. (1990)   'Is Social Policy a Problem in a Socialist Country?' in Deacon and Szalai 1990, pp. 51–62.

Kukathas, C. and Lovell, D. (1991)   'The Significance of Civil Society', in Kukathas, Lovell and Maley 1991, pp. 18–40.

Kukathas, C., Lovell, D. and Maley, W. (eds) (1991)   *The Transition from Socialism* (Melbourne: Longman Cheshire).

Kupchan, C. (ed.) (1995)   *Nationalism and Nationalities in the New Europe* (Ithaca, N. Y.: Cornell University Press).

Kusin, V. (1977)   'Czechoslovakia', in M. McCauley (ed.), *Communist Power in Europe 1944–1949* (London: Macmillan), pp. 73–94.

Lane, D. (1978)   *Politics and Society in the USSR* (London: Martin Robertson).

Lane, D. (1982)   *The End of Social Inequality* (London: Allen and Unwin).

Lane, D. (1985)   *Soviet Economy and Society* (Oxford: Blackwell).

Latynsky, M. (1992)   'Poland – May 27, 1990', in Garber and Bjornlund 1992, pp. 95–111.

Lavigne, M. (1995) *The Economics of Transition* (London: Macmillan).

Lefort, C. (1977) 'La premiere revolution anti-totalitaire', *Esprit*, no. 1, pp. 13–19.

Lemke, C. and Marks, G. (eds) (1992) *The Crisis of Socialism in Europe* (Durham, N.C.: Duke University Press).

Lemon, A. (1995) 'In Russia, a Community Divided', *Transition*, vol. 1, no. 4, pp. 12–18.

Lentini, P. (1994) *Statistical Data on Women in the USSR* (Glasgow: Lorton House).

Lentini, P. and McGrath, T. (1994) 'The Rise of the Liberal Democratic Party and the 1993 Elections', *Harriman Institute Forum*, vol. 7, no. 6, pp. 1–12.

Lewis, P. (ed.) (1992) *Democracy and Civil Society in Eastern Europe* (New York: St Martin's Press).

Lewis, P. (1993) 'Democracy and its Future in Eastern Europe', in D. Held (ed.), *Prospects for Democracy* (Cambridge: Polity), pp. 291–311.

Lewis, P., Lomax, B. and Wightman, G. (1994) 'The Emergence of Multi-party Systems in East-Central Europe', in Pridham and Vanhanen 1994, pp. 151–88.

Ligachev, Ye. (1993) *Inside Gorbachev's Kremlin* (New York: Pantheon).

Lijphart, A. (ed.) (1992) *Parliamentary versus Presidential Government* (New York: Oxford University Press).

Linz, J. (1994) 'Presidential or Parliamentary Democracy: Does It Make a Difference?' in Linz and Valenzuela 1994, pp. 3–87.

Linz, J. and Valenzuela, A. (eds) (1994) *The Failure of Presidential Democracy* (Baltimore: Johns Hopkins University Press).

Lipset, S. (1959) 'Some Social Requisites of Democracy: Economic Development and Political Legitimacy', *American Political Science Review*, vol. 53, no. 1, pp. 69–105.

Lissyutkina, L. (1993) 'Soviet Women at the Crossroads of Perestroika', in Funk and Mueller 1993, pp. 274–86.

Liu, A. (1986) *How China is Ruled* (Englewood Cliffs: Prentice Hall).

Los, M. (ed.) (1990) *The Second Economy in Marxist States* (London: Macmillan).

Lovenduski, J. and Woodall, J. (1987) *Politics and Society in Eastern Europe* (London: Macmillan).

Lowenhardt, J. (1995) *The Reincarnation of Russia* (Durham, N.C.: Duke University Press).

Lucky, C. (1993/4) 'Table of Presidential Powers in Eastern Europe', *East European Constitutional Review*, vols 2/3, nos 4/1, pp. 81–94.

Lucky, C. (1994) 'Table of Twelve Electoral Laws', *East European Constitutional Review*, vol. 3, no. 2, pp. 65–77.

Lydall, H. (1986) *Yugoslav Socialism* (Oxford: Oxford University Press).

Malloy, J. and Seligson, M. (eds) (1987) *Authoritarians and Democrats* (Pittsburgh: University of Pittsburgh Press).

Manning, N. (1992) 'Social Policy in the Soviet Union and its Successors', in Deacon et al. 1992, pp. 31–66.

Marnie, S. (1993) 'The Social Safety Net in Russia', *RFE/RL Research Report*, vol. 2, no. 17, pp. 17–23.

Marples, D. (1987) *Chernobyl and Nuclear Power in the USSR* (London: Macmillan).

Martin, K. (1994) 'Central Asia's Forgotten Tragedy', *RFE/RL Research Report*, vol. 3, no. 30, pp. 35–48.

Marx, K. and Engels, F. (1970) *The German Ideology* (London: Lawrence and Wishart).

Mason, D. (1992) *Revolution in East-Central Europe* (Boulder: Westview).

Matthews, M. (1991) '*Perestroika* and the Rebirth of Charity', in Jones, Connor and Powell 1991, pp. 154–71.

McAdams, M. (1992) *Croatia* (Sacramento: CIS Monographs).

McAuley, M. (1992) *Soviet Politics 1917–1991* (Oxford: Oxford University Press).

McFaul, M. (1993) *Post-Communist Politics* (Washington D.C.: Center for Strategic and International Studies).

McGregor, J. (1993) 'How Electoral Laws Shape Eastern Europe's Parliaments', *RFE/RL Research Report*, vol. 2, no. 4, pp. 11–18.

McGregor, J. (1994) 'The Presidency in East Central Europe', *RFE/RL Research Report*, vol. 3, no. 2, pp. 23–31.

McIntosh, M., Abele Mac Iver, M., Abele, D. and Smeltz, D. (1994) 'Publics Meet Market Democracy in Central and East Europe, 1991–1993', *Slavic Review*, vol. 53, no. 2, pp. 483–512.

McIntyre, R. (1988) *Bulgaria* (London: Pinter).

McLean, L. and Garber, L. (1992) *The October 13 1991 Legislative and Municipal Elections in Bulgaria* (Washington D.C.: National Democratic Institute for International Affairs).

McLellan, D. (1980a) *The Thought of Karl Marx* (London: Macmillan).

McLellan, D. (1980b) *Marxism after Marx* (London: Macmillan).

McLellan, D. (ed.) (1988) *Marxism: Essential Writings* (Oxford: Oxford University Press).

McMahon, E. (1992) 'Slovenia – April 7 and 21, 1990', in Garber and Bjornlund 1992, pp. 65–74.

Medvedev, G. (1991) *The Truth about Chernobyl* (New York: Basic Books).

Medvedev, Z. (1969) *The Rise and Fall of T. D. Lysenko* (New York: Columbia University Press).

Medvedev, Z. (1990) *The Legacy of Chernobyl* (Oxford: Blackwell).

Melia, T. (1992) 'Hungary – March 25, 1990', in Garber and Bjornlund 1992, pp. 39–64.

Mendeloff, D. (1994) 'Explaining Russian Military Quiescence: The "Paradox of Disintegration" and the Myth of a Military Coup', *Communist and Post-Communist Studies*, vol. 27, no. 3, pp. 225–46.

Mestrovic, S. (1994) *The Balkanization of the West* (London: Routledge).

Meth-Cohn, D., with others (1993) 'The New Left', *Business Central Europe*, vol. 1, no. 6, pp. 7–9.

Meyer, A. (1984) *Communism* (New York: Random House).

Michta, A. (1994) *The Government and Politics of Postcommunist Europe* (Westport: Praeger).

Mihalka, M. (1995a) 'Creeping Toward the East', *Transition*, vol. 1, no. 1, pp. 80–5.

Mihalka, M. (1995b) 'The Bumpy Road to Western Europe', *Transition*, vol. 1, no. 1, pp. 73–9.

Millard, F. (1992) 'Social Policy in Poland', in Deacon et al. 1992, pp. 118–43.

Millard, F. (1994) *The Anatomy of the New Poland* (Aldershot: Elgar).

Miller, J. (1993) *Mikhail Gorbachev and the End of Soviet Power* (London: Macmillan).

Miller, R. (ed.) (1992a) *The Developments of Civil Society in Communist Systems* (Sydney: Allen and Unwin).

Miller, R. (1992b) 'Civil Society in Communist Systems: An Introduction', in Miller 1992a, pp. 1–10.

Miller, R. and Rigby, T. H. (eds) (1986) *Religion and Politics in Communist States* (Canberra: Australian National University).

Molyneux, M. (1990) 'The "Woman Question" in the Age of Perestroika', *New Left Review*, no. 183, pp. 23–49.

Moore, B. (1966) *Social Origins of Dictatorship and Democracy* (Boston: Beacon).

Morgan, R. (ed.) (1985a) *Sisterhood is Global* (Harmondsworth: Penguin).

Morgan, R. et al. (1985b) 'Hungary', in Morgan 1985a, pp. 289–92.

Morrison, J. (1994) *Vladimir Zhirinovskiy* (Washington D.C.: National Defense University).

Morvant, P. (1995a) 'Unemployment: A Growing Problem', *Transition*, vol. 1, no. 6, pp. 46–50.

Morvant, P. (1995b) 'Bearing the "Double Burden" in Russia', *Transition*, vol. 1, no. 16, pp. 4–9 and 60.

Mushaben, J. (1984) 'Swords to Plowshares: The Church, the State and the East German Peace Movement', *Studies in Comparative Communism*, vol. 17, no. 2, pp. 123–35.

Musil, J. (ed.) (1995) *The End of Czechoslovakia* (Budapest: Central European University Press).

Nadais, A. (1992) 'Choice of Electoral Systems', in Garber and Bjornlund 1992, pp. 190–203.

Nathan, A. (1990) *China's Crisis* (New York: Columbia University Press).

Nogee, J. and Donaldson, R. (1988) *Soviet Foreign Policy since World War II* (Oxford: Pergamon).

Nourzhanov, K. (1994) 'The Elections in Kazakhstan', *Centre for Middle Eastern and Central Asian Studies Bulletin*, vol. 1, no. 1, pp. 3–4.

Nove, A. (1986) *The Soviet Economic System* (Winchester, Mass.: Allen and Unwin).

Nove, A. (1992) *An Economic History of the USSR 1917–1991* (Harmondsworth: Penguin).

Obrman, J. (1992) 'The Czechoslovak Elections', *RFE/RL Research Report*, vol. 1, no. 26, pp. 12–19.

Obrman, J. (1993) 'Military Reform in the Czech Republic', *RFE/RL Research Report*, vol. 2, no. 41, pp. 37–42.

O'Connor, J. (1973) *The Fiscal Crisis of the State* (New York: St. Martin's Press).

O'Donnell, G. (1973) *Modernization and Bureaucratic Authoritarianism* (Berkeley: Institute of International Studies, University of California).

O'Donnell, G., Schmitter, P. and Whitehead, L. (eds) (1986) *Transitions from Authoritarian Rule* (Baltimore: Johns Hopkins University Press).

Offe, C. (1984) *Contradictions of the Welfare State* (London: Hutchinson).

Offe, C. (1991) 'Capitalism by Democratic Design? Democratic Theory Facing the Triple Transition in East Central Europe', *Social Research*, vol. 58, no. 4, pp. 865–92.

Ogden, S. (1989) *China's Unresolved Issues* (Englewood Cliffs: Prentice Hall).

Okolicsanyi, K. (1993) 'Hungary's Misused and Costly Social Security System', *RFE/RL Research Report*, vol. 2, no. 17, pp. 12–16.

Orttung, R. (1995a) 'Battling Over Electoral Laws', *Transition*, vol. 1, no. 15, pp. 32–6.

Orttung, R. (1995b) 'Yeltsin's Most Dangerous Rival', *Transition*, vol. 1, no. 22, pp. 17–18.

Osiatynski, W. (1994) 'Decommunization and Recommunization in Poland', *East European Constitutional Review*, vol. 3, nos 3–4, pp. 36–41.

Pakulski, J. (1991) *Social Movements* (Melbourne: Longman Cheshire).

Pakulski, J. (1993) 'East European Revolutions and "Legitimacy Crisis"', in Frentzel-Zagorska 1993, pp. 67–87.

Pannier, B. (1995) 'A Step Back for Democracy', *Transition*, vol. 1, no. 11, pp. 62–6.

Pano, N. (1968) *The People's Republic of Albania* (Baltimore: Johns Hopkins University Press).

Panova, R., Gavrilova, R. and Merdzanska, C. (1993) 'Thinking Gender: Bulgarian Women's Im/possibilities', in Funk and Mueller 1993, pp. 15–21.

Park, A. (1994) 'Ethnicity and Independence: The Case of Estonia in Comparative Perspective', *Europe-Asia Studies*, vol. 46, no. 1, pp. 69–87.

Pataki, J. (1993a) 'A New Era in Hungary's Social Security Administration', *RFE/RL Research Report*, vol. 2, no. 27, pp. 57–60.

Pataki, J. (1993b) 'Hungary', *RFE/RL Research Report*, vol. 2, no. 40, pp. 50–2.

Pavkovic, A., Koscharsky, H. and Czarnota, A. (eds) (1995)   *Nationalism and Post-Communism* (Aldershot: Dartmouth).

Pehe, J. (1993)   'Czechoslovakia: Toward Dissolution', *RFE/RL Research Report*, vol. 2, no. 1, pp. 84–8.

Pei, M. (1994)   *From Reform to Revolution* (Cambridge: Harvard University Press).

Pelczynski, Z. (1988)   'Solidarity and "The Rebirth of Civil Society" in Poland, 1976–81', in Keane 1988, pp. 361–80.

Perez, L. (1988)   *Cuba: Between Reform and Revolution* (New York: Oxford University Press).

Petrova, D. (1993)   'The Winding Road to Emancipation in Bulgaria', in Funk and Mueller 1993, pp. 22–9.

Pipes, R. (1974)   *Russia under the Old Regime* (Harmondsworth: Penguin).

Poggi, G. (1978)   *The Development of the Modern State* (London: Hutchinson).

Popper, K. (1957)   *The Poverty of Historicism* (London: Routledge and Kegan Paul).

Powell, D. (1991)   'Aging and the Elderly', in Jones, Connor and Powell 1991, pp. 172–93.

Pravda, A. (1986)   'Elections in Communist Party States', in S. White and D. Nelson (eds), *Communist Politics* (London: Macmillan), pp. 27–54.

Pravda, A. (ed.) (1992)   *The End of the Outer Empire* (London: Sage).

Pribylovskii, V. (1992)   *Dictionary of Political Parties and Organizations in Russia* (Washington D.C.: Center for Strategic and International Studies).

Pridham, G. (ed.) (1984)   *The New Mediterranean Democracies* (London: Cass).

Pridham, G. and Lewis, P. (eds) (1996)   *Stabilising Fragile Democracies* (London: Routledge).

Pridham, G. and Vanhanen, T. (eds) (1994)   *Democratization in Eastern Europe* (London: Routledge).

Prifti, P. (1978)   *Socialist Albania since 1944* (Cambridge, Mass.: MIT Press).

Pryde, P. (1991)   *Environmental Management in the Soviet Union* (Cambridge: Cambridge University Press).

Pye, L. (1966)   *Aspects of Political Development* (Boston: Little Brown).

Rabkin, R. (1991)   *Cuban Politics* (New York: Praeger).

Rady, M. (1992)   *Romania in Turmoil* (London: Tauris).

Ramet, P. (ed.) (1989)   *Religion and Nationalism in Soviet and East European Politics* (Durham, N.C.: Duke University Press).

Ramet, S. (1993)   (Book review), *American Political Science Review*, vol. 87, no. 2, pp. 526–7.

Ramet, S. (1995)   *Social Currents in Eastern Europe* (Durham, N.C.: Duke University Press).

Rau, Z. (ed.) (1991a)   *The Reemergence of Civil Society in Eastern Europe and the Soviet Union* (Boulder: Westview).

Rau, Z. (1991b)   'Introduction', in Rau 1991a, pp. 1–23.

Rau, Z. (1991c)   'Human Nature, Social Engineering, and the Reemergence of Civil Society', in Rau 1991a, pp. 25–50.

Reddaway, P. (1983)   'Policy towards Dissent since Khrushchev', in T. H. Rigby, A. Brown and P. Reddaway (eds), *Authority, Power and Policy in the USSR* (London: Macmillan), pp. 158–92.

Reddaway, P. (1993)   'The Role of Popular Discontent', *National Interest*, no. 31, pp. 57–63.

Reid, E. (1995)   'The Russian Federation Constitutional Court', *Coexistence*, no. 32, pp. 277–303.

Reisch, A. (1993a)   'The Hungarian Army in Transition', *RFE/RL Research Report*, vol. 2, no. 10, pp. 38–52.

Reisch, A. (1993b)   'The Central European Initiative: To Be or Not To Be?' *RFE/RL Research Report*, vol. 2, no. 34, pp. 30–7.

Reisinger, W., Miller, A., Hesli, V. and Maher, K. (1994) 'Political Values in Russia, Ukraine and Lithuania: Sources and Implications for Democracy', *British Journal of Political Science*, vol. 24, pt 2, pp. 183–223.

Remington, R. (1971) *The Warsaw Pact* (Cambridge, Mass.: MIT Press).

Remington, T. (ed.) (1994a) *Parliaments in Transition* (Boulder: Westview).

Remington, T. (1994b) 'Introduction: Parliamentary Elections and the Transition from Communism', in Remington 1994a, pp. 1–27.

Rhodes, M. (1993) 'The Former Soviet Union and the Future: Facing Uncertainty', *RFE/RL Research Report*, vol. 2, no. 24, pp. 52–5.

Riasanovsky, N. (1984) *A History of Russia* (New York: Oxford University Press).

Rigby, T. H. (1982) 'Introduction: Political Legitimacy, Weber and Communist Mono-organisational Systems', in Rigby and Feher 1982, pp. 1–26.

Rigby, T. H. (1988) 'Staffing USSR Incorporated: The Origins of the Nomenklatura System', *Soviet Studies*, vol. 40, no. 4, pp. 523–37.

Rigby, T. H. (1990) *The Changing Soviet System* (Aldershot: Edward Elgar).

Rigby, T. H. (1991) 'Mono-organisational Socialism and the Civil Society', in Kukathas, Lovell and Maley 1991, pp. 107–22.

Rigby, T. H. (1992) 'The USSR: End of a Long, Dark Night?', in Miller 1992a, pp. 11–23.

Rigby, T. H. and Feher, F. (eds) (1982) *Political Legitimation in Communist States* (London: Macmillan).

Riggs, F. (1988) 'The Survival of Presidentialism in America: Para-constitutional Practices', *International Political Science Review*, vol. 9, no. 4, pp. 247–78.

Robinson, N. (1995) *Ideology and the Collapse of the Soviet System* (Aldershot: Elgar).

Rose, R. (1991) *Bringing Freedom Back In* (Glasgow: University of Strathclyde).

Rose, R. (1995) 'Russia as an Hour-Glass Society: A Constitution without Citizens', *East European Constitutional Review*, vol. 4, no. 3, pp. 34–42.

Rose, R. and Haerpfer, C. (1994a) 'Mass Response to Transformation in Postcommunist Societies', *Europe-Asia Studies*, vol. 46, no. 1, pp. 3–28.

Rose, R. and Haerpfer, C. (1994b) *New Russia Barometer III: The Results* (Glasgow: University of Strathclyde).

Rose, R. and Mishler, W. (1994) 'Mass Reaction to Regime Change in Eastern Europe: Polarization or Leaders and Laggards?' *British Journal of Political Science*, vol. 24, pt 2, pp. 159–82.

Rosenberg, T. (1995) *The Haunted Land* (New York: Random House).

Roskin, M. (1993) 'The Emerging Party Systems of Central and Eastern Europe', *East European Quarterly*, vol. 27, no. 1, pp. 47–63.

Rostow, W. (1960) *The Stages of Economic Growth* (Cambridge: Cambridge University Press).

Rostow, W. (1971) *Politics and the Stages of Growth* (Cambridge: Cambridge University Press).

Rueschemeyer, D., Huber Stephens, E. and Stephens, J. (1992) *Capitalist Development and Democracy* (Cambridge: Polity).

Rueschemeyer, M. (ed.) (1994) *Women in the Politics of Postcommunist Eastern Europe* (Armonk, N.Y.: Sharpe).

Rush, M. (1993) 'Fortune and Fate', *National Interest*, no. 31, pp. 19–25.

Rusinow, D. (1977) *The Yugoslav Experiment 1948–1974* (London: Hurst).

Sabbat-Swidlicka, A. (1993) 'The Polish Elections: The Church, the Right and the Left', *RFE/RL Research Report*, vol. 2, no. 40 (8 Oct.), pp. 24–30.

Sakwa, R. (1990) *Gorbachev and his Reforms* (Hemel Hempstead: Philip Allan).

Sakwa, R. (1993) *Russian Politics and Society* (London: Routledge).

Scarpetta, S. and Reutersward, A. (1994) 'Unemployment Benefit Systems and Active Labour Market Policies in Central and Eastern Europe: An Overview', in Boeri 1994, pp. 255–307.

Schenk, C. (1993) 'Lesbians and their Emancipation in the Former German Democratic Republic: Past and Future', in Funk and Mueller 1993, pp. 160–7.

Schopflin, G. (1993a) 'Culture and Identity in Post-Communist Europe', in White, Batt and Lewis 1993, pp. 16–34.

Schopflin, G. (1993b) *Politics in Eastern Europe* (Oxford: Blackwell).

Schwartz, H. (1993a) 'The New East European Constitutional Courts', in Howard 1993, pp. 163–207.

Schwartz, H. (1993b) 'The New Courts: An Overview', *East European Constitutional Review*, vol. 2, no. 2, pp. 28–32.

Secretariat of the Economic Commission for Europe (1990) *Economic Survey of Europe in 1989–90* (New York: United Nations).

Seton-Watson, H. (1961) *The New Imperialism* (New York: Capricorn).

Seton-Watson, H. (1965) *Nationalism Old and New* (Sydney: Sydney University Press).

SEV Sekretariat (1990) *Statisticheskii Ezhegodnik Stran–Chlenov Soveta Ekonomicheskoi Vzaimopomoshchi* (Moscow: Finansy i Statistika).

Shafir, M. (1985) *Romania* (London: Frances Pinter).

Shafir, M. (1993) 'Romanians and the Transition to Democracy', *RFE/RL Research Report*, vol. 2, no. 18, pp. 42–8.

Shearman, P. (1994) 'Reimagining Russian National Identity', unpublished paper.

Shearman, P. (ed.) (1995) *Russian Foreign Policy since 1990* (Boulder: Westview).

Sher, G. (1977) *Praxis* (Bloomington: Indiana University Press).

Shils, E. (1991) 'The Virtue of Civil Society', *Government and Opposition*, vol. 26, no. 1, pp. 3–20.

Shugart, M. (1993) 'Of Presidents and Parliaments', *East European Constitutional Review*, vol. 2, no. 1, pp. 30–2.

Siklova, J. (1990) 'Women and Ageing under Real Socialism', in Deacon and Szalai 1990, pp. 192–200.

Sillince, J. (ed.) (1990) *Housing Policies in Eastern Europe and the Soviet Union* (London: Routledge).

Simon, J. (1993) 'Post-paternalist Political Culture in Hungary: The Relationship between Citizens and Politics during and after the "Melancholic Revolution" (1989–1991)', *Communist and Post-Communist Studies*, vol. 26, no. 2, pp. 226–38.

Singleton, F. (1985) *A Short History of the Yugoslav Peoples* (Cambridge: Cambridge University Press).

Singleton, F. (ed.) (1987) *Environmental Problems in the Soviet Union and Eastern Europe* (Boulder: Rienner).

Skocpol, T. (1979) *States and Social Revolutions* (Cambridge: Cambridge University Press).

Slater, W. (1994a) 'The Diminishing Center of Russian Parliamentary Politics', *RFE/RL Research Report*, vol. 3, no. 17, pp. 13–18.

Slater, W. (1994b) 'Female Representation in Russian Politics', *RFE/RL Research Report*, vol. 3, no. 22, pp. 27–33.

Slay, B. (ed.) (1993) 'Roundtable: Privatisation in Eastern Europe', *RFE/RL Research Report*, vol. 2, no. 32, pp. 47–57.

Slider, D. (1994) 'Politics outside Russia', in White, Pravda and Gitelman 1994, pp. 266–84.

Smart, C. (1990) 'Gorbachev's Lenin: The Myth in Service to Perestroika', *Studies in Comparative Communism*, vol. 23, no. 1, pp. 5–21.

Smith, A. (1991) *National Identity* (London: Penguin).

Staar, R. (1989) 'Checklist of Communist Parties in 1988', *Problems of Communism*, vol. 38, no. 1, pp. 47–68.

Staar, R. (ed.) (1993) *Transition to Democracy in Poland* (New York: St Martin's).

Staniszkis, J. (1995) 'In Search of a Paradigm of Transformation', in Wnuk-Lipinski 1995a, pp. 19–55.

Stastna, J. (1995) 'New Opportunities in the Czech Republic', *Transition*, vol. 1, no. 16, pp. 24–8 and 61.

Stepan, A. and Skach, C. (1993) 'Constitutional Frameworks and Democratic Consolidation: Parliamentarianism versus Presidentialism', *World Politics*, vol. 46, no. 1, pp. 1–22.

Stokes, G. (1993) *The Walls Came Tumbling Down* (New York: Oxford University Press).

Sword, K. (ed.) (1990) *The Times Guide to Eastern Europe* (London: Times Books).

Szacki, J., Glowacka, I., Liro, A. and Szulczewska, B. (1993) 'Political and Social Changes in Poland', in Jancar-Webster 1993a, pp. 11–27.

Szajkowski, B. (ed.) (1981) *Marxist Governments* (3 vols, London: Macmillan).

Szajkowski, B. (ed.) (1994) *New Political Parties of Eastern Europe, Russia and the Successor States* (Harlow: Longman).

Szakolczai, A. and Horvath, A. (1992) 'The Discourse of Civil Society and the Self-Elimination of the Party', in Lewis 1992, pp. 16–31.

Taras, R. (ed.) (1992a) *The Road to Disillusion* (Armonk, N.Y.: Sharpe).

Taras, R. (1992b) 'The "Meltdown" of Marxism in the Soviet Bloc', in Taras 1992a, pp. 3–17.

Tarrow, S. (1989) *Struggle, Politics and Reform* (Ithaca: Center for International Studies, Cornell University).

Tarrow, S. (1994) *Power in Movement* (Cambridge: Cambridge University Press).

Tatu, M. (1970) *Power in the Kremlin* (New York: Viking).

Teague, E. (1994) 'Russia and Tatarstan Sign Power-sharing Treaty', *RFE/RL Research Report*, vol. 3, no. 14, pp. 19–27.

Thirkell, J., Scase, R. and Vickerstaff, S. (eds) (1995) *Labour Relations and Political Change in Eastern Europe* (London: UCL Press).

Tigrid, P. (1975) 'The Prague Coup of 1948: The Elegant Takeover', in T. Hammond (ed.), *The Anatomy of Communist Takeovers* (New Haven: Yale University Press), pp. 399–432.

Tilly, C. (1993) *European Revolutions 1492–1992* (Oxford: Blackwell).

Tismaneanu, V. (ed.) (1990) *In Search of Civil Society* (New York: Routledge).

Tismaneanu, V. (1992) *Reinventing Politics* (New York: Free Press).

Todres, V. (1995) 'Bashkortostan Seeks Sovereignty – Step by Step', *Transition*, vol. 1, no. 7, pp. 56–9.

Tokes, R. (ed.) (1979) *Opposition in Eastern Europe* (London: Macmillan).

Tolz, V. (1990) *The USSR's Emerging Multiparty System* (New York: Praeger).

Tolz, V. and Wishnevsky, J. (1993) 'Russia after the Referendum', *RFE/RL Research Report*, vol. 2, no. 19, pp. 1–5.

Tolz, V., Slater, W. and Rahr, A. (1993) 'Profiles of the Main Political Blocs', *RFE/RL Research Report*, vol. 2, no. 20, pp. 16–25.

Touraine, A. (1981) *The Voice and the Eye* (Cambridge: Cambridge University Press).

Touraine, A. (1985) 'An Introduction to the Study of Social Movements', *Social Research*, vol. 52, no. 4, pp. 749–87.

Touraine, A. (1994) 'European Countries in a Post-national Era', in C. Rootes and H. Davis (eds), *Social Change and Political Transformation* (London: UCL Press), pp. 13–26.

Treml, V. (1991) 'Drinking and Alcohol Abuse in the USSR in the 1980s', in Jones, Connor and Powell 1991, pp. 119–36.

Turner, B., Hegedus, J. and Tosics, I. (eds) (1992) *The Reform of Housing in Eastern Europe and the Soviet Union* (London: Routledge).

Vachudova, M. (1993) 'The Visegrad Four: No Alternatives to Cooperation?', *RFE/RL Research Report*, vol. 2, no. 34, pp. 38–47.

Vachudova, M. and Fisher, S. (1993) 'The Czech and Slovak Republics', *RFE/RL Research Report*, vol. 2, no. 40, pp. 44–9.

Valencia, M. and Frankl, P. (1993) 'Power to the People?', *Business Central Europe*, vol. 1, no. 5 (Oct.), pp. 60–2.

Vinton, L. (1993a) 'Walesa Applies Political Shock Therapy', *RFE/RL Research Report*, vol, 2, no. 24, pp. 1–11.

Vinton, L. (1993b) 'Poland Goes Left', *RFE/RL Research Report*, vol. 2, no. 40 (8 Oct.), pp. 21–3.

Vinton, L. (1993c) 'Poland', *RFE/RL Research Report*, vol. 2, no. 40, pp. 56–9.

Vinton, L. (1993d) 'Poland's Social Safety Net: An Overview', *RFE/RL Research Report*, vol. 2, no. 17, pp. 3–11.

Vogel, H. (1975) 'Bulgaria', in Hohmann, Kaser and Thalheim 1975, pp. 199–222.

Vogel, L. (1983) *Marxism and the Oppression of Women* (London: Pluto).

Volgyes, I. (ed.) (1974) *Environmental Deterioration in the Soviet Union and Eastern Europe* (New York: Praeger).

Walker, R. (1993) *Six Years that Shook the World* (Manchester: Manchester University Press).

Waller, J. M. (1994) *Secret Empire* (Boulder: Westview).

Waller, M. (1981) *Democratic Centralism* (Manchester: Manchester University Press).

Waller, M. (1993) *The End of the Communist Power Monopoly* (Manchester: Manchester University Press).

Wang, J. (1992) *Contemporary Chinese Politics* (Englewood Cliffs: Prentice Hall).

Waters, E. (1993) 'Finding a Voice: The Emergence of a Women's Movement', in Funk and Mueller 1993, pp. 287–302.

Weiner, M. and Huntington, S. (eds) (1987) *Understanding Political Development* (Boston: Little Brown).

Wheaton, B. and Kavan, Z. (1992) *The Velvet Revolution* (Boulder: Westview).

White, S. (1979) *Political Culture and Soviet Politics* (London: Macmillan).

White, S. (1991) *Gorbachev and After* (Cambridge: Cambridge University Press).

White, S. and Hill, R. (1996) 'Russia, the Former Soviet Union and Eastern Europe: The Referendum as a Flexible Political Instrument', in M. Gallagher and P. Uleri (eds), *The Referendum Experience in Europe* (London: Macmillan, forthcoming).

White, S., Batt, J. and Lewis, P. (eds) (1993) *Developments in East European Politics* (London: Macmillan).

White, S., Gardner, J. and Schopflin, G. (1987) *Communist Political Systems* (London: Macmillan).

White, S., Gill, G. and Slider, D. (1993) *Politics in Transition* (Cambridge: Cambridge University Press).

White, S., Pravda, A. and Gitelman, Z. (eds) (1990) *Developments in Soviet Politics* (London: Macmillan).

White, S., Pravda, A. and Gitelman, Z. (eds) (1994) *Developments in Russian and Post-Soviet Politics* (London: Macmillan).

Whitefield, S. (ed.) (1993) *The New Institutional Architecture of Eastern Europe* (New York: St Martin's).

Williamson, P. (1985) *Varieties of Corporatism* (Cambridge: Cambridge University Press).

Wishnevsky, J. (1993) 'Russian Constitutional Court: A Third Branch of Government?', *RFE/RL Research Report*, vol. 2, no. 7, pp. 1–8.

Wnuk-Lipinski, E. (ed.) (1995a) *After Communism* (Warsaw: Institute of Political Studies, Polish Academy of Sciences).

Wnuk-Lipinski, E. (1995b) 'Is a Theory of Post-Communist Transformation Possible?' in Wnuk-Lipinski 1995a, pp. 5–18.

Wohlfeld, M. (1995) 'The WEU as a Complement – Not a Substitute – for NATO', *Transition*, vol. 1, no. 23, pp. 34–6 and 64.

Wolchik, S. (1991) *Czechoslovakia in Transition* (London: Pinter).

Wolchik, S. and Meyer, A. (eds) (1985) *Women, State and Party in Eastern Europe* (Durham, N.C.: Duke University Press).

Woodall, J. (1982) *The Socialist Corporation and Technocratic Power* (Cambridge: Cambridge University Press).

Woodard, C. (1995) 'The Internet's Explosive Expansion', *Transition*, vol. 1, no. 18, pp. 84–7.

Wolff, R. (1956) *The Balkans in our Time* (Cambridge: Harvard University Press).

Yasmann, V. (1993a) 'The Russian Civil Service: Corruption and Reform', *RFE/ RL Research Report*, vol. 2, no. 16, pp. 18–21.

Yasmann, V. (1993b) 'Where Has the KGB Gone?', *RFE/RL Research Report*, vol. 2, no. 2, pp. 17–20.

Yasmann, V. (1993c) 'Corruption in Russia: A Threat to Democracy?', *RFE/RL Research Report*, vol. 2, no. 10, pp. 15–18.

Yasmann, V. (1993d) 'The Role of the Security Agencies in the October Uprising', *RFE/RL Research Report*, vol. 2, no. 44, pp. 12–18.

Yasmann, V. (1994) 'Security Services Reorganized: All Power to the Russian President?', *RFE/RL Research Report*, vol. 3, no. 6, pp. 7–14.

Ziegler, C. (1987) *Environmental Policy in the USSR* (Amherst: University of Massachusetts Press).

Ziegler, C. (1991) 'Environmental Protection in Soviet–East European Relations', in DeBardeleben 1991a, pp. 83–100.

Zubek, (1994) 'The Reassertion of the Left in Post-communist Poland', *Europe-Asia Studies*, vol. 46, no. 5, pp. 801–37.

Zukin, S. (1975) *Beyond Marx and Tito* (London: Cambridge University Press).

Zwick, P. (1983) *National Communism* (Boulder, Colo.: Westview).

Index

Index